Red
Phoenix
Rising

Red
Phoenix
Rising

The Soviet
Air Force in
World War II

Von Hardesty

and

Ilya Grinberg

University Press of Kansas

© 2012 by the University Press of Kansas

Published by the University Press of
Kansas (Lawrence, Kansas 66045),
which was organized by the Kansas
Board of Regents and is operated and
funded by Emporia State University,
Fort Hays State University, Kansas State
University, Pittsburg State University,
the University of Kansas, and Wichita
State University

The paper used in this publication meets
the minimum requirements of the
American National Standard for
Permanence of Paper for Printed
Library Materials Z39.48-1984.

Library of Congress
Cataloging-in-Publication Data

Hardesty, Von, 1939–
Red phoenix rising : the Soviet Air Force
in World War II / Von Hardesty and Ilya
Grinberg.
p. cm. — (Modern war studies)
Includes bibliographical references and
index.
ISBN 978-0-7006-1828-6 (cloth : alk. paper)
1. World War, 1939–1945—Aerial
operations, Soviet. 2. World War,
1939–1945—Aerial operations, German.
3. Soviet Union. Raboche-Krest?ianskaia
Krasnaia Armiia. Voenno-Vozdushnye
Sily—History—World War, 1939–1945. 4.
Germany. Luftwaffe—History—World
War, 1939–1945. I. Grinberg, Ilya, 1955–
II. Title.
D792.S65H36 2012
940.54'4947—dc23   2011042399

British Library Cataloguing in
Publication Data is available.

Printed in the United States of America

10 9 8 7 6 5 4 3 2
The paper used in this publication is
recycled and contains 30 percent post-
consumer waste. It is acid free and
meets the minimum requirements of the
American National Standard for
Permanence of Paper for Printed Library
Materials Z39.48-1992.

To Patricia Hardesty and Roza Grinberg

CONTENTS

A photo section follows page 206.

ACKNOWLEDGMENTS

The authors wish to acknowledge those who generously offered assistance during the preparation of *Red Phoenix Rising: The Soviet Air Force in World War II*. James F. Gebhardt and Richard Muller provided expert knowledge on the Soviet Air Force and the *Luftwaffe,* respectively; their critical analyses and willingness to share key data are profoundly appreciated. The research for this book, by design, reached out to representatives of a whole new generation of scholars in the Russian Federation and Ukraine who greatly enhanced our knowledge of Soviet airpower in World War II: Vladislav Antipov, Oleg Bezverkhniy, Michael Bykov, Vitaliy Gorbach, Sergey Isayev, Dmitriy Kyenko, Sergey Kuznetsov, Dmitriy Linevich, Oleg Rastrenin, Valeriy Romanenko, Andrey Simonov, Vasiliy Tashkevich, Michael Timin, Igor Utkin, and Igor Zhidov. For the special maps used in this book, we wish to acknowledge the work of Terry Higgins and Zach Downey-Higgins. In addition, we are grateful to Konstantin Chirkin, Carl-Fredrick Geust, Dmitriy Karlenko, Oleg Korytov, Aleksey Pekarsh, Gennadiy Petrov, Valeriy Romanenko, Thomas Salazar, Hans-Heiri Stapfer, and Glen Sweeting for generously supplying photographs for the book.

At the University Press of Kansas, Michael Briggs deserves special thanks for his oversight of and enthusiasm for this study of the Soviet Air Force. Other staff at the press deserve mention as well for their numerous and substantive contributions, including Susan Schott, Larisa Martin, and Linda Lotz. Finally, thanks to indexer Patricia N. Hardesty.

ABBREVIATIONS AND TERMS

ADD	*Aviatsiya Dalnego Deystviya*, or long-range aviation
ALSIB	Alaska-Siberian route
BAD	*Bombardirovochnaya Aviatsionnaya Diviziya*, or bomber air division
BAK	*Bombardirovochnyy Aviatsionnyy Korpus*, or bomber air corps
BAO	*Batalion Aerodromnogo Obsluzhivaniya*, or airfield service battalion
BAP	*Bombardirovochnyy Aviatsionnyy Polk*, or bomber air regiment
BG	Bomber group
BS	Bomber squadron
DBA	*Dalnebombardirovochnaya Aviatsiya*, or long-range aviation
DBAD	*Dalnebombardirovochnaya Aviatsionnaya Diviziya*, or long-range bomber air division
Front	Russian term for a group of armies, equivalent to a British or American Army Group, or the military zone they occupy (e.g., Western *Front*, 1st Belorussian *Front*, Bryansk *Front*)
Front	theater of operations (e.g., Western Front, Eastern Front)
front	front line
GBAP	*Gvardeyskiy Bombardirovochnyy Aviatsionnyy Polk*, or Guards bomber air regiment
GIAD	*Gvardeyskaya Istrebitelnaya Aviatsionnaya Diviziya*, or Guards fighter air division
GIAK	*Gvardeyskiy Istrebitelnyy Aviatsionnyy Korpus*, or Guards fighter air corps
GIAP	*Gvardeyskiy Istrebitelnyy Aviatsionnyy Polk*, or Guards fighter air regiment
GKO	*Gosudarstvennyy Komitet Oborony*, or State Defense Committee
GNBAP	*Gvardeyskiy Nochnoy Bombardirovochnyy Aviatsionnyy Polk*, or Guards night bomber air regiment

GOSPLAN   *Gosudarstvennaya Planovaya Komissiya*, or State
            Planning Commission
GSAK   *Gvardeyskiy Smeshannyy Aviatsionnyy Korpus*, or
            Guards mixed air corps
GShAD   *Gvardeyskaya Shturmovaya Aviatsionnaya Diviziya*, or
            Guards ground attack air division
GShAK   *Gvardeyskiy Shturmovoy Aviatsionnyy Korpus*, or Guards
            ground attack air corps
GShAP   *Gvardeyskiy Shturmovoy Aviatsionnyy Polk*, or Guards
            ground attack air regiment
HSU   Hero of the Soviet Union, the highest award for
            bravery in combat
IAD   *Istrebitelnaya Aviatsionnaya Diviziya*, or fighter air
            division
IAK   *Istrebitelnyy Aviatsionnyy Korpus*, or fighter air corps
IAP   *Istrebitelnyy Aviatsionnyy Polk*, or fighter air regiment
JG   *Jagdgeschwader*, or fighter wing
KG   *Kampfgeschwader*, or bomber wing
KGB   *Komitet Gosudarstvennoy Bezopasnosti*, or State
            Committee for National Security
LG   *Lehrgeschwader*, or operational training unit
MPVO   *Mestnaya Protivovozdushnaya Oborona*, or local air
            defense
NBAD   *Nochnaya Bombardirovochnaya Aviatsionnaya Diviziya*,
            or night bomber air division
NKAP   *Narodnyy Komissariat Aviatsionnoy Promyshlennosti*, or
            People's Commissariat of Aviation Industry
NKVD   *Narodnyy Komissariat Vnutrennikh Del*, or People's
            Commissariat of Internal Affairs
Osoaviakhim *Obshchestvo sodeystviya oborone i aviatsionno-*
            khimicheskomu stroitelstvu SSSR (loose translation,
            Society for Assistance to Defense and Aviation-
            Chemical Construction of the USSR), an institution that
            existed from 1927 to 1948 and trained Soviet youth in a
            number of military skills
PTAB   *Protivotankovaya aviatsionnaya bomba*, or antitank air
            bomb
PVO Strany *Protivovozdushnaya Oborona Strany*, or National Air Defense

RAB	*Rayon Aerodromnogo Bazirovaniya*, or air-basing region
RAG	*Rezervnaya Aviatsionnaya Gruppa*, or reserve air group
RAP	*Razvedyvatelnyy Aviatsionnyy Polk*, or reconnaissance air regiment
RKKA	*Raboche-Krestyanskya Krasnaya Armiya*, or Workers' and Peasants' Red Army
RS	*Reaktivnyy snaryad*, or rocket projectile
SAD	*Smeshannaya Aviatsionnaya Diviziya*, or mixed air division
SAK	*Smeshannyy Aviatsionnyy Korpus*, or mixed air corps
SBAD	*Skorostnaya Bombardirovochnaya Aviatsionnaya Diviziya*, or high-speed bomber air division
SBAP	*Skorostnoy Bombardirovochnyy Aviatsionnyy Polk*, or high-speed bomber air regiment
SG	*Schlachtgeschwader*, or ground attack wing
ShAD	*Shturmovaya Aviatsionnaya Diviziya*, or ground attack air division
ShAK	*Shturmovoy Aviatsionnyy Korpus*, or ground attack air corps
ShAP	*Shturmovoy Aviatsionnyy Polk*, or ground attack air regiment
ShKAS	*Shpitalnogo, Komarnitskogo aviatsionnyy skorostrelnyy*, or rapid-firing aviation machine gun (7.62mm) designed by Shpitalnyy and Komarnitskiy
ShVAK	*Shpitalnogo, Vladimirova aviatsionnaya krupnokalibernaya*, or large-caliber aviation cannon (20mm) designed by Shpitalnyy and Vladimirov
Stavka	High Command for Soviet armed forces in the war
StG	*Sturzkampfgeschwader*, or dive-bomber wing
TsAMO RF	*Tsentralnyy Arkhiv Ministerstva Oborony Rossiyskoy Federatsii*, or Central Archive of Ministry of Defense of the Russian Federation
VA	*Vozdushnaya Armiya*, or air army
VNOS	*Vozdusnogo Nablyudeniya, Opovescheniya i Svyazi*, or air observation, warning, and communications
VVS	*Voyenno-vozdushnyye sily*, or Soviet Air Force
ZG	*Zerstorergeschwader*, or heavy fighter wing

INTRODUCTION

Airpower played a pivotal role in shaping the course and final outcome of World War II. Some prewar air theorists had prophesied that the airplane would be the decisive weapon in any future war. Even if this vision failed to materialize, airpower—in its various operational modes—made a powerful and enduring impact on the conduct of warfare. In the popular mind, of course, military aviation was associated with many of the dramatic episodes in the war—the Battle of Britain, the launching of the bold Doolittle raid, the sinking of Japanese carriers at the Battle of Midway, the debut of the first operational jet fighters, and the long and costly strategic bombing campaigns against Germany and Japan. Most dramatic of all was the use of the B-29 Superfortress to drop atomic bombs on Hiroshima and Nagasaki, a singular moment that ushered in the nuclear age. After 1945 a flood tide of books, documentaries, and movies chronicled or showcased the crucial role of the airplane in war. The particular role of aviation in World War II became a familiar theme.

The United States and Great Britain employed airpower in a strategic way, and in large measure their air forces enjoyed considerable independence from other branches of the military. By contrast, Germany and the Soviet Union clearly subordinated their air assets to the ground forces. Fighting on the Continent, often in vast and varied geographic settings, both these nations were forced to place a strong emphasis on combined arms operations—and how well this approach was perfected decided the outcome of the war.

In the prewar years the Soviet Union pursued a rapid advance of its air arm, which peaked by the spring of 1941. However, such expansion was not properly backed up by the training of aircrews, logistics, spare parts, and radio communications, not to mention doctrinal views on the application of airpower in modern mobile warfare. Technologically, the Soviet Union was not yet ready to support the quantitative and qualitative aspects of rapidly growing air forces. Doctrinal views, which were linked very tightly with ground forces, also shifted toward

direct subordination to army commanders, which led to the decentralization of airpower and, as a result, its low efficiency. When the
Soviet Union was attacked on June 22, 1941, the Soviet Air Force—
Voyenno-vozdushnyye sily (VVS)—located in western frontier military
districts, was practically annihilated. However, the huge loss of aircraft did not necessarily translate to the loss of pilots. Scrambling
every possible resource from the vast inner territories of the country
and quickly reorganizing, the VVS followed the pattern of the ground
armies and reemerged within a few months of its near defeat to become a tough fighting force. As time passed and lessons were learned,
many organizational and tactical changes materialized. Like the
ground forces, the VVS actively emulated the superior tactics of the
Germans. From a loosely organized juggernaut on the eve of Barbarossa, the VVS forged a strong and unified command during the Battle of Moscow; other organizational and operational reforms followed
at Stalingrad, in the skies of Kuban, in the battle for Kursk, and finally
in the decisive drive to Berlin. The VVS emerged as the largest opera-
tional-tactical air force in the world by the end of the war in May 1945.
Although always embedded in combined arms operations, the VVS
achieved strategic success in a broader context of quantitative superiority, improved performance and quality, coordination between
branches of aviation and with ground forces, perfected command and
control, and proper integration of military and economic planning.
This became an important, if not always acknowledged, chapter in the
air war of World War II.

For myriad reasons and until recent decades, there has been minimal attention in the West to the importance of the air war on the Eastern Front. The fighting in the East—to the degree it was vaguely
comprehended—remained a shadowy domain where Nazi Germany
and the Soviet Union engaged in a titanic and merciless ground war.
"The paucity of detailed information on the war available in the English language," David M. Glantz has observed, "reinforce[d] the natural
American (and Western) penchant for viewing the Soviet-German war
as a mere backdrop for more dramatic and significant battles in western theaters, such as El Alamein, Salerno, Anzio, Normandy, and the
Bulge."[1] Overcoming this formidable mind-set—in scholarship and in
popular writing—has been difficult in the continuing quest to understand fully the history and impact of World War II.

One could argue that among all the themes in World War II, the history of the Soviet Air Force has been the least chronicled or understood. At best, the air war in the East has been approached as a backdrop story. This new study offers a coherent overview of this lost chapter in the history of World War II. As such, it derives its inspiration from Von Hardesty's 1982 work *Red Phoenix: The Rise of Soviet Air Power, 1941–1945.*[2] It was something of a pathfinder for its time, part of a small and growing library of studies on Soviet airpower to appear in the West. Hardesty was faced with the challenge of reconstructing the story at a time when Russian archival resources were still closed. Russian-language memoirs were available, always keyed to the official Soviet accounts of the war; nonetheless, these were valuable for their detail and perspective. Like other historians, Hardesty made ample use of the memoirs of German veterans, which were a mix of accurate storytelling and transparent bias. On the eve of the fall of communism, the history of the Soviet Air Force was still viewed in the West "through a glass darkly." In the decades after the collapse of the Soviet Union, there has been a dramatic shift in the historiography of the war on the Eastern Front: archival sources became more accessible for a time, and most important, a new generation of Western and Russian historians and commentators emerged to chronicle in great detail the history of the war in general and the air war in particular. What resulted from these myriad studies was a more candid view of the air war. For the first time, the air war between the VVS and the *Luftwaffe* could be understood in a more complete and authoritative way.

Red Phoenix Rising, by design, offers in one volume a new and more authoritative account of the Soviet Air Force in World War II. Such an overarching study required a certain degree of selectivity when it came to content and focus. The task was to identify the core themes and episodes to evoke a clear sense of the air war in the East. Accordingly, certain Soviet air operations were not covered in detail, most notably those of the naval air arm, the operations in the North, and the role of the VVS in the final offensives against Japan in the Far East. The narrative of *Red Phoenix Rising*, at its core, sheds light on a sequence of fundamental air operations that shaped the course of the air war in the East. These air operations, considered in total, provide not only a chronicle of Soviet airpower but also an avenue to assess how the Soviet Air Force managed to reorganize and mobilize the necessary air assets to defeat the *Luftwaffe*. Moreover, such a formal study must contend with the persistent problem of contradictory data on aircraft inventories, sorties flown in the various air operations, and actual combat losses on both sides. Surviving records—personal memoirs, air unit reports, and formal histories—often give diverging accounts. Consequently, *Red Phoenix Rising* offers the most authoritative figures based on archival sources. The authors acknowledge that the fog of battle can be only partially dispersed in this critical area of inquiry.

The need for an exhaustive account of the Soviet Air Force, written in English, remains compelling. *Red Phoenix Rising*, it is anticipated, will provide a catalyst to achieve this worthy goal.

Chapter One

An Arduous Beginning

The Soviet Union passed abruptly from peace to war at 0330 hours on Sunday, June 22, 1941. Thirty handpicked *Luftwaffe* bomber crews, flying He 111s, Ju 88s, and Do 17Zs in groups of three, struck ten Soviet airfields in the predawn darkness. As the first wave of a skillfully planned preemptive air strike, the German bombers approached the western periphery of the Soviet Union at maximum altitude to avoid detection. Once over the Soviet territory, the attackers swept down on their targets at the very moment German artillery signaled the advance of a ground force consisting of 3.8 million men. This initial air strike aimed to create havoc at the forward Soviet air bases. At sunrise, the major *Luftwaffe* force of 500 bombers, 270 dive-bombers, and 480 fighters hit sixty-six airfields containing nearly three-quarters of the Soviet combat aircraft.[1] Wave after wave of German aircraft struck Soviet airfields with only token resistance from interceptors or antiaircraft fire. There were only isolated air alerts. No effort had been made to disperse the numerous aircraft deployed at these forward airfields. Only a few Soviet fighters managed to escape the fury of the *Luftwaffe*. Soviet air divisions faced near annihilation within the space of one day—the 9th SAD (*Smeshannaya Aviatsionnaya Diviziya,* or mixed air division) of the Western Special Military District lost 347 planes out of 409 deployed, the 10th lost 180 out of 231, and the 11th lost 127 out of 199 as the devastating raid unfolded.[2]

The Soviet Air Force (*Voyenno-vozdushnyye sily,* or VVS) had been caught by surprise. Its movements in the wake of this aerial assault were incoherent and sluggish, much like those of a large animal stricken by sudden and repeated blows. At one airfield, attacking *Luftwaffe* fighters discovered more than 100 VVS aircraft—bombers, fighters, and reconnaissance planes—parked in long rows, as if on display. In the course of twenty minutes, German fighters made repeated sweeps of the airfield, destroying the aircraft in place.[3] Soviet airpower became effectively paralyzed, which allowed the *Luftwaffe* mastery of the air and the freedom to strike at will Soviet defensive fortifications, rail junctions, troop groupings, and communications.

The German strategy, dubbed ominously Operation Barbarossa, gave expression to Adolf Hitler's projected *coup de main* against the hated Bolshevik regime of Joseph Stalin. The initial phase of the elaborate war plan called for a preemptive air strike by the *Luftwaffe*. Four air fleets, or *Luftflotten*, constituted this formidable air armada of approximately 2,790 aircraft—945 bombers, 345 dive-bombers, 1,036 single-engine fighters, 93 twin-engine fighters, 120 reconnaissance aircraft, and 252 transport and liaison planes.[4]

With the *Luftwaffe* in firm control of the air, the German army moved into Russia along three diverging avenues of conquest—toward Leningrad in the north, Moscow in the center, and Kiev in the south. If successful, the massive German offensive in the East would eliminate a potential enemy and hasten the end of the war on German terms. Implicit in this ambitious blueprint was an optimistic vision of a quick triumph. Soviet Russia, in Hitler's estimate, was highly vulnerable: "We have only to kick in the door and the whole rotten structure will come crashing down."[5]

For the few Soviet pilots who managed to get airborne that morning, they faced the daunting task of air combat with the battle-seasoned *Luftwaffe*. Those who entered into air combat encountered skilled pilots such as Werner Molders, who had eighty-two victories to his credit, fourteen in Spain and sixty-eight on the Western Front. Before his death in an accidental air crash in November 1941, Molders would notch another thirty-three victories against the VVS. Not all German pilots possessed Molders's skills, but many took full advantage of their superior training and equipment to become aces. Many roaming Messerschmitt Bf 109s, typically flying in formations of two or four aircraft, found the demoralized VVS fighter units only capable of sporadic and uncoordinated resistance, many fleeing on the approach of the German fighters.

In a vortex of burning airfields and widespread confusion, isolated Russian air units did strike back in a reactive mode that I. V. Timokhovich described as "spontaneous, uncoordinated and purposeless."[6] Some Soviet bombers, spared destruction in the opening hours of the war, were ordered out to stem the relentless German advance: VVS commanders at the front, following confusing directives from Moscow, recklessly sacrificed numerous frontline bombers in the vain hope of destroying *Luftwaffe* staging areas. At 1315 hours, three groups of nine SB bombers, drawn from the 130th SBAP (*Skorostnoy Bombardirovochnyy Aviatsionnyy Polk,* or high-speed bomber regiment), attacked German targets north of Brest. This became a desperate sortie, one pursued with no fighter escort. Upon reaching their targets, the VVS bombers encountered fierce antiaircraft fire. The formation dispersed under this withering response. Once the Soviet bombers were dispersed, four Bf 109 fighters made a concerted attack. Even in the face of this onslaught, all three VVS bomber groups managed to attack their targets, including a *Luftwaffe* airfield at Biala-Podliaska. The price for the bold raid proved to be very high. While leaving the target area, the Soviet bombers were attacked by a large formation of Bf 109s (perhaps as many as thirty fighters), and twenty of the twenty-seven VVS bombers were lost.[7]

The high attrition suffered by Soviet bombers on the first day of Operation Barbarossa left an indelible impression on both sides—an image of *Luftwaffe* aerial dominance on an unparalleled scale. SBs and DB-3s often appeared in waves and routinely without fighter escort. Their desperate aim was to interdict the advancing German army at crucial road and river crossings. In the pursuit of these near-suicidal sorties, the Soviet bombers attempted to hit the German targets from altitudes of 10,000 to 12,000 feet (3,000 to 4,000 meters), an approach altitude prescribed in their prewar training. Some sorties were flown at lower altitudes from 3,000 to 5,000 feet (900 to 1,500 meters). With their slow approach speeds, especially at lower altitudes, the Soviet bombers became easy targets for German antiaircraft batteries. German fighter pilots and flak crews watched in amazement as the unescorted Soviet aircraft made repeated sweeps and endured severe losses. For example, Captain Lozenko's squadron of the 24th SBAP, 13th BAD (*Bombardirovochnaya Aviatsionnaya Diviziya,* or bomber air division), performing bomb runs from an altitude of 6,000 feet (1,800 meters), encountered fierce antiaircraft fire and attacks by up to twenty Bf 109 fighters. This squadron lost eight bombers out of fifteen. Two other groups of the 13th BAD, led by Major Nikiforov and Captain Sukhanov, bombed concentrations of German troops at Kossuv from

3,000 feet (900 meters). Eighteen SB bombers out of nineteen were lost to enemy fighters and antiaircraft fire.[8]

Once ordered to attack a German target, the VVS bombers doggedly maintained their course. The destruction of Soviet bombers continued into July. On July 9, when his airfield was attacked by twenty-seven Soviet bombers, Major Guenther Luetzow of the *Luftwaffe's Jagdgeshwader* (JG) 3 took to the air with his unit and shot down the entire regiment in an intense fifteen-minute aerial skirmish, without taking a loss.[9] One *Luftwaffe* fighter unit, II/JG 51, scored sixty-three aircraft on the ground and twenty-eight in the air in one day.[10]

There was no frame of reference for the *Luftwaffe's* air triumph on June 22 and the subsequent phases of Operation Barbarossa. For the Soviet Union, it was an air debacle of unprecedented scope. Chaos and devastation had overwhelmed the forward air defenses. The marauding *Luftwaffe* bombers with their fighter escorts flew their sorties with utter abandon. Even as they looked out upon burning aircraft and grappled with a shattered communications network, local air commanders still managed to organize resistance, even as they evacuated surviving aircraft and air personnel.

The formidable German *Wehrmacht* brought untold destruction and chaos to the Soviet Union's defenses in the western borderlands. This new combat arena for World War II—the Russian Front—now extended from the Baltic to the Black Sea, a total of 1,800 miles (2,900 kilometers), and it would soon expand.

Once the Germans began to tally the results of their opening air assault, the air triumph surpassed their boldest expectations. At 1330 hours, General Franz Halder recorded in his diary 800 Soviet aircraft destroyed, compared with German losses of only 10! By the end of the day, the tally had reached over 1,200 aircraft—800 on the ground, and the rest in the air.[11] One German archival source recorded German losses for the day at 63 aircraft.[12] During the next twenty-four hours, another 1,000 Soviet aircraft (or perhaps twice that number) were destroyed, totaling around 4,000 VVS and DBA (*Dalne-bombardirovochnaya Aviatsiya,* or long-range aviation) aircraft alone by the end of the first week of the war.[13]

The German estimates for VVS losses were not uniform or necessarily consistent. Erhard Milch, for example, recorded in his diary the destruction of 1,800 Soviet aircraft on the first day, another 800 on the second, 557 on the third, 351 on the fourth, and 300 on the fifth.[14] Even Hermann Goering, a man often prone to hyperbole, found the first reports of Soviet losses for June 22–24 to be suspect. Fearing exaggeration, he ordered a hurried recount with verification. The subsequent recount, to his amazement, added 300 Soviet aircraft to the original figure.[15] One Russian archival source, in fact, revealed that on the second day, VVS losses had reached a total of 3,922 aircraft, with the downing of 78 enemy aircraft. This particular Russian source may well be close to reality.[16] Whatever the actual count, the *Luftwaffe* achieved firm control of the air in the first week of the war. German air units now shifted to a different role—one of ground support of the *Wehrmacht* as it continued its rapid advance into Soviet territory along three corridors.

The genesis of Operation Barbarossa could be traced back to Directive 21, issued by Hitler on December 18, 1940, although the actual decision to launch the invasion came in the complex and shifting wartime circumstances in the first half of 1941. Named after the legendary Frederick Barbarossa (Red Beard), who had marched to the Holy Land in 1190, the plan called for "armored spearheads" to penetrate deeply into the hinterland of the Soviet Union, destroy the Red Army, and erect "a barrier against Asiatic Russia."[17] The word *Barbarossa* itself evoked a historical meaning, which historian John Erickson describes as "arrogant in its recall of medieval splendors and menacing in its hints of medieval cruelties."[18]

Ironically, the *Wehrmacht*—with its mobility, massive striking power, and battle experience—advanced into the Soviet Union in 1941 one day after the date chosen by Napoleon for the invasion of tsarist Russia in 1812. The ambitious campaign to bring down the Soviet regime involved a series of envelopment battles west of the Dvina and Dnieper Rivers, the capture of the Baltic republics and Leningrad, the liquidation of surviving Soviet forces around Moscow, and concluding forays in the Volga and Caucasus regions.[19]

Germany's dramatic victories over France, Poland, and Yugoslavia in 1940–1941 fueled an attitude of supreme confidence in Berlin, where the defeat of Stalinist Russia was considered inevitable and a key factor in launching the Nazi New Order. The epic Russo-German war would become one of the most fateful and decisive military struggles in history—and aviation would play a vital role in deciding the final outcome.

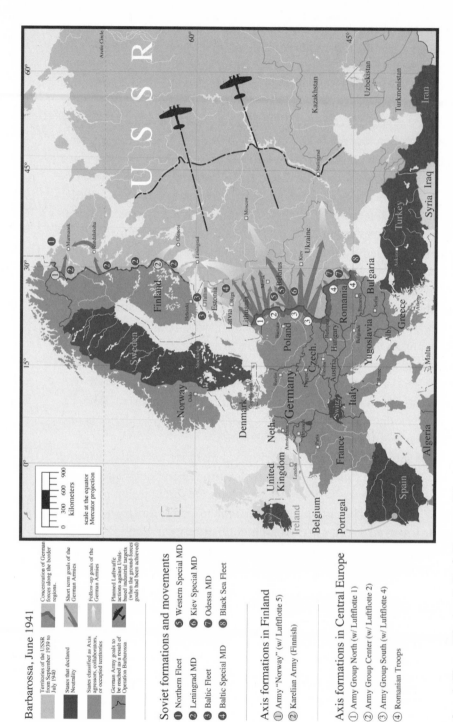

Barbarossa, June 1941

Territories of the USSR from September 1939 to July 1940.

States that declared Neutrality.

States classified as Axis aggressors, collaborators, or occupied territories.

German Army goals to be reached as a result of Operation Barbarossa.

Concentration of German forces along the border regions.

Short term goals of the German Armies.

Follow-up goals of the German Armies.

Planned Luftwaffe actions against Urals-based industrial targets (when the ground-forces goals had been achieved).

scale at the equator
Mercator projection

0 300 600 900
kilometers

Soviet formations and movements

❶ Northern Fleet   ❺ Western Special MD
❷ Leningrad MD   ❻ Kiev Special MD
❸ Baltic Fleet   ❼ Odessa MD
❹ Baltic Special MD   ❽ Black Sea Fleet

Axis formations in Finland

① Army "Norway" (w/ Luftflotte 5)
② Karelian Army (Finnish)

Axis formations in Central Europe

① Army Group North (w/ Luftflotte 1)
② Army Group Center (w/ Luftflotte 2)
③ Army Group South (w/ Luftflotte 4)
④ Romanian Troops

Map. 1 (Terry Higgins & Zach Downey-Higgins © 2011 [based on Russian source material supplied by the authors])

One key precondition for the launching of Operation Barbarossa had been a careful program of aerial reconnaissance. In fact, systematic overflights of Soviet territory had begun early in 1941. High-altitude *Luftwaffe* reconnaissance aircraft made repeated sweeps over the western periphery of the Soviet Union. And they provided for the Soviets telltale signs of German intentions. Airfields were photographed in detail and studied, along with antiaircraft batteries, roads, and storage facilities. One German reconnaissance aircraft, equipped with a camera and exposed film of Soviet territory, crashed near Rovno on April 15. Despite these aerial incursions, which reached a high frequency by June, Stalin forbade Soviet fighters or antiaircraft units to intervene. Later, many of the Soviet officers who survived the fighting wrote bitterly about the lack of preparedness in the months preceding the war.[20]

The first reports of *Luftwaffe* air strikes reached the Defense Commissariat in Moscow shortly after 0330 hours on June 22. General G. K. Zhukov, destined to play a major role in the war as a Soviet commander, passed the information on to Stalin shortly afterward. The latter's initial reaction was to view the attacks as "a provocation on the part of the German generals."[21] Three hours earlier, he had approved a confusing directive to the frontier military districts after a day of discussion about the growing menace on the western border. Issued through Marshal S. K. Timoshenko, the People's Commissar of Defense, it warned the military districts of a possible German attack on June 22–23. The directive called for local commanders to take concrete steps to assure combat readiness: troops were secretly to man the fire points of fortified districts; aircraft were to be dispersed and camouflaged before dawn on June 22; all units were to be placed at combat readiness; and other measures, such as the blacking out of towns and installations, were to be implemented.[22] These same commanders, however, were told in explicit terms to take no other steps without special authorization.

The belated directive by Timoshenko mirrored certain half measures taken largely in response to the overwhelming weight of intelligence data suggesting a German invasion, but they failed to make the grim prospects of war clear to Soviet commanders. Coming just after midnight, the Timoshenko directive did little to reduce the vulnerability of the Soviet Air Force. In some areas, air commanders adopted

An aerial photo, one frame in a sequence from high altitude, taken by a
Luftwaffe reconnaissance aircraft over the western periphery of the
Soviet Union, May 1941. A closer look reveals a Soviet fighter at the
lower left, shadowing the German intruder. (From the collection of Von
Hardesty)

a passive posture, ordering their air units not to intercept or fire on German aircraft found in Soviet airspace unless the enemy aircraft attacked. With dawn, many Soviet aircraft at forward airfields were still in place on their crowded runways. Only in isolated places, mostly in the more remote sectors in the South, did local air commanders have the time and the resolve to disperse substantial numbers of their aircraft prior to the arrival of the *Luftwaffe*.[23]

By 0715 hours on the morning of June 22, Timoshenko, after further consultation with Stalin, issued a second directive.[24] At this point the full brunt of German ground forces had fallen on the exposed and disorganized Soviet defenses in the western periphery. War now raged from the Baltic Sea to Ukraine as German mechanized spearheads penetrated deeply into the Soviet Union. Overhead, the *Luftwaffe* swept toward its various targets with massive and lethal concentrations of firepower. Soviet air defenses appeared almost nonexistent as the communications network collapsed and Moscow lost effective contact with the frontier. In this murky and ever-deepening crisis, Timoshenko directed "active offensive operations" to begin against the invading German troops where they had violated the border. Soviet aircraft, at that very moment facing the full fury of the *Luftwaffe*, were ordered on the offensive, to "destroy with powerful blows" the enemy aircraft and ground forces. For the first time, Moscow permitted the VVS to conduct air strikes to a depth of 100 miles (160 kilometers) into German territory.[25] This belated move only dramatized the impotence of Soviet airpower in facing the formidable challenge of the *Luftwaffe*.

A MOSAIC OF AIR WARFARE

The failure of the Soviet Air Force to respond effectively to Operation Barbarossa cannot be explained narrowly in terms of German military prowess or the widespread disorientation that befell Soviet arms in the wake of such a massive and unprecedented preemptive air strike. Ironically, the seeds for the catastrophe had been planted in the immediate prewar context. In the spring of 1941, certain missteps and delays in modernization created a context of vulnerability. These subtle and pervasive factors—largely concealed to the intelligence-gathering organs of the German military—profoundly shaped and conditioned the capacity of the VVS to operate effectively in this extreme national emergency. In fact, the crushing losses and humiliating retreat witnessed in June had their origins in the critical period from the end of 1940 to the eve of the invasion. During this time frame, the VVS wrestled—often with minimal success—with the challenges of adapting new technologies and rapid expansion. This chaotic process cast a long shadow over Soviet military fortunes.

The transition program to a whole new generation of modern aircraft had occupied a pivotal place in prewar Soviet efforts at modernization. Combat readiness, properly understood, rested squarely on the shift to newer and more effective combat aircraft. In fact, this specific effort was at the epicenter of a wide-ranging program of modernization and expansion. Soviet air planners in the prewar years aimed to gain technical parity with all potential enemies, in particular the German air force. The rapid pace of refinement in aircraft technology—designs, engines, and armament—placed a priority on modernization. For the Soviet Union, national security required a viable air arm to achieve and sustain air supremacy in any future war emergency. And there were other related factors at play in the formula for preparedness—new air tactics, the building of airfields, increased aircraft production and logistics, the training regimen of pilots and ground crews, and perfection of the communications network to assure optimal command and control along the vast borderlands of the Soviet Union. On the eve of the war, the VVS—as opposed to its popular image—was indeed a dynamic entity, keenly alert to the pressing requirement to make the transition to newer types of technology.

As it turned out, the calendar became a powerful ally for the German war planners. The *Luftwaffe* took full advantage of the fact that the Soviet transition program was still in motion. Even those VVS air units targeted to receive the newer-type warplanes faced frequent delays and difficulties. Rapid expansion of the VVS called for the formation of 104 new air regiments, bringing the number of combat-ready airplanes to over 22,000. Such a hasty pace of growth was warranted by neither the production of new aircraft nor the training of new cadre. As a result, about 25 percent of the regiments existed on paper only. Air regiments of all branches of the VVS consisted of sixty to sixty-four aircraft. Their organizational structure was not well suited to mobile warfare, and it stymied any effort to disperse warplanes in the event of an emergency or an air attack.[26] There were many "teething" problems with the new aircraft, which became evident only during the field tests. The aviation factories experienced chronic problems with the shift to serial production, most notably, low output. The prewar plan had called for 22 fighter regiments (out of 106) to be equipped with modern aircraft by summer.[27]

By June 1941, the Soviet aviation industry had manufactured a variety of newer model warplanes: 1,289 MiG-3s, 322 LaGG-3s, 335 Yak-1 fighters, 458 Pe-2 bombers, and 249 Il-2 Shturmoviks. However, the final acceptance of these aircraft from the aviation factories and their eventual deployment to frontline air units had been slow—even glacial—in pace. From January 1 to June 20, 1941, the VVS received only 706 of the new-type aircraft, including 407 MiG-3s, 29 LaGG-3s, 142 Yak-1s, and 128 Pe-2s.[28] Although success had been achieved, there was a noticeable lack of momentum. By one estimate, only eight fighter regiments had made the full transition and could be considered combat ready. Of these air units, five had been assigned the MiG-3, one the LaGG-3, and two the Yak-1.[29] Transition training for pilots and ground crews also had proceeded slowly. Problems with the new bombers, for example, the Pe-2s, were troublesome. Although the speed of the Pe-2 was greater than that of the He 111 and Ju 88, it was inferior in the critical categories of payload, range, and defensive armament. Derived from a high-altitude fighter design, the Pe-2 possessed minimal payload and range, along with a high landing speed that led to many mishaps. Soviet pilots complained that it was a difficult aircraft to control in emergency situations when one engine was shut down or failed. The VVS faced the *Luftwaffe* with a whole new generation of advanced fighters, ground attack aircraft, and tactical bombers, but this critical upgrade did not necessarily transfer into heightened preparedness.

The VVS training regime remained less than adequate, reinforcing a technical and tactical vulnerability the seasoned *Luftwaffe* airmen would fully exploit.[30] As early as the mid-1920s, the VVS had inaugurated a massive program of training for air and ground crews. The number of air personnel skyrocketed from 33,000 in 1929 to 110,000 in 1935. New flight schools were opened in 1937. The rapid expansion, however, did not reverse a lingering deficit in skilled command and flight personnel. Often there were more aircraft than trained personnel to fly and maintain them. On the eve of Operation Barbarossa, notwithstanding the many advances in the training program, the VVS faced a critical need for trained flight commanders at the squadron and regimental levels. During the first three months of 1941, pilots of the Baltic Special Military District (*Pribaltiyskiy Osobyy Voennyy Okrug*) clocked, on average, 15.5 hours in the air, pilots of the Western Special Military District (*Zapadniy Osobyy Voennyy Okrug*) clocked 9 hours, and those of the Kiev Special Military District (*Kievskiy Osobyy Voennyy Okrug*) only 4 hours.[31] Retraining on the newer types of aircraft had been steady but slow: on June 22, 1941, only 932 pilots out of 2,800 had completed their scheduled transition training.[32] Such a melancholy pattern of transition training—glacial in pace and short of any acceptable standard of combat readiness—had its predictable consequences when the hour of reckoning with the enemy arrived.

In April 1941, General A. V. Nikitin, head of the VVS Organization and Manning Directorate, took the time to conduct an inspection of the 12th BAD of the Western Special Military District. A veteran of the Russian Civil War and an experienced military pilot, Nikitin found the retraining program proceeding at a glacial pace. He discovered that 104 of the 139 crews of the 12th BAD had completed only part of their retraining.[33] For talented and highly motivated officers such as Nikitin, the prewar setting prompted no small measure of foreboding. Part of the inertia in training stemmed, no doubt, from the purges of the military in the late 1930s, when no fewer than three VVS air commanders and many midlevel air officers had been arrested, imprisoned, or executed. These purges were still a vivid memory. Any functioning air officer, in particular one in a command position, displayed a prudent caution toward the transition program—an understandable reflex to avoid failure, since accidents of any kind could be interpreted by the ubiquitous political officers as evidence of "wrecking" or "sabotage." Consequently, retraining flights were few in number and lacking in complexity. Nikitin's complaints led to a call from the top for an accelerated program of retraining, but his objections about the "impermissibility of such a faulty retraining method" came too late.

A whole new generation of Soviet fighter and ground attack aircraft, however, did show great promise. The fact that these aircraft designs had appeared in advance of Barbarossa offered a strategic advantage to the VVS. These new aircraft reflected the work of a younger generation of aircraft designers—Sergei Ilyushin, Alexander Yakovlev, Artem Mikoyan, Mikhail Gurevich, and Semyon Lavochkin. Their designs signaled a concerted drive to achieve technical parity with the *Luftwaffe* and other major air forces of the world. In the 1930s, aircraft design had advanced in a dramatic fashion with the embrace of streamlined silhouettes, closed cockpits, and retractable landing gears; the expanded use of aluminum components; and the development of more powerful and reliable engines. Keeping pace was a challenge, and air planners understood that technical backwardness in this critical realm of technology could compromise national security. Among these new designs was the aforementioned MiG-3 (along with smaller numbers of the earlier version MiG-1), which sported a modern silhouette and represented a technical advance over designs of the interwar years. Other new fighter types were the Yak-1 and LaGG-3, which had also reached forward air units in small numbers. The remarkable Il-2 Shturmovik ground attack airplane had become operational, and it was destined to play a decisive role in Soviet combined air-army operations later in the war. As the transition program moved ahead in spurts, VVS air units soon contained an odd mix of old and new warplanes, all deployed in a confusing and haphazard fashion.

Overall, the prewar growth of the VVS had been dramatic. This expansion mirrored similar trends throughout the Soviet military. The creation of new air regiments put considerable pressure on the existing administrative and logistics structures. The recruitment and training of pilots, ground crews, and other technical specialists presented formidable challenges. To ensure effective leadership, seasoned pilots were transferred to these new air units. This had certain consequences that air planners were slow to realize. For instance, older units suddenly found themselves weakened and demoralized. Moreover, the newly minted pilots often reached their assigned regiments not as officers but as sergeants. This innovation had been initiated by Timoshenko and approved by Stalin himself, who took a keen interest in some of the proposed reforms for the Soviet Union's air arm. All these factors created an atmosphere of uncertainty and low morale.

The low level of combat readiness in the various military districts generated no small amount of anxiety for air planners, in particular those VVS leaders who feared a German invasion in the near term. Disorder prevailed among the forward elements of the Soviet Air Force. For example, in the Western Special Military District, the fighter air arm displayed only minimal efficiency. The emphasis had been on a rather hurried program of conversion training, and that training had been accompanied by a number of accidents. Operational air units had been allowed to engage in gunnery practice only occasionally—an approach that lacked discipline and high standards. Moreover, there was an inadequate supply of bombs and ordnance either for training or, more ominously, for actual operations in case of a war emergency. The logistics dilemma was not unique to this particular district. Too often, bomber crews lacked experience in long-distance sorties to perfect their skills in navigation and targeting. The ability to conduct reconnaissance flights was very limited. At the time, the 313th and 314th RAPs (*Razvedyvatelnyye Aviatsionnyye Polki,* or reconnaissance air regiments) were making the transition to the newer Yak-2 and Yak-4 aircraft. The 314th RAP first received these new models in April, and by June, it had only six combat-ready crews.[34]

The mix of old and new technology created unforeseen problems, reinforcing the general mood of disorientation. In the Kiev Special Military District there were similar telltale signs that the VVS was not combat ready on the eve of the war. For example, there was a preponderance of older types of fighters and bombers (I-16s, I-153s, SB bombers). Not all phases of training had been completed. The training program for the newer-type aircraft had been ineffectual on many levels. Only a small segment of the pilots and ground crews had been introduced to the MiG-3, Yak-1, Yak-2, Yak-4, Pe-2, and Su-2 aircraft. Consequently, flying experience with the new technology was minimal at best. In the Baltic Special Military District there was even a lack of proper training with the older generation of aircraft such as the I-16 and I-153 fighters. In this same district, only two regiments had received the newer MiG-3 fighters, and the parallel transition to the new generation of bombers had been just as slow and ineffectual. In fact, the active air regiments in this sector could conduct sorties only in daytime, in good weather, and at lower altitudes. The capacity to launch night missions was limited.[35] In the Baltic, the *Luftwaffe* would encounter a force severely compromised and extremely vulnerable.

Many of these inadequacies related to an unforgiving calendar, and they were mirrored elsewhere in the forward VVS air units. The VVS faced formidable problems with aircraft maintenance, supply, and the availability of spare parts. The Western Special Military District, for example, experienced chronic difficulties maintaining the SB and Su-2 bombers, as well as smaller numbers of the obsolete TB-3 heavy bombers. Even frontline I-16 and I-153 fighters and I-15bis ground attack airplanes were often poorly serviced. On forward airfields in the Kiev Special Military District, training proved to be haphazard and ineffectual, especially with regard to the proper techniques for gunnery and bombardment with the newly acquired advanced models, which had reached frontline units in small numbers. Many air units, such as the 52nd and 48th SBAPs, simply lacked modern types of aircraft and training, making them extremely vulnerable on the eve of the war.[36] For those air units fortunate enough to receive new aircraft, there was only minimal training, which made them ineffective once the war began.

On the eve of the war, the rapid expansion of VVS air units required the building of new airfields and the modernization of existing bases. This program took place after the signing of the Nazi-Soviet Pact in August 1939. For example, in the newly acquired territory of Western Belorussia, there had been a concerted drive to build new air force facilities as part of a larger program to consolidate the Soviet hold on the territory. Some seventy airfields, in fact, had been built in this time frame, but only thirty of them had adequate stockpiles of fuel and ordnance.[37] There had been a certain asymmetry to this airfield construction, with the forward and rear areas well developed but the central sector almost devoid of aerodromes—an area that included Vilnius, Pinsk, Minsk, and other key cities. In a parallel fashion, there was an effort to construct simple landing fields to allow the dispersal and maneuver of air units in an emergency, but this effort—like so many others in the spring of 1941—had been only partially implemented. Forty-six airfields were under construction or being expanded, which meant limited maneuver for air units, leaving only fifteen to seventeen airstrips for the 9th, 10th, and 11th SADs within 6 to 25 miles (10 to 40 kilometers) from the border.[38] Most of these airfields, it turned out, lacked proper storage for aviation fuel, ammunition, and other vital supplies. And oddly, the airfields with the largest and most complete storage facilities were close to the frontier and exposed to a preemptive strike. Adding to the context of vulnerability was the absence of effective communications between these forward airfields and the VVS command structure in the rear.

The deployment of antiaircraft batteries to protect the operational VVS airfields also proved to be haphazard, even though, in theory, this was considered a vital dimension for the air defense of the frontier. The Kiev Special Military District, for example, displayed little efficiency in this realm of preparedness. Moreover, there had been little progress in fashioning a systematic program for the camouflaging of aircraft. This vulnerability was evident in the Baltic Special Military District in the critical months leading up to the war. German aerial reconnaissance had photographed many of the key Soviet air bases in the weeks prior to the invasion, offering a telltale sign of their intentions. The absence of an effective net of antiaircraft batteries severely compromised any Soviet effort to oppose a systematic preemptive air strike. This lack of a viable air defense did not escape notice in the weeks leading up to June 22, when German reconnaissance aircraft made repeated sweeps over the frontier zones of the Soviet Union.

The precise nature of the German threat had not been fully comprehended by frontal air commanders, let alone their aircrews. Little had been done to carefully study the organizational, tactical, and technical capabilities of the enemy. This reality remained outside official military pronouncements and training documents. On one level, an abstract one, a certain body of information had been gathered via intelligence and existed on paper, but this had not been translated into any systematic program of study. German air operations in the West since 1939 offered a vast arena for study, but this crucial task had not been achieved by the spring of 1941. Moreover, the VVS had not made use of foreign reports and analyses on the *Luftwaffe* air operations in the West. Such work required time and dedication, all of which was missing in the context of 1941. Only in the last two months of peace—literally, in the eleventh hour—did the VVS belatedly launch a formal and systematic analysis of German airpower. By contrast, German reconnaissance had studied VVS aircraft, airfields, communications, and logistics in great detail. Knowledge of one's enemy is a vital factor in war, and it would be in this realm that the VVS found itself severely compromised.[39]

Yak-2 of the 136th SBAP, Berdichev airfield. (From the collection of Hans-Heiri Stapfer)

In the period leading up to the war, the VVS High Command had experimented with the problem of command and control for an air force deployed over a vast geographic area. The task was daunting—given the enormity of the fronts. Adding to the problems was the fact that most air officers lacked any practical or combat experience. The Western Special Military District possessed a skilled staff, as evident in war games going back to 1940. In fact, frontal aviation units had participated in four large exercises with army ground forces. These exercises provided meaningful training, but the experience offered little understanding of actual air operations against a formidable and experienced enemy. In the Baltic sector, the training regimen at the air division level included useful exercises with radios. However, there was no realistic training on the efficient modes of evacuation and re-basing of air units—a skill that would be highly prized in the summer of 1941. Moreover, VVS frontal units required additional rehearsal on how best to coordinate bomber and fighter sorties, along with proper command and integration of air defense units. All these training

I-16 of the 89th IAP and I-153 of the 46th IAP in the background. (From the collection of Hans-Heiri Stapfer)

efforts revealed serious problems in the realm of communications—the coordination of forward command posts as well as regimental and division air units. War descended on these fronts before this critical dimension of combat readiness had been perfected.[40]

In retrospect, the Germans clearly enjoyed superior intelligence in the months leading up to the invasion. This key factor allowed the *Luftwaffe* to execute a series of sudden and paralyzing air strikes against forward VVS air units. The Soviets had taken a series of steps to achieve greater combat readiness, but the disorderly nature of these transitions, along with the shortage of time, did little to enhance Soviet military fortunes. The image of VVS aircraft destroyed in place on the morning of June 22 offered an enduring picture of Soviet vulnerability. What this familiar image did not reveal was the capacity of the VVS to reorganize and resist. And much of that residual strength had its origins in the immediate prewar period.

I-153 of the 160th IAP destroyed at Loschitsa airfield, Minsk area. (From the collection of Hans-Heiri Stapfer)

A SUDDEN COUNTERATTACK

For the Soviets, there was the urgent question of how best to counter the unfolding German air campaign. This became an immediate and perilous mandate for surviving VVS air units near or in the direct path of the invasion corridors. Even with the near complete breakdown of the command and control structure, the VVS made an effort to launch effective counterstrokes against the invaders. Timoshenko issued a third directive at 2115 hours Moscow time. This order from the Commissariat of Defense called on the Soviet military—now roughly redefined into the Northwestern, Western, and Southwestern *Fronts* and coextensive with the avenues of invasion—to go on the offensive and carry the war into enemy territory. Ironically, this projected counteroffensive to push the German forces back from the frontier coincided with the collapse of Soviet forward defenses. At Minsk and in

MiG-3 of 15th or 31st IAP, 8th SAD, Keidany (Kedainiai) airfield. I-153 of
the 61st ShAP is in the background. (From the collection of Hans-Heiri
Stapfer)

other sectors, the Soviet army faced encirclement and disintegration.
The Soviet Air Force, already in ashes, was simply incapable of providing sustained air support for offensive operations.

The deployment of Soviet airpower was keyed to the five new
military zones: the Northern *Front* (formerly the Leningrad Military
District) covering Leningrad and environs, the Northwestern *Front*
(formerly the Baltic Special Military District), the Western *Front*
(organized from the Western Special Military District), the Southwestern *Front* (centered on the Kiev Special Military District), and the
Southern *Front* (hurriedly set up on June 25 in the wake of the
invasion and based on the Odessa Military District). In addition, the
Soviets possessed independent army units and reserves. The VVS fit
into this fluid organization as a major air component. The sudden and
dramatic advance of the German forces largely compromised or even
shattered this initial structure. As the necessary shift to defensive
warfare took place, *Stavka,* the Soviet High Command, would redefine
these *Fronts* to reflect the ebb and flow of the conflict.

German soldiers inspect a downed Su-2 light bomber on a main road west of Bryansk, near Dubrovka, September 1941. (From the collection of Von Hardesty)

For Nazi Germany, the acquisition of air supremacy in the first hours of the invasion evoked a mood of supreme confidence and the belief that Operation Barbarossa would be a success. This stridency and optimism rested initially on the preemptive air strikes of the *Luftwaffe,* arguably the most dramatic and devastating in the history of airpower. Throughout the summer of 1941, German air units maintained effective control of the skies. The dominance of German airpower stemmed from several factors: modern, fast, and technically advanced aircraft; seasoned pilots and aircrews; superior combat tactics; well-developed command and control; and efficient intelligence.

By contrast, the VVS had been caught off guard, had endured enormous material losses, and now faced the prospect of losing even the capacity to offer resistance. In terms of organization, availability of modern aircraft types, and consistent pilot combat experience, the Soviet air arm faced distinct disadvantages. This inferiority to the *Luftwaffe,* so dramatically manifest in the opening stages of the war, made any sustained countermove extremely difficult. Moreover, fateful con-

Adolf Hitler, Hermann Goering, and Albert Kesselring (then commander of *Luftflotte* 2) during the Barbarossa campaign, conveying a mood of supreme confidence about the war in the East. The dramatic successes of the *Luftwaffe* prompted Hitler to order a temporary reduction in combat aircraft production. (From the collection of Valeriy Romanenko)

tingency planning in the prewar period only enhanced the enemy's potential to achieve air dominance. Moscow had deployed a large number of VVS air units very close to the frontier, a move that created a context of extreme vulnerability that the *Luftwaffe* cleverly exploited. The preparatory air reconnaissance work by skilled German aircrews had been systematic and effective, revealing the positioning and strength of Soviet air units.

It has been estimated that, prior to Operation Barbarossa, the VVS possessed 7,133 aircraft in the five western military districts. The long-range bomber command consisted of a total of 1,339 aircraft, and these assets were stationed in the European part of the Soviet Union. The Soviet naval air arm, deployed in the Northern, Baltic, and Black Sea Fleets, constituted another sphere of airpower, numbering some 1,445 aircraft. Accordingly, Soviet aviation may have numbered just under 10,000 aircraft (not counting auxiliary aviation) on the eve of the war.[41] Whatever the precise figures and actual deployment, Soviet aviation appeared formidable in quantitative terms. Once the *Luftwaffe* unleashed its many combat sorties against Soviet forward airfields, the quantitative edge became drastically reduced or neutralized. Soviet aircraft losses were enormous, and there were accompanying problems with communications and logistics—leading to near paralysis. One report suggested that of the 880 aircraft inventoried by the Northwestern *Front* on June 22, only 550 were left by June 25.[42] Only 10 to 20 aircraft were operational for each regiment. The entire 7th SAD reported only 60 aircraft surviving the German onslaught. SB medium bombers of the 7th SAD had, on average, 50 percent of their engine lives left. This factor also limited a program of sustained operations against the advancing Germans. There were severe gaps in logistical support, particularly ammunition supply. In some instances, VVS air units had ammunition for only one to two days. Frantic efforts to deliver ammunition and other supplies from Estonia and other rear areas were compromised by a dearth of ground transportation. No real command and control was provided from the leadership of the VVS Northwestern *Front* due to the absence of communication and the lack of initiative. Retreat was often necessary, there was a catastrophic breakdown in communications between air units and army commanders, combat missions against the enemy were difficult or often impossible to launch, and many VVS aircraft remained on the ground, exposed to repeated air raids by the *Luftwaffe*.[43]

All the widely dispersed VVS air bases, in fact, faced formidable threats in the opening days. Some were merely neutralized by the *Luftwaffe*; others were only partially so, allowing some measure of air counterattack. One example was the 9th SBAP of the 9th SBAD (*Skorostnaya Bombardirovochnaya Aviatsionnaya Diviziya,* or high-speed bomber air division) at Panevezhis airfield. This air regiment endured the loss of seven bombers and another fourteen damaged on the ground during the Germans' predawn attack at 0420 hours. Thirty minutes later, following orders from Division Headquarters, twenty-five of the remaining bombers took off for the assigned target of Tilsit rail station. At 0620 the Soviet bombers dropped their ordnance on the target from an altitude of 25,000 feet (7,500 meters). Other groups of this regiment hit troop concentrations from 13,000 feet (4,000 meters) with the loss of three aircraft due to antiaircraft fire. The remaining twenty-two aircraft landed at their airfield at 0710, only to take off again for a new base of operations. This sortie was the first Soviet air strike at German territory and also the first sortie performed according to prewar plans.

At 0540 hours, the 46th SBAP (from the 7th SBAD) deployed eighteen bombers of the 2nd and 3rd squadrons to attack German troop concentrations in the Tilsit area. Each of these squadrons lost five bombers with their crews; another two crash-landed at their airfields, with several crew members killed and wounded. According to the plan, the 46th was to appear over the target, together with the 9th SBAP, under the cover of fighters from the 10th IAP (*Istrebitelnyy Avi-atsionnyy Polk,* or fighter air regiment). However, the fighter cover did not materialize due to the fact that they had to fight for their lives fending off the German assault on their own airfield in Siauliai. The bombers of the 46th fell prey to the skilled pilots of II/JG 53 and I/JG 54. The results were grim, but typical, for this formative period of the war. The attrition in Soviet bombers, it should be noted, was due in part to the lack of consistent fighter cover. Even in this desperate situation, the bomber regiment managed to keep formation and shoot down one of the attacking German fighters.[44] Other conditioning factors were the confusing directives from above and the Soviet High Command's inability to mobilize decisive counterblows until noon on June 22. In retrospect, some air commanders acted decisively, taking the initiative in a climate of confusion; others did not. Although the losses endured by VVS air units were heavy and debilitating, the advancing German juggernaut learned that the Soviets possessed a remarkable capacity to strike back under extreme pressure.

THE SAGA OF THE 123RD FIGHTER AIR REGIMENT

In the midst of this vast military catastrophe, there were isolated instances in which VVS air units responded with extraordinary courage and even managed to inflict significant losses on the *Luftwaffe*. One stellar example was the 123rd IAP, posted at Kobrin near the strategic fortress of Brest. First organized in 1940 near Orsha, the 123rd possessed fifty-eight aircraft on the eve of the invasion, staffed with a coterie of eighty-seven pilots. These aircraft were mostly obsolescent types, such as I-15s and I-153 biplanes, but the air regiment had just received twenty Yak-1s, a monoplane fighter of modern design. The arrival of these new fighters reflected a long-range plan to refit VVS air units at or near the frontier. The newly minted Yak-1s had been manufactured at an aviation plant in distant Saratov. At Kobrin, the transition to these new aircraft ran into unforeseen problems with logistics, in particular the supply of proper aviation fuel. When an inspector from the VVS High Command arrived at the base on June 19 to oversee transition training with the Yak-1 fighters, he discovered there was a stockpile of only 2,000 pounds (1,000 kilograms) of the necessary fuel available, a grim fact that severely compromised training and combat readiness. Other complexities made life at the air base at Kobrin less than optimal: there were persistent delays in the construction of hangars and other facilities, the absence of effective antiaircraft batteries, and problems supplying key air staff and technical personnel. Kobrin's organization and capabilities reflected the plight of many forward Soviet air bases—outwardly functional, but in no way combat ready to face a menacing *Luftwaffe* poised like a coiled spring just over the horizon.[45]

Major Boris N. Surin commanded the 123rd Air Regiment. He impressed the frontline personnel with his forceful style and his manifest skills as a fighter pilot. On the eve of Barbarossa, Surin displayed a keen awareness of the dangers that beset the VVS in the frontier areas in 1941. As early as May, he observed the regularity of German reconnaissance flights over Brest and surrounding areas, a telltale sign of impending military action or outright war. Surin spoke boldly about the apparent danger, telling his airmen that "war was inevitable, a mere question of time."[46]

With Brest as a logical target, Surin took some meaningful steps to prepare for air combat. As late as June 21, he test-flew one of the Yak-1s to gain familiarity with the new fighter. Other senior members of the regiment underwent similar training. Even as these test flights proceeded, Surin ordered some precautionary moves to get the Kobrin air base in a heightened state of readiness, not knowing the German aerial assault was just hours away. Aircraft were dispersed and camouflaged. Select members of the technical staff were briefed on the dire contingency of rapid withdrawal and the procedures for the destruction of equipment, fuel, and supplies—to deny the enemy the use of any abandoned war materiel. Family and nonessential personnel were evacuated to the rear. Surin's most experienced pilots were restricted to the airfield and ordered to be ready for any contingency. All these steps were taken without specific instructions from higher air force authorities.

At the second hour on the first day, the 123rd IAP received its first alert—a signal that was simultaneously vague and ominous. Two hours passed. Then word reached Kobrin of a German air attack on nearby Brest. Surin quickly ordered his air regiment into action at dawn. These repeated sorties continued into the morning as the 123rd sought out the enemy in the skies over Brest. There were at least ten separate engagements with the *Luftwaffe* in those early hours. Moreover, archival records for the air regiment list some initial triumphs, including the downing of two Ju 88 bombers and two Messerschmitt Bf 109 fighters without the loss of any Soviet aircraft. By 1300 hours, the pilots of the 123rd claimed thirty enemy aircraft downed, with the loss of six VVS fighters. That same afternoon, ten He 111 bombers and eleven Bf 109 fighters hit Kobrin, leaving only fifteen aircraft on the field operational. Given the circumstances, the 123rd withdrew to an airfield near the city of Pinsk.[47]

During one air battle, Surin with two escorts attacked ten enemy aircraft. He scored his first air victory, downing a Bf 109. Pilots of the 123rd flew repeated sorties, making necessary return flights to Kobrin for refueling and rearming. Surin flew repeated sorties on June 22, but in the end he fell victim to *Luftwaffe* fighters. On his last sortie, he was seriously wounded and attempted to return to Kobrin, only to lose consciousness and crash. His leadership on the first day had been inspirational to his air regiment. The air battles over Brest were often sudden and violent, with opposing warplanes caught up in spiraling dogfights at various altitudes. The more experienced German fighter pilots benefited from the element of surprise, their more technically advanced fighters, and superior tactics. Nonetheless, the spirited attacks by pilots of the 123rd gave evidence of the residual strength of the VVS and its determination to mount a credible opposition to the *Luftwaffe*.

One of the most alarming tactics employed by Soviet pilots was the *taran,* or the deliberate ramming of an enemy plane. In fact, the 123rd IAP initiated this perilous maneuver as early as 1000 hours on that first day: in an attempt to save fellow pilot G. N. Zhidov from enemy attack, P. S. Ryabtsev successfully downed a German aircraft with this extraordinary tactic near Brest and then managed to parachute to safety. As the air battles unfolded, it turned out, he was not alone: on the same day, I. I. Ivanov of the 46th IAP rammed a German He 111 bomber with his I-16 fighter in the Zholkva region, a move he employed after his ammunition had been exhausted. However, Ivanov did not survive this bold exploit.[48] The *taran* can be traced to August 26, 1914, at the beginning of World War I, when famed Russian aviator P. N. Nesterov rammed the plane of Austrian Baron von Rosenthal. Both Ryabtsev and Ivanov, along with a recorded eight other fighter pilots, followed in the tradition of Nesterov on the first day of Operation Barbarossa.[49]

The *taran* required great skill and no small amount of courage to execute. The deed was always a voluntary act. In the popular mind, it reflected a higher calling of patriotism, the willingness to place one's own life in harm's way to achieve a tactical victory. The pilot consciously embraced this option only in extreme situations. Typically, the favorite script for the *taran* called for the ramming of the control surfaces of an enemy aircraft—with the slow-moving German bombers being the preferred targets. The Soviet pilot accomplished this feat by approaching from the rear, adjusting to the speed of the enemy plane at close quarters, and then pushing the tip of his propeller into the opponent's rudder or elevator. As soon as firm contact was made, the Soviet pilot would drop away quickly, fearing he might become entangled in the stricken aircraft as it spun out of control. The resulting impact on the enemy aircraft and on the Soviet fighter was never predictable. Frequently, both fell into a spin. If propeller damage was minimal, the Soviet pilot might even retain control of his fighter and land safely.

Ryabtsev's heroic exploit on June 22, like all ramming maneuvers, differed from the kamikaze attacks employed by the Japanese toward the end of World War II in the Pacific, although both were motivated by patriotism and desperation. For the Soviets, the tactic pivoted on certain practical considerations. While never an official directive, the *taran* became a live option when there was no hope of knocking down an enemy plane by other means. As noted, if the Soviet pilot was as skillful as he was bold, he might survive, as did Ryabtsev and many others, by parachuting to safety after executing the high-risk maneuver. Some chose to fly their now crippled aircraft to the ground, which proved to be the less predictable option. For the Soviets, the trade-off in the brutal calculus of air combat meant the loss of an obsolete prewar I-16 or I-15 for the downing of a modern He 111 or Ju 88. In time, ramming became an established, if unconventional, air combat technique.

The 123rd IAP, like other forward air units, had begun the critical transition to modern-type fighters. By June 21, around 412 Yak-1s had been manufactured, but certainly not all of them had reached the air regiments.[50] This sleek monoplane became the baseline technology for the Yak series (Yak-7, Yak-9, and the highly effective Yak-3 variants). Fast and highly maneuverable, the Yak-1 was a quantum leap over prewar models, although its debut had been marked by many problems. In addition, some veteran pilots regarded the Yak-1 as too lightly armed with its ShVAK 20mm and two ShKAS 7.62mm machine guns, even though the rate of fire for these guns matched or surpassed Western technology at the time.[51] There were also racks for arming the Yak-1 with six rockets, mounted under the wings. Yaks had entered operational life with other nagging problems, such as chronic fuel leaks, defective cockpit canopies, and critical shortages in replacement engines, radiators, and other key spare parts. Still, the first-generation Yak fighters showed great promise. Although Soviet fighters were still constructed of wood and metal components at this stage of the war, the Yak fighters—if fully armed and properly maintained—were effective interceptors. For Major Surin, the Yaks would have utility.

The desperate heroics of the 123rd IAP on the opening day of the war offered a dramatic counterpoint to the grim reality of Soviet paralysis and disorderly retreat in face of the German air juggernaut. Now forced on the move, the 123rd continued the uneven struggle, flying a number of improvised missions in defense of Pinsk on the second day. That day, the 123rd recorded three downed Ju 88 bombers. The interlude at Pinsk proved short-lived owing to the ever-advancing German army. Forced to flee again, the 123rd moved farther to the east; surviving pilots flew to Bobruysk as ground crews and nonflying personnel traveled by foot, truck, or train along the crowded corridors of retreat. Throughout July and August, the 123rd remained a viable fighting force in a sequence of combat assignments from providing air cover for the vital Moscow–Leningrad rail link to the strategic defense of Moscow itself. In the skies over Moscow, pilots of the 123rd flew 480 daytime sorties and 78 night missions.[52] Chaos and constant movement became routine for the hard-pressed air regiment as the summer came to a close.

THE AIR WAR IN THE NORTH AND WEST

Not all VVS air units in the northern sector were necessarily caught off guard by the devastating German aerial assault. Ten days prior to the invasion, the air units of the Baltic Special Military District had gone on alert with a series of war maneuvers.[53] During this exercise, ground troops and air defense elements had been tested. Sensing the impending crisis, the military council for the district had stated: "Today, as never before, we must be in full combat readiness. Many commanders do not understand this point. They should fully and clearly realize that we should be ready for any combat task and at any time."[54] Other steps followed as the invasion hour neared. On June 15, Colonel General F. I. Kuznetsov signed a directive to establish the means to notify the troops of any large-scale violation of the border by the German army.[55] Three days later, he set up a procedure to initiate air defenses in full combat readiness, a measure designed to protect vital bridges and communications links from enemy air strikes. Kuznetsov also organized around-the-clock monitoring of enemy movements and communications. On June 19, the People's Commissariat of Defense issued orders for the camouflaging of aircraft, hangars, and buildings at key airfields. This order, if prudent and welcome, had arrived belatedly the day before the German invasion. Notwithstanding the directive from Moscow, the military district had ordered certain preparatory steps on its own: "Aircraft on the airfields must be dispersed and camouflaged in the woods and bushes, avoid parking them in lines, and put all aircraft in combat readiness."[56]

At the time, air forces of the Baltic Special Military District consisted of five air divisions, each possessing from 170 to 316 aircraft. All were mixed air divisions with fighter, ground attack, and bomber regiments. Overall, the district had 1,211 combat aircraft at its disposal.[57] Looking closer, it was apparent that the transition to modern types had been slow at best, with older fighters and bombers making up most of the inventory and only 156 newer aircraft types (MiG-3, Pe-2, and Il-2).[58] Only two regiments had made the full transition to the late-model MiG-3 aircraft. In addition, there were a handful of modern Pe-2 bombers available. The complement of new Il-2 Shturmoviks for the 61st ShAP (*Shturmovoy Aviatsionnyy Polk,* or ground attack air regiment) had arrived, but these aircraft remained in crates and unassembled. Some of the ground attack pilots for the Il-2 Shturmoviks had been assigned to the aviation plant at Voronezh for transition training at the time of the invasion.

This same military district contained a total of seventy-one air bases. The network included twenty-one permanent aerodromes. The remainder of the airfields were uneven in quality; some were primitive landing strips with only temporary structures in place. On the eve of hostilities, there were twenty-three airfields under construction for the installation of concrete runways. One modern aerodrome was located at Kaunas in Lithuania. Ironically, the facility had been constructed in the interwar years by German specialists. Here and in other sectors of the Northwest, the VVS met the enemy with a flotilla of mostly obsolete aircraft, flying I-153, I-15, and I-16 fighters and SB medium bombers. Whenever possible, forward air units deployed these outclassed aircraft to attack German mechanized units. At this juncture, the I-153 fighter was also deployed as a ground attack aircraft. On the Baltic coast, near Riga, efforts were made to hit seaborne transports. Heroic efforts were even made to hit enemy airfields and staging areas near Memel.[59] The task of attacking German bombers en route to their targets became an uncertain undertaking. Routinely, these marauding enemy bombers approached their targets with a robust fighter escort. *Luftwaffe* airmen at this stage of the war enjoyed the advantage of being on the offensive; they could choose the optimal moment to attack, and they possessed superior training and experience. Given the disruptive context at Soviet airfields, the VVS offered isolated—if often spirited—opposition at best. Soviet losses were predictably high. On the second day of the invasion, the VVS frontal air commanders were able—often under extremely difficult circumstances—to move threatened air regiments to rear areas. The *Luftwaffe* kept the pressure up in the early phases, with sorties of six to eighteen bombers (Ju 88s, Do 215s, He 111s, and Bf 110s) hitting Soviet airfields. The ubiquitous Bf 109 fighters offered necessary protection from any marauding Soviet fighters. Given the accuracy of German intelligence and the incipient chaos on the ground, a huge number of VVS aircraft were destroyed in place at targeted airfields. In this northern sector of the front, efforts were made to rebase surviving fighters on the second day. Some success was achieved in moving certain threatened air assets to second and third echelons of defense. This hurried effort at rebasing proved to be an arduous undertaking, as it was pursued under fire and without efficient leadership by local air commanders.[60]

On the Western *Front*, a pattern of extreme vulnerability became evident. The deployment of six air divisions, one air corps, and four separate air regiments defined the operational capabilities of Soviet frontal aviation. On the morning of June 22, there were six air divisions consisting of twelve fighter regiments and eighteen bomber regiments available—a force supplemented with two ground attack and two reconnaissance regiments plus an array of reserve aircraft, for a total of 1,909 aircraft, of which 1,022 were fighters and 887 were bombers.[61] On paper, this was a relatively large air arm. However, VVS operations in this *Front* would prove to be ineffectual. The impact of repeated *Luftwaffe* blows in air battles and the strafing of airfields proved to be substantial: 538 aircraft were lost on the first day,[62] and a total of 1,163 aircraft were lost over the course of the first eight days. During July, the surviving VVS air elements engaged in a series of defensive air battles as the Germans advanced eastward toward Bobruysk. Efforts were made, sometimes with success, to attack the German mechanized units operating at the cutting edge of the invasion along the Pruzhany–Bereza axis and in the area of Molodechno, Baranovichi, Minsk, and Bobruysk. Here—and elsewhere—the Red

Army air units were active. Throughout these opening stages of the war, the task of coordinating VVS air units with the army proved extremely difficult, a situation made worse by the inability of the Soviet command to establish a secure line of defense to thwart the German advance.

The opening hours of Barbarossa led to many tragic incidents on the Soviet side. Across the entire swath of the Soviet frontier, the VVS—in particular at the level of small air units—reacted clumsily to the lethal blows of menacing *Luftwaffe* fighters and bombers. In the Pskov region, for example, one air base endured a chaotic five-day ordeal fending off enemy air attacks.[63] With the war just a week old, the VVS command ordered a mission to the forward air base at Pskov to assess its actual war footing—operational aircraft, personnel, fuel, supplies, ammunition, and spare parts. Major J. S. Stadnik piloted the inspection team in a PS-84 transport, or "Douglas" (a copy of the DC-3). He discovered on his final approach to the airfield that he could not lower the plane's landing gear. He then decided to circle the field as he and the crew worked in vain to resolve this unwelcome technical glitch. Now in plain sight and cruising slowly at low altitude, the visiting transport—notwithstanding its red star livery—prompted alarm among the pilots and ground crews looking skyward. A MiG-3 interceptor quickly took off and attempted to shoot down the circling intruder. This attack was joined by steady small-arms fire from machine guns and rifles. After several hits, Major Stadnik abandoned his efforts to lower the landing gear and executed an emergency landing, setting the aircraft down on its belly. Except for bullet holes and bent propellers, the Douglas had reached the runway more or less intact. No one on board had been seriously injured. Later, a group of thirty to thirty-five air personnel were able to raise the Douglas and repair the landing gear, a spirited effort carried out under the threat of enemy air attack. Colonel T. S. Toropchin—the no-nonsense air division commander and Hero of the Soviet Union—had arrived on the airfield just prior to the crash landing. He observed the event with anger and frustration and claimed that all the fools circling the airfield should be shot down. On approach, Toropchin had not received a warning, if indeed one had been sent. The loss of communication created a serious crisis.

In the meantime, a patrolling flight of MiG-3s landed. No sooner had they touched down than a group of Dornier bombers suddenly attacked the nearby train station at low altitude, scoring a number of direct hits. Several MiG and I-153 fighters rose to make a belated response, but this counterattack took place some six to seven minutes after the enemy bombers had departed. In the aftermath of the raid and in response to the many calamities of the day, the local commander, Major General T. F. Kutsevalov, ordered Toropchin to muster all the base personnel for a dressing down, which meant pulling everyone off duty for the reprimand. The angry critique lasted for one hour.

On the same day, another Douglas and an SB bomber were fired on from the ground by their own forces. In the evening, two MiG-3s and two I-153s took off following a flare signal toward an approaching twin-engine aerial target. Upon return, one of the pilots reported that an enemy He 111 had been downed. General Kutsevalov immediately went to inspect the site, only to find that it was their own DB-3F bomber returning from a reconnaissance mission. At 0200 hours on July 1, a Dornier Do 215 swept over the field three times, dropping illumination bombs. One I-153 fighter rose to intercept the Dornier but failed to make contact. Then, on the morning of July 2, two Do 215s bombed the airfield despite low-cast clouds, dropping bombs from 300 to 450 feet (100 to 150 meters). Patrolling VVS fighters had failed to detect them. Moreover, there was no alert or guidance from the ground. Subsequent German attacks over the next few days inflicted serious damage, with no effective response by the local defenses. There had been a systematic failure to identify the enemy and react effectively. These episodes mirrored the chaos at isolated Soviet air bases in the opening phases of Operation Barbarossa.

Sporadic action over the airfield near Pskov persisted from July 1 to 5, with MiG-3 and I-153 fighters scrambling to challenge attacking enemy aircraft. Often VVS aircraft stationed at the airfield ranged out as far as Velikiye Luki on patrol. On occasion, German bombers stealthily used cloud formations to shield attacks. At the nearby rail station, patrolling Soviet fighters missed two low-flying German aircraft that managed to reach their target and hastily retreat. On the night of July 4, the airfield faced an attack by He 111 bombers. One defending MiG-3 fell under friendly fire from the ground and was forced to make an emergency landing. The attacking He 111s escaped. Four

MiG-3s and one U-2 aircraft were burned on the ground. One bright moment came when Captain Bakhchivandzhi shot down one enemy aircraft and returned unhurt. Of the twenty-three MiG-3 fighters at the airfield, only seven remained operational at the close of July 4. On the following day, two Bf 109s strafed the field, making nine passes. Despite a clear signal for takeoff, none of the available MiGs and I-153s managed to get airborne to intercept the enemy aircraft.

The after-action report looked critically at the performance of air and ground personnel during the five-day assault on the beleaguered airfield near Pskov. Certain vexing problems stood out, which only enhanced the combat efficiency of the *Luftwaffe* fighter and bomber crews. The gap in experience and technique was obvious, creating a situation in which the heroism and determination of the defenders were not adequate to stem the tide. On certain occasions, such as during the attack on the rail station, the antiaircraft batteries had failed to act. Frequently, command points had functioned awkwardly, as in the case of radio communications. This critical new tool was rarely exploited as a way to organize defenses. There were moments when stupidity prevailed, such as the case of a command point sounding an alarm with a rocket when the men spotted a flock of geese at 6,500 feet (2,000 meters). Too often there were no debriefings of the aircrews, which allowed mistakes to continue unabated. This near total loss of command and control meant that functional command fell to rank-and-file pilots. For instance, a regimental engineer fired flares to launch a flight of interceptors when he supposedly spotted the enemy near the airfield. These and other complaints gave the report an impressive candor and honesty regarding the failures at one forward air base. Indeed, what happened at Pskov mirrored the grim realities of the opening phase of the war, when the *Luftwaffe* enjoyed air supremacy.

A COUNTERSTROKE AT LENINGRAD

The Northern *Front* was charged with the defense of Leningrad. This military district became the locale for some of the most spirited air operations against the enemy in the first days of the war. The Karelian peninsula, situated northwest of Leningrad, had been seized by the Soviets in the Winter War with Finland in 1939–1940. Now an ally of

Nazi Germany, Finland was prepared to engage in what it called the "Continuation War" to reclaim its lost territory. In May 1941, the German and Finnish governments reached a cooperative agreement on joint operations in any impending conflict. The *Luftwaffe* first appeared over the Leningrad sector in the early hours of June 22, when twelve aircraft, flying in three groups, dropped mines in the Gulf of Finland. The following night, the air raid sirens warned the citizens of Leningrad of an impending German air attack, but no massive raid materialized. Being remote from the enemy breakthrough zones, the Leningrad Military District and the Red Banner Baltic Fleet enjoyed a brief reprieve. By the second week of the war, however, this area would be drawn into the vortex of battle.

Once the war became a reality, Major General Alexander A. Novikov found himself at the epicenter of VVS air operations against the *Luftwaffe* and allied Finnish air units. Novikov was a talented aviator and a resourceful leader who managed, in the grim days of June, to launch a series of attacks on Finnish targets as opposed to adopting a more passive defensive tactic. Novikov's aggressive posture won him plaudits in Moscow and set the stage for his elevation to overall VVS commander a year later.[64] For Novikov, there were many challenges in these opening hours. His impulse was to act decisively— even in a context of widespread confusion and uncertainty. Yet he was constrained by the defensive posture adopted in Moscow. There was a standing order that no military unit was to engage in any provocative act against the Germans or their allies. Novikov, however, chose to adopt an aggressive approach to the enemy in this awkward and confusing context. German air units had been allowed to rebase at several Finnish airfields, which, to any sober-minded observer, was a clear indication of intent. In the days leading up to the war, German reconnaissance flights became more active, with regular and unmolested forays over Soviet territory. While these flights gave the enemy detailed information on the deployment of Soviet air units, the VVS command lacked any authoritative data on the deployment and strength of German and Finnish air units. Some frontline VVS air units lacked even accurate maps of adjacent Finnish-controlled territory. During these uncertain hours, the VVS air units under Novikov's command operated under distinct disadvantages.

On the night of June 24, Novikov learned of a downed Ju 88 in his region. This particular aircraft type had routinely been employed by the *Luftwaffe* for aerial reconnaissance and photography. Marauding Ju 88s, in fact, had been frequent intruders in Soviet airspace for weeks. For Novikov, the downed Ju 88 confirmed the *Luftwaffe's* intention to gain air supremacy over Leningrad. Accordingly, Novikov sought the green light from authorities in Moscow to launch air strikes. He was turned down. Even in the first hours of the war, VVS air units were denied permission to violate the borders of either Finland or Romania, which was still technically neutral. Soon, however, this policy was reversed with a directive from *Stavka*, signed by Marshal Timoshenko: the VVS was ordered to begin air sorties against the enemy's airfields in southern Finland, in particular Turku, Malmi, Parvu, and other targets in Karelia. Air units from the Northern *Front* and the Baltic Fleet were placed under Novikov's direct command for these offensive operations.[65]

On the morning of June 25, Novikov ordered a series of air attacks against enemy airfields in Finnish territory. He deployed a force consisting of twelve bomber regiments and five fighter regiments to attack selected Finnish bases. This bold strike, however, revealed the chaotic scene in the border areas. At one juncture, 37 SB bombers of the 72nd SBAP flew to their targets in groups of three, without fighter cover, and made four bomb runs from altitudes of 6,000 to 9,000 feet (2,000 to 3,000 meters). Such sorties were very risky without the proper fighter escorts. It is estimated that as many as 263 Soviet bombers and 224 fighters and ground attack aircraft participated in these wide-ranging daylight raids, hitting as many as eighteen Finnish airfields.[66] This level of activity alone showed Novikov's remarkable ability to mobilize counterstrikes under extreme conditions. These surprise raids of the VVS and naval aviation caught the German and Finnish air units off guard, with squadron records indicating that some damage had been inflicted on enemy aircraft, hangars, and storage buildings.

Air action continued through June 25 as local VVS commanders hurriedly worked to sustain the improvised air operations. And, as it turned out, the High Command in Moscow took notice of the aggressive VVS air commander in the Leningrad sector of the front. The effort to stem the *Luftwaffe* offensive, however, came with a high price: one source lists Soviet losses as twenty-three bombers and eleven fighters—perhaps a low figure, but suggestive that the VVS had assumed a sustained offensive posture against the enemy.[67] Despite these losses, especially to bombers without fighter cover, Novikov and his command continued the air campaign into July, though with less intensity. Some enemy bases were attacked as many as eight to ten times in this period. Soviet records acknowledge the loss of 40 aircraft, versus 130 German and Finnish aircraft destroyed (a figure obtained in part with the use of aerial photography).[68] Soviet flying personnel suffered grievous losses, with more than a hundred airmen and five squadron commanders killed in action. Yet the raids stymied enemy plans, forced the withdrawal of some aircraft to the rear, and—most important—interrupted or delayed projected enemy air attacks on Soviet aerodromes in the Northern *Front*.

Novikov had opted for massed attacks on selected Finnish targets, and he achieved some measure of success. At Turku, for example, VVS bombers destroyed between thirty and forty aircraft and two administration buildings on June 25. Around Turku, Soviet bombers hit the railway station and populated centers as well, with the goal of bringing the war to Nazi Germany's erstwhile ally. More than fifty-five people were killed and numerous buildings destroyed. Finnish aircraft losses, however, were minimal. One problem Soviet bomber crews faced was incomplete intelligence on the exact location of enemy airfields; however, the relative weakness of Finnish air defenses allowed Soviet bombers some measure of freedom in seeking out targets. By contrast, *Luftwaffe* air units were more effective in downing Soviet aircraft. Overall, the VVS scored only marginal success in these sorties, a consequence of inexperience (some crews had only 100 hours of training), ineffectual air reconnaissance, poor planning on a tactical level, obsolescent aircraft, and, on occasion, the reckless deployment of air elements too close to the frontier, among other factors.

For Novikov and his chief of staff, General A. P. Nekrasov, these air raids represented a logical and necessary response to a dire national emergency. The *Luftwaffe* had shattered the forward network of Soviet airfields. The posture of Soviet airmen in this sector had been bold and aggressive in the face of a powerful enemy.

THE AIR STRUGGLE IN THE SOUTH

On June 22, the German army and its allies drove deep into Ukraine, using occupied Poland and Romania as stepping-off points. This massive offensive operation called for the crossing of the Bug River, which constituted a natural barrier running along the Soviet border. Pressing forward, this phase of Operation Barbarossa soon threatened the ancient city of Kiev. During the summer campaign, Hitler's armies would set the stage for the envelopment of Kiev, reach the gates of Odessa, and occupy the Soviet-held Crimea. Separating the action in the South from the war in the North were the Pripyat Marshes, a large swath of swamps and waterlogged terrain stretching from Belarus into northern Ukraine. This legendary forested region was (and is) part of the Pripyat River basin, a major tributary of the Dnieper River. The marshes, with their pine forests, floodplains, and immense bogs, cover more than 104,000 square miles (270,000 square kilometers), posing a formidable challenge to any form of mechanized warfare. In practical terms, this inhospitable region separated the emerging Eastern Front into two halves, giving the southern arena of conflict a peculiar isolated character in the opening weeks of the war. In the region below the Pripyat Marshes, chaos descended on the Soviet side just as it did in the North. *Luftwaffe* sorties proved very effective in neutralizing forward defensive positions, disrupting communications, and prompting great disorder.

The Southern and Southwestern *Fronts* took on the formidable and complex task of defending the approaches to Kiev. This arena of combat was vast. It also became the site for some unexpected tactical triumphs against the *Luftwaffe*. The VVS air units deployed to these two *Fronts* were organized into air divisions. The 14th, 15th, 16th, 17th, and 63rd SADs; the 18th DBAD (*Dalnebombardirovochnaya Aviatsionnaya Diviziya*, or long-range bomber air division); the 19th and 62nd BADs; the 36th, 44th, and 64th IADs (*Istrebitelnyye Aviatsionnyye Divizii*, or fighter air divisions); and the 315th and 316th RAPs in the Southwestern *Front* amounted to an impressive 1,901 aircraft (1,674 serviceable). The Southern *Front* (formerly the Odessa Military District) possessed 962 aircraft (798 serviceable).[69] They were often stationed near the frontier. As forward air units, they were organically linked to the various armies assigned to guard the border. For example, the 15th and 16th SADs were assigned to the Soviet 6th Army, the 63rd IAD was assigned to the 26th Army, and the 44th and 64th IADs were assigned to the 12th Army. And in the rear, air divisions were attached to armies in the Crimea and the North Caucasus regions, giving the Soviets a measure of echeloned air defense. They would feel the full brunt of the German attack in the South.

Air action in the South against the *Luftwaffe* soon took on an unanticipated ferocity, reflecting in part the influence of geography and the surprising capacity of local air commanders to mobilize resistance. On the night of June 21–22, air commanders reacted as best they could to confusing directives from Moscow. They faced the challenge of achieving a heightened level of combat readiness while not engaging in any "provocative acts" against the enemy. As dawn approached on June 22, meaningful steps had been taken to disperse aircraft and begin the process of camouflaging aircraft and buildings. These eleventh-hour steps, belated and largely ineffectual, did not seriously hinder the inevitable *Luftwaffe* assault.

The first *Luftwaffe* strikes at the frontline airfields of the Southwestern *Front* did not deal a serious blow to VVS units in the area. However, a dearth of competent leadership from divisional and regimental commanders in organizing rebasing to rear airfields and a failure to organize air defenses led to repeated strikes during the next two days and the destruction of significant numbers of aircraft at those same airfields. Still, the VVS in the South managed to launch a spirited pattern of air action against a superior foe. The reasons were multiple. First, the relative strength of the two opposing air forces was more advantageous to the Soviets, notwithstanding the *Luftwaffe*'s edge in terms of experience and tactics. Second, VVS air units took advantage of their more favorable airfield situation, which allowed them to disperse air units farther from the border than was possible in the Western *Front*. Finally, in the South, a number of energetic local commanders acted forcefully, as Novikov had at Leningrad, ordering dispersal and camouflage efforts. So, when the *Luftwaffe*'s 400-plus aircraft appeared at dawn and attacked some twenty-three airfields,[70] the VVS's capacity to offer resistance had been greatly enhanced. Many regiments were able to avoid surprise attacks at their airfields and met the enemy in the air. However, the *Luftwaffe*'s trademark was persistence in achieving its objectives. Soviet airfields were attacked methodically during the day, and this approach paid off. The Soviet command had no plan for dispersing aviation to alternative airstrips. Nor was it technically possible to do so, due to the ongoing construction and modernization of the airfield network. Consequently, the destruction of Soviet aviation on the ground was just a matter of time: if the first enemy air strike was not successful, then the desired results would be achieved on the second, third, or even tenth attempt. The 17th IAP, located at Velitsk airfield, was finished by the third day of the war.[71] In three days, losses of aircraft on the ground alone stood at 237 in the Southwestern *Front*. Poor organization of numerous aspects of combat also led to substantial noncombat-related losses: from June 22 to August 10, 242 aircraft were lost or damaged due to accidents or other incidents.[72]

The Soviet defenders perceived any enemy movement eastward as an ultimate threat to the cities. Population centers were considered to be of strategic importance and required a spirited defense. For the enemy, however, the urban centers were not the primary targets. Instead, the *Wehrmacht* was intent on the encirclement and annihilation of the Red Army. One of the objectives of Operation Barbarossa was to destroy the main Russian forces in western Russia and prevent their retreat into the depths of the vast Russian territory. The Soviet fixation on defending the cities at this stage of the war proved costly.

One Soviet airman, the commander of the 87th IAP, Major I. S. Suldin, wrote a vivid account of the air war in the South.[73] He remembered that at 0430 hours his unit received a report that German bombers had attacked a number of frontier towns—what was later revealed to be the first wave of a bombardment campaign against key Soviet targets. Suldin's regiment was immediately placed on alert. Pilots, ground crews, and aircraft specialists rushed to prepare the regimental aircraft for action. Within twenty minutes, these frenzied predawn preparations stopped abruptly with the approach of a two-engine airplane in the distance. The approaching aircraft was partially obscured in the morning darkness. At first, some onlookers took the unidentified aircraft to be one of their own SB bombers with the division commander on board, inspecting their alert preparedness. Soon they realized the plane was indeed an enemy aircraft, and once it was in view, they recognized it as a *Luftwaffe* Ju 88 bomber. Startled and desperate, the airmen on the field opened fire with their personal weapons. However, it was too late. The low-flying Ju 88 bombed the parked Soviet aircraft. In one lethal pass, the enemy bomber destroyed seven of the ten parked aircraft, killed two pilots, and wounded two of the ground crew. For Suldin, the war arrived with a nerve-shattering suddenness on June 22, just as the sun appeared on the eastern horizon.

Losses were recorded throughout the network of Soviet air bases as they, too, endured the air assault from the *Luftwaffe*. The aircrews of the 66th Ground Attack Aviation Regiment, attached to the 6th Army, considered the alert to be just another training exercise and arrived too late. The tragic result was the loss of thirty-four of the regiment's sixty-three aircraft. Flight personnel of one fighter regiment, the 17th IAP of the 14th IAD, attached to the 5th Army, had taken leave to visit their families in Kovel and missed the action on the first day. The enemy bombers were therefore met by only a token force of alert flights. The overall pattern of chaos, however, was punctuated by occasional triumphs. For example, the 164th IAP of the 15th Air Division intercepted a group of German bombers and escorts flying to their target, downing four bombers and one fighter. In these desperate hours of the first day, senior Lieutenant I. I. Ivanov of the 46th IAP of the 14th Air Division took drastic action. He rammed his I-153 into a German bomber, and both the attacker and prey fell to the earth in flames.[74]

However, the aerial battles over Ukraine had just begun. Despite losses in the air and on the ground, air units of the Southwestern and Southern *Fronts* did not lose their combat capacity. Airfields in depth offered a mode of defense because they were often outside the range of the *Luftwaffe*. The 17th, 19th, and 44th Air Divisions were located near the old border and would prove to be a formidable force to counter the advancing Germans. The *Luftwaffe* did not gain aerial supremacy here. They retained the initiative but could not stop or minimize the Soviet air strikes at the forward and rear units of the advancing *Wehrmacht*.

Air units of the Southwestern *Front* engaged in a series of fierce combat sorties between June 22 and August 8, an interlude when Soviet military fortunes were on the wane, a time of paralysis and retreat. Here, as elsewhere, Soviet airmen faced great difficulty launching air sorties and, in turn, establishing effective coordination with ground forces. The nagging problem with signals, the absence of

Soviet TB-3 heavy bombers in flight. In total, 818 of these four-engine giants were built in the 1930s. By the beginning of the war, they were obsolete, with their slow cruising speed and minimal defensive armament. Marauding *Luftwaffe* fighters and antiaircraft artillery quickly reduced their numbers in the early weeks of the war. As a consequence, the remainder were restricted to night and transport duties. (From the collection of Valeriy Romanenko)

radios, and the general breakdown in the communications net haunted the defensive moves of the VVS. Yet there were moments of measured success: spirited attacks against German mechanized forces, the strafing of advancing tanks and armored columns, and the harassment of infantry concentrations. There were also concerted efforts to neutralize the enemy's fixed positions, such as artillery batteries and operational airfields. At Kovel, Lvov, Tarnopol, Chernigov, Rovno, and Kiev, VVS air units managed to make an appearance, often in an offensive mode.[75] Even the bomber elements appeared to challenge the German forces.[76] There were even night missions, flown by SB bombers and R-5 aircraft, to harass enemy airfields and troop concentrations. Huge losses accompanied these actions, especially among the bomber units, but the VVS in the South displayed a certain

Crew members in front of an SB bomber before a combat sortie, July 5, 1941. Left to right: Junior Lieutenant N. Duritko, Junior Lieutenant D. Seleznev, and Lieutenant N. Ovchinnikov. SB crews suffered heavy losses, often flying near-suicide missions without fighter escorts. (From the collection of Valeriy Romanenko)

aggressiveness that set it apart. All these actions—aggressive and unanticipated—gave the advancing German forces pause. A key factor in allowing the VVS to launch a multiplicity of sorties, and even to provide cover for the retreating Red Army, was the enormity of the landscape. Time and distance offered the beleaguered air defenders the options of movement, rebasing, and countermoves.

THE ENEMY AT THE GATES OF MOSCOW

As the summer of 1941 drew to a close, the VVS—and the larger Soviet military—found itself in great peril, beleaguered on many fronts, and uncertain about the prospects for survival. Yet, in the midst of endless reversals and humiliations, the VVS fought back and displayed a residual strength that now alarmed many observers of all ranks in the Ger-

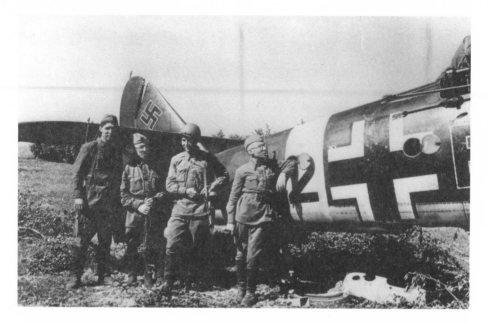

Rare moment of triumph for the VVS in the summer of 1941. This HS 126 of 9.(H)/LG 2 was lost on July 11 in the Meshki area. The third person from the left is Konstantin Simonov, war correspondent of the *Krasnaya Zvezda* (*Red Star*) newspaper and famous Soviet poet and writer. (From the collection of Dmitriy Karlenko)

man military. The enemy now occupied a huge swath of Soviet territory—almost all of European Russia, Belorussia, and Ukraine. Two major cities, Leningrad and Moscow, held out, but the enemy appeared poised to conquer them, perhaps before the onset of winter. Few in the West gave the Soviet defenders much chance of survival. The unleashing of Operation Barbarossa, like the 1940 campaign in France, was characterized by rapid breakthroughs, dramatic victories with the VVS as the chosen victim, and a series of encirclements by the enemy. The lethal impact of Barbarossa was evident on the first day when the *Luftwaffe* bombers assaulted 66 of the 100 VVS airfields situated in forward areas from the Baltic region to Odessa on the Black Sea.[77] Under General Ritter von Leeb, Army Group North occupied the Baltic republics in July in a campaign coordinated with the Finns, who advanced into their former territory in Karelia. On August 16, the Germans overran Novgorod and within a week reached Krasnogvardeysk, on the outskirts of Leningrad. Within a month, the Germans placed Leningrad under siege, which turned out to be one of the most protracted (900 days) and costly phases of the war for the Soviet defenders. In the South, the Germans scored additional successes, but with much more difficulty. Army Group South, commanded by Field Marshal Karl von Rundstedt, advanced into the vast territory of Ukraine, threatening to capture Kiev. Colonel General M. P. Kirponos held out bravely but ultimately fell victim to the German encirclement, a disaster aided in part by Moscow's unwillingness to let Kirponos withdraw to the East in time. Kiev, the ancient capital of the Russian state, was captured by the advancing *Wehrmacht*. Subsequently, Army Group South pushed on toward Rostov and into the Crimea. The summer campaign had also seen the bombing of Moscow by the *Luftwaffe*, evoking a heightened sense of crisis and doom in the Soviet capital. At that moment, few in the West gave the Soviet regime any chance of surviving in the face of such overwhelming force.

For the VVS in August 1941, there were signs of resiliency—even renewal. Indeed, the Nazi blitzkrieg had achieved dazzling tactical victories, but in a strategic sense, the enemy had been denied a clear and decisive victory. The reality was more than just a trade of land for time, a tactic by the defenders to stall the inevitable. The Soviet military—and the VVS—fought desperately, even in the face of enormous losses. The VVS remained severely weakened and disorganized, but it persisted as a viable force. Over time, the war emergency had strengthened the popular will to survive. Already in motion that month was the evacuation of key war industries to the East. On the eve of the battle for Moscow, the VVS could still muster 1,716 combat aircraft.[78] Another factor, concealed in the confusion of Soviet reversals, was the survival of a significant number of VVS pilots, other air personnel, and technicians. Thus, in the prolonged struggle ahead, the Soviet Air Force would not face, as one might have expected, an acute shortage of flight crews. Like Britain in 1940, the enemy had not destroyed Soviet airpower, although it had inflicted severe punishment. As long as the VVS survived, there was the hope of renewal and perhaps ultimate victory.

The reasons for the Soviet reversal were complex and multiple. On the eve of the war, there were many systemic weaknesses in the air arm—this was the background reality. The VVS had inaugurated a process of transition to new aircraft, methods, and organization. Such a commitment certainly expressed a mood of urgency, but it brought in its wake no small amount of confusion and vulnerability to the operational air units. The calendar itself became a cruel master, with little time to make changes in advance of the German invasion. Wittingly or unwittingly, Operation Barbarossa came at a time of profound weakness and disorientation for the Soviet Air Force.

On the eve of the war, the VVS leadership lacked maturity and clear purpose. Going back to the late 1930s, there had been numerous turnovers in top and midlevel personnel, along with reformulations of structure. Barbarossa exposed the outdated character of the entire VVS organizational structure, which was ill suited to meet the strategic and tactical demands of effective air defense, in particular against the veteran *Luftwaffe*. None of the threatened forward sectors possessed adequate resources. Moreover, the airfield net on the western periphery had rapidly evolved into a large matrix of facilities, some in close proximity to the new borders established in the aftermath of the Nazi-Soviet Pact of 1939. Forward operational airfields, perhaps as many as 382, were very congested with the clutter of newly arriving aircraft and numerous construction projects under way.[79] One key indicator of the enhanced vulnerability of the Soviet air arm in June 1941 was the fact that the VVS deployed no fewer than twenty different types of warplanes. The air force organization lacked a clear focus, which was mirrored in the ineffectual training program and the haphazard pattern of maintenance. Local air commanders displayed great inertia when it came to combat readiness, failing to disperse and camouflage operational aircraft. Eleventh-hour directives from Soviet High Command to enhance readiness were implemented slowly, if at all.

There was no settled sense of air theory in place in 1941 to provide a baseline for organization, operations, or training. In fact, the emphasis had shifted from bombers to fighters and ground attack aircraft designs, but this critical redefinition of priorities had not been properly translated into a functioning air doctrine. At the meeting of top aviation and army commanders on December 23–31, 1940, often conflicting positions were voiced about the optimal organizational structure, centralization of command and control, methods of achieving air superiority, efficiency of air strikes at enemy airfields, and coordination between aviation and ground forces. Even recent lessons of combat operations in Europe were interpreted differently.[80]

The Communist Party under Joseph Stalin's leadership had stressed preparedness. Yet Operation Barbarossa made a mockery of the perceived Soviet military capacity. At the supreme moment of crisis, the Soviet military leadership acted with hesitation and ignorance. Gross deficiencies in equipment, training, and organization emerged as the Soviets clumsily, if heroically, fought back. There is a popular notion that the travails of Soviet airpower—if not the entire calamity of the military—can be blamed on the Stalinist purges of the late 1930s. Certainly, the purges of 1937–1939 had a negative impact on the VVS leadership. Successive air commanders—Ya. I. Alksnis, Ya. V. Smushkevich, and P. V. Rychagov—had been arrested and executed. Pilot training, ground services, equipment, and organization were all deficient by *Luftwaffe* standards. Stalin's repression reached the middle and lower levels of the VVS command structure, creating a mood of conditioned passivity among the cowed survivors. This atmosphere precluded initiative and boldness in the face of new wartime challenges.

Going into World War II, no modern air force had experienced the scale and ferocity of the purge of the VVS officer corps. The crisis in leadership, however, was more complex; it cannot be attributed solely to purges in the prewar years. Other problems that beset the VVS included inadequate and uneven funding for the rapidly expanding air force, a lack of upward mobility for talented junior officers, numerous reorganizations, confusion over air doctrine, and the too-rapid expansion of leadership cadres for the entire military, including the VVS. These factors, not just the purges, created significant confusion within the ranks—a fatal disorientation that was exposed during the German offensives in the summer of 1941.[81]

The VVS aircraft inventory, by one reckoning, numbered 7,133, but this total included 919 aircraft—a dramatic 13 percent—deemed defective or inoperative. Within this inventory, there were 1,448 newer-type aircraft.[82] These advanced warplanes were crowded into forward air bases with the more numerous older designs, creating a widespread pattern of congestion. Only about 208 aircrews were properly trained to operate the newer-type aircraft.[83] Given the variety of designs and the many field modifications, the VVS inventory contained at least twenty distinct types of warplanes. There were chronic problems with logistics, especially the timely availability of sufficient quantities of spare parts. All these aircraft were deployed in a large and poorly coordinated air base network, with many of the airfields positioned close to the frontier. In fact, the number of operational airfields had been expanded in June 1941 (for a total of 477 permanent and forward operational airfields), only adding to the confusion.[84] The layering of forward air defenses was further compromised by the presence of premodern aircraft. For example, many bomber units flew the slow and obsolescent DB-3 and TB-3 types. There were only nine modern Pe-8 four-engine bombers, four of which were not serviceable.[85] This general pattern of obsolescence was true of the fighter arm as well, though on a less dramatic scale. For example, based at Chernovtsi were sixty-seven older I-16 and I-153 types and sixty-four new-model MiG-3s. At Dolubovo airfield, only 6 miles (10 kilometers) from the border, where the 126th IAP was stationed, fifty MiG-3s shared the tarmac with twenty-three I-16s.[86] Sadly, for Soviet fortunes, most of these aircraft—old or new—were neither dispersed nor properly camouflaged. Consequently, one of the most dramatic and lingering memories of Operation Barbarossa would be the countless number of VVS aircraft destroyed in place in the opening hours of the war.

The VVS entered the crucible of war with an amalgam of old and new aircraft. The concerted efforts at reorganization and expansion evoked a context of poor integration as local air commanders faced a mixed inventory of old and new warplanes. Training had been piecemeal and ineffectual. There had been logistical problems, particularly the availability of spare parts. Many of the forward air commanders were inexperienced. Prior to the war, no less than 43 percent of the commanders at all levels had been posted at their air bases for less than six months.[87] Air doctrine was in a fluid state; there was no clear focus, and it failed to reflect the operational and strategic significance of airpower. Moreover, this lack of precision was reflected in the training program. Few airmen fully comprehended the technical and tactical character of the enemy air units poised for attack across the frontier. The efforts to bring forward air units to full readiness had proved to be too late and incomplete. Air reconnaissance—a crucial factor—failed to comprehend the full extent of the enemy threat. All these inefficiencies mirrored an obsolete organizational structure then in place. Large reserves were absent.

Once hostilities were under way, the mismanagement and lack of initiative of forward air commanders resulted in the failure to relocate forward-based aircraft, which led to huge losses of aircraft. Directives to put the VVS on high alert came belatedly, as did Timoshenko's second directive on response actions. Most of the combat-ready units charged with the response were already devastated by that time. The command and control system collapsed, and only a few units acted on the initiative of their commanders.[88]

The ultimate fate of the VVS—as well as the larger Soviet military—would rest on the State Defense Committee's crucial decision, in early July 1941, to evacuate Soviet war industries to the East. The herculean effort to transplant more than 1,500 industrial enterprises beyond the Ural Mountains at the height of the German invasion marks one of the Soviets' most impressive wartime achievements. The migration of workers and industrial machinery beyond the reach of the German army required enormous effort and organization. These cadres of workers and skilled specialists numbered around 10 million, and they experienced great hardships in the winter of 1941–1942. After making the difficult trek eastward, they faced the enormous challenge of resuming industrial production in the most primitive conditions.[89] During 1942, the relocated plants produced nearly 25,000 aircraft. Most of these were newer models: Il-2s, Pe-2s, and Yak-1s. The rebirth of the Soviet Air Force after 1942 stemmed from this remarkable achievement. But the hidden strength of the Soviet Union was less than apparent to both sides in the summer of 1941.

The German juggernaut advanced eastward in what appeared to be an irreversible tide. With the approach of autumn, there were doubts that Moscow could be saved. If the Soviet capital fell to the invaders, few believed the Soviet regime could survive.

Chapter Two

The Air Battle for Moscow

For *Stavka*, the Soviet High Command, the war in the summer of 1941 appeared grim, the apprehension being that the nation was on the cusp of Armageddon as the German juggernaut had moved relentlessly across the breadth of European Russia, placed Leningrad under siege, overrun Kiev and much of Ukraine, and advanced through Smolensk to the western edge of Moscow. Among all the extraordinary reverses, the fall of Smolensk to the Germans on July 16 evoked a new mood of foreboding: for the first time, Moscow fell within the range of German bombers. The pending German conquest of the Soviet capital, many outsiders prophesied, would signal yet another triumph for German arms and set the stage for the collapse of the Bolshevik regime.

The *Luftwaffe*—flying on the cutting edge of Operation Barbarossa—had neutralized Soviet airpower, provided air support to the *Wehrmacht* in a series of vast ground offensives, and managed to thwart Soviet counterstrokes. But even in this moment of apparent triumph, the *Luftwaffe* faced new challenges. The enormity of the Russian Front, then extending for 1,800 miles (2,897 kilometers), dwarfed any wartime scenario experienced in the West. Communications and logistics, not to mention the coordination of widely separated air units supporting the three-pronged assault corridors, quickly became problematic; indeed, the sheer vastness of the geography reduced the effectiveness of the technologically advanced *Luftwaffe* to narrow targeted zones of combat. Airpower—even with a lavish deployment of aircraft and crews—could never be coextensive with the front. And for the entire German juggernaut—infantry, mechanized units, and airpower—there was the melancholy realization that the Soviets possessed a surprising residual strength, the ability to counterattack fiercely even in the aftermath of catastrophic defeats. For the *Luft-*

waffe, there had been the difficult role of a fire brigade, called on to save the day in dire emergencies.

Tactical air warfare had proven essential, and in ways not fully anticipated by prewar planners. With each passing week, though, it became more and more evident that the hard-pressed *Luftwaffe* possessed only a finite capacity to deal with the dire and ever-shifting challenges of the Russian Front. However, this primary tactical role for German airpower came to an abrupt end on July 19, 1941, when Hitler issued Führer Directive 23, which launched a strategic bombing campaign to raze the Soviet capital, hitherto untouched by the war. This sudden move aimed to bring the war to the center of "Bolshevik resistance" and prevent any "orderly evacuation of the Russian government apparatus."[1] There was now a dramatic shift to strategic air warfare. Hurriedly, air elements from *Luftflotte* 2 took up positions in the East to bolster the overall striking power of German aviation. On the eve of the aerial assault, He 111, Do 17, and Ju 88 bombers from *Fliegerkorps* II and *Fliegerkorps* V assembled at forward airstrips at Minsk, Orsha, and Shatalovka.

To reach Moscow, German bomber crews faced the formidable task of flying missions of roughly 250 to 375 miles (400 to 600 kilometers), depending on their departure point.[2] Such a concerted bombing offensive placed unusual logistical demands on the *Luftwaffe*, including the daunting challenge of keeping widely scattered bomber units properly supplied with fuel, ordnance, spare parts, and effective maintenance. German bomber crews would fly a total of seventy-six nighttime and eleven daytime missions, an effort that extended over several months and into 1942. The effort to fulfill Führer Directive 23 came at a time when the striking power of the *Luftwaffe* had declined dramatically. Moreover, the altered German air strategy unfolded in a broader context of operational disarray and confusion. Constant movement and attrition in aircraft and aircrews had severely compromised the viability of German airpower. For example, the headquarters for one German air element, *Fliegerkorps* VIII, had shifted no fewer than eighteen times. Such frontline demands slowly and perceptively exhausted German aircrews and sapped their morale, a growing crisis that was largely concealed by the bright glare of tactical victories in the opening weeks of the invasion.[3]

The first raid on Moscow took place on the night of July 21–22, an aerial assault unfolding over five hours. Flying in four separate waves, some 195 German aircraft struck the Soviet capital with high-explosive and incendiary bombs. Soviet records chronicled 130 people killed and another 241 severely injured in this raid. While spectacular as an air raid, the *Luftwaffe* managed to inflict only minor physical damage on the Soviet capital, with most of the ordnance dropped on widely scattered targets in a chaotic fashion. The following night, a flotilla of 115 German bombers returned to the skies over Moscow. A third raid followed on July 24 with 100 aircraft. Alexander Werth, the renowned British journalist, observed these opening raids at ground level, one of a small coterie of Western journalists in Moscow that fateful summer. He took pains to record the spirited response of the Soviet air defenses—the ubiquitous searchlights, the intense array of tracer bullets from antiaircraft batteries, and the roaming fighter interceptors. In fact, he observed that the Moscow challenge to the *Luftwaffe* surpassed anything he had experienced in the bombing of London. The first nights of the bombing campaign, as it turned out, proved to be the high point in the assault on Moscow. Soon the German bombing missions became more desultory and arbitrary, never achieving the massive scale of the 100-bomber raid of August 11, 1940.[4] There would be no replication of the London Blitz.

The *Luftwaffe*'s air raids on Moscow, despite all their drama, set the stage for, ironically, the first major defeat of German arms in the East. The aerial battle in the skies over Moscow, as it turned out, raged episodically for months, even as a fierce struggle ensued on the ground. In late September, the Germans unleashed Operation Typhoon, a wide-ranging operation on the western periphery of the Soviet capital. Once stalled, the Germans faced an aggressive Soviet counteroffensive in December—a bloody campaign that faltered only with the severe winter of 1941–1942. Moscow's resistance had an enormous psychological impact on both sides at this crucial phase of the war. For the Soviets—as for the British in 1940—the mobilized resistance to the *Luftwaffe* evoked in the popular mind an extraordinary moment of heroism and national determination.

MOSCOW — IN HARM'S WAY

The larger struggle for the Soviet capital extended roughly from the summer of 1941 to April 1942. More than 7 million soldiers were caught up in the vortex of this fierce battle. Both armies fought during the legendary Russian winter, an extreme and unforgiving context that caused enormous suffering on both sides. The Soviet Union paid a high price to thwart the advance of the *Wehrmacht*. In his November 6 speech at the Mayakovskiy metro station, Stalin himself openly admitted the great loss of life in the defense of the Soviet Union: "In four months of the war we lost 350,000 killed, 370,000 missing, and have 1,020,000 wounded men."[5] Precise figures for the attrition on both sides are difficult to pinpoint, given the chaotic nature of the war in the East. Yet Moscow—unlike Paris two years before—stopped the advance of Nazi Germany. For the Soviet Union, as well as the Allied cause itself, this was indeed a momentous turning point in the war.

The Soviet resistance at Moscow had been foreshadowed in the prewar years. In the 1930s, as war with Nazi Germany became a potential threat, the air defense of the Soviet capital took on a high priority. Soon this planning acquired institutional expression with the creation of the PVO Strany (*Protivovozdushnaya Oborona Strany*), or National Air Defense). This newly organized air defense force included radar detection, searchlight units, antiaircraft batteries, and fighter interceptor air units. Organizationally separate from the VVS, the PVO's key task was defending urban and industrial centers in the Soviet Union. At the time of Operation Barbarossa, there were thirteen distinct PVO regions or zones that operated within the confines of the military districts. At Moscow, the air defenses were echeloned to provide optimal air cover. Fighter interceptors were deployed within 75 miles (120 kilometers) of the Kremlin. General M. S. Gromadin took command of the Moscow PVO zone in February 1941. Among his assets was the 6th IAK (*Istrebitelnyy Aviatsionnyy Korpus*, or fighter air corps), organized in June 1941, just before the German invasion, and commanded by Colonel I. D. Klimov. Klimov's fighter air units possessed a significant number of late-model fighter interceptors. The 6th IAK had an operational inventory of 389 aircraft, 175 of which were newer types such as the MiG-3, LaGG-3, and Yak-1 fighters. In terms of training and combat efficiency, the pilots of this air corps surpassed their counterparts in frontal aviation units.

As the threat of a German aerial assault became real, Moscow's PVO units geared for day and night interdiction of enemy bombers.[6] The larger PVO network consisted of an echelon of defensive rings, with the outermost ring located about 124 miles (200 kilometers) from the center of Moscow. The airfields were located up to 75 miles (120 kilometers) from the city. Each ring included a cadre of men and women from VNOS (*Vozdushnogo Nablyudeniya, Opovescheniya i Svyazi*, or air observation, warning, and communications).[7] Closer to the city, elements of the 6th IAK were deployed. All the approaches to the center of Moscow were defended by a network of searchlights and antiaircraft batteries. The innermost ring was festooned with barrage balloons, a tactic intended to force enemy bombers to fly at higher altitudes. One odd and technically uncertain measure was the employment of acoustic devices, shaped like megaphones, aimed toward the sky to pick up any telltale noise from approaching bomber engines. Moscow had been fitted with these layered defenses by mid-July 1941.[8]

Fear of an air attack on Moscow had surfaced in the first week of the war. On the morning of June 24, an unidentified aircraft appeared on the western approaches to the city, prompting the air defense system to come alive. Fighter interceptors and antiaircraft artillery tracked the intruder for over an hour, only to learn that the plane was in fact a Soviet PS-84 (later designated Li-2) civilian transport. These transports had been manufactured as licensed copies of the American Douglas DC-3 aircraft. The intruding airplane sustained some damage when defensive fire scored several hits, but the crew managed to land without any loss of life. That evening, General M. S. Gromadin was summoned to the Kremlin and had to endure a painful dressing-down, but he was let off with a warning.[9] The criticism focused on the fact that the fighter interceptors had failed to respond to this slow-flying aircraft—what would have happened if it had been a *Luftwaffe* bomber?[10]

When the German air raid took place on July 21–22, Muscovites felt for the first time the lethal cutting edge of German military might, one that tested all the defensive systems in place. The city itself had been organized in depth to resist any onslaught by German bombers. Local civil defense became the responsibility of the MPVO (*Mestnaya Protivovozdushnaya Oborona*, or local air defense), which had been organized in 1932. Air raid warnings were given via sirens and the public-address system, the latter an elaborate system fostered under the Communist regime to instruct and mobilize the populace. With the advent of war, steps were taken to black out all public buildings, adapt the subway system as a convenient chain of air raid shelters, and cover the roofs of Moscow's ubiquitous wooden buildings with an inflammable, rubberized tar paper. To prevent any massive fire within the city, there was a concerted effort to expand the number of fire stations. Firefighters were equipped with special uniforms and equipment, including canvas gloves and metal pincers to pick up and remove incendiaries. The MPVO worked assiduously to prepare for the coming aerial assault by turning schools into field hospitals. Each district (*rayon*) had its own air raid battalion, which became an important entity for mobilizing thousands in the defense of the capital. This network reached down to the apartment level, where MPVO operatives were recognizable by their red armbands. At the center of Moscow was the Kremlin, a key historical precinct with enormous political and symbolic importance. The plan to conceal the fortress was thoroughgoing, with the golden cupolas of the Kremlin cathedrals painted and camouflage netting stretched over other buildings. The Kremlin walls were disguised as apartment facades with the use of contrasting colors. Lenin's tomb was reshaped with scaffolding to appear as a two-story building. The MPVO, with its cadre of 600,000 workers, worked tirelessly to transform the outward appearance of many key areas of the city.[11] The link between the searchlight batteries and the antiaircraft gun crews was carefully orchestrated. Many of the searchlight units were composed of women. They combed the skies for incoming aircraft to determine their altitude and direction and then signaled this vital information to the antiaircraft batteries.[12] The program of massed mobilization was reinforced by a genuine and powerful upsurge of patriotism among Muscovites.

The air defense network, if outwardly intimidating, possessed certain weaknesses. On a human level, Soviet civil and military personnel lacked combat experience. By contrast, the *Luftwaffe* air units that appeared over the city were fully acquainted with the tactics for night bombardment. Many of the German bomber crews had flown in the Battle of Britain. Although the city's skillful mass mobilization assured a robust effort to resist the *Luftwaffe*, the Soviet defenders lacked optimal training. Some of the PVO fighter interceptor regiments possessed a mix of new and obsolescent aircraft, which in practical terms brought no small measure of confusion and severely compromised the Soviet effort at air interdiction. Upon closer examination, some PVO air units fell short of any high standard of combat readiness. Colonel N. A. Kobyashov of the 6th IAK reported that he possessed 494 pilots, but only 417 were prepared for combat duty; of these, only 88 pilots had been trained for night missions, and only 8 had been properly trained for night operations on the newer aircraft types. No less important, the Soviets lacked a sufficient quantity of radios for instant communication and proper coordination. Where radios were not available, ground observers were dependent on telephones to alert the defense network of the number and direction of approaching enemy bombers. Primitive land signals, such as large cloth arrows pointing in the direction of a target, were widely used. Unlike London in 1940, however, Moscow did have an operational radar warning network.[13]

Steps were taken on the eve of the bombing raids to reinforce PVO air units in the Moscow sector. Additional aircraft were assigned to the 6th IAK, a prudent move to meet the impending emergency. By July 17, the number of aircrews had been expanded from 585 to 708 (those deployed for night missions increased from 76 to 133). Although the 6th IAK still had some 289 fighters of the older generation (I-16s and I-153s), the quantity of newer types increased dramatically to include 220 MiG-3s, 82 LaGG-3s, and 117 Yak-1s. At the same time, steps were taken to expand the number of observation posts and antiaircraft stations—the latter was considered a high priority; in the second half of July, the 1st Corps of the PVO was fitted with new 85mm and 37mm guns. All these changes had been achieved quickly and substantially strengthened Moscow's air defenses.

Aerial reconnaissance by the *Luftwaffe*—routinely thorough and systematic—preceded the bombing raids. By Soviet reckoning, a total of eighty-nine reconnaissance missions were flown over Moscow and its suburbs.[14] Nine of these missions were flown at altitudes exceeding 22,000 feet (7,000 meters), allowing the German reconnaissance planes to complete their missions largely outside the range of Soviet guns and fighter interceptors. In fact, the Soviets downed only two enemy reconnaissance aircraft over Moscow in the first month of the war. Once the bombing campaign began on the night of July 22, the relative quiet gave way to intense air action. In this context, the Soviet air defenses found themselves hard-pressed. Waves of German bombers appeared over the city, many carrying bomb loads of up to 5,500 pounds (2,500 kilograms). Not only did the German bomber crews encounter the probing searchlights and artillery fire; they also had to contend with night fighters, flying more than 170 nighttime sorties during the initial raid.[15] German aircraft losses mounted with each raid.

The bombing of Moscow offered a context for Soviet defenders to employ certain unconventional air tactics, most notably *taran,* or the deliberate ramming of enemy aircraft. Margaret Bourke-White introduced Westerners to this tactic in her celebrated book *Shooting the Russian War,* which chronicled the story of Viktor Talalikhin.[16] On August 8, 1941, the young and inexperienced Talalikhin, attached to the PVO 177th IAP, rammed a German bomber, becoming the first Soviet air hero to execute a *taran* at night. While on a night patrol in an I-16 fighter, Talalikhin spotted a German He 111 bomber at an altitude of around 15,000 feet (4,600 meters). As he approached the enemy aircraft to attack, the German pilot abruptly swerved out of the line of fire and dived to a lower altitude. Talalikhin managed to retain visual contact and continue his pursuit, but his guns had little effect. At around 7,500 feet (2,300 meters), Talalikhin had exhausted his ammunition. For several seconds he followed the He 111 in a mood of futility, pondering his next move. After some hesitation, he maneuvered his fighter to within 30 feet (9 meters) of the rudder and rear control surfaces of the enemy bomber, intending to ram the aircraft. As the threat to ram became apparent, the German gunner opened fire. At such close range, his fire was intense and accurate, piercing the right side of Talalikhin's cockpit and searing his right arm. Simultaneously, Talalikhin opened his throttle and rammed into the rear of the He 111, striking its control surfaces. The German bomber abruptly spun out of control and crashed. Now flying upside down and out of control, Talalikhin managed to free himself from his damaged fighter and parachute into the night sky. He landed in a small lake, the survivor of a bold and high-risk maneuver.[17]

Bourke-White interviewed Talalikhin at length and, with the permission of the military authorities, photographed the twenty-three-year-old pilot at several public fetes held in his honor. The Soviet propaganda organs gave considerable attention to Talalikhin, who ap-

Viktor Talalikhin greets his mother after his celebrated ramming of a German bomber during the *Luftwaffe*'s assault on Moscow, summer 1941. (From the collection of Von Hardesty)

peared in public in his dress uniform with his bandaged right hand clearly visible. The young Talalikhin did not survive the war. On October 27, he died in aerial combat over Moscow. For the Soviets in 1941, the feats of Talalikhin and others provided a measure of pride in a dark period of military defeat.

One official Soviet source claimed the destruction of thirty-seven German bombers over Moscow in the month of August 1941.[18] As with all data on aircraft losses generated in a wartime context, that figure may be exaggerated. But the fact remained that Soviet air defenses were taking their toll of *Luftwaffe* aircraft assigned to the bombing campaign. German aircrews discovered how challenging it was to breach the layered air defenses on the approach to the Soviet capital.

Luftwaffe pilot Richard Wernicke flew in the Moscow air offensive and reported how shocked he was at the intensity of the antiaircraft fire: "It was terrible; the air was full of lead, and they were firing very accurately. We hadn't seen anything like this before."[19] By one esti-

Luftwaffe airmen look in amazement at an He 111 bomber damaged in an aerial ramming by an I-16 Soviet fighter. Despite severe damage to the central section and control surfaces, the German bomber made it back to its home base. (Courtesy of Glen Sweeting)

mate, about 40 percent of all Soviet antiaircraft batteries were concentrated around Moscow, one visible atop the roof of the Moskva Hotel next to the Kremlin and others placed more discreetly adjacent to potential high-value targets around the city. There was even an antiaircraft battery protecting Stalin's dacha in the remote suburbs. Wernicke also noted the continued threat from Soviet fighter interceptors. They appeared in large numbers and challenged the *Luftwaffe* in an aggressive and lethal fashion. The continued air-to-air threat troubled Wernicke and other German airmen who flew their missions confident that Soviet airpower had been largely neutralized.[20]

In comparison to subsequent Anglo-American strategic bombing missions over Europe, the German air assault on Moscow did not amount to a major aerial campaign on an urban center. Yet these bombing missions created an interlude of extreme hardship for the So-

For this He 111 crew, the war is over, summer 1941. (From the collection of Von Hardesty)

viet capital. At the time, the German raids appeared to be a prelude to the eventual conquest and occupation of the city. Stalin ordered the evacuation of certain segments of the government and industries (and even had Lenin's body moved from Red Square) to rear areas. The Kremlin itself had been hit with sixteen high explosives and numerous incendiaries.[21] An interim report on the bombings issued by the security police (NKVD) on November 24, 1941, noted that there had been no fewer than ninety raids in the first five months. The *Luftwaffe* had dropped 1,521 demolition bombs and 56,620 incendiary bombs on Moscow. The incendiary bombs posed a special threat, with a recorded 1,539 major fires that destroyed 402 apartment buildings and damaged another 852. The fear of a citywide conflagration—one that might equal the great Moscow fire during the Napoleonic invasion—prompted some innovative measures: civil defense officials placed workers, mostly young women, on rooftops to toss off small incendi-

Atop a building overlooking Red Square and the Kremlin, a soldier stands alert with binoculars to sight incoming German bombers, Moscow, 1941. (From the collection of Von Hardesty)

ary bombs before they ignited a fire. This same NKVD report noted that 1,327 Muscovites had died in the air raids, with 1,931 seriously injured and 3,122 slightly injured.[22]

By the end of August, the Soviets had achieved another remarkable feat that went largely unnoticed in the West: the evacuation of hundreds of war plants and their workers to distant eastern locales. This herculean task was conducted under the most severe pressure, during a time of general retreat across the entire expanse of European Russia and Ukraine and while Moscow itself was under aerial bombardment. The evacuation led to temporary shortages in planes, equipment, and ammunition. The project was led by the Council for Evacuation, set up by the State Committee for Defense on June 24, 1941. To coordinate the vast undertaking, Stalin appointed N. A. Voznesensky, then the head of GOSPLAN (the same entity that oversaw industrial planning). He was assisted by A. N. Kosygin, future premier of the Soviet Union. The whole endeavor, controlled from the top down, was complex and chaotic at certain junctures. Plants had to be stripped of machine tools, which were then loaded on trains and trucks for removal.

This 37mm antiaircraft gun crew, defending Moscow, prepares to meet the aerial assault of the *Luftwaffe*. Antiaircraft artillery played a significant role in the elaborate defense of Moscow. (From the collection of Von Hardesty)

The workforce followed the plant equipment, and it was no small task to coordinate the transport, housing, and feeding of all these people as they traveled across the expanse of the Soviet Union. German reconnaissance aircraft spotted the mass movement of materiel and people, but they were slow to comprehend its character or implications. By one estimate, a total of 1,523 factories (1,360 directly related to war production) were removed to safer environs in the Volga River region, Siberia, and Central Asia. Many aviation plants, the core of the aviation sector, became part of this migration. In the end, the Soviet Union had managed to preserve a huge portion of its war-making potential in the summer and fall of 1941.[23]

THE CRISIS DEEPENS — OPERATION TYPHOON

The belated German assault on Moscow, code-named Operation Typhoon, began at 0530 hours on September 30, 1941. Field Marshal Fedor von Bock's Army Group Center planned a double envelopment of Soviet troops guarding the approaches to Moscow. German pincers, advancing to the north and south of the Smolensk–Moscow highway, were to close the trap at Vyazma, while another panzer spearhead moved below Bryansk toward Orel. Once these initial encirclements were completed, the Germans would be in a position to make the final assault on the Soviet capital some 80 miles (130 kilometers) away. The German High Command remained optimistic about Operation Typhoon's potential for success. It represented a concerted effort to bring the war in the East to a dramatic conclusion.

The goals for Operation Typhoon had been laid out in Directive 35, a document that Hitler approved and signed on September 6, 1941. The aim of the operation was the destruction of Soviet forces west of Moscow. German planners were alert to the onset of winter, which was just weeks away, and they mobilized a large force to ensure quick success. Once launched, Operation Typhoon attempted a double encirclement of the Soviet defenders in the Vyazma sector, a maneuver that required the deployment of powerful armored assets on the flanks of the Soviet defensive line. Accordingly, the German Fourth and Eighth Armies, supported by the Fourth and Third Panzer Groups, were at the cutting edge of the offensive. To augment this force, the Second Panzer Group was moved from the Kiev area. Vyazma found itself at the epicenter of the targeted zone. The German offensive aimed to penetrate Soviet defenses quickly and deeply. Never before had three panzer groups moved on the offensive in this fashion, and there was great optimism for a decisive victory. Army Group Center, now reinforced, consisted of 1,929,406 men organized into seventy-eight divisions, including fourteen panzer divisions with 2,304 tanks. The *Luftwaffe* aimed to provide air support from *Luftflotte* 2 under Field Marshal Albert Kesselring, an air armada of 1,320 aircraft (720 bombers, 420 fighters, 40 ground attack planes, and 140 reconnaissance aircraft).[24]

Facing the Germans' Army Group Center were three Soviet *Fronts*—the Western, Bryansk, and Reserve *Fronts*—with a total of 1,250,000 men. The VVS deployed some 568 aircraft (210 bombers, 285 fighters, 36 Shturmoviks, and 37 reconnaissance aircraft).[25] During the initial phases of the battle, a total of 368 bombers of the DBA were thrown into the action, along with air assets from PVO Moscow (423 fighters and 9 reconnaissance aircraft).[26] Given these Soviet deployments, the VVS and the *Luftwaffe* were nearly equal numerically: 1,368 Soviet aircraft facing 1,320 from the *Luftwaffe*. The Soviet operational plan called for a spirited defensive effort on all sectors west of Moscow. At this stage of the war, however, Soviet planning was compromised by faulty and incomplete intelligence on enemy intentions. The logical approach for the advancing German forces, keyed to a known deployment of one large panzer group, was the Smolensk– Yartsevo–Vyazma road. Following this assumption, *Stavka* concentrated forces in this sector, but this anticipated arena of battle never materialized. The Germans had skillfully regrouped their forces, covertly moving the Fourth Panzer Group from the Leningrad area. This meant the Germans would strike in two places, not one. The *Stavka* had determined the time of the offensive, but it lacked detailed and timely data on its direction. The Third Panzer Group moved north of the Yartsevo–Vyazma road, which allowed forward movement between the Soviet 19th and 30th Armies; meanwhile, the Fourth Panzer Group was advancing south of this road between the Soviet 24th and 30th Armies, south of Roslavl. Consequently, the main German offensive hit the Soviet lines at a vulnerable point. The Germans achieved local numeri-

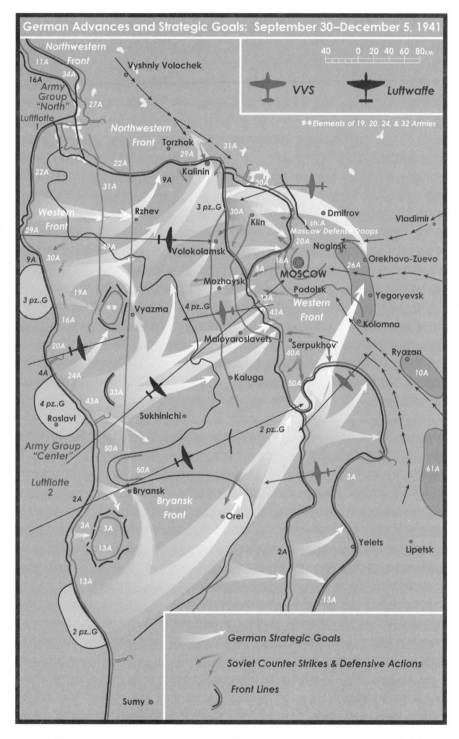

Map 2 (Terry Higgins & Zach Downey-Higgins © 2011 [based on Russian
source material supplied by the authors])

cal superiority and enjoyed the advantage of surprise. In this asymmetrical situation, there were twelve German divisions moving forward against only four Soviet divisions. It would be in this context that General Heinz Guderian, commander of the Second Panzer Group, moved out two days ahead of the main advance on September 30 by the Third and Fourth Panzer Groups, with massive air support from the *Luftwaffe*. Guderian enjoyed good weather and passable roads during his decisive operation. For the Soviet defenders, there was great confusion as new enemy armies appeared out of nowhere, and they moved hurriedly in this chaotic scene to close breaks in their defensive lines.[27]

In fact, the German offensive had been launched ahead of the *Rasputitsa* ("time without roads"), the heavy rainy season that occurred in central Russia each autumn. This shift in weather had a devastating impact on both armies, turning the region into a vast, muddy, impassable terrain. Most Russian roads were primitive, in reality just dirt passageways without roadbeds. Only wide-track vehicles could move on these muddy arteries, and then only with great difficulty. This situation ended with the coming of the Russian winter, which offered its own severe weather. Shortly after the first snow fell on October 6, it melted, adding to the sorry state of the roads. Often the *Rasputitsa* has been viewed as the major factor compromising the Germans' success in the East in 1941–1942. Although the rainy season was indeed a critical factor, it was not necessarily the decisive one. The abrupt change in weather afflicted the Soviet defenders in equal measure. The *Rasputitsa* favored neither combatant in those fateful weeks in the fall of 1941. Both sides faced the daunting challenge to deploy or to concentrate their armies. Logistics became a nightmare in this muddy stalemate. Moreover, the German offensive in the East had already stalled in a significant way. In retrospect, another key factor— and arguably the decisive one—was the aggressive posture of the Soviet military. The beleaguered Soviet defenders managed to rally against these formidable odds. At enormous cost and sacrifice, the Soviets offered fierce resistance, a display of residual strength and determination that set the stage for Nazi Germany's first major defeat in World War II.

For three months, the Soviets had traded geography for time. Time indeed was now short, dictating a shift from strategic retreat to the

Table 1. Composition of Soviet and German Air Forces during the Defense of Moscow, September 1941

| | Red Army VVS | | | | |
Aircraft Type	Frontal Aviation[a]	Long-Range Aviation	Fighter Aviation PVO	Total	Luftwaffe
Bomber	210[b]	368	—	578	720[c]
Fighter	285	—	423	708	420[d]
Shturmovik	36	—	—	36	40
Reconnaissance	37	—	9	46	140[e]
Total	568	368	432	1,368	1,320

a. There were 272 airplanes in the ranks of the VVS Western *Front*, 126 in the Reserve *Front*, and 170 in the Bryansk *Front*.
b. The Western *Front* had 28 TB-3 bombers.
c. Including about 250 Ju 87s.
d. Including 50 Bf 110s.
e. Including the reconnaissance airplanes of army aviation.

manning of fixed, echeloned defenses at Moscow. The defense of the Soviet capital occupied Stalin's full attention on the eve of Operation Typhoon. On his orders, the Stavka reorganized Soviet forces facing Army Group Center into the Western, Bryansk, and Reserve *Fronts*. The composition of forces at this juncture revealed a rough parity (see Table 1), notwithstanding the offensive posture of the *Luftwaffe* and its vast superiority in terms of experience.[28]

The oft-repeated notion that the Soviets used mainly outdated aircraft types in the Battle of Moscow is misleading. On the contrary, the number of modern types (Yak-1, MiG-3, LaGG-3, Pe-2, and Il-2) was constantly growing. VVS commanders also managed to implement changes in command and organization. For instance, General F. G. Michugin, commander of the VVS Western *Front*, concentrated all available air divisions under his control, removing them from the subordination of army commanders. For the first time since the beginning of the war, his staff officers started to analyze aerial combat and tactics. However, there were many unsolved issues, the high rate of accidents being one of them. By contrast, *Luftflotte* 2 had 1,320 aircraft, nearly half of which, according to Soviet sources, consisted of bombers.[29] Even with this approximate numerical parity between the air forces, the *Luftwaffe* excelled in tactical air operations and, in particular, the efficient concentration of air assets in the breakthrough corridors. German air superiority proved to be overwhelming.

By September, both air forces had experienced a dramatic drop in the number of operational aircraft. The long summer campaign produced a low serviceability rate among German air units assigned to frontline duty, a condition aggravated by persistent logistical problems, primitive airfields, and the debilitating regimen of maintaining air operations over the vast, ever-advancing Russian Front. The deterioration of German airpower in the East could be measured in the attrition rate of *Fliegerkorps* VIII at Moscow. During the brief interlude of August 10–21, this air corps took heavy losses in the effort to interrupt Soviet traffic on the Moscow–Leningrad railroad. Owing to the unanticipated aggressiveness of Soviet air units, *Fliegerkorps* VIII lost 10.3 percent of its frontline combat aircraft. Moreover, another 54.5 percent of its combat aircraft inventory was damaged but repairable. In human terms, 3.9 percent of the flying personnel had been killed, another 5.7 percent wounded, and 2.9 percent missing, for a total casualty rate of 12.5 percent. And this German attrition occurred at a time when Soviet airpower had been severely weakened and was on the defensive.[30]

Although surviving Soviet and German accounts of aircraft losses are often contradictory, there is ample evidence that the *Luftwaffe* had suffered significant attrition at this point in the war. By August 31, unrecoverable losses had skyrocketed to 1,320 combat aircraft. The pattern of heavy attrition extended to reconnaissance aircraft, with 170 aircraft destroyed and another 127 damaged. Added to this melancholy toll for the *Luftwaffe* were 197 transport and liaison aircraft. The long summer campaign had been exhausting, with minimal opportunity to reinforce forward units and reserves.[31]

The VVS also faced problems in sustaining air operations. There were critical shortages in day bombers and ground attack aircraft. This problem was evident on the eve of Operation Typhoon, when the VVS possessed only five Shturmovik (ground attack) regiments for deployment at the Western, Bryansk, and Reserve *Fronts*.[32] Nevertheless, Air Commander General P. F. Zhigarev could muster a significant number of fighters for frontal aviation. He could also count on the 6th IAK of the PVO at Moscow. In addition, the six newly organized *Stavka* RAGs

The highly versatile German Bf 109 did not survive early air operations on the Eastern Front. High attrition in aircraft and aircrews punctuated the triumphal advance of German armies in the East. (From the collection of Dmitriy Karlenko)

(*Rezervnaya Aviatsionnaya Gruppa,* or reserve air groups) included 60 to 100 aircraft in each and provided the VVS defenders at Moscow with some modest reinforcements. For the long run, the VVS, along with the 6th IAK PVO enjoyed the benefits of flying from established airfields around Moscow: Vnukogo, Fili, Tushino, Khimki, and the Central Aerodrome.[33] With the advent of the *Rasputitsa* and the Russian winter, the possession of good basing facilities would become a distinct advantage, although this was not necessarily a reality at this point in the war. Good basing facilities were in short supply and not well positioned. On September 7, General G. A. Vorozheykin, the VVS chief of staff, ordered his logistical command to develop a plan to improve the situation. He demanded 125 new landing strips and the construction of temporary wooden hangars at existing airfields to assure better operations in adverse weather.[34]

Moscow's historic Central Aerodrome was located on the Leningrad highway and adjacent to Petrovskiy Palace, once the temporary quarters for Napoleon in 1812. The fabled airfield had been the epicenter of civil, military, and experimental aviation in the prewar years and boasted a vast complex of aircraft hangars, runways, and factories. The 11th and 12th GIAPs (*Gvardeyskiy Istrebitelnyy Aviatsionnyy Polk,* or Guards fighter air regiment) flew from the Central Aerodrome during the dramatic weeks of the aerial assault on Moscow. During this national emergency, the regimental headquarters was housed in dugouts, and the available combat aircraft were camouflaged and dispersed. The Soviet pilots took their meals at the nearby Zhukovskiy Air Force Academy, which occupied a portion of the Petrovskiy Palace. The most intense air action for the two regiments took place in November, just as the German army reached the western periphery of Moscow. Soviet pilots flew repeated strafing sorties against German infantry and mechanized units. Typically, these sorties lasted twenty minutes or less, so pilots flew multiple missions each day. The Central Aerodrome was one of the established fields caught up in the maelstrom of the air war over Moscow.[35]

The VVS played an active role just prior to the German offensive. Air units assigned to the Western *Front* flew 4,101 sorties and delivered 831 tons of bombs on enemy positions during September. The Soviets also claimed to have destroyed 120 enemy aircraft on the ground and another 89 in air combat.[36] The Reserve and Bryansk *Fronts* recorded similar levels of air activity. Bombers from the DBA followed the same pattern. According to the Soviet records, the 81st BAD, down to a mere forty operational aircraft by September 30, hit the staging airfields for the *Luftwaffe*'s air raids on Moscow. More than 80 percent of these strikes took place at night.

Night bombing, mostly by U-2 biplanes in the tactical zones, became commonplace in 1941. Attacks were frequently launched in extreme weather, but the ideal conditions for bombing sorties were long moonlit or starry nights. The U-2s approached their targets singly at predetermined intervals, usually five to fifteen minutes apart, and at varying altitudes ranging from about 700 to 5,000 feet (200 to 1,500 meters).[37] Although the bomb loads were light (up to 441 pounds, or 200 kilograms), the U-2s made a significant impact on German troops by maintaining a sustained air presence over the battle zone.[38]

Such harassment raids worked well because the U-2—a prewar biplane design—was highly maneuverable, and its slow speed made night interception by the fast German fighters a difficult undertaking. VVS pilots would often stop their engines and glide stealthily to the target, dropping their bombs by hand. Any campfire or other German target sighted became fair game. These ubiquitous night attackers—nicknamed "sewing machines" or "duty sergeants" by the German troops—forced the enemy on all fronts to take precautions, lose sleep, and, on occasion, suffer the destruction of a storage area or fuel depot. Sometimes the Germans' only warning of an incoming Soviet fragmentation bomb was the wind whistling through the wing struts of a low-flying U-2.[39]

In the opening days of Operation Typhoon, the Germans struck southwest of Bryansk toward Orel, a drive spearheaded by Guderian's Second Panzer Group. The Germans quickly established a breakthrough corridor, pierced the Soviet tactical defense zone, and advanced rapidly toward Orel. They were countered by the 1st Guards Rifle Corps, consisting of the 6th Guards Rifle Division, the 5th Guards Rifle Division (moved from the Western *Front*), the 4th Tank Brigade, the 11th Tank Brigade, and the 6th Reserve Air Group with two fighter regiments, one ground attack regiment, and one regiment of Pe-2 dive-bombers. There were also four air divisions from long-range aviation and the special-purpose 81st Bomber Air Division, commanded by Colonel A. Ye. Golovanov.[40] Long-range aviation interdicted the advancing German reserves while frontal aviation attacked the first echelons of the advancing German troops. Most of the sorties were strafing missions, designed to slow down the pace of the German advance. Tank crews under the command of Colonel M. Ye. Katukov performed effectively and practically annihilated the German Fourth Panzer Division, which had only thirty-eight serviceable tanks by October 16. Aviation also gained some success. On October 10, six Il-2s and twelve MiG-3s of the 6th RAG strafed the German airfield at Orel. They appeared unexpectedly and claimed seventy-five airplanes destroyed on the ground and six in the air.[41] However, Guderian's breakthrough distracted Soviet command from the fact that the western axis was the shortest route to Moscow from the West.

On October 2, a follow-up German drive began to the north against the Soviet Western *Front*. With good weather, the *Luftwaffe* mounted some 1,387 sorties that day.[42] The German panzer units managed to advance through the Soviet defenses. *Luftwaffe* aircraft enjoyed local

air superiority, being able to linger over the battle zone for long periods of time against only token resistance from the VVS. The dearth of
antiaircraft batteries placed Soviet defenses in greater jeopardy. For
example, units of the 29th Army of the Western *Front* faced the advancing German army with no antiaircraft elements.[43] Consequently,
the *Luftwaffe* displayed great effectiveness, operating in large groups
and inflicting massive blows on Soviet army units caught in the corridors of advance.

Aircraft of the Western *Front* and the 6th IAK of the Moscow PVO
hit advancing German motorized units in the Yukhnov sector. Pilots of
the 6th IAK executed ground attack sweeps against the enemy with
their twin-engine Pe-3 aircraft. By October 7, the deputy commander
of the VVS, P. S. Stepanov, arrived with the aim of concentrating airpower in the sector. Soviet air assets increased dramatically with the
addition of an air regiment of Il-2 Shturmoviks, along with two regiments of MiG-3 fighters equipped with RS (*reaktivnyy snaryad*, or
rocket projectile) rockets and one regiment of Pe-2 dive-bombers. Additional reinforcements on that day included one ground attack and
three fighter air regiments. On the following day, the augmentation in
airpower continued with the addition of one ground attack regiment,
four fighter air regiments, and one bomber regiment with Pe-2 dive-
bombers. Most of the fighters were equipped with RS rockets for
strikes against enemy ground targets. From October 2 to 10, Soviet aviation of the Western *Front* flew a total of 2,850 sorties. These air operations, in reality, became virtually the only way to slow the German
advance toward Moscow. As a result of the Soviet air strikes, the German advance was slowed down significantly (German forces covered
the 31 miles [50 kilometers] from Yukhnov to Medyn in six days).
However, this came at a high price, especially for Shturmovik units,
which averaged one loss per 8.6 sorties.[44]

Nevertheless, the repeated German blows had shattered the entire
forward structure of Soviet defenses in the Vyazma and Bryansk sectors. The German advance quickly gained momentum. Orel fell on
October 3 after bitter fighting. By the end of the first week, Bryansk
had been taken, and forward units of the Second Panzer Group had
reached the outskirts of Tula. On October 7, the advancing Germans
successfully closed the trap at Vyazma, encircling a large contingent
of Soviet troops. The *Stavka*'s refusal to allow retreat, fearing panic and

disintegration, had kept Soviet forces in place in the Vyazma sector. This tactic assisted the Germans' aim of trapping them. It also afforded the *Luftwaffe* a multitude of static targets with little or no VVS air cover in the first days of Operation Typhoon. For the Soviet regime, this was the moment of truth, and no effort was spared to blunt the German offensive. Committed in force, the VVS steadily increased its air activity, flying 700 sorties against the advancing Germans in the opening week. Soviet aircraft of various types airlifted men and material from rear areas to reinforce the precarious defenses.[45] During these frantic opening days, VVS aircraft transported 5,500 troops and thirteen tons of supplies to the forward defense zones.[46] At several crucial moments, and against the hovering menace of the *Luftwaffe*, General G. K. Zhukov ordered massive air strikes against German tanks and motorized units. Soviet bomber units, already depleted by the carnage of the summer campaign, also flew numerous sorties against the enemy.

At Moscow, the VVS managed to provide the German ground forces with an unpleasant surprise—the Il-2 Shturmovik. Small numbers of these effective ground attack planes had reached frontal air units prior to Operation Barbarossa, but they had not made any significant impact. For the first time at Bryansk, the Il-2 "Ilyushas," as the Soviet pilots called them, made an appearance in force, boldly attacking German infantry and tanks. Guderian's Second Panzer Group at Orel, according to one German account, faced an aggressive display of Soviet airpower: "Enemy air activity was very lively, with Soviet bombers and ground attack aircraft flying in small formations of three to six planes."[47] Guderian found himself under air attack on October 4, shortly after his plane landed at Sevsk airfield, an experience repeated shortly afterward when he moved forward with the Third Panzer Division.[48]

The *Luftwaffe*, even in the face of concentrated Soviet air sorties, remained supreme. According to the Soviets, the Germans flew more than 4,000 combat sorties in the first nine days of October against the Western *Front* alone. At the same time, the *Luftwaffe* renewed its attacks on Moscow, flying forty-one missions over the Soviet capital between November 15 and December 5, 1941. In the course of these raids, Soviet air defenses claimed an average of thirty to forty enemy planes destroyed per day.[49] Soviet accounts recorded many extraordinary acts of bravery and sacrifice by VVS aircrews. These same histor-ical sources also candidly pointed to "serious shortcomings" of the So-viet Air Force, particularly in the crucial sphere of coordinating air and ground actions. Under the chaotic conditions of retreat, commu-nications broke down, and VVS air division commanders frequently directed air operations with minimal contact or interaction with ground commanders.[50]

By October 10, Soviet troops of the Western, Bryansk, and Reserve *Fronts* had retreated to the Mozhaysk Line, a secondary tier of de-fenses situated a mere 50 miles (80 kilometers) west of Moscow. The Germans offered no reprieve, applying constant pressure on the re-grouping Soviet forces. At this crucial juncture, the Western and Re-serve *Fronts* were combined into a single Western *Front* and placed under Zhukov's command. Stalin's choice of the talented and tough-minded Zhukov reflected a realistic appraisal of the extreme peril fac-ing the Soviet Union. Stalin could no longer blissfully allow political orthodoxy and cronyism to be criteria for the selection of military commanders. The caprice of the purges had ceased by 1941, but their destructiveness had not been exorcised. Earlier, Zhukov had displayed considerable organizational skill and military leadership at Leningrad, prompting Stalin to select him as commander of the Soviet defenses at Moscow. With Zhukov's appointment, a war-generated pragmatism prevailed in the higher Soviet military councils.[51]

Having successfully enveloped the Soviet defensive group at Vyaz-ma, Army Group Center began a spirited assault against the Mozhaysk Line. Rather than assault this position directly, the Germans applied pressure on its flanks, at Kalinin (Tver) in the North and at Kaluga in the South. Under these grim circumstances, Zhukov's debut as overall commander did not bring immediate success. On October 12, German forces occupied Kalinin; two days later, Kaluga fell, forcing the Soviets to abandon Mozhaysk for fear of another envelopment. Fierce battles raged on the ground and in the air along the path of the advancing German spearheads. Borodino, the site of the dramatic battle with Napoleon in 1812, fell after bitter fighting; Tula, the pivot for Soviet de-fenses southwest of Moscow, found itself momentarily surrounded.

The fall of Moscow now appeared imminent. On October 19, Stalin ordered a state of siege, which threatened execution for "spies, wreck-ers, diversionists, and agents provocateur."[52] On the same day, Field

Marshal von Bock reported to the German High Command that Army Group Center had captured 573,000 prisoners at Vyazma. At this moment of ultimate peril, Stalin ordered a number of government offices to evacuate to Kuybyshev (modern day Samara), a move accompanied by contingency plans to relocate important armaments factories out of the Moscow area. The Moscow Communist Party organization, the State Defense Committee, and the *Stavka* remained to organize the capital's defenses.

Beginning on October 12, a *levee en masse* of more than 450,000 Muscovites, three-quarters of them women, began the construction of massive defensive fortifications, tank traps, and trenches on the outer ring of the city. "Communist Battalions," consisting of 12,000 untrained civilian volunteers, also moved into "gaps" along the front lines in a desperate effort to stem the German advance. As these emergency measures were implemented, a panic of sorts gripped the populace, prompting many to flee the city in advance of the German troops. The Communist regime, hoping to firm up the shattered confidence of the Red Army and the civilian population, blended patriotic appeals and explicit threats to those who digressed from duty in word or deed.[53]

On October 17, it was announced that Stalin remained in Moscow. This reality, combined with the iron discipline of the party organization and the NKVD, helped instill a tenuous sense of confidence. Stalin's famed speech, delivered in the Mayakovskiy subway station on the night of November 6, provided another significant gesture of defiance. The Soviet leader spoke confidently of ultimate victory—and made a direct appeal to Russian nationalism, reminding the people of past heroes such as Alexander Nevskiy, Dmitriy Donskoy, and Generals Suvorov and Kutuzov, who had led Russia against past invaders.

Even as Moscow prepared for the German assault, the Russian weather, up to this time only a feared specter, intervened to halt Operation Typhoon. First, there were steady rains mixed with snow, which turned roads and airstrips into impassable bogs as the mud sometimes reached a depth of 3 feet (1 meter).[54] Suddenly, the *Luftwaffe*'s *Luftflotte* 2 found itself nearly immobilized as the offensive entered the second half of October. From October 18 to the beginning of November, the German army made little progress, although at this juncture it was less than 50 miles (80 kilometers) from Moscow. Again, Soviet resistance, not just the extremes of weather, halted the Germans during this period. Threatened with encirclement, the Red Army held on to Tula with fierce determination. At Kaluga, Volokolamsk, and other points west of Moscow, Soviet troops held on and harassed the enemy.

Winter frost and snow finally arrived in mid-November, abruptly ending the muddy season. The frozen ground allowed easy mobility once again, and the Germans renewed their stalled offensive. But the changing weather brought new rigors as one of the worst winters in memory descended on both sides. Soon, movement ceased again. The subzero temperatures brought untold hardships to the German army, which was not properly equipped or clothed for the extremes of the Russian winter.

The *Luftwaffe* operated under the most primitive field conditions, a situation now made worse by the deluge of snow, fog, and freezing temperatures. Airstrips had to be continually cleared of snow. Starting the aircraft engines, particularly liquid-cooled engines, became nearly impossible in the extreme cold. Ground crews found even routine maintenance almost impossible when their exposed skin froze to metal. Rubber tires at these extreme temperatures became brittle and deteriorated rapidly with use. Ground crews frequently had to work in the open or in unheated areas, and their tools had to be heated before use; engines and armament defied the elaborate efforts of skilled technicians to make them operative, and work efficiency dropped sharply. There were no manuals or established procedures to accommodate the impact of "General Winter" on *Luftwaffe* operations.[55]

Even in these dire conditions, the VVS managed to increase the tempo of its air operations to exploit the enemy's immobility. Dropping out of low clouds, Soviet aircraft repeatedly hit the hard-pressed German troops. Soviet air units, long accustomed to cold-weather flying, controlled the skies above the frozen ground. In the month of November, VVS units deployed on the Western *Front* flew 5,232 sorties (781 of which were night sorties). Soviet records suggest a total of fifty German aircraft destroyed and damaged on the ground and another thirty-three downed in air combat.[56]

With the arrival of inclement weather, the number of *Luftwaffe* sorties had been reduced. In turn, this decline in air sorties slowed the advance of German ground forces. By contrast, the VVS increased its daily sorties. This augmentation in Soviet air operations was not nec-

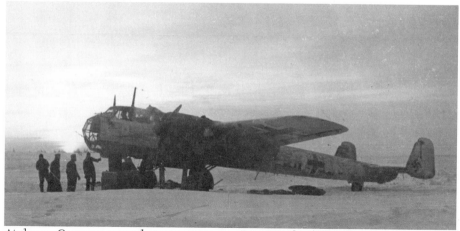

At dawn, German ground crews prepare a Do 17Z of 8./KG 3 for a combat mission, winter 1941–1942. To sustain air operations in such extreme weather, the *Luftwaffe* adapted the cold-weather flying techniques pioneered by the Soviets in the prewar years. (From the collection of Von Hardesty)

essarily a consequence of better air basing. Instead, it reflected an aggressive posture embraced by forward VVS aircrews. One general with the *Wehrmacht*'s XXXIX Panzer Corps lamented, "The Russians were attacking us in aircraft of all types during the most severe weather." The willingness and impressive ability of Soviet airmen to launch sorties in all kinds of weather and to make full use of all types of aircraft made a visible impact on the battle. On October 21, Colonel S. A. Khudyakov, chief of staff for the VVS of the Western *Front*, directed VVS air units to assume an active role, whatever the weather conditions at the front. The 6th IAK PVO had flown 1,151 sorties from October 4 to 9 and another 2,736 sorties from October 9 to 14. The 6th IAK's attrition rate was high as a result of weather-related accidents and enemy action, but the enhanced operational work continued.[57]

The seemingly invincible *Wehrmacht* now found itself nearly frozen in place, exhausted, and incapable of sustaining the drive on Moscow. The campaign in the East had placed enormous strain on the entire German war machine, a fact that became apparent only with the sudden collapse of Operation Typhoon. If Soviet casualties and losses in 1941 appeared catastrophic, German losses were mounting steadily as well. By September 25, 1941, German casualties reached 534,000, with

This American-built P-40 fighter (RAF designation Tomahawk II) was delivered to the VVS by the British. It was flown by Lieutenant S. G. Ridnyi, flight commander of the 126th IAP (6th IAK PVO), Moscow area, December 1941. Ridnyi achieved twenty-one aerial victories overall; of these, one individual and nine shared were achieved while flying the Tomahawk. (From the collection of Valeriy Romanenko)

more than one in five being killed.[58] Russia proved to be more formidable in its defensive capabilities than either Great Britain or France in 1940. Although Soviet resistance was uneven, it displayed a ferocity and toughness unparalleled in the West. The enormity of the landscape appeared to absorb the German infantry, mechanized units, and aircraft with ease. The military triumphs of the Germans, now projected over four months, had ended in exhaustion rather than inevitable victory. The vast stage for the war, the enormity of the landscape, had taxed the German army in ways beyond the frame of reference for western Europe. The vision of Operation Barbarossa had proven foolhardy and ill-fated. Moreover, there was the Soviet defenders' unanticipated capacity to hang on, to mobilize the residual strength of the country, and to impressively—even fiercely—resist the invader.

The desperate plight of the invaders in October–November has been summarized well by Albert Seaton: "Infantry companies, twenty men strong, led by second lieutenants or sergeants, were bearded and filthy, not having bathed or changed their clothes for months. Tormented by lice, they lay all day cramped and stiff in the narrow weapons pits filled with water, and their feet so cold that they had lost all feeling. Sickness and cold caused more casualties than enemy action. Rain fell incessantly and the *Luftwaffe* seemed unable to cope with the Soviet Air Force fighters and bombers which dropped out of the low clouds, bombing and machine gunning."[59] These privations were soon intensified by a logistics crisis. The unfolding crisis continued into December 1941 as the desperate, ill-clad German troops attempted to maintain themselves against a revitalized Soviet air and ground offensive.

The vaunted power of the *Luftwaffe* also proved illusory in the face of these challenges on the Eastern Front. The air supremacy achieved in June–July 1941 quickly dissipated, as the strains of a 2,000-mile (3,200-kilometer) front took their toll. With increasing commitments in the West, the *Luftwaffe* had few reserves to sustain a prolonged air support role in the East. At the end of 1941, Hitler withdrew Kesselring's *Luftflotte* 2 from the support of Army Group Center at Moscow to meet new requirements in the Mediterranean theater. Up to that time, the *Luftwaffe*, even with a beginning strength of 3,000 aircraft, found itself incapable of performing multiple assignments in the vast arena of combat. In 1941, the *Luftwaffe* deployed about two aircraft per mile on the Eastern Front, compared with ten to fifteen per mile in earlier campaigns in Poland, France, and the Balkans.[60]

During the first month of the war, the *Luftwaffe* had flown an average of 2,500 or sometimes 3,000 sorties per day. During the summer, German aircrews had displayed considerable skill and efficiency—destroying VVS machines on the ground and in the air, providing effective ground support, and covering ever-extending lines of communication.[61] But the serviceability of the *Luftwaffe* aircraft inventory began to decline perceptibly by the end of the summer, a condition that became even more critical during Operation Typhoon (October–November 1941), when bad weather intervened to halt nearly all aerial operations. Combat losses mounted steadily, prompting concern within the operational units. Though crippled, the VVS continued to operate and, in some sectors, make *Luftwaffe* operations difficult. The use of *taran*

This Bf 110D (3U + CM) of 4./ZG 26 was downed on the Kalinin *Front* in late fall–winter 1941. (Photo by P. Ryapasov; from the collection of Dmitriy Karlenko)

only added to German frustrations over the Soviets' doggedness and resilience. The use of Messerschmitt Bf 110s, He 111s, and Ju 88s for ground strafing resulted in unexpected and unacceptable losses.[62]

Again, the German frame of reference for offensive operations, forged in the triumphal campaigns in the West and in Poland, was ill-suited to meet the unfolding realities of the harsh Eastern Front. The *Luftwaffe* approached the Russian winter of 1941–1942 exhausted, overextended, and depleted in numbers. At best, the German air arm—despite unparalleled victories—had only a tenuous hold on tactical air superiority. The German High Command had been surprised at the capacity of the Soviets to strike back suddenly and often effectively, which prompted no small amount of confusion among the ground forces. While faced with the menace of a catastrophic German breakthrough at Moscow during the second week of October, the VVS made a bold air strike on enemy airfields. Soviet intelligence had learned that the *Luftwaffe* was planning a mass attack on the Western *Front* on October 12, aimed at industrial centers, airfield complexes, rail terminals, and logistical support facilities. The Soviets estimated that more than 1,500 planes would participate. To blunt this enemy raid, the *Stavka* ordered the hard-pressed VVS to mobilize a preemptive strike for the night of October 11–12, to be followed by an air raid on the morning of October 12. The *Stavka* directive, part of a larger blueprint for VVS air operations for the period October 11–18, called for VVS air units to hit *Luftwaffe* staging airfields along the northwestern, western, and southwestern axes leading to Moscow. This plan drew heavily on the existing frontal and long-range bomber units deployed around Moscow.

According to the Soviets, the preemptive air strikes achieved dramatic success, descending with force on *Luftwaffe* airfields at Vitebsk, Smolensk, Orel, Orsha, Siversk, and other points. The reported tally for October and November reached 300 aircraft, a figure not confirmed by German accounts.[63] Although exact figures remain elusive, this whole operation reflected boldness and resourcefulness on the part of the Soviet Air Force in the most difficult climatic conditions.

The causes for the ultimate failure of the German offensive outside Moscow, according to historian Dmitry Khazanov, are vividly apparent in the diary of von Bock, then in charge of Army Group Center. Writing on December 7, von Bock noted that the abrupt arrival of bad weather, the paralysis of railroad links to the forward areas, and the unanticipated fierce resistance of the enemy blended to first stall and then reverse the German army's advance on the Soviet capital. Khazanov noted that the weather in October–November had been severe, with temperatures below average. Yet these same conditions prevailed on the Russian side, making air operations difficult to sustain. Only the Russians' prewar experience with cold-weather flying techniques offered a decided advantage.[64] Khazanov further observed that von Bock had not fully comprehended the other forces at play on the Russian side that made the defense of Moscow such a success. A key factor was the manifest achievement of the entire PVO air defense network around the capital—always alert and fierce in terms of its resistance to the enemy. Soviet fighter interceptors played a dramatic role, but the effectiveness of antiaircraft batteries was extraordinary, the one source of opposition remembered most vividly by German airmen. And with the bad weather and cloud cover in October–November, German bomber crews were compelled to fly at lower altitudes of 1,650 to 3,300 feet (500 to 1000 meters), which enhanced the danger posed by antiaircraft batteries. For the first time, the Soviet side made effective use of radio communications to coordinate the air defense effort; this tool became more prominent with training and combat experience. In retrospect, the key factor in the war was the mobilization of human and material resources. The defense of Moscow was strengthened by the timely arrival of reinforcements from rear areas and skillful maneuver of troops from less threatened areas to the front.[65] By the first week of October, the Soviets possessed 508 bombers, 180 ground attackers, 948 fighters, and 80 reconnaissance aircraft—a total of 1,716 serviceable aircraft. By December, there were 590 bombers, 164 ground attackers, 1,010 fighters, and 65 reconnaissance aircraft—a total of 1,829 serviceable aircraft. This level of aircraft inventory suggests the impressive intrinsic strength of the VVS at the end of 1941.[66]

The renewed production of warplanes was placed under the supervision of People's Commissar of the Aviation Industry A. I. Shakhurin. It was during this time that Stalin sent his famous telegram to the directors of the plants manufacturing the Il-2 Shturmovik, saying, "These aircraft are [as] essential to the Red Army as air and bread." The highly centralized and disciplined war production program eventually made a decisive impact, allowing the Soviet Union to equip its burgeoning air force with vast numbers of a variety of modern aircraft designs.[67]

THE SOVIET COUNTEROFFENSIVE

Operation Typhoon had pushed forward in October–November against an increasing tempo of Soviet resistance. The ferocity of the Soviet defenders soon matched the extremes of weather to slow the German advance. On November 27, German troops reached within 19 miles (30 kilometers) of the center of Moscow, occupying the last tram stop at the edge of the city at Khimki. This became the high-water mark for the invaders. Farther south, the German forces failed to occupy the city of Tula, a key objective in the planned ground assault on Moscow. A turning point in the Moscow campaign was now in the making. By the beginning of December, the German offensive against Moscow was in deep trouble. The overall complexity of the situation was apparent as the Germans managed to achieve some triumphs in the South, despite the collapse of the effort at Moscow: Army Group South advanced from the Dnieper River to the Sea of Azov and made some initial forays into the Crimea. On November 21, German forces occupied the city of Rostov, which placed them on the threshold of the Caucasus. However, these victories only added to the strategic problems facing German arms. The *Wehrmacht* now faced the problem of overextension. This vulnerability was dramatized by the Soviet counterattack that quickly recaptured Rostov and compelled the German army's first major retreat in the East. In its episodic fury, this retreat typified the overall crisis of Operation Typhoon. Four days later, Guderian wrote in his journal a fitting epitaph for the German assault: "The offensive on Moscow has ended. All the sacrifices and efforts of our brilliant troops have failed. We have suffered a serious defeat."[68]

Guderian's grim assessment of German military fortunes at Moscow coincided with the Soviet decision to launch a winter counteroffensive. Bloodied by more than five months of war, the Soviet army remained viable despite its reduced numbers and equipment shortages. Sensing an opportune moment, Stalin called on his troops to roll back the invaders. Timely reinforcements from Siberia and the *Stavka*'s reserves gave the Soviets enhanced striking power for a counterattack against a weakened and vulnerable enemy. Nine new armies began to arrive at the end of November from formation sectors as distant as Lake Onega in the North and Astrakhan in the South. This reality on the ground reflected the Soviet effort to achieve total or permanent mobilization. As such, frontline Soviet army and air units endured great hardships, often fighting out of encirclements and in extreme weather to blunt the enemy's advance.

At the beginning of December, Soviet armies in the Moscow axis consisted of 718,800 men, 5,900 field guns and mortars, 415 rocket launchers, and 667 tanks.[69] Zhukov approached the counteroffensive with the reinforced Kalinin and Southwestern *Fronts* on his northern and southern flanks. For the air war, the VVS had in the western sector alone (the VVS of the Kalinin, Western, and Southwestern *Fronts*, as well as the strength of the 6th IAK PVO and DBA units) 1,393 aircraft (910 listed as operational), against an estimated 580 *Luftwaffe* aircraft.[70]

At dawn on December 5, troops of the Kalinin *Front* went over to the offensive, crossing the frozen Volga River against stubborn German resistance. The following day, Soviet troops from the Western and Southwestern *Fronts* joined the battle. Now the Russian counteroffensive moved forward along the entire Moscow Front, a distance

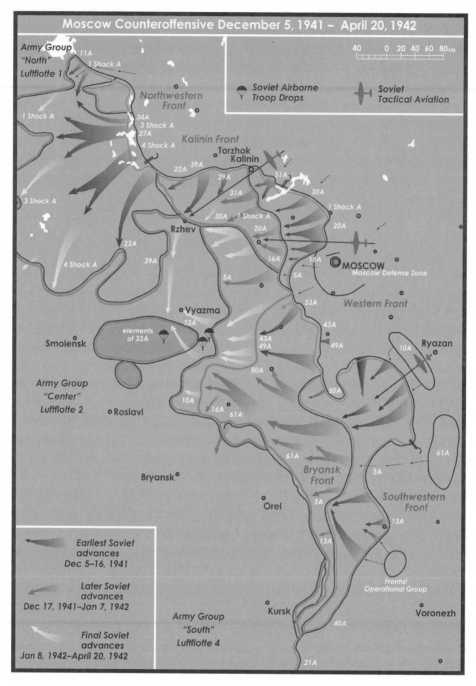

Map 3 (Terry Higgins & Zach Downey-Higgins © 2011 [based on Russian source material supplied by the authors])

of 560 miles (901 kilometers), stretching from Kalinin in the North to Yelets in the South. Fierce fighting erupted along the length of the Soviet advance, and the Soviets quickly made dramatic progress through mobile pursuit and flanking tactics. Despite poor weather—low clouds, fog, and snowstorms—the VVS covered the Soviet advance in force.

The German army then fell back in disorder. Fighting became brutal and exacting. Soviet troops pierced the tactical zone of the enemy defenses during the first three days, despite aggressive opposition and the numbing cold. For the first time, the Russians had advanced in force and threatened the Germans with encirclement in several sectors. By December 9, Soviet air reconnaissance confirmed a massive withdrawal of German troops west of Klin. Fearing entrapment, many German units along the front withdrew in panic, abandoning their guns, tanks, and equipment along the snow-drifted roads. At Kaluga, a city earmarked by Hitler to be defended at all costs, the Germans offered stubborn opposition, which forced the Soviet attackers to take the city street by street and house by house in some of the heaviest fighting of the war. At Kaluga, there was already ample evidence of the brutality of the Russo-German War, now in its sixth month: Soviet troops found seven men and one woman, accused of partisan warfare, hanging from a gallows in the main square. In other places, the retreating German troops torched buildings, large and small, in an effort to make Russia a landscape of charred ruins.

Along the entire sweep of the Moscow Front, both armies struggled against the bitter cold and the heavy snow.[71] For the Germans, who lacked cold-weather clothing, proper equipment, and lubricants for operation in subzero temperatures, the impact of winter was more severe and debilitating. Frostbite took a fearful toll of German soldiers. By contrast, Soviet replacements from Siberia and the Far East arrived west of Moscow fully equipped with winter-issue, fighting in their white-camouflage combat clothing designed for maximum protection against the rigors of the Russian climate.[72] There was also the timely employment of T-34 tanks and Katyusha rocket launchers.

Moscow confidently announced on December 11 that the German drive on the capital had been pushed back. A week later, the momentum of the counteroffensive began to slow perceptibly, but the Soviets had recaptured the cities of Klin, Kalinin, Yelets, Kaluga, and Volokolamsk; forced Guderian's panzers back from besieged Tula; and now threatened the encirclement of the forward elements of Army Group Center. Fearing a total collapse of the German forces at Moscow, Hitler ordered his troops on December 16 to stand fast "without retreating a step." This move, taken against the urging of many of his generals, stiffened German resistance, particularly in the center in the Rzhev–Gzhatsk–Vyazma triangle located between Smolensk and Moscow. Here the residual strength of the German army once again asserted itself against the determined but faltering Soviet counteroffensive. There would be no repetition of the retreat of Napoleon's *Grande Armee* of 1812.

In this altered context of German retreat, the resuscitated Soviet air arm made a dramatic, if limited, show of force on the western approaches to Moscow in December 1941. The VVS demonstrated in this uncertain and complex setting its formidable potential as a tactical air arm and the capacity to conduct combined arms operations in a major offensive. On the first day, the VVS attacked German troop concentrations and artillery positions in support of the advancing 31st Army on the Kalinin *Front*. After the fall of Kalinin, Soviet air units flew support missions between December 17 and 26 to assist five armies in the northwest sector in a drive on Rzhev. Frontal air units made 1,289 combat sorties in close air support missions, reconnaissance flights, and sporadic attacks on retreating troops in rear areas. During these actions, Soviet fighters claimed sixteen air victories over the *Luftwaffe*.[73] General S. I. Rudenko, who replaced General N. K. Trifonov as VVS commander for the Kalinin *Front* in January 1942, displayed energy and skill during the winter counteroffensive. His subsequent career would include command of the 16th Air Army at Stalingrad, Kursk, and Berlin.

At Tula, located on the southwest approach to Moscow, General F. Ya. Falaleyev assumed command. Here the VVS's major goal was the destruction of Guderian's Second Panzer Group, now in retreat. In the Tula sector, the *Stavka* deployed a concentration of ground forces drawn from the Western and Southwestern *Fronts*, which included the 50th and 10th Armies plus some cavalry units. During the first ten days of the offensive, the Soviet forces pushed the enemy back 50 to 60 miles (80 to 160 kilometers). Soviet air units made a valiant effort to destroy Guderian's tanks. On the Southwestern *Front*, the VVS had

208 operational aircraft in nine air divisions, while the Western *Front* could muster eight air divisions with 242 serviceable combat aircraft of mixed composition. The VVS of the Kalinin *Front* had only five regiments with 49 serviceable aircraft.[74] Even with this modest number of operational aircraft, the VVS played an important role during December in this sector. Despite the unfavorable weather, the aviation of the Southwestern *Front* flew around 1,500 combat sorties alone, while the VVS of the Western *Front* took to the air 5,066 times and scored a significant tally of enemy tanks and vehicles, according to Soviet records.[75] The steady air pressure from VVS units also restricted the general movement of German troops, now in desperate retreat, and compelled them to feverishly set up antiaircraft defenses.

During the December counteroffensive, the *Stavka* attempted to slow the German retreat with the use of airborne troops. On the night of December 15, 415 men were dropped behind German lines in the northwestern district of Teryayeva Sloboda. The VVS aimed to block the escape route west of this spot in coordination with the advancing 30th Army. Although some Soviet sources describe this operation as successful, there is evidence that it failed to achieve its purpose. It was a bold maneuver, but it lacked organization, coordination, and adequate cover from VVS fighter squadrons. The Soviet paratroopers suffered heavy casualties and only narrowly escaped annihilation.[76] In January 1942, another paratroop drop numbering 2,000 men took place at Medyn, near Tula. Such operations, launched under severe weather conditions, displayed boldness and heroism, if not efficiency.[77] For the air operations over the crucial Western *Front* of General Zhukov, the VVS concentrated nearly 80 percent of its strength. Aviation from the Moscow Air Defense Zone (PVO) joined with frontal air units to assist the 5th, 33rd, and 43rd Armies in breaking through the enemy's defenses. Fighting in this sector had been bitter, and progress had been slow for the Soviet armies until late December 1941. By January 4, 1942, the Soviet 43rd Army had retaken Borovsk and Maloyaroslavets, two key cities located on a line directly south of Mozhaysk.

During these difficult days, General N. F. Naumenko commanded the Soviet air operations in the Western *Front* (he would be replaced by General S. A. Khudyakov on February 7, 1942). A veteran of the Winter War with Finland, Naumenko went on to command the 4th Air

Army briefly in the Kuban and then the 15th Air Army at the Battle of Kursk. The 6th IAK (PVO), commanded by Colonel I. D. Klimov (and, after November 1941, by Colonel A. I. Mitenkov), played a prominent role in the defense of Moscow and the subsequent Soviet winter offensive. While maintaining its role as the protector of Moscow proper, the 6th Fighter Air Corps assisted VVS frontal aviation in the vital air support role, attacking enemy troops, airfields, and railroad centers.[78] During November, this unit alone, according to Soviet records, destroyed 170 enemy aircraft; in December, it destroyed another 80 planes.[79] The 6th Fighter Air Corps switched to ground attack missions in December as the *Luftwaffe*'s threat to Moscow diminished. Between December 9 and 14, during a period of heavy snow and extreme cold, fighter pilots from this air defense unit harassed retreating columns of enemy troops at various points west of Moscow, including the areas around Klin and Solnechnogorsk.[80] This flexible use of PVO air units in the Soviet counteroffensive complemented their earlier heroics in the defense of Moscow in the summer and fall of 1941. A total of twenty-three fliers from the 6th Fighter Air Corps received the Gold Star, Hero of the Soviet Union, during the battle for Moscow.[81]

Along with the 6th IAK, other air units participated in the assault on retreating German infantry and tanks. Reserve air groups (under Generals A. A. Demidov and I. F. Petrov) joined selected bomber units from long-range bomber aviation to bolster Soviet airpower during the defensive struggle at Moscow and the subsequent general offensive. The mobilization of all available units for these crucial operations provided Soviet air commanders with valuable experience in coordinating diverse forces over a vast geographic area. Not only had Soviet aviation survived in 1941; it had also conducted offensive operations in extreme winter conditions, to the surprise of an enemy that now appeared to be something less than invincible.

At the time, the Moscow Military District had sufficient air strength to form a special air group under the command of N. A. Sbytov. Once it was reinforced by the 46th BAP (*Bombardirovochnyy Aviatsionnyy Polk*, or bomber air regiment), equipped with the fast Pe-2 aircraft, and by the 65th and 243rd ground attack regiments flying Il-2s, Sbytov's air group entered combat along the Mozhaysk Line in support of the Soviet 5th Army. During the defensive stage of the Battle of Moscow, additional reinforcements came from military school instructors and recent graduates of *Osoaviakhim* pilot training courses, who were thrown into night-flying air regiments equipped with U-2, R-5, and R-Z aircraft.[82] Three-fourths of VVS frontal aviation, in fact, was flown in this offensive. Tactical air sorties prevailed, with sustained attacks by day and night on retreating German troop columns or at their defensive strongpoints. The 180th IAP, for example, flew a total of 208 sorties over an eight-day period. Even the weather favored the Soviets at this juncture, with a spell of good flying weather in early December. In the shifting meteorological conditions, the VVS made excellent use of the slower, obsolete R-5, R-Z, and U-2 aircraft. Joining the fray was the 6th IAK, a PVO air unit contributing support to the Soviet 20th Army.[83] All these trends reflected the aggressive mode of Soviet airpower during difficult winter operations. Moreover, this pattern of reinforcement became a telltale sign of the impressive residual power of Soviet military aviation. Only half a year had passed since the VVS endured the first blows of Operation Barbarossa.

The first phase of the Soviet counteroffensive at Moscow lasted thirty-three days. It included air action south and north of the central sector. The VVS flew a total of 7,210 combat sorties in the Western and Kalinin *Fronts* in direct support of the ground forces.[84] The VVS's newfound flexibility was evident in its systematic attack on German rear areas by DBA elements; these bombers—often at high risk and with uneven fighter escorts—hit troop concentrations, supply depots, and mechanized units. Soviet archival materials suggest the special and increasingly vital role of the *Shturmoviki*, the aircrews flying the remarkable Il-2 Shturmovik.[85] Under severe conditions, the Soviet air units demonstrated an impressive capacity for maintaining flight operations. Only the most extreme weather—heavy snowstorms or fog—grounded Soviet operational aircraft. Low clouds and marginal visibility proved challenging, but these were not insurmountable obstacles for the low-flying VVS pilots who were intent on attacking the retreating enemy columns.

Faced with the challenge of sustaining air operations during a general winter offensive, the VVS mobilized the necessary organizational and logistical elements to assure success. There were failures and inefficiencies as the technique was refined. With each advance, there was the need to rebase air units and assure their resupply. With the recapture of Klin, there was the luxury of using a newly liberated aero-

For winter operations, this SB bomber was fitted with ski landing gear. FAB-250 bombs are attached to the bomb racks under the wing center section. (From the collection of Valeriy Romanenko)

drome, but elsewhere, there was the daunting task of establishing airfields under the most primitive conditions. In some cases, aircraft were equipped with skis to operate from snow-covered and frozen airstrips.[86]

Getting supplies such as ordnance and fuel to air units proved to be no easy task. Pilots and ground crews often lived in improvised and primitive conditions. The Soviet Union, with its prewar experience in arctic flying, had developed techniques for the cold-weather starting of aircraft engines. This technical knowledge paid huge dividends—more often than not, VVS aircraft were airborne, while *Luftwaffe* ground crews failed to overcome the severe weather conditions. In other technical areas, however, VVS personnel demonstrated fewer skills, most notably with the use of radios for coordinated combined arms warfare. Only episodically were radio communications used effectively in this phase of the war.[87]

THE NEW YEAR ARRIVES — 1942

At Moscow, the *Stavka* had deployed its small rump air force against the enemy along the main avenues of attack. Frontal aviation alone flew 70 percent of its sorties against the northern grouping, a concentration of airpower that made a significant contribution to the advance of Soviet ground forces in this dangerous sector. Along the entire front, VVS air units, often using two crews for each aircraft in around-the-clock operations, accelerated the pace of the counteroffensive. In the enemy rear, attacking Soviet aircraft created confusion by applying pressure to retreating units, command posts, and lines of communication. As *Luftwaffe* sorties diminished in the severe winter months, the VVS managed to establish a measure of air supremacy.

Stalin still hoped to annihilate the German army before the end of winter, to repeat Russia's great triumph against Napoleon. Before a conclave of top leaders at the Kremlin on January 5, Stalin announced his decision to launch a general offensive. The bold plan called for the envelopment of Army Group Center, then situated between Smolensk and Moscow; the lifting of the siege of Leningrad; and the liberation of the Donets Basin and the Crimea. From January to April 1942, the Soviets attempted a sequence of attacks to make this ambitious scheme for ultimate victory a reality. In the end, they faltered and suffered enormous losses.

West of Moscow, Army Group Center held on in January–February 1942 and successfully resisted the Soviet effort to close the trap at Smolensk. To the north at Leningrad and to the south at Kerch, the Soviet general offensive also proved inconclusive. The *Wehrmacht*, though exhausted and vulnerable, proved resilient. For the Soviet armed forces, the general offensive exposed their own strategic weaknesses. The strain of prolonged conflict, the enormous losses in men and materiel, and the lack of adequate reserves made the general offensive a difficult, and ultimately impossible, undertaking. By the spring of 1942, it was apparent to both sides that the war was going to be a prolonged one.

During offensive operations in December–March 1942, the VVS, by its own account, flew a total of 59,385 sorties against Army Group Center (10,150 during counteroffensive operations, and 49,235 during general offensive operations). This high level of air action, even adjusted for probable Soviet exaggeration, reveals the remarkable vitality of the VVS during the difficult months of the 1942 general offensive.[88] Frontal aviation, according to Soviet sources, played a significant role in this offensive against Army Group Center. Between January 4 and 7, 1942, for example, VVS frontal aviation units attacked forward *Luftwaffe* airfields at Rzhev and Velikiye Luki; during this period of transition, increasing numbers of transport aircraft were making an appearance to resupply hard-pressed German ground units. Participating in the raid were the 5th GIAP and 193rd IAP, drawn from General Petrov's air group.[89] The Soviets claimed they destroyed nine Ju 52s on the ground and one Do 217 in aerial combat. The element of surprise and the impressive capability of the VVS to operate in poor weather were key elements to the Soviet success.

Although the rigors of combat and weather drastically reduced the total number of available VVS aircraft, the proportion of newer types increased. The VVS Western *Front* inventory, for example, numbered 360 by December 5: 69 Pe-2s and Pe-3s, 16 SBs and Ar-2s, 4 DB-3s and TB-3s, 45 R-5s and R-Zs, 14 U-2s, 54 Il-2s, 10 Yak-1s, 4 Yak-7s, 40 LaGG-3s, 46 MiG-3s, 20 I-16s, and 38 I-153s.[90] This meant that only 38 percent of the inventory consisted of obsolete models. The Soviets accelerated this process of transition to newer models in the summer and fall of 1942, once aircraft production in the newly relocated aviation factories reached full capacity.

Soviet chroniclers of the winter offensive have described a quickening of air combat activity during February and March 1942. In February, they recorded 67 air battles in the Moscow region involving 344 aircraft. During March, 258 air battles took place in wide-ranging combat encounters, which saw 656 Soviet aircraft committed against 971 German planes. The Soviets explain this increased tempo of air combat by pointing to the aggressive posture they assumed during this period.[91] Viewed from this historical perspective, the Soviet air arm, though still numerically inferior to the *Luftwaffe*, managed to take the initiative against Army Group Center. Soviet pilots flew combat missions along the entire German salient from Smolensk to the approaches of Moscow, attacking enemy troops, tanks, communication centers, and airfields.

German accounts, however, suggest a much lower level of combat activity by the VVS in the early months of 1942. Walter Schwabedissen, a *Wehrmacht* veteran and postwar commentator on this cam-

Yak-1 of squadron commander of the 123rd IAP, G. N. Zhidov. He ended the war with sixteen personal and thirteen shared victories. (From the collection of Igor Zhidov)

paign, acknowledged that by the turn of 1941–1942, the Soviet Air Force had survived the impact of Operation Barbarossa and projected a renewed vitality. Soviet units, however, varied in combat aggressiveness, depending on the time and the circumstances. The shift to a more offensive orientation became apparent in the summer, rather than the spring, of 1942. Soviet fighter units showed a new confidence as their aircraft approximated the performance of German models. The Soviet ground attack arm, in particular, became stronger and more aggressive as 1942 progressed.[92]

At the start of the war, VVS combat aircraft were austerely equipped compared with *Luftwaffe* airplanes. The Soviets introduced radios during 1941–1942, a technological leap of great significance for VVS planners, who strove to improve the control and discipline of air operations. With radio control techniques, the VVS command structure gained a powerful tool to coordinate air and ground operations. Some Soviet accounts attribute the increased effectiveness of VVS frontal aviation in the winter offensive to this radio air direction teamwork.[93] German accounts, however, have recorded that the system was primitive and poorly run.[94] Since the transmissions were made by voice, the *Luftwaffe* monitored them regularly and exploited the information to its advantage.

In the first year, VVS reconnaissance aviation experienced growth and refinement. Accurate and current data on the enemy became an operational requirement of the highest priority—a function made more critical by the immense size of the front, which stretched from Murmansk to the Black Sea. On June 22, 1941, in the military districts along the western periphery, the VVS possessed a mere seven reconnaissance regiments and one separate long-range or strategic reconnaissance regiment. This segment of the air force had some 269 operational aircraft. One critical weakness of the force was the fact that only 13 percent of the pilots were adequately trained to fly in complex weather conditions, and only 3 percent were trained for night sorties. Many of the aircraft assigned to the reconnaissance regiments were obsolescent types, such as the prewar R-5. The regiments also suffered extensive losses in the opening months of Operation Barbarossa. Later, more modern aircraft types, such as MiG-3s and Pe-2s, were assigned reconnaissance duty.[95]

The battle for Moscow became the arena for some fundamental changes in the organization of Soviet airpower.[96] For the first time, the Soviets organized their rear services for an arduous winter offensive. A total of seven new air basing regions (*Rayon Aerodromnogo Bazirovaniya,* or RAB) were organized, consisting of thirty airfield service battalions (*Batalion Aerodromnogo Obsluzhivaniya,* or BAOs), nine airfield engineer battalions, and other support units. Soviet rear services also established large storage depots along the front at intervals of 150 to 250 miles (241 to 402 kilometers) to serve the forward airfields. The organizational difficulties were enormous, given the disruption following the invasion, but the ruthless application of centralized control began to pay off.

A network of airfields was established, technical and logistical personnel were distributed, and stores of ammunition, fuel, and foodstuffs were funneled in a rational fashion toward the frontline airfields. Moreover, the entire logistical command was organized to serve an advancing, offense-oriented air arm. Mobile railway aviation workshops provided the flexibility required for offensive operations. The entire system, by definition, was designed to sustain a massive counteroffensive rather than a number of static or territorially based air units. These pragmatic efforts at mobilization and centralization anticipated the great Soviet air offensive operations of 1943–1945.

The Soviet winter offensive brought in its wake an important and precedent-laden conflict at Demyansk. In February 1942, in the seam between Army Group North and Army Group Center, the advancing

Soviet troops encircled the German II Army Corps, a force numbering around 100,000 men. The Soviet advance also swept around another smaller pocket of German troops at Kholm, just southwest of Demyansk. The Demyansk–Kholm region, located south of Lake Ilmen, offered a challenge to both armies with its numerous forests and swamps. During the January–February Soviet assault on the exposed right flank of Army Group North, heavy snows fell in the region, blunting both Soviet mobility and German efforts to stabilize their defensive positions. As part of the general offensive, the Soviet effort in the Demyansk sector placed Army Group Center in distinct jeopardy of encirclement by the northern wing of the Soviet pincer movement. Fierce fighting accompanied Soviet penetration into the area.

Faced with a crisis of considerable magnitude in mid-February, Hitler boldly ordered his encircled forces to remain in place rather than acquiesce to their urgent requests for permission to attempt a breakout. The continued occupation of the Demyansk pocket, as Hitler correctly reasoned, diverted Soviet attention from Army Group Center. Moreover, Hitler became convinced that the *Luftwaffe* and its air transport command could sustain the pockets through an airlift of reinforcements and supplies. Once conditions permitted, it was assumed that the encircled pockets could be rescued by establishing a land corridor.[97]

Now called on to execute an emergency airlift during the Russian winter, the *Luftwaffe* responded with an impressive vigor and capacity for improvisation. The smaller Kholm pocket, with its constricted area and lack of adequate airfields, posed a real problem. Initial efforts to land Ju 52 transports ended in disaster, since the small Kholm airfield fell within the range of enemy guns. The *Luftwaffe* then resorted to airdrops and the use of gliders to supply the 3,500 soldiers there.

The larger Demyansk pocket posed enormous obstacles for any effort of resupply in the midst of an enemy offensive and severe weather. *Luftflotte* 1, assigned to Army Group North, had only one air transport group at the outset of the crisis. Demyansk, it was quickly determined, required a minimum of 300 tons of food and materiel daily.[98] By February 19, a total of seven air transport groups were available for the airlift, an air flotilla that was steadily reinforced during late February and March. Given the aircraft's low serviceability in winter operations, the *Luftwaffe* needed to deploy 500 Ju 52s for the airlift to ensure 150 operational aircraft, each loaded with two tons of cargo, to meet the daily requirement.[99]

Of the two fields within the Demyansk pocket, the one suitable for airlift operations was a former VVS air base located at Demyansk; the other, at Peski, was little more than an emergency strip. To save Demyansk, both airfields had to be prepared for maximum use even in the absence of adequate ground facilities. The *Luftwaffe* began its airlift effort in an atmosphere of urgency. Various ad hoc measures followed to initiate the vital flow of materiel. The Soviets quickly moved forward, like a coiled spring, applying intense pressure on both pockets—setting up antiaircraft batteries on the approaches to Demyansk and deploying fighter units for air interdiction.

The Demyansk airlift worked, but barely. It established the fateful precedent of using airpower to supply surrounded troops even during the rigorous Russian winter. From January 1942 to the final removal of the Soviet threat to Demyansk early in 1943, the *Luftwaffe* flew a total 64,844 tons of ammunition, supplies, weapons, spare parts, and fuel. Moreover, German reinforcements amounting to more than 30,000 troops reached Demyansk by way of the airlift, while return flights brought out more than 35,000 wounded. During the most critical phase in late winter and spring (February 18–May 19, 1942), the *Luftwaffe* managed to deliver an average of 302 tons per day, narrowly exceeding the daily needs of Demyansk. The price tag for the entire airlift was high: 265 aircraft lost. In addition, *Luftwaffe* transports assigned to the airlift consumed 42,155 tons of aviation fuel and 3,242 tons of lubricants.[100]

Throughout the Demyansk airlift operations, German fighters made repeated sweeps over the approach and return routes, providing essential fighter cover for the slow-flying Ju 52s. Soviet antiaircraft batteries, however, displayed considerable skill against the German transports, often with mobile, self-propelled guns. Consequently, the danger from antiaircraft fire compelled the Ju 52s, which formerly flew in pairs at low levels, to cross the enemy zone in groups of twenty to forty aircraft at altitudes ranging from 6,000 to 8,000 feet (1,800 to 2,400 meters).

German fighters and transports found VVS fighters in the Demyansk operation to be unaggressive. The VVS always avoided direct contact with fighter escorts or large groups of Ju 52s, preferring to attack stragglers or single, unprotected transports. This assessment of Soviet fighter units fits the *Luftwaffe*'s overall negative estimate of VVS fighter air operations during 1941–1942. Yet these same sources are quick to acknowledge the prowess of VVS pilots in low-level bombing and strafing attacks, which, according to one German spokesman, "invariably resulted in German personnel and aircraft losses."[101] Within a year, the VVS brought these same skills for surprise attack, along with a much more aggressive fighter interceptor role, to Stalingrad, where an "air blockade" worked with Soviet ground forces to annihilate a German pocket three times as large as the one at Demyansk.

Soviet sources have remained largely silent about the role of VVS fighter units over Demyansk in 1942. One source, a memoir by Major General F. A. Kostenko, describes in graphic detail the aggressive role assumed by Soviet fighter units over Demyansk the following winter. At that time (February–March 1943), a renewed Soviet offensive to destroy the German army grouping at Demyansk began in earnest. Kostenko's account suggests that VVS fighters, largely late-model Yaks (Yak-7bs) with some La-5s, flew cover for Il-2 Shturmoviks, which were often used to draw German fighters into air combat. Against Bf 109s and Fw 190s, the VVS in this sector deployed some of its best fighter units. The results, as Kostenko records, were often quite successful. VVS fighters displayed occasional skill at resisting sweeps by enemy fighters (normally six to twelve aircraft) to clear the air prior to the arrival of German bombers. Soviet fighter pilots, many now proudly flying with the "Guards" designation, boldly challenged German fighters for control of the air.[102] As Kostenko points out, the enemy again anticipated easy victories, but the skies over Demyansk were now hotly contested, thanks to Kostenko's 1st IAK as well as the 6th Air Army, which had been unavailable in 1942 during the crucial first days of the Demyansk encirclement. Part of the success of the German Demyansk airlift rested on the anemic state of Soviet fighter aviation in the winter of 1941–1942.

Both sides had learned their respective lessons at Demyansk. The *Luftwaffe* victory—once disembodied from its accompanying high costs—became an illusory model for subsequent German airlift operations. With the advent of Stalingrad, Hitler and the German High Command turned to this precedent to bolster their contention that a large encircled army grouping could be resupplied effectively by air. The

Soviets, always keen to perfect their skills at combined arms operations, learned at Demyansk the requirements for an air blockade. By the time of Stalingrad, the VVS would possess the requisite aircraft and battle experience to attempt another air blockade on a larger scale.[103]

THE SOVIET TRIUMPH AT MOSCOW

For the Soviets, the winter counteroffensive achieved the fundamental objective of removing, at least temporarily, the German threat to Moscow. But the larger goal of destroying Army Group Center was not achieved, despite extraordinary effort and sacrifice. The VVS claimed the destruction of more than 1,400 enemy aircraft.[104] If true, this was a singular accomplishment for an air force that had suffered the worst air defeat in military history in the summer and fall of 1941. The struggle for Moscow signaled a new phase in the epic Russo-German War. Moscow endured a long—if uneven—bombing campaign that began in July 1941 and extended into 1942. During the long winter months, the Soviet forces pushed the Germans back as far as 240 miles (386 kilometers) in some sectors, inflicting, by Moscow's reckoning, 300,000 casualties. German tallies of war losses confirmed the high attrition. General Halder, chief of the general staff, listed 1,005,000 Germans killed, wounded, or missing by the end of February 1942. The war now entered a new phase, one in which the Soviet Union's residual strength— vast reserves of manpower, enormous productive capacity, permanent mobilization, and the capacity to wage total war—would play out against a still formidable and ruthless occupying army.

During defensive operations, the *Stavka* demonstrated greater effectiveness in the use of airpower. By the beginning of October, VVS air units had been deployed from several *Fronts,* the Moscow Military District, fighter aviation of PVO, bombers from DBA, and assets from the newly formed RAGs. Command and control of these air units achieved a new level of efficiency. Under *Stavka* leadership, airpower was concentrated in the main sectors of combat, a harbinger for future operations. By the second week of December, an estimated 46 percent of VVS air strength had been moved to the Moscow region, where Soviet air units conducted operations around the clock, hitting advancing enemy units.

Soviet air commanders learned valuable lessons on how to coordinate and sustain air operations under extreme conditions. Forging closer ties and collaborating with ground forces stood as another achievement of the Moscow battle. Creating a program of genuine combined arms warfare, however, remained an elusive goal. There were still other lessons to be learned, such as the management of logistics and supplies, the use of radios for effective communication, counteroffensives, fighter aircraft tactics, and so on. The battle for Moscow, with all its stresses and sacrifices, allowed the VVS to gain valuable combat experience that would cast a long shadow over subsequent battles with the enemy. Attempts were made to coordinate these air operations with the larger goals of the *Fronts*. Yet in practical terms, the VVS suffered considerable losses and failed to provide consistent support for the ground forces. As the counteroffensive unfolded, the organizational divide widened. By February 1942, up to 75 percent of all serviceable aircraft were under the control of air force commanders of combined arms armies. The capabilities of frontal aviation were thus significantly limited. During this period, most important targets were attacked by only four to six strike aircraft.[105]

The role of Soviet airpower in the defense of Moscow was an important, if not necessarily decisive, factor in shaping the final outcome of the battle. For the first time, air commanders acquired experience in the organization and operational deployment of aviation in a major wartime campaign. This wartime crucible extended over months, involved defensive and offensive operations, required movement across a vast geography, and took place in shifting extremes of weather. There were technical and institutional failures that compromised any effort at a quick recovery. The demands of the conflict necessitated changes in leadership and even reorganization in times of extreme peril.

Bloodied in the first six months of the war, the VVS managed to preserve itself and exercise a measure of command and control over its finite air assets. It even pressed for air supremacy in the winter of 1941–1942. Soviet airpower—though drastically weakened in the first phase of Operation Barbarossa—had proven to be resilient.

Chapter Three

Stalingrad

The second year of the war gave birth to a fierce struggle for the city of Stalingrad, the ancient trading town on the Volga River known in prerevolutionary times as Tsaritsyn. Epic in scope and meaning, this bloody conflict endured for 199 days, beginning in July 1942 and ending in February 1943. For Nazi Germany, the battle became a military catastrophe of the first order. The *Wehrmacht* had pushed eastward to the Volga River, only to falter with the partial conquest of the city and then see its veteran Sixth Army encircled and systematically destroyed.

Stalingrad represented a turning point in the trajectory of Allied fortunes in the war. For Nazi Germany, the battle became an Armageddon in terms of its scale, unfathomable brutality, and fateful consequences. The *Wehrmacht* suffered an irreversible loss of initiative in the East. Each side took measure of the unfolding character of the Russo-German War, with its tally of human lives and the squandering of vast material resources. Lessons were learned and relearned by Soviet war planners in this fiery crucible, and even in triumph, there was the sobering realization in Moscow that a formidable invader still occupied Soviet territory and possessed the means to continue the relentless and unforgiving struggle. In strategic terms, Hitler's vision of conquering the North Caucasus and the Baku oil fields had been thwarted. Stalingrad also exposed the finite and now severely weakened war-making capacity of Nazi Germany.

The epochal struggle at Stalingrad involved aviation on both sides. Each side deployed airpower at crucial moments in an effort to decide the outcome of the battle. On the eve of Stalingrad, the VVS continued to face the arduous tasks of reorganizing and exercising proper command and control of its expanding air power. During the long Soviet winter offensive in 1941–1942, the VVS had been pressed to the limit.

Soviet pilots were often outnumbered and outclassed by the enemy, but the abundant heroism and dedication of Soviet air and ground crews remained impressive. Yet heroism alone could not carry the day. There had been a lack of efficient coordination of aviation and ground forces. The VVS had employed a number of ad hoc measures to enhance efficiency, but these fell short of solving the fundamental problems. Now with the prospect of a new German offensive, there was an urgent need for reform of the Soviet air arm. In the spring of 1942, there would be a major reorganization of the VVS, a pivotal series of initiatives in organization and tactics that would shape Soviet air operations for the rest of the war.

The ensuing air war saw the Soviet air arm increasingly display more effective air combat tactics. Soviet factories, with their augmented production of warplanes, and the timely arrival of Lend-Lease aid soon set the stage for the VVS to gain the numerical strength and the technical means to challenge the *Luftwaffe* for air supremacy. At Stalingrad, there would be an intense struggle by the VVS to gain the tactical initiative, even to successfully execute a large-scale "air blockade" to thwart the *Luftwaffe* in its attempt to resupply the encircled Sixth Army. Historians routinely divide the air war at Stalingrad into two distinct phases: a defensive stage, beginning in July 1942 and extending into the fall, in which the VVS endeavored to blunt German air and ground operations on the Don and at Stalingrad; and the Soviet counteroffensive, lasting from November 19, 1942, to February 2, 1943, which encircled and destroyed General Friedrich Paulus's Sixth Army.[1] Over Stalingrad, especially during the Soviet counteroffensive, a new mood of confidence animated Soviet pilots and aircrews. No longer did the VVS view the *Luftwaffe* as invincible. This shift in attitude alone signaled a vital change and a key harbinger of the future.

The two phases of the Stalingrad conflict were uneven for the VVS in terms of air operations. During the defensive stage, Soviet sorties against the enemy were occasional at best and offered no serious challenge to the *Luftwaffe*'s air supremacy. This reduced level of air action by the VVS contrasted sharply with the fierce ground resistance offered by the Soviets on the approaches to Stalingrad. Only in the second phase, beginning with the November 19 Soviet counteroffensive, did the full brunt of Soviet airpower fall with a vengeance on the overextended German positions. By the fall of 1942, the Soviet aviation industry had regained its productive capacity, supplying a steady stream of newer-model warplanes. In addition, there was now a new reserve of Lend-Lease aircraft to add to the mix. Stalin prudently channeled the growing number of VVS aircraft into the Air Corps of the *Stavka* Reserve. Stalingrad became an important testing ground for the reorganized VVS command structure to make effective use of these resources.

THE RENEWAL OF SOVIET AIRPOWER

The imperative for a reorganization of the VVS weighed heavily on the *Stavka* and air force commanders in the spring of 1942. There was a shared sense of urgency to address many of the problems evident in the air arm.[2] Already, the Germans were planning a second summer offensive. A renewed German drive, perhaps against Moscow, would place an enormous burden on the hard-pressed Soviet Air Force. The aviation industry, now safely relocated beyond the Urals after extraordinary human effort and sacrifice, had gained momentum in the winter months and was able to reach (and soon pass) prewar production levels. This meant a steady flow of modern combat aircraft during the coming months.[3] With the aim of transforming the air arm into a powerful strike force, the *Stavka* decided to refashion the structure, operational character, and tactics of the air force. The effort to reorganize the VVS in 1942 was not necessarily a war-induced phenomenon. During the interwar years, in fact, the world's major air forces had pursued reforms in response to new technologies and to emerging threats both perceived and real. The form and purpose of airpower, of course, had been an obsession for many air planners in the prewar decades, a process that may have originated in World War I. In 1940, in fact, the VVS had initiated a dramatic set of reforms at the end of the purge era that sought to enhance national security in a world increasingly threatened by war. The air force organization, along with logistics, airfield construction, design bureaus, and the aviation industry itself, had experienced significant changes. For the operational VVS, however, the 1940 reforms had preserved, even reinforced, a pattern of decentralization. This reality, along with the perpetuation of political controls via the commissar system (following the purges), only weakened the overall posture of Soviet airpower.

The survival of the Soviet regime, however, rested squarely on the ability to forge an effective military, one that included a powerful air arm. There were major challenges that weighed heavily on the VVS leadership, including a list of myriad tactical and organizational deficiencies. The pressing issue was how the bitter lessons of the first year of the war now shaped and conditioned the process of renewal. The priority of integrating VVS air units into the ongoing operations of the ground forces remained a fundamental task. The quest to achieve an optimal concentration of forces in both defensive and offensive campaigns defined *Stavka* planning at this critical phase of the war.[4] At the beginning of 1942, there was a pressing requirement to mobilize and deploy powerful air groups to support the active *Fronts*. Air Commander Colonel General P. F. Zhigarev, in a directive of January 25, openly recognized the inadequacies, in particular the tendency to disperse existing air assets among the various *Fronts*. Any reform would be aimed at finding an organizational structure that would allow for the concentration of airpower.[5] Later, on March 15, Zhigarev wrote in a report to Stalin that the VVS required organizational unity—for him, that was the pathway to success. A single command would allow the more decisive application of airpower, the ability to maneuver effectively, and, when appropriate, the ability to execute powerful blows against the enemy. Moreover, Zhigarev proposed the creation of "five operational air armies."[6] The clarion call for the highest military leadership to act quickly and decisively had been made.

A major transformation of the VVS structure and operational principles quickly followed. The first decree came from the People's Commissariat of Defense on May 5, 1942, creating the 1st Air Army.[7] Earlier, on April 11, 1942, General A. A. Novikov had replaced Zhigarev as VVS commander. The decision to appoint Novikov reflected Stalin's wartime preference to place proven military commanders at key positions. In the prewar context, many appointments had reflected political concerns over professionalism. Zhigarev assumed command of the VVS in the Far East, a reassignment that reflected the fact that, in the end, it did not mean the end of his military career, although his tenure as air commander had coincided with a time of retreat and retrenchment. The selection of Novikov, as events unfolded, proved to be an inspired choice. Novikov quickly took charge of the VVS and presided over a series of far-reaching reforms of the Soviet air arm. Novikov's ascent to the top had been rapid. He had first attracted attention in the opening months of the war at Leningrad, where he demonstrated initiative as a commander. In February 1942, he assumed the post of first deputy commander of the VVS, a short-term assignment that sent him to the various *Fronts* to coordinate air operations as part of the Soviet general offensive then in progress. Returning to Moscow in the second half of February, Novikov helped plan air operations on the western axis. In March, he moved to the North to plan and lead VVS air operations in the area of the Volkhov and Leningrad *Fronts*. With subordinate air commanders drawn from frontal aviation, long-range aviation, and the Air Corps of the *Stavka* Reserve, Novikov planned and executed the first massed air strikes in support of troops on two *Fronts*. For this strategic achievement, he was appointed commander of the Red Army Air Force and, concurrently, Deputy People's Commissar of Defense.

While Novikov pushed energetically to modernize the VVS, he did not emulate the *Luftwaffe* in any slavish fashion. Expediency dictated selective borrowing. The rites of copying, always with refinements, reflected the elasticity of the Bolshevik ideological program in the interwar years. Being behind the *Luftwaffe* at the outset of the war in technical and operational terms was not unique to the Soviet Air Force. During the Battle of Britain, for example, the Royal Air Force had made a series of changes in air tactics to conform to the *Rotte* and *Schwarm* formations. The VVS, by necessity, struggled with the same problem, among others, making similar tactical adjustments in 1942–1943. Through the Air Force Military Council, Novikov organized the War Experience Analysis and Generalization Section to systematically study the "lessons" of the air war in the East. In part, this meant a close scrutiny of *Luftwaffe* organization, tactics, and equipment. The larger task, however, required an adaptation to the peculiarities of the Eastern Front, that is, changes in the lockstep Soviet air doctrine, which dictated the building of a strong tactical air force.

To achieve these ends, Novikov blended proven *Luftwaffe* techniques with what could be described as indigenous notions of air combat. The VVS under Novikov forged many innovations, and over time, these reforms narrowed and closed the gap in equipment and technique with the *Luftwaffe*, a fact later acknowledged by General Adolf Galland.[8] There were also areas in which the VVS surpassed the *Luft-*

waffe in both technique and experience, such as cold-weather air operations. Novikov began his tenure as Air Commander (a post he would hold for the duration of the war) with a group of able associates. His first deputy was Major General G. A. Vorozheykin. Serving as chief of staff, General F. Ya. Falaleyev became an important operational leader; he would hold this post until June 1943, when he was replaced by his deputy, General S. A. Khudyakov.[9] Other important and long-term assignments included General F. I. Zharov (Rear Services), General A. K. Repin (Engineering-Technical Service), General I. P. Turkel (Inspector-General), General N. S. Shimanov (Political Directorate), General A. V. Nikitin (Air Formations Directorate), and General I. P. Zhuravlev (Air Operations Directorate). These men provided continuity in VVS leadership in the period of rapid expansion after 1942.

Soviet military planners viewed VVS organization in 1941–1942 with a critical eye, seeing a persistent pattern of inferior performance and poor coordination. Some of this disarray, of course, stemmed from Operation Barbarossa's disruption of the command and logistics structure. At Moscow, however, the situation had stabilized enough to test the existing air force organization. Enormous problems continued throughout the winter, particularly with air operations for any general offensive. The increased scope of the war required better command and control, more effective means of mobilizing air resources, and improved training for aircrews. Another critical sphere of reorganization was the subordination of fighter air components assigned to air defense under the command structure of PVO Strany. These timely and far-reaching changes began in January 1942, with the aim of fashioning a more efficient single command.[10]

Spearheading the entire program of reform was the Air Force Military Council, a group of high-ranking officers charged with oversight of both the military and the political affairs of the VVS. This group reviewed a series of staff proposals in 1942 for the improvement of the air force's central administration. As a consequence, the various sections and directorates were redefined, including the creation of the aforementioned War Experience Analysis and Generalization Section, with A. A. Vasilyev as section chief.[11] The sweep of reform altered rear services as well, which included the important spheres of airfield construction and technical and supply functions. All these changes extended the work of the 1940 reorganization program.

Steps were taken in March 1942, at the time of Novikov's appointment, to reorganize the bomber command. The aim was to create a separate air arm for strategic aviation under the direct supervision of the *Stavka*. This move, of course, reflected Stalin's desire to exercise close control over his air force and, in this case, the rudiments of an independent strategic air force. As such, the newly organized bomber command had its own command structure, communications, and logistical supply system. Though independent, the bomber command assumed many tactical missions in the war, flying sorties for the various *Fronts*. Although this command had been named long-range bomber aviation (DBA), prior to March 1942, it possessed only a depleted fleet of medium-sized bombers at the end of the first winter of the war. During the previous summer, the DBA had struck Berlin in a bold effort to bring the war home to the enemy, a symbolic gesture much like the Doolittle raid on Tokyo in 1942. The Berlin raids had been planned and conducted under the overall command of Major General S. F. Zhavoronkov of the naval air arm of the Baltic Fleet. A joint task force drawn from the Baltic Fleet and the DBA, flying DB-3s and DB-3Fs, had operated from Saaremaa (Osel) Island. There had also been an independent air strike with Pe-8 bombers. But the prevailing climate in *Stavka* planning circles favored tactical, not strategic, bombing. Such an inclination pivoted on wartime expediency and on Soviet air doctrine, which, after a brief flirtation with Douhet's concept of strategic bombing at the end of the 1930s, had shifted toward tactical bombing. The Soviets remained interested in long-range bombers and even requested Lend-Lease shipments of Boeing B-17 bombers.[12] But this technology was denied. Instead, the United States made available to the VVS in 1942 a significant quantity of A-20 and B-25 medium bombers. These bombers reinforced the tactical focus of Soviet aviation during the war. The Soviet aviation industry also committed itself to production of the marginally effective Il-4 (DB-3F) bomber in 1942, in the hope of expanding its inventory of bomber aircraft. In many ways, the decision of the VVS to define a largely tactical role for its bomber units reflected circumstance as much as air doctrine. In 1942 it was often necessary to improvise to strengthen the bomber force: Li-2 transports, for example, were modified to carry bombs and then thrown into combat.[13]

After March 1942, the new structure for long-range aviation was the ADD, or *Aviatsiya Dalnego Deystviya*. As successor to the DBA, the newly formed "strategic aviation" component operated in direct subordination to the *Stavka* command. Major General A. Ye. Golovanov assumed the post of ADD commander, with Lieutenant General M. I. Shevelev as chief of staff. The ADD bomber command initially had seven bomber air divisions, one transport air division, and one reserve air brigade. In May 1943, the ADD underwent further reorganization and expansion, adding eight bomber air corps consisting of two divisions each (each division, in this case, consisting of two regiments). Later, in December 1944, the ADD became the 18th Air Army, with Golovanov as commander, but now subordinated to Novikov rather than directly to Stalin himself.

Bomber operations remained an important, if problematic, dimension of Soviet airpower during the war. Interestingly, Stalin took a special interest in the service, even personally assigning bombing targets to General Golovanov.[14] Unlike the British or the Americans, however, there was no concerted drive to deploy a large long-range bomber force. The ADD's eventual reorganization into the 18th Air Army enshrined strategic aviation in an institutional way, but this move in no way compromised the tactical and operational character of VVS bomber sorties. For certain, the Pe-8—a large, four-engine Soviet bomber—existed, but in modest numbers. The commitment to the tactical and operational deployment of bombers left the VVS with little real capacity for strategic bombing in 1945. The issue of strategic aviation would be addressed only at the very end of the war.

The creation of air armies (*Vozdushnaya armiya,* or VA) became a fateful move at the very epicenter of the Novikov reforms. The new structure soon became a powerful tool to give expression to the idea of the VVS as a component in combined arms warfare. Novikov, with the active involvement of air commanders such as I. A. Vikulenkov and S. A. Khudyakov, sought to use air armies, which were always subject to augmentation and flexible assignments to active *Fronts*, as a tool for centralized control of VVS air operations.[15] Such an organizational change assured that Soviet airpower, now on the threshold of rapid expansion, could be concentrated quickly in strategic theaters of conflict for maximal effect. And these same air armies would be the vehicles for forging new air tactics, experimenting with new technologies, and making full use of modern aircraft types.

Mobile air armies under centralized control provided the VVS with enormous flexibility in all future campaigns. The 1st Air Army, with General T. F. Kutsevalov as commander, first appeared in May 1942. It combined the air units of the Western *Front* for the purpose of "heightening the striking power of aviation and allowing the successful application of massed air strikes."[16] In its initial formulation, the 1st Air Army possessed modest strength: three fighter air divisions (210th, 202nd, and 203rd IADs), one mixed air division (215th SAD), one ground attack division (214th ShAD), a training air regiment, a long-range air reconnaissance squadron, a liaison squadron, and a night bomber air regiment equipped with U-2s (renamed Po-2 in 1944). Although army aviation, per se, was scheduled to be phased out, this did not take place quickly. Other air armies took shape during the spring and summer of 1942: the 2nd, 3rd, 4th, and 8th Air Armies in May; the 5th and 6th in June; the 14th and 15th in July; and the 16th in August. By November, three more air armies had been organized (the 7th, 13th, and 17th), completing the dramatic transformation of Soviet frontal aviation. Except for regimental air units performing reconnaissance and liaison work, all operational aircraft of the VVS entered the mobile air armies.

Air armies gave the Soviets the capability to achieve a rapid buildup of airpower to meet the shifting requirements of battle. This capability became crucial in the last stages of the war (1943–1945), when large-scale summer and winter offensives along a 2,000- to 2,500-mile (3,200- to 4,000-kilometer) front required the swift orchestration of forces to keep the enemy off balance. The demise of army aviation (*Armeyskaya aviatsiya*) and the older frontal air command (*VVS Fronta*) meant that control of the VVS passed to the air army commander, who was subordinate in operational terms to the *Front* commander. By working as an air deputy to the *Front* commander, the VVS air army commander was able to coordinate his air operations more effectively with the *Front* commander's requirements for either defensive or offensive action.

No less important for the ultimate success of the air armies was the creation in 1942 of the Air Corps of the *Stavka* Reserve. Again, the Air Force Military Council assumed a leading role in the establishment of this powerful air reserve.[17] Each reserve air corps normally consisted of two or more air divisions with a total strength of 120 to 270 aircraft.

Armed with the latest-model aircraft, the Air Corps of the *Stavka* Reserve numbered thirteen air corps at the end of 1942 and comprised twelve fighter, eleven ground attack, one mixed, and seven bomber air corps by the end of the war.[18] These strategic air reserves served as a conduit from the aviation industry to the air armies. They reinforced VVS aviation at crucial junctures in the war, augmenting air armies according to the requirements defined by the *Stavka*. Such a system gave the air armies an impressive capacity for maneuver and concentration.

With an ample supply of reserves, the average air army grew dramatically in size within a short period of time. During the 1942–1943 period, as the VVS challenged the *Luftwaffe* for the strategic initiative in the air, an air army normally consisted of 900 to 1,000 aircraft. By 1944–1945, the average reached 1,500, and for the final campaigns on the approaches to Berlin, the size of participating air armies mushroomed to 2,500 to 3,000. The formidable air production allowed the Air Corps of the *Stavka* Reserve to make massive augmentations in frontline air strength, sending more than 3,000 aircraft (eleven air corps) forward to buttress the 1st, 3rd, 4th, and 16th Air Armies during the important Belorussian campaign in June–August 1944.[19]

The creation of the air armies affirmed the important principle of concentrating air assets for pivotal operations. Yet this move proved to be less than complete if examined in actual operational terms. Voices of reform called for a few powerful air armies to be placed under the direct control of the VVS air commander. This redeployment of air assets would have allowed the optimal concentration of airpower as needed for both offensive and defensive operations. Air armies were routinely subordinated to *Front* commanders. Any shift of air units from one air army to another was a complicated affair, always pursued with reluctance, notwithstanding the ruling principles of mobility and concentration of forces. Any shifts required the direct approval of the *Stavka*, which took time. Any concentration of air armies under one command allowed greater mobility and less dependence on reserves. In fact, the reserves played a key role, acting in reality as mobile air armies that could be thrown into combat as required. Consequently, ground commanders retained a strong measure of control over air assets even with the Novikov reforms. This pattern reflected either a reluctance to transfer too much power to VVS air army commanders or a fear of Stalin and the *Stavka*, or both.

Along with the creation of the air armies, the VVS began a gradual shift to homogeneous air units at the division and regimental levels. Air commanders argued for such units, particularly in fighter regiments, to provide greater efficiency, more effective maintenance and supply, and better training of air and ground crews. This type of organization facilitated centralized control of Soviet airpower. In 1941, VVS air regiments typically numbered sixty to seventy aircraft, but this was later reduced to twenty or more aircraft as part of a process of consolidating force levels. By 1943, VVS fighter air regiments began to appear with inventories of a single type of aircraft, but this single type often included more than one variant of a given design. For example, the 812th IAP, its parent division, the 265th IAD, and the 3rd IAK were equipped with different Yak fighter models: Yak-1, Yak-7B, and Yak-9T, along with advanced Yak-9U and Yak-3 models later in the war. For tactical reasons, Shturmovik air divisions retained their composite character, with one fighter regiment attached for escort and reconnaissance duty. Novikov endeavored to reshape VVS squadron, regiment, and division configurations to meet the exigencies of air combat.

THE FATEFUL DRIVE TO
THE VOLGA RIVER

After the abortive Soviet offensive at Demyansk and Kharkov in May–June 1942, the German High Command ordered Army Group B under von Bock to begin the long-awaited German summer offensive. Stepping off in the Bryansk sector on June 28, Army Group B moved toward Voronezh. Concurrently, Army Group A, under the command of Field Marshal Wilhelm von List, attacked through the Donets Basin toward the Volga River. Across the flat, almost limitless steppe of the eastern Ukraine, German panzer units pushed forward in clouds of dust and in sweltering heat. Overhead, the *Luftwaffe*, resuming its customary ground support role, attacked the retreating Russians in force. Having overrun the Soviet defenses on the Don, the Germans, with Paulus's Sixth Army as a spearhead, managed to reach the Stalingrad oblast (region) by July 12. To the south, German forces moved into the Caucasus.

Captain T. D. Kartuzov, commander of the 1st squadron of the 36th IAP, awaits the signal to begin a combat sortie from the Kuleshovka airfield in the Rostov–Don area, January 17, 1942. (From the collection of Thomas Salazar)

Moscow reacted in a desperate effort to halt the German advance, sending reinforcements to Voronezh and organizing the defenses of Stalingrad. The *Luftwaffe*, deployed along the attack zones of the German Army Group South, possessed 1,640 aircraft (970 bombers, 510 fighters, and 160 reconnaissance aircraft).[20] By contrast, the VVS found itself awkwardly situated to meet the challenge, being outnumbered by nearly four to one in the attack zones.[21] The *Stavka* sent an operational group under P. S. Stepanov to organize the air defense of Stalingrad. Stalin feared a possible collapse of Soviet defenses. In the face of the unfolding crisis, he issued Order No. 227 (July 28), which stated: "*Ni shagu nazad*" (not a step backward). The decree was harsh and determined. For potential "deserters" or "panic mongers," there was swift retribution. It was also patriotic in its appeal, committing the Red Army to the strategic defense of Stalingrad—a city hitherto out-

Pilots of the 210th ShAP stand next to the Il-2 flown by their commander, Major N. A. Zub, Southern *Front,* March 1942. The slogan on the fuselage reads "Death to fascist occupiers!" Major Zub was killed in action over the Kuban in July 1943 on his 381st sortie. (From the collection of Valeriy Romanenko)

side the arena of combat. At the moment of this decision, Paulus's Sixth Army was approaching the great bend in the Don River.

The city of Stalingrad occupied a narrow strip of land nearly 25 miles (40 kilometers) long on the west bank of the Volga. In earlier times, the city had been an important tsarist military and trading center; now, in 1942, it was a burgeoning industrial center with a population of 500,000. The historic city had been renamed from Tsaritsyn to Stalingrad (the city of Stalin) because Joseph Stalin had led the Bolshevik forces there during the Civil War following the Bolshevik Revolution. The terrain on the approach to Stalingrad from the west resembled a tabletop, giving way at the city's perimeter to a series of hills and ridges. Winding through this asymmetrical geography was the deep Tsaritsa Gorge. In the middle of Stalingrad, overlooking the Volga River, was the hill known as Mamayev Kurgan. The long, tightly arranged urban strip that was Stalingrad proper looked out on a bend in Volga and the vast, flat

A. V. Shashko, a navigation officer with the 2nd IAP, stands next to a LaGG-3 fighter in the Kharkov area, May 1942. (From the collection of Dmitriy Karlenko)

terrain stretching to the east. Once the German summer offensive began, the city acquired strategic importance, since its loss would sever the north-south waterway between Moscow and the Caucasus.

The *Stavka* had moved slowly to prepare the defenses of the threatened city. Not until July 14 did Moscow place Stalingrad on a war footing. The previous summer, during the hectic days of Operation Barbarossa, the Soviet authorities had ordered the construction of three defensive lines on the western perimeter of the city, but these projects remained unfinished. Work had resumed in late June, just on the eve of Army Group B's thrust eastward. Other defensive measures followed in the wake of the German advance, including the creation of a people's militia, the organization of partisan groups, and the evacuation of children. All these measures fell under the aegis of the Stalingrad *Front*, which had been created by the *Stavka* on July 12. Since German air raids, as expected, preceded the main assault on the city, desperate efforts were made to provide adequate air cover. The 8th Air Army of the former Southwestern *Front* assumed an important role in the air defense of Stalingrad.

A LaGG-3 fighter of the 2nd IAP prepares for takeoff from an airfield in the Kharkov region, May 1942. (From the collection of Dmitriy Karlenko)

P. S. Stepanov, the *Stavka* representative, inspected the situation at Stalingrad and reported to Moscow that the entire network of air defenses was inadequate. He toured the various airfields and established communications with the PVO command for Stalingrad. The 102nd IAD (PVO) possessed a mere ninety-four aircraft, mostly obsolete I-15 and I-16 types.[22] The newer Yak and Lavochkin types were in short supply, and Stepanov appealed to Air Commander Novikov and the *Stavka* for the immediate deployment of a fighter regiment equipped with Yak-1s. This appeal did not go unheeded: Novikov ordered a fighter air regiment from Moscow to Stalingrad, and the *Stavka* deployed ten fighter air regiments, nine ground attack regiments, and three bomber regiments to reinforce the 8th Air Army.[23] For frontline air commanders, these timely reinforcements were most welcome and necessary. The fact that nearly 75 percent of the aircraft in these regiments represented the newest models—Yak-1, Yak-7b, Il-2, and Pe-2—prompted greater confidence in the VVS's ability to frustrate the *Luftwaffe* at Stalingrad.

Already, the Novikov reforms were shaping the character of the VVS response. General F. Ya. Falaleyev, appointed VVS chief of staff in July, spearheaded a number of crucial operational changes. During the first week of his tenure as chief of staff, Falaleyev issued a directive instructing all frontal air commanders to concentrate their aviation along the main avenues of Soviet army operations. He worked tirelessly to make the VVS an effective weapon. No longer would it be dispersed to perform myriad tasks without reference to larger combat priorities. The diffusion of Soviet airpower had led to extraordinary attrition and minimal efficiency during the first year of the war.

Falaleyev's directive embodied the ongoing effort to centralize Soviet air operations. VVS strikes against secondary targets were still possible, but only after the larger requirements had been met. Reflecting Novikov's stress on competence and efficiency, he pushed for better operational planning. This meant greater use of air reconnaissance. For the headquarters staff in Moscow, there was the difficult task of walking a tightrope between the increased need for centralization and the desire to encourage initiative among frontline air commanders. VVS personnel, from squadron to division levels, were now displaying high morale and renewed confidence in their struggle with the *Luftwaffe*. At the same time, the Soviet air commanders, still intimidated by the purge era and fearing retribution for any mistakes that might result from excessive battlefield "initiative," exercised caution in all things. Men such as Falaleyev encouraged a higher level of flexibility, but these problems defied any permanent solution.

Stalin himself monitored VVS air operations through daily briefings. These reports, based on the major air operations of the previous day, provided a profile of missions flown and targets hit, the number of air battles, a summary of German and VVS losses, and an evaluation of VVS effectiveness. Through these summaries, Stalin also learned about *Luftwaffe* air actions and deployment. Two high-ranking air force officers prepared the summaries after a systematic study of accumulated reports from the field. General N. A. Zhuravlev, "who possessed the ability to say a great deal in a little space," wrote the final version of the briefing report for Stalin.[24]

Being assigned to the *Stavka* involved hard work. Novikov and a small group of senior commanders briefed Stalin on a regular schedule. All activity at the *Stavka* was subordinate to the will of Stalin, who

received detailed reports on the vast enterprise of the war. His deci-
sions were all-encompassing in their impact, dealing with both major
and minor issues. For the most part, Stalin preferred to have a limited
coterie of talented subordinates around him. As Supreme Commander, he could be petty and vindictive and always exacting in his
demands, but he was a quick learner of the military art. By the time of
the Stalingrad crisis, the *Stavka* had achieved a higher level of efficiency and demonstrated the capacity to plan complex defensive and
offensive operations.

For Novikov and the other high-ranking officers who prepared the
regular briefings, there were the inevitable and tension-filled encounters with the Supreme Commander in the Kremlin, where he maintained both an apartment and an office in a "little corner" near the
Supreme Soviet. Colonel General S. M. Shtemenko, who worked at
Supreme Headquarters, relates in his memoirs the context and the
procedure:

> We entered the small room of the chief of the personal guard
> through Poskrebyshev's [Stalin's personal secretary's] office and
> from there into the Supreme Commander-in-Chief's suite. On the
> left side of the office, not far from the wall, stood a long,
> rectangular table. We used to roll out the maps on it and use
> them to make a report on each Army Group in detail, starting
> with the one where major action was taking place at that given
> moment. . . . At the end of the table, in the corner, there was a
> large globe on the floor. I must say that in the hundreds of times
> I visited the office, I never once saw the globe used during a
> discussion of operational questions. In addition to the Supreme
> Commander-in-Chief, as a rule, members of the Politburo and
> members of *Stavka* were present at these briefing sessions. . . .
> Usually, all civilians present sat along the table against the wall
> facing us, the military, and the huge portraits of Suvorov and
> Kutuzov which hung on the opposite wall of the office. Stalin
> used to pace up and down along the table on our side as he
> listened. From time to time, he would go over to his desk, which
> stood far back on the right, take two cigarettes, tear them open,
> and stuff his pipe with tobacco.[25]

During these intense sessions, Stalin reviewed the overall situation and the various directives proposed to the *Stavka*. These directives, after being corrected and/or supplemented, were signed by Stalin and the chief of the General Staff. In response to military emergencies, a *Stavka* directive would be transmitted immediately to the front from a nearby communications room. For Shtemenko, Novikov, and others, the planning sessions could last until 0300 or 0400 hours, typifying the "rigid work schedule that Stalin had established and no one could change." Such a regimen, according to Shtemenko, required "enormous physical and moral resources . . . which not every man could take, the more so because, as a rule, men were dismissed from the General Staff for the slightest mistake with all the ensuing consequences."[26]

At this stage in the war, there were acute problems with Soviet fighter operations at the front. General S. I. Rudenko complained that fighter cover for ground attack aircraft lacked discipline. Inexperienced fighter pilots frequently abandoned their assigned positions in the heat of battle, making fighter protection occasional at best. When fighters and Shturmoviks broke formation singly, they exposed themselves to the ever-present danger of German fighters. Moreover, few of Rudenko's fighter pilots were prepared for the rigors of air combat, and they lacked technical knowledge about their new aircraft, since their brief transition training had afforded them little opportunity to learn the nuances of their planes. Under the immense pressures of the German invasion, training had been abbreviated to meet the wartime emergency. Two-thirds of the pilots in the 220th IAD, for example, arrived at Stalingrad with minimal flight experience in the newer Yak and Lavochkin fighter aircraft.[27] They also knew little about the region's geography, giving them no particular advantage as defenders.

Given these concerns, Novikov endeavored to bring greater efficiency to all VVS air operations. At the front, he gave considerable attention to air control, an area that started to show improvements with the use of radio. In the rear, Novikov saw a clear need to improve training methods. His War Experience Analysis Section, providing detailed information on *Luftwaffe* strengths in equipment and tactics, was helpful in reshaping VVS training along more realistic lines. Always energetic, Novikov visited frontline airfields and spoke at length with unit commanders and pilots. Many of these visits prompted him to order immediate changes to improve operational effectiveness. With typical Bolshevik rigor, Novikov always checked that the various levels of the air force command structure complied with his instructions.[28] A. S. Yakovlev observed in his memoirs that Novikov had a profound sense of duty and single-mindedness about defeating the *Luftwaffe*.[29] He was animated as well by a pragmatism and willingness to learn. These qualities made him an effective air commander, one who never allowed himself to be trapped by the prewar operational modes that had brought the VVS close to the point of extinction.

On August 23, Novikov made his first appearance at the Stalingrad *Front* as part of a special commission of high-ranking officials sent from the *Stavka* in Moscow. G. M. Malenkov, Stalin's wartime associate and member of the State Defense Committee (*Gosudarstvennyy Komitet Oborony*, or GKO), had arrived in the city on August 12 with General A. M. Vasilevskiy, then chief of the General Staff. Already, the *Luftwaffe* had placed Stalingrad under bombardment, and German troops were moving forward across the Don. During these critical days, the *Stavka* worked desperately to stem the German advance. By August 20, General A. Ye. Golovanov had completed the relocation of five of his ADD divisions from Moscow to the Stalingrad area.

Overhead, the *Luftwaffe* still ruled supreme, and on the ground, the *Wehrmacht* continued its advance. As commander of the newly formed 16th Air Army, Rudenko faced critical problems at Stalingrad in the defensive stage. This air army had been formed by order of the State Defense Committee on August 8, 1942, but because of the complicated situation on the front, the process proved slow. Various air units arrived at the front below full strength. The 228th ShAD (*Shturmovaya Aviatsionnaya Diviziya*, or ground attack air division), for example, entered battle with only one-third of its prescribed complement of combat aircraft. By September 4, the 16th Air Army had only 152 serviceable aircraft, which included 42 fighters, 70 Shturmoviks, and 31 light bombers. By this time, Soviet air assets at the Stalingrad axis had 738 aircraft—113 day bombers, 71 night bombers, 241 Shturmoviks, and 313 fighters—organized in the 8th Air Army, 16th Air Army, and 102nd IAD PVO. They were supplemented by 150 to 200 bombers of the ADD.[30] Most flight crews of the 16th Air Army were inexperienced. VVS air units were quickly assigned to frontline airfields and began their duties at once, flying reconnaissance, providing air support for the ground troops, and attacking enemy positions. Confusion prevailed in this climate of frenzied emergency measures. There was little in the way of effective communication between the arriving VVS air units and the army hierarchy. In the rear areas, the logistics problems mounted as the Soviet army attempted to stem the German advance. On September 4, the 16th Air Army had three logistical support units (the 23rd, 35th, and 80th RABs), along with seventeen airfield servicing battalions (BAOs) and assorted depots for fuel and spare parts. Despite some aircraft reinforcements, supply problems continued to sharply curtail the combat effectiveness of the 16th Air Army.[31]

Air battles over the western approaches to Stalingrad arose suddenly. Only in rare instances did the VVS come away from these fierce encounters as the clear victor. Although losses were great on both sides, the *Luftwaffe* managed to sustain its control of the skies. The Soviet 434th IAP, for example, flew 611 combat sorties in September (5,225 total for the 16th Air Army), participated in forty-eight air battles, and claimed eighty-two enemy aircraft downed. This level of air action reduced the 434th's serviceability dramatically, and by the end of the month, one-third of its combat aircraft were in serious disrepair.[32]

With mounting losses in fighters on the Soviet side, Rudenko ordered VVS fighter pilots in this defensive stage to avoid enemy fighters and strike at bombers and reconnaissance planes. The *zasada,* or "ambush," became a new VVS technique to hit these more vulnerable enemy aircraft. A number of experienced VVS pilots, operating normally in the new *para* (pair) formation, awaited German bombers along their flight routes to Stalingrad. Along with the piecemeal use of new tactics, VVS pilots continued to practice some old ones, such as ramming, which had proved successful in the first months of the war. The renewal of the ramming phenomenon at the time of overall *Luftwaffe* air supremacy and devastating air raids on the city of Stalingrad grew out of a mood of desperation. On September 14, I. M. Chumbarev, a young pilot flying a Yak-1 with the 237th IAP, was on an ambush sortie near his airfield. While patrolling in his assigned zone, he intercepted a Focke Wulf Fw 189 reconnaissance plane. The Fw 189 had arrived over the field undetected, flying in and out of the heavy cloud cover to perform its mission. At around 3,500 feet (1,000 meters), Chumbarev drew in on the enemy aircraft, with radio assistance provided by observers on the ground. Chumbarev rammed the German aircraft from behind and below, sending it to its destruction. Wounded in the head, Chumbarev nevertheless maintained effective control of his plane and landed it in a field near some Soviet troops.[33]

On September 19, the VVS recorded two additional rammings—one by V. N. Chenskiy of the 283rd IAD, who managed to down a German aircraft and then parachute to safety, and a second by L. I. Binov of the 291st IAD, who downed a Bf 110 and, like Chumbarev, guided his crippled aircraft safely to the ground.[34] For the Soviets, these men represented the highest expression of bravery. Rather than abandoning an unequal struggle, they chose to do whatever they could to destroy enemy aircraft. Despite such heroics, the VVS did not seriously challenge the *Luftwaffe* over Stalingrad in September–October 1942. Beyond the Volga, however, the VVS moved resolutely to gather its resources for the anticipated winter offensive against the Germans.

The 8th Air Army, commanded by General T. T. Khryukin, also assumed an active role. Once the German army began its crossings of the Don River on August 17, this newly organized air army moved forward to help annihilate the enemy groupings. Attack groups, often consisting of thirty Pe-2s and Il-2 aircraft covered by ten to fifteen Yak-1 or La-5 fighters, struck the advancing Germans. Between August 18 and 22, VVS pilots flew more than 1,000 sorties against enemy river crossings. Some ground attack pilots flew as many as three sorties per day during these operations. Such an intense level of air action slowed, but did not stop, the enemy.

On August 23, the German army, with massive air support, finally established a breakthrough at Stalingrad. Elements of the XIV Panzer Corps breached the Stalingrad *Front* between the Soviet 4th Tank Army and the 62nd Army and advanced to Rynok. By 1600 hours, the advancing German force reached the Volga River in the Yerzovka–Rynok sector. This thrust by the enemy established a wedge of 5 miles (8 kilometers). Once the Germans reached the Volga—a key objective—they turned south toward the city of Stalingrad. Aerial reconnaissance for the Soviets proved ineffectual at this critical juncture, denying the *Stavka* and local commanders precise knowledge of the enemy's movements and tactical successes. Not until the evening did General Khryukin order the 228th and 206th ShADs and the 270th BAD to attack the advancing Germans. He ordered the VVS units into action with these words: "A large group of enemy tanks and motorized infantry is advancing toward Stalingrad. Your orders are to scramble and then destroy the enemy convoy before it reaches Stalingrad. Combat sorties are to be made until nightfall." As a consequence, the Il-2s shifted their attention from targeting airfields to attacking German mobile forces on the approaches to Stalingrad. VVS pilots demonstrated a fierce determination in these sorties as they flung themselves at the enemy. During one sortie near Rynok, the deputy squadron commander of the 766th ShAP of the 206th ShAD, Junior Lieutenant Shevchenko, rammed his damaged Il-2 into a concentration of German forces.[35]

The city of Stalingrad itself endured a series of fierce German air attacks. VVS fighters, then deployed to blunt the German ground offensive to the Volga River, were unable to effectively challenge this powerful aerial assault. General A. I. Yeremenko, at that time commander of the Southeastern *Front*, recorded a vivid account of the destruction: "We were astonished on August 23 with the nightmarish quality of the German air raids. Fiery clouds filled the sky. The oil storage tanks were hit, which ignited huge flames with corrosive smoke moving across the cityscape. Burning oil in torrents flowed to the surface of the Volga River, burning streamships. The asphalt streets melted in this vortex of heat and smoke. Sidewalks burst instantaneous into fiery passageways with telegraph poles appearing like burning matches. Buildings and factories were consumed in the fiery conflagration, emerging as skeletons."[36] VVS fighters had failed to protect the city in an effective way. Certain PVO air units and the headquarters of the 8th Air Army were evacuated to other side of the Volga River. During the day, the *Luftwaffe* had enjoyed air supremacy, flying 2,000 sorties.[37]

In late September, the German offensive led to the occupation of much of the city of Stalingrad, now largely a vista of rubble and charred ruins. Named Deputy Supreme Commander in Chief, General G. K. Zhukov had assumed command of the crucial Stalingrad defense on August 29. As plans in Moscow went forward to organize a major counteroffensive, bitter fighting took place within the precincts of Stalingrad itself, as each side attacked and counterattacked with infantry, tanks, artillery, and airpower. Zhukov had little success dislodging the Germans, who had positioned themselves at key points and along the high bluffs. Bitter fighting continued for weeks as the

The *Luftwaffe* bombs Stalingrad in advance of the German assault on the city. (From the collection of Von Hardesty)

Valeriya Khomyakova, a pilot of the 586th IAP (PVO), stands near her Yak-1 fighter. On a night mission on September 23, 1942, Khomyakova shot down a Ju 88. This was the first and only night aerial victory by a female fighter pilot. (From the collection of Von Hardesty)

Captain M. D. Baranov of the 183rd IAP in the cockpit of his Yak-1 after achieving his twenty-fourth aerial victory. He was awarded the Gold Star, Hero of the Soviet Union, on August 12, 1942. Baranov was killed in an air accident on January 15, 1943. (From the collection of Dmitriy Karlenko)

two sides battled for the rubble of factories—often floor by floor, room by room. On Mamayev Kurgan, occupied by General V. I. Chuikov's 62nd Army, there was fierce bloodletting amidst a maelstrom of sustained artillery fire. The Central Railroad Station changed hands three times. The Germans shelled Soviet reinforcements crossing from the east bank of the Volga around the clock; the Russians returned the artillery fire on German-held positions. After taking the Stalingrad tractor plant, with a loss of more than 3,000 men, the Germans cut Chuikov's sector in two, coming within 400 yards (366 meters) of the Volga. The climactic German drive against Chuikov's 62nd Army took place on November 11, but it failed. Chuikov and the Stalingrad defense managed to hold on.

VVS air assets, drawn from the 8th Air Army and the ADD, supported the fierce defense of Stalingrad. Soviet air strikes hit one enemy sector after another with Il-2 Shturmoviks in low-level sweeps. Between September 27 and October 8, the 8th Air Army flew nearly 4,000 sorties.

This Bf 109 found its end in the ruins of Stalingrad. (Courtesy of the Center for Documentation of Modern History of Volgograd Region [TsDNIVO], fond 13226, opis 1, delo 1496)

Novikov also ordered an intensification of night attacks by the 8th and other participating air armies. In a directive issued on October 22, 1942, Novikov instructed each ground attack and fighter air regiment to train five crews for night sorties. These specially trained aircrews were also expected to fly in the difficult winter weather conditions that would soon descend on the region. During the defensive stage of the battle for Stalingrad, Il-2 Shturmoviks scored 406 night sorties.[38]

The VVS experimented at this time with a radio vectoring network. Air Commander Novikov put the system into operation along the Don *Front*, using air units from the 16th Air Army. Earlier, as a frontal air force commander at Leningrad, Novikov had introduced a system of ground-based radio stations—a novelty at the time for the austerely equipped Soviet air units. Now in the crucible of Stalingrad, Novikov continued the effort in the hope of tightening the control of VVS air operations. Such experimentation in the crisis period of late September required confidence on the part of Novikov in the system's efficacy. To ensure proper use of the new radio technology, he sent two high-ranking officers to the 16th Air Army to set up the communica-

This Il-2 flown by A. V. Chuvikov shows the inscription "Za Otradnova" (for Otradnov), Western *Front*, 1942. On one dramatic mission, Otradnov—though mortally wounded—managed to land his aircraft successfully. (From the collection of Valeriy Romanenko)

tions network—General V. N. Zhdanov, deputy commander of the 13th Air Army (Leningrad *Front*), and General G. K. Gvozdkov, VVS Headquarters Signal Directorate chief. Both men, accompanied by specialists, helped the 16th Air Army command prepare field instructions on the use of a radio guidance system. Novikov monitored the program even as he attended to the pressing needs for the air defense of Stalingrad.[39]

Once the radio guidance system had taken shape, it provided a powerful new weapon. Fighter guidance radio stations were placed adjacent to the front, about 1 to 2 miles (1.6 to 3.2 kilometers) from the forward line at intervals of 5 to 6 miles (8 to 9.6 kilometers). Each station maintained contact with fighter pilots in the air, the various airfields, and the command posts of the 16th Air Army. The radio station network, which was subdivided into command and information stations, soon allowed the command of the 16th Air Army to receive situation reports quickly. Control and response became much more effective, and the radio stations expanded their scope to include ground attack operations as well. Novikov took advantage of the situation to exploit the training possibilities of the program. He called up twenty-five commanders and deputy commanders of reserve fighter air regiments to participate in the radio control guidance operations. From this pivotal experiment, VVS Headquarters in Moscow developed a field manual, *Instruktsiya dlya Voyenno-Vozdushnykh sil po upravleniyu, opoveshcheniyu i navedeniyu samoletov po radio* (instructions to the air force on controlling, informing, and guiding airplanes by radio).[40]

As the defensive stage of the struggle for Stalingrad drew to a close, the VVS had augmented its fighting capacity. By November 1942, it had 5,335 aircraft (4,408 serviceable), with 828 aircraft (516 serviceable) in the 8th and 16th Air Armies committed to Stalingrad.[41] Nearly three-quarters of combat aircraft were now of modern design, a reflection of the growing productivity of the aviation industry. This enhanced strength in modern aircraft made an impact at the fronts, where air regiments now boasted three rather than two squadrons. The transition to new air tactics was under way. The organization of the VVS command structure and the creation of the air armies soon promised that airpower would assume a larger role in the projected Soviet offensive.[42]

The war context in these months became desperate. The overall transition to new and more effective air tactics—in large part an adaptation to the enemy's superior operational techniques—proved to be haphazard in the context of 1942. Air commanders had to impose top-down control and then regularize a whole series of radical new approaches to air combat. Many of these changes were implemented in isolated situations where reform-minded pilots were eager to improve their air tactics in light of experience. Making such changes across the board, however, meant abandoning old habits and overcoming the normal inertia that always accompanied any type of reform. One surviving document of the war, a set of orders from the chief of staff of the 8th Air Army (Colonel Seleznev) dated August 18, 1942, allows us to understand in a vivid way the urgency of the transition to new air tactics. The document, sent to all regimental and divisional commanders, began with a candid analysis of how the *Luftwaffe* had exercised air dominance. The chief of staff reminded his local air commanders that German fighter pilots routinely used surprise and close proximity to VVS aircraft before they fired, a technique that often proved effective. Moreover, *Luftwaffe* aircrews chose to enter air combat only when they enjoyed numerical superiority and often lured VVS fighters into traps. The use of two- and four-fighter aircraft formations assured tactical success for the enemy. In all things, the *Luftwaffe* displayed great discipline, always moving in force at decisive moments. The enemy also used radio communications. While on the attack, German warplanes were echeloned and deployed in such a fashion to achieve optimal results. By maintaining a clear grasp of the battle zone, the *Luftwaffe* was able to husband its air resources to hit VVS rear areas and inflict considerable damage and disorientation. The portrayal of the *Luftwaffe* was accurate and complimentary. The Germans' tactics offered a clear standard for air combat technique. By contrast, Seleznev concluded, the VVS had displayed a melancholy pattern of poor organization, lack of initiative, and lapses in discipline and coordination. VVS fighter pilots—despite repeated orders, Seleznev complained—had not flown consistently in two-aircraft (*para*) formations, which set the stage for many disasters in dogfights with the enemy.

To counter these conditions, new orders were laid out clearly and forcefully for all air units in the 8th Air Army. Instructions on the new air tactics were to be delivered to all forward air units both verbally and in written form. No operational air unit was exempt from these high-priority directives. Prior to combat sorties, fighter and ground attack commanders were to coordinate their plans, and this planning was to be detailed. The two-aircraft formation for fighters was now mandatory, with an accompanying stress on mutual support in air battle. Combat order was to be disciplined, with attention to echeloned flights. Aircraft should be dispersed in such a way as to retain visual contact whenever possible. Wherever possible, radio communications should be used to ensure contact and coordination. He called for greater accuracy in all bombing missions and for careful planning and the use of stealth for all sorties. In air combat, fighters should use vertical maneuver. Finally, efforts should be made to neutralize the trump card of the German fighters—their use of vertical maneuver. This was to be achieved by VVS fighters deployed in pairs or in groups at different altitudes. And while engaged in air combat, VVS pilots were ordered to sustain the advantage of altitude at all times. These and other prescriptions were outlined by the chief of staff in this detailed and remarkable document. What is apparent in Colonel Seleznev's analysis and remedies is a clear critique of the VVS at a moment of critical transition in the war. Seleznov ended his communication with the statement that all air commanders bore the responsibility for implementing these orders.[43]

The shifting fortunes of the *Luftwaffe* and the Soviet Air Force in the skies over Stalingrad can best be measured in small-unit action or even the experiences of individual pilots. The recollections of one *Luftwaffe* fighter pilot, Heinrich von Einsiedel, offers a mirror on this reality.[44] The great-grandson of Otto von Bismarck, Einsiedel came to his flying career with an aristocratic pedigree of unrivaled stature. He also reflected the impulse of many young men in his social class to choose the elite *Luftwaffe* over other branches of the German military. His experiences in the opening days of the Stalingrad campaign give witness to the diverging character of the two competing air forces. While flying over Stalingrad on a warm August day in 1942, he caught sight of the approaching enemy. He remembered "a light haze over the Steppes" as he circled high over the enemy in his Bf 109. Then an intense air battle ensued. "Every German Stuka, every combat airplane was surrounded by clusters of Russian fighters," he recalled. One Russian fighter pilot attempted to evade Einsiedel by diving down to 10 feet (3 meters) above the ground. Still on his tail, Einsiedel fired accurately, even as "his machine vibrated with the recoil of its guns." There was no escape for the Russian pilot—"a streak of flame shot from the petrol tank of the Russian plane. It exploded and rolled over on the ground. A broad, long strip of scorched steppe-land was all that it left behind."[45]

For Einsiedel, his initial air victory set the stage for further action. He spotted a cluster of Soviet fighters above him and gave chase, scoring yet another victory. At that moment, however, his fate was sealed: "As I turned around to look for Russian fighters, I saw their blazing guns eighty yards behind me. There was a terrific explosion and I felt a hard blow on my foot. I twisted my Messerschmitt and forced it up into a steep climb." He evaded the enemy, returning to his base with a badly damaged plane. Less than a week later, however, Einsiedel was less fortunate in an air battle with the VVS. He was attacked by several

Russian fighters that managed to cripple his engine, forcing him down over Russian-held territory. He was soon captured and taken away as a prisoner of war.[46]

Einsiedel had engaged in air combat with great confidence, a mood that still animated the German air arm even in the face of a diminishing capacity to provide adequate air cover for the ground forces. The grim reality was becoming increasingly apparent to all German airmen, however: they had failed to assert dominance over the pivotal Stalingrad sector. Einsiedel and others like him could destroy Soviet aircraft, but the pressure from the VVS continued unabated. The German airmen still enjoyed a marginal advantage over the Soviets in terms of tactics, technology, and experience, but these factors did not equate with control of the skies. Against the *Luftwaffe*, the Soviets were able to reinforce their forward air groups with remarkable speed and effectiveness. The *Luftwaffe* did not possess such residual strength; its losses in aircraft and air personnel were irreversible. As Einsiedel learned, the VVS could flood the combat zone with overwhelming numbers. Also, in this context, the Soviet air arm now displayed increased skill and aggressiveness. A turning point had been reached, and it was now evident in the struggle for Stalingrad.[47]

THE SOVIET COUNTEROFFENSIVE

The Soviet army opened the second phase of the battle for Stalingrad on November 19, 1942, with a powerful counteroffensive. The strategy called for the troops of the Southwestern *Front* to begin the attack on the northern perimeter of the German salient. The 5th Tank Army spearheaded the advance, in close coordination with a massive artillery barrage. After five days, the troops of the Southwestern *Front* reached Kalach, situated on the Don directly west of and behind the German Sixth Army. The northern pincer had covered a distance of 93 miles (150 kilometers). Troops of the Stalingrad *Front*, acting as the southern pincer, moved off on November 20 and had advanced 71 miles (114 kilometers) by the end of the fifth day. They captured the small town of Sovetskiy on November 23, closing the trap on the German Sixth Army.

The role of the VVS in this first stage of the counteroffensive

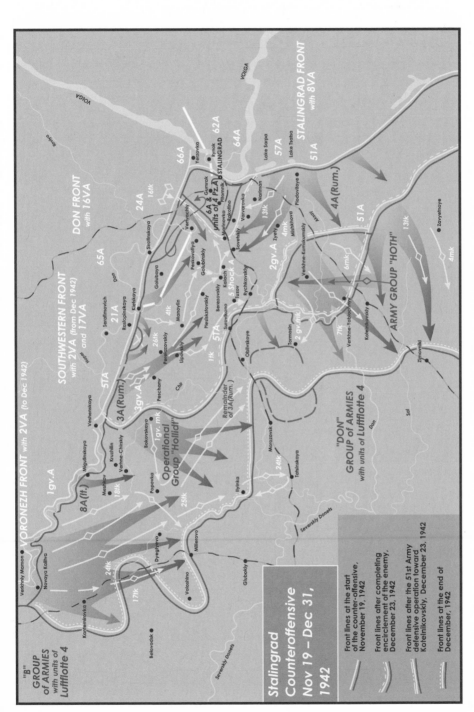

Map 4 (Terry Higgins © 2011, adapted from *Dragons on Bird Wings*, vol. 1, Aviaeology 2006)

turned out to be rather limited, despite elaborate efforts to position Soviet airpower for a concentrated blow. Poor weather—low clouds and
fog—reduced VVS sorties to a mere 1,000 for the first four days of the
offensive. Once the weather improved, VVS air activity increased dramatically; 5,760 combat sorties were claimed by the 16th, 17th, and
8th Air Armies for the period November 24–30. Against the *Luftwaffe's*
1,400 aircraft (600 supporting Army Group A, and 800 supporting
Army Group B),[48] the VVS had a total of 1,414 aircraft, of which 1,027
were serviceable.[49] Although numerical parity had been achieved, 426
of the Soviet combat aircraft (U-2s, R-5s, and SB bombers) were obsolete and assigned to night operations. These machines, deployed
around and adjacent to the German salient, were organized in the 2nd,
16th, 17th, and 8th Air Armies, along with elements of the ADD and
PVO. At the onset of the counteroffensive, however, these air units
faced critical problems. Moved hastily to improvised airfields close to
the breakthrough zones, they encountered enormous difficulties in
sustaining air operations. The Soviet rear services in late 1942 still
faced an acute shortage of trucks and air transport. Aviation fuel, ammunition, spare parts, and other supplies reached the frontline units
only with considerable effort. Although denied an active role in the
immediate breakthrough, the VVS quickly assumed a vital part in the
Soviet drive to maintain the encirclement and destroy the German
Sixth Army. In a message to General Zhukov dated November 12,
Stalin asserted that the VVS should be called on to make a maximum
effort. In fact, Stalin saw airpower as a crucial component in achieving
a breakthrough: "The experience of war . . . indicates that we can
achieve a victory over the Germans only if we gain air supremacy."[50]

Novikov's report to Zhukov on the VVS's low state of preparedness
on the eve of the counteroffensive prompted Stalin's statement on the
role of Soviet airpower. Despite concerted efforts to bolster the VVS in
the Stalingrad region, there were persistent problems with a logistical
system that was not yet fully capable of meeting the requirements of
a major offensive. Novikov's report, for example, indicated that in the
second week of November, the VVS was down to two rations of fuel
and faced an acute shortage of ammunition. Not only were there
shortfalls in fuel and munitions; General Rudenko also claimed that
the percentage of inoperable aircraft remained quite high. The 16th
Air Army, for example, had 329 aircraft on November 19, but 80 were

grounded for repairs. This same situation prevailed in the other air armies. Although the number of combat aircraft increased steadily, Rudenko and other commanders realized that the inadequate base for aircraft repairs, especially a shortage of engines, slowed the tempo for rebuilding the VVS.[51]

Novikov played a key role in preparing air armies for the counter-offensive, working closely with *Stavka* representatives in Stalingrad—Generals G. K. Zhukov, A. M. Vasilevskiy, and N. N. Voronov. With the principal army commanders, Novikov prepared detailed battle plans, discussed the optimal uses of airpower, and established procedures for the efficient interaction between the VVS and the ground forces. At the same time, he planned specific air operations with his air army commanders at Stalingrad: General S. A. Krasovskiy of the 17th Air Army (Southwestern *Front*); General S. I. Rudenko, 16th Air Army (Don *Front*); and General T. T. Khryukin, 8th Air Army (Stalingrad *Front*).

On November 12, Stalin had set forth the primary goals for the VVS in offensive operations at Stalingrad. The air force would first concentrate its actions in the breakthrough zones, clearing out enemy aircraft and providing effective air cover. With the advance of Soviet troops, the VVS would strafe and bomb German forces as part of a combined arms effort to penetrate the enemy's tactical defense zone. Once the German defenses had been shattered, the VVS air units would pursue retreating troops in a sustained fashion to prevent any enemy effort to reestablish a stable defensive line. Such a blueprint for an aggressive use of airpower displayed boldness at a time when the VVS was still inferior to the *Luftwaffe* in terms of aircraft quality and combat technique.

The Soviet plan called for first concentrating air assets at decisive points and then forging the efficient coordination of air action with artillery, tanks, and infantry. The Infantry Combat Manual, issued on November 9, 1942, gave definition to this emerging concept of an "air offensive," which consisted of the preparatory phase and the support phase. Aviation was to provide continuous support of the infantry with concentrated fire.[52] At Stalingrad, the 17th Air Army supported the 5th Tank Army and the 21st Army on the main axis of their advance. In like manner, the 16th Air Army flew in support of the 65th Army, and the 8th Air Army deployed 75 percent of its operational aircraft to assist the 50th Army. The 16th Air Army under Rudenko provides a representative profile of the VVS at the opening of the

Stalingrad counteroffensive. First organized in August–September 1942, the 16th Air Army had 107 fighters, 102 Shturmoviks, 117 night bombers (all U-2, R-5, and R-Z types), and 3 reconnaissance aircraft as of November 19. Only 249 of the 329 aircraft were operational, but Rudenko received a modest increment of 10 Yak fighters just before the offensive began.[53] During November, the 16th Air Army flew a total of 2,847 sorties. Rudenko targeted two-thirds of these sorties against German airfields and claimed 63 enemy aircraft destroyed. In 32 recorded air battles, the 16th Air Army claimed 33 German planes downed; Soviet losses were listed at 35 aircraft.[54]

The overall strength of the VVS at Stalingrad was 1,414 combat aircraft, about equal to the opposing *Luftflotte* 4. While the *Luftwaffe* enjoyed "qualitative superiority," Rudenko pointed to the VVS's rapid transition to newer aircraft types: for example, at the time of the counteroffensive, the 16th Air Army had achieved a 73 percent transition overall, and nearly 97 percent within the fighter inventory. Of its 107 fighters, only 9 were the less effective LaGG-3s. The Shturmovik units had been completely reequipped with the modern Il-2s.[55] Moreover, the 16th Air Army obtained two divisions of Pe-2 bombers at the end of November, which greatly enhanced the striking power of Rudenko's force.[56]

The Soviet pincer movement had trapped more than 300,000 German troops within an area about the size of Connecticut.[57] To maintain the envelopment and systematically annihilate the German pocket, the *Stavka* ordered an increased level of VVS air operations. Consequently, the Soviet counteroffensive brought an inevitable clash with the *Luftwaffe*, which had now become a vital weapon for the relief and protection of Paulus's Sixth Army. In the crucial days after November 19, Novikov remained at the forward control posts, together with General Vasilevskiy.

In a context of urgency and growing peril, the German High Command decided to mobilize the *Luftwaffe* for an airlift operation to sustain Paulus's trapped army. Historians debate the wisdom of this fateful decision, which was based in part on the apparent success of the Demyansk experience, as well as Hermann Goering's bold assurances that the *Luftwaffe* could do the job. Many *Luftwaffe* commanders, including General Freiherr von Richthofen, questioned the *Luftwaffe*'s capacity—even in warm weather—to meet the challenge.

Richthofen and others argued forcefully against the airlift option, seeing Demyansk as a costly undertaking, not an analog for the salvation of the Sixth Army.[58] In retrospect, the option of ordering Paulus to attempt a breakout in the immediate aftermath of the encirclement appears to be wise counsel. Yet it must be remembered that the Russians planned not merely to trap Paulus at Stalingrad but also to prevent any German action on the ground to liquidate the problem, either by Paulus's escaping west or by a relief force's breaking through the Soviet ring. When Field Marshal Erich von Manstein attempted the latter tactic on December 12, he was halted short of his goal. In fact, by the end of December, the Russians had moved the Germans farther back toward the West, capturing the vital Morozovskaya and Tatsinskaya airfields, used as major staging areas for the airlift. Standing in place at Stalingrad fit well into Hitler's peculiar mind-set in 1942, which coincided with Stalin's own attitude of no retreat. "Once a German soldier has taken his position," Hitler stated, "there is no power in the world strong enough to dislodge him."[59] The German High Command fatefully ordered a massive airlift. The lingering historical question is why the airlift failed.

The German Sixth Army required 750 tons of supplies per day. This level of support, given the winter conditions and the finite resources of the *Luftwaffe*, simply could not be achieved. To meet such a goal, 375 Ju 52 transports, each with a load of 2 tons, would have to land daily in the pocket. With the normal operational readiness of 30 to 35 percent, the *Luftwaffe* would have to deploy 1,050 Ju 52s.[60] No possibility existed that the *Luftwaffe* could mobilize such an enormous flotilla of air transports. Beyond the question of numbers, there was the unpredictability of the Russian weather. Severe cold and heavy snow made any airlift difficult in November–December 1942. After further consultations, the Germans reduced the daily airlift goal to 300 tons per day, less than half the total Paulus required.[61] Before even this lower goal could be achieved, the German airlift command for Stalingrad had to obtain additional transport aircraft. All available Ju 52s, He 111s, and Ju 88s were ordered to the East. From the Office of the Chief of Training, some of the most experienced flight instructors in the *Luftwaffe* were assigned on an emergency basis to the airlift. Even Ju 86s, used for training purposes, were deployed to airlift duty, along with small numbers of He 177s, Fw 200s, and Ju 290s. A mood of desperation prevailed among German aircrews. This was evident in the fact that the *Luftwaffe* briefly considered the use of freight gliders— DFS 230 and GO 244 types. The idea proved impracticable because of inadequate ground facilities.[62] The formidable task of coordinating the Stalingrad airlift began to gain momentum after November 25, 1942, the first day weather permitted resupply by air to the Sixth Army. At staging areas at Zaporozhye and Kirovograd, Ju 52s and other aircraft assigned to transport duty were converted for winter operations. Once this was completed, they were moved east toward Morozovskaya and Tatsinskaya airfields, which were 125 and 155 miles (200 and 250 kilometers), respectively, from Stalingrad. Eventually, these fields became congested and quite inadequate for servicing the sudden increase of transports. Goods accumulated, and many Ju 52s proved to be inadequately prepared for airlift duty. General von Richthofen observed the growing difficulties with alarm and requested that the Sixth Army be ordered to break out. Hitler refused.[63] The flight to the *Kessel*, or pocket, normally took fifty minutes. On November 30, the three-engine Ju 52s, later to be joined by a large number of He 111s, followed a radio beacon to Pitomnik airfield within the pocket. Upon landing, the transports were quickly unloaded. Wounded men were then taken aboard for the flight back to Morozovskaya or Tatsinskaya. General Martin Fiebig headed this airlift operation in an atmosphere of urgency and growing frustration.

Many of the Ju 52s were old, ill suited for cold-weather operations, and lacking in armament and radios. Aircrews with varying skills hurriedly arrived from other combat sectors and from training schools in Germany. Some were veterans; others had only minimal experience. Many faced the demanding airlift missions without winter clothing.[64] There were constant problems with sudden snowstorms, which made the approach to, landing at, and departure from Pitomnik hazardous undertakings. The attrition in transports as a result of accidents grew with the onset of severe winter weather. Air traffic control faced the enormous challenge of directing large numbers of transports into and out of the primitive airfield at Pitomnik on a daily basis. The first flights there began on November 25, and after two days, the airlift had delivered 130 tons of materiel. By December 17, the airlift had achieved an average of 84.4 tons per day; on the best day, 289 tons were moved into the pocket with 154 transports.[65]

The Ju 52 transport was an essential *Luftwaffe* aircraft, shown here
being loaded with supplies for encircled German soldiers at Demyansk.
Later, the transport was a mainstay for air relief operations to Stalingrad
in 1942–1943. (From the collection of Von Hardesty)

Problems grew with the airlift each day. The flight corridors
quickly became aerial gauntlets, haunted by VVS fighters and swept
by salvos of Soviet antiaircraft fire. The rigors of the Russian winter
once again frustrated the German will and resourcefulness. There
were low clouds, fog, snowstorms, ice damage, and numbing cold.
Ground crews at Pitomnik, often on reduced rations, worked long
hours against formidable obstacles: the airstrip had to be cleared repeatedly of drifting snow, fingers froze to aircraft engine parts, and gas
masks had to be worn to prevent frostbite. There was an alarming increase in pilot error, leading to frequent accidents. Goods piled up,
adding to the congestion. Pressure from marauding VVS ground attack
aircraft and Soviet artillery increased with each passing day as the ring
around the *Kessel* tightened. Shortages in medicine, ammunition, and
food gradually sapped the encircled Sixth Army of its fighting efficiency and morale.[66] Soviet and German accounts of the Stalingrad airlift differ on the extent of *Luftwaffe* losses. Most Soviet sources list
more than 1,000 German aircraft destroyed in the air and on the
ground, with about 80 percent of them being transports and
bombers.[67] Against the German airlift attempt, lasting from November
19, 1942, to February 2, 1943, the VVS claimed 35,920 sorties flown,

which, by their estimate, surpassed the number of German sorties by about two to one. Instead of 300 tons of supplies reaching the trapped German Sixth Army each day, the Soviet air blockade allowed, on average, only 50 to 80 tons of resupply per day.[68]

VVS fighters hit the German transports both in the air and on the ground. On November 30, for example, fighters from the 283rd IAD, with Colonel V. A. Kitayev in command, intercepted seventeen Ju 52s, escorted by four Bf 109s, over Gumrak airfield in the pocket. They destroyed five of the Ju 52s and one Bf 109. On some days, these *Okhot-niki,* or free hunters, destroyed up to half the German transport "caravans." These VVS aircraft showed equal skill as fighter-bombers. On December 2, they destroyed seventeen transports on the ground within the pocket, and between December 10 and 13, they claimed another eighty-seven transport planes. The Il-2 Shturmoviks, being faster than the Ju 52s, reversed their role on occasion and intercepted Ju 52s en route to the pocket.[69] One German account acknowledged the loss of around 488 aircraft, along with 1,000 flight crew personnel: 266 Ju 52s, 42 Ju 86s, 165 He 111s, 9 Fw 200s, 5 He 177s, and 1 Ju 290. Besides the grievous loss of machines and personnel, the failure of the Stalingrad airlift resulted in a serious interruption of the *Luftwaffe* training program, for many experienced flight instructors were lost at Stalingrad.[70]

The German High Command made one serious effort to relieve the Sixth Army at Stalingrad. Army Group Don, under von Manstein, attempted to break the encirclement on December 12, 1942, in the Kotelnikovo region southwest of the pocket. This drive pushed forward slowly until December 21, but then faltered in the face of stiff Soviet resistance. The 8th Air Army alone flew 1,694 sorties between December 19 and 23 to help stop the relief effort.[71] To stem von Manstein's drive and simultaneously apply pressure on the pocket, the VVS marshaled all available air units. Such an orchestration of airpower demonstrated again the growing efficiency of the VVS command structure.

From Karpovka, within the pocket, the German Sixth Army prepared to move out to link up with von Manstein, whose position at one point was a mere 25 to 30 miles (40 to 48 kilometers) away. VVS combat aircraft, drawn from the 8th and 16th Air Armies, then struck the enemy positions at Karpovka. On the morning of December 16, at the height of the battle, 100 VVS airplanes strafed the Germans. To the south, the Soviets applied additional pressure to disrupt the German effort to liberate the Sixth Army at Stalingrad. Here the *Stavka* activated the Southwestern *Front*, hoping to strike at von Manstein's rear. Part of this offensive operation included VVS air strikes at the Morozovskaya and Tatsinskaya airfields. Soviet air operations, both day and night, maintained constant pressure on the German positions.

On Christmas Eve, at the height of the Soviet counterattack, the Germans lost the Tatsinskaya airfield. No single event in the somber days of December brought greater dismay to General Fiebig or more fateful consequences for the airlift operation. The Soviets signaled the attack on Tatsinskaya with an artillery barrage on the fog-shrouded morning of December 24. Fiebig, along with Richthofen, had appealed to Hitler to allow the evacuation of the airfield the previous week. They had observed the Soviet buildup with alarm, and now the dreaded attack materialized, threatening destruction to a massive number of Ju 52s crowded at the airfield. After a few minutes of Soviet artillery fire, Fiebig ordered the immediate evacuation of the German transports, even as Soviet tanks and infantry approached. In an atmosphere of poor visibility and near panic, the Ju 52s took off. Two transports collided in midair, and a large number of aircraft piled into one another on the ground. Fiebig himself narrowly escaped at the last moment as Soviet tanks overran the airfield. A total of 56 transports were lost. Out of this debris field of wrecked and burning aircraft, some 124 transports managed to escape.[72]

In the air, Soviet pilots earned a reputation for persistence and bravery during this period. One example of this fierce dedication was N. Abdirov of the 808th ShAP of the 17th Air Army, who flew his aircraft into a group of German tanks. He received the title of Hero of the Soviet Union posthumously. Soviet accounts of the air war at Stalingrad provide numerous examples of individual feats of bravery, and German recollections confirm the Soviet aggressiveness in the air. German troops respected the Shturmovik units for their courage and determination. Abdirov's spectacular feat demonstrated in sharper focus the overall toughness of the Soviet ground attack arm. Many air units earned the elite "Guards" designation for their combat sorties in this period.[73]

At Zverevo, near the last staging airfields and still within range of

German aircraft captured in the Stalingrad area. One of them (Ju 52/3M on the left) has already been rebadged with red stars. Beginning in the spring of 1943, more than a dozen Ju 52s were used by the VVS and the civil air fleet for transport duties in the rear. By October 1943, a total of thirty-one captured German aircraft were in service. As a precaution, such aircraft were used solely in the deep rear. (From the collection of Valeriy Romanenko)

the Ju 52s, the Germans built another airstrip to supply Pitomnik. Zverevo was 2,000 feet (600 meters) long and 100 feet (30 meters) wide and occupied a former cornfield. The runway consisted of hard-packed snow. For the construction of the Zverevo landing strip, there were no rollers available; everything had to be improvised. German troops, with the aid of the local population, managed to carve out this airfield under the most difficult circumstances. At first, the ground crews lived in snow huts; these were later replaced by tents and crudely constructed wooden barracks.[74] Snowstorms, constant companions, interrupted activity for days at a time. On occasion, heavy snow drifted over the Ju 52s, which had to be dug out by hand. Austere and storm-ridden, Zverevo became a makeshift emergency airfield, carved out of an icy wasteland.

The organization of the Soviet air blockade had displayed careful planning and stewardship of finite resources. Four zones were de-fined, each with specific boundaries and functions. The first zone be-came the outer front of the encirclement. There, along the periphery, were the German airfields—Morozovskaya, Tatsinskaya, Salsk, Novo-cherkassk, and Rostov—used as stepping-off points for the airlift. The 17th and 8th Air Armies assumed air interdiction responsibilities for the first zone. The second zone, or ring zone, consisted of the area be-tween the outer and inner fronts. Over this zone, the Germans estab-lished air corridors for the airlift. Depending on whether the Germans flew out of Morozovskaya or Tatsinskaya, the flight to the pocket cov-ered around 200 miles (320 kilometers). The VVS subdivided the sec-ond zone into five sectors, and the 16th and 8th Air Armies, along with the 102nd IAD PVO, deployed fighters to each. Thus, every VVS unit became thoroughly acquainted with its sector, yet the subdivision al-lowed for mobility and adaptation. The VVS command aimed to pro-vide a powerful air defense system that took maximum advantage of Soviet airpower. Ringing the pocket, the third zone encompassed a band varying in width up to 19 miles (30 kilometers).[75] Here, the Sovi-ets constructed a series of antiaircraft positions along the anticipated flight paths of German transports. During the period of the air block-ade, these positions were strengthened and redeployed to maximize antiaircraft fire. Soviet antiaircraft gunners also provided an effective curtain of fire against approaching German transports, often com-pelling them to veer off or delay their landings. At the same time, So-viet fighters, always close at hand, sought out targets of opportunity, particularly slow-moving transports in a landing pattern.

The fourth zone was the pocket itself. Besides Pitomnik, the Ger-mans operated four other airstrips within the pocket—Gumrak, Basargino, Voroponovo, and Bolshaya Rossoshka.[76] These airstrips, with their own fighter interceptors, maintained the vital but precari-ous lifeline of the Sixth Army. On the ground, the Soviets moved re-lentlessly to reduce the area of encirclement and occupy these crucial airfields. Above, VVS fighters endeavored to destroy approaching and departing German transports. Constant pressure from VVS Shtur-moviks and bombers made operations from these airstrips difficult at best.

Initially, the German aircraft crossed over to the pocket singly or in small groups, approaching Stalingrad from different directions and often without fighter escort. Within the pocket were forty fighters, mostly Bf 109s, to provide a measure of air cover adjacent to the landing zones. The *Luftwaffe* air transport command mobilized sixty to seventy transports per day for airlift duty; once the operation was in full stride, this level increased to 100 to 150. Between November 25 and 30, 1942, the VVS applied significant pressure on the ever-growing number of transports of the German airlift. Soviet fighters appeared along the air corridors, attacking the Ju 52s along the 200-mile (322-kilometer) pathway to Stalingrad. These attacks were sudden and, in the absence of German fighter escorts, very effective. Meantime, the VVS struck the German airfields within the pocket on a regular basis. On November 28, the Soviets destroyed twenty-nine enemy aircraft at Gumrak and Bolshaya Rossoshka.[77]

The Germans moved quickly to counteract the rising tempo of VVS air operations. Fighters were assigned to escort the beleaguered transports wherever possible. To provide additional range, Bf 109s and Bf 110s were equipped with supplementary fuel tanks. Again, the Russian environment of vast distances and extreme weather compelled adaptation. Each successive effort appeared more desperate and less effective. Behind the organization of the Soviet air blockade was the imperative to use the full force of combat aircraft. At Demyansk, the VVS had used obsolete U-2 aircraft for the night bombing of the encircled German troops. This tactic was embraced again at Stalingrad, with great effectiveness. Bomber units, drawn from the ADD, were deployed for raids at night, when the slow-moving Soviet aircraft operated in relative freedom, attacking German airfields at low altitudes. The VVS now had the capacity for sustained around-the-clock operations. Bomber units normally flew to their targets from airfields situated 40 to 60 miles (64 to 96 kilometers) from the front lines. Fighters, by contrast, were positioned much closer—12 to 31 miles (19 to 50 kilometers). Depending on the mission, Soviet bombers attacked their targets in regiment-sized units, consisting of thirty to forty aircraft.[78]

The tempo of bomber attacks increased dramatically in the final month of the Stalingrad siege. To make the work of the U-2s and the bombers more effective, the Soviets moved large numbers of artillery up to the front lines, where they focused much of their attention on German airfields.[79] Once in place, Soviet firepower on the ground and in the air exerted massive and sustained pressure on the enemy. To maintain such pressure, the Soviets devised an elaborate and effective scheme for air-ground control. At Kotluban airfield, the 16th Air Army established a radio command post for the interdiction of German transports. This command post directed operations for the 16th Air Army and maintained regular contact with the corresponding command post for the 8th Air Army. Novikov vigorously pursued a goal of coordination that brought Kotluban into a larger scheme of guidance. Radio control stations, all linked to Novikov's headquarters, became a kind of a nervous system for the VVS air operations at Stalingrad. In the four zones, these ground radio stations maintained contact with Soviet fighters, now equipped with radio sets for the first time, and later with ground attack aircraft. This enabled the Soviets to maintain radio guidance for their combat aircraft over the front lines and with the rear airfields. This served the dual purposes of command and information gathering.

At Stalingrad, the Germans observed with alarm the general upgrading of the Soviet signal communications service. Whereas in 1941 most VVS air operations had been poorly executed, complicated by the absence of radios, the VVS now displayed impressive skills in orchestrating their combat sorties. Along with radios, the Soviets now employed radar, telephones, and Teletype. Moreover, the VVS adapted various aircraft for liaison, courier, and command duties. The progress achieved at Stalingrad led to the decision to equip all fighters with radios.[80]

In early January 1943, the Germans converted a primitive airstrip at Salsk into another major staging area for the airlift to Stalingrad. Salsk was little more than a frozen field that had been cleared of snow for *Luftwaffe* air operations. It was rough, poorly equipped, but spacious. It was also vulnerable to Soviet air attack. The approach route to Stalingrad from Salsk was about 250 miles (400 kilometers) long, near the outer limit of the Ju 52's range.[81] On January 9, 1943, the hastily constructed airfield became the scene of one of the more spectacular raids by VVS Shturmoviks. By this date, the Germans had collected up to 150 aircraft at Salsk.[82] These airplanes were parked in a congested fashion, and the whole operation, as reflected in its layout, had a disorderly, makeshift quality.

Knowing the airfield's vulnerability to attack, the Germans quickly assigned both fighters and flak units to Salsk. On two occasions, Soviet fliers from the 622nd ShAD attempted to strafe the Salsk field but were repulsed. To hit this target, the VVS decided in early January to resort to a sudden, low-level attack by a small number of heavily armed Il-2s. On January 2, Captain I. P. Bakhtin led seven Il-2s, escorted by a squadron of Yak-1 fighters, toward Salsk. Once the Il-2s passed over the German lines, they descended to treetop altitude at full speed, hoping to avoid enemy interceptors and detection by antiaircraft units. Suddenly, Bakhtin and his group made one strafing run over the field out of the clouds, then repeated it six times. The German defenses were caught off guard, and before a concerted response could be mustered, seventy-two German aircraft had been destroyed. The Soviets admitted the loss of only four aircraft in this raid.[83] The raid on Salsk symbolized the increased striking power of the VVS at Stalingrad, the impressive ability of VVS units to operate in marginal weather conditions, and the enlarged range of VVS air operations, which now included German rear areas. Bakhtin and three others received the Gold Star, Hero of the Soviet Union, for their bravery. Other attacks, by day and at night, were made at Bolshaya Rossoshka, Karpovka, and Gumrak. When Erhard Milch, representing the German High Command, arrived at Taganrog on January 16, 1943, to inspect the airlift operation, he quickly saw its desperate state. By this date, Salsk itself was in danger of being overrun on the ground, and Paulus's capitulation was two weeks away.

The VVS interceptors over the pocket soon demonstrated a new lethality in downing German aircraft. Colonel I. D. Podgorny, commanding eighteen fighters from the 235th IAD, attacked sixteen Ju 52s en route to Pitomnik. During the initial encounter, Podgorny's fighters shot down nine Ju 52s; five crashed in flames, and the rest made emergency landings. Eight German airmen were taken prisoner. Seven Ju 52s turned back, but the Soviet fighters pursued them with relentless determination, shooting down all but one. By January 1943, the VVS had made the German airlift extremely difficult. German fliers discovered that distance, severe weather, and primitive airfields were not the only hazards. The VVS had assumed an aggressive air combat presence around Stalingrad. For the *Luftwaffe*, the attrition in aircraft and aircrews became a matter of deep concern.

From the beginning of the air blockade, Soviet fighters attacked German transports from "ambush." For example, the 16th Air Army in the northwest sector organized ambushes at Pichuga, Kotluban, and Kachalinskaya. At first, these ambushes amounted to regular patrols by VVS fighters along the air corridors to Stalingrad. They attacked single planes, artillery positions, and moving targets on the ground. Once losses occurred, the Germans shifted their tactics. Fighter escorts were now provided, and transports were flown in larger groups for maximum protection against the marauding VVS fighters. Also, the number of night flights by German transports increased dramatically. The VVS countered by reassigning its fighters in pairs to the airspace adjacent to the German airfields within the pocket. This was done to catch the German transports at their most vulnerable moments—landing or taking off—when their airspeed and defensive capability were sharply reduced.

In time, the Soviet radio control stations acquired enough sophistication to provide accurate early warnings. As soon as the German transports were spotted crossing the belt separating the outer and inner front lines, VVS fighter and Shturmovik units were alerted. Combat aircraft and aircrews were maintained on a constant alert status, enabling them to scramble quickly to intercept the enemy. The goal was to arrive over the German airfields or designated positions along the air corridor to Stalingrad at the optimal time. Speed was combined with a shrewd use of weather conditions. Soviet fliers, particularly the ground attack pilots, took full advantage of clouds to effect sudden sweeps on unsuspecting German transports attempting to negotiate the difficult approaches to Pitomnik. Another favorite VVS tactic was to attack at dusk. These same conditions, of course, provided cover and protection for the German transports. The VVS, however, had the natural advantage of place, the choice of time and target, and overwhelming numbers. By contrast, German aircrews faced the disadvantage of flying over enemy territory in poor weather and frequently without fighter escorts. Moreover, they operated from primitive airstrips lacking proper maintenance.

The VVS quickly expanded the role of the *Okhotniki*. Volunteers were accepted from among the most talented and experienced pilots to join these units. They had to possess consummate flying skills and excellent marksmanship and demonstrate aggressiveness as fighter pilots. Now *Okhotniki* were created out of each fighter aviation division. In groups, most often in *para* or *zveno* (flight) formations, they

Aces of the legendary 9th GIAP, 8th Air Army, after the Stalingrad battle. Left to right, with their wartime air victories (personal + shared): regiment commander L. L. Shestakov (16 + 8; Hero of the Soviet Union [HSU], killed in action March 13, 1944), I. G. Korolyev (7 + 3; HSU), A. I. Plotnikov (5 + 1; killed in action February 17, 1945), Golubev, A. N. Karasev (25 + 9; HSU), N. V. Kostyrko (10; killed in action July 20, 1943), unknown, A. V. Alelyukhin (34 + 6; 2 HSU), I. Ya. Serzhantov (14 + 8; HSU, died on April 29, 1943), unknown, V. D. Lavrinenkov (35 + 11; 2 HSU), I. V. Timofeenko (19 + 6; HSU), Ye. M. Ivanov (9; killed in action April 24, 1944), Ye. P. Dranischev (19; HSU, killed in an air accident August 20, 1943). (From the collection of Dmitriy Karlenko)

were deployed to specific regions to attack targets of opportunity. They roamed the air corridors to Stalingrad, attacking German transports and their fighter escorts with swiftness and efficiency. The pilots of each group became familiar with their areas of patrol, and they flew the latest models of Soviet fighter aircraft—Yak-9s and La-5s—to allow the full exploitation of their skills. These elite units quickly established a reputation for aggressiveness and air combat skill. As a consequence, the Germans began to shift the majority of their flights to nighttime or periods of bad weather that provided some cover without unduly increasing the danger of landing in the pocket.

Having lost the airfields at Tatsinskaya and Morozovskaya in December 1942, the German High Command faced a grim situation at the beginning of 1943. For the Soviets, this was an occasion to push for the liquidation of the German Sixth Army. The encirclement proved to be effective, despite von Manstein's relief effort. The distance between the external and internal lines had been widened, deepening the geographic isolation of Paulus's troops and making the success of the airlift more problematic. Events moved swiftly to force the capitulation of the German forces at Stalingrad. On the ground, the relentless pressure of the Soviet army reduced the area of the pocket. Within the city, a brutal struggle continued as the exhausted and poorly supplied troops under Paulus attempted to hold out against the gathering weight of the Soviet army.

The VVS intensified the air blockade along the air corridors and struck repeatedly at the remaining airfields held by the Germans at Stalingrad. German airfields at Pitomnik, Bolshaya Rossoshka, Karpovka, and Gumrak faced the increasing tempo of VVS attacks by day and night. VVS fighters were moved up to airfields within 15 to 30 miles (24 to 48 kilometers), while bombers and ground attack aircraft were moved to within 40 to 60 miles (64 to 96 kilometers) of the pocket to allow sustained operations. At night, U-2s roamed over the beleaguered German airstrips, dropping bombs on transports as they unloaded their cargoes. In January 1943, the superiority in numbers reached a level that allowed the entire 16th Air Army, with 600 combat aircraft, to be deployed exclusively in support of the 65th Army. The VVS was now able to send bombers in groups of forty to hit enemy positions.[84]

When the Germans rejected the demand for surrender, the Soviets launched their final drive on January 10, 1943. After furious fighting, Soviet troops occupied the western approaches to the city on January 12. A second offer to surrender was made and again rejected. As the circle closed, the quantity of firepower from air and artillery units intensified. With the help of radio guidance stations, the accuracy of Soviet fire improved even as it became more concentrated.

On January 24, Pitomnik itself fell. This calamity sealed the fate of the German garrison. Pitomnik was the last working airfield after the January 10 offensive. Only Gumrak remained, and it lacked the size and operational status to continue the airlift. With the loss of Pitom-

Containers like this one were used to drop food, medical supplies, and ammunition for encircled German troops in Demyansk and the Stalingrad area. (From the collection of Valeriy Romanenko)

nik, the Germans no longer had a link with the outside. The airlift was reduced in the last two weeks of January to airdrops by parachute, many of which fell into Soviet hands.

The assault on the reduced German pocket, now almost coextensive with the city, began on January 22. Two days later, the Soviets reached the western edge of Stalingrad. By January 25, they had linked up with the 62nd Army under General Chuikov, cutting the enemy sector in half. Now the German units began to surrender. Finally, Field Marshal Paulus, in command of the northern group, capitulated on January 31. On February 2, the last remnants of the German Sixth Army surrendered.

AT THE CUTTING EDGE

The evolving character of Soviet airpower became manifest at Stalingrad. The changes can best be measured by the combat experience of certain small air units, such as the 434th IAP (later the 32nd GIAP). First organized in July 1941, the 434th was destined to become one of the elite VVS air regiments during the course of the war. The first commander of the regiment, Major Alexander A. Koryagin, reflected the talented cadre of pilots assigned to the unit. The 434th was initially posted to the Leningrad *Front* in the difficult summer months of 1941. As the war progressed, Major Koryagin was joined by some of the most experienced and skilled fighter pilots in the VVS, a deliberate effort to transform the 434th into an elite air unit. Initially, the pilots and technicians of the air regiment took custody of modern LaGG-3 fighters with their M-105 engines. In the first months of the war, the 434th expanded its aircraft inventory to include Yak-1 and MiG-3 fighters, although transition training proved to be hurried and less than ideal (some pilots gained only twelve hours of flight time on each of the new fighters). The initial numerical strength of the 434th IAP was two squadrons, a total of twenty aircraft. At Leningrad, the pilots of the 434th flew air cover, engaged in strafing attacks on advancing German infantry and mechanized forces, and conducted reconnaissance missions. The first air victory came on September 11, when Koryagin downed a *Luftwaffe* Bf 109 near Demyansk. However, the overall success of the air regiment at this stage of the war was limited, in no small measure a consequence of its small size, its few late-model aircraft, and its combat inexperience.[85]

While attached to the Leningrad *Front*, the 434th IAP engaged in a quickened pattern of combat operations. Sorties flown increased steadily, reaching fifty-six on September 17 and another seventy-five on the following day. As in other air units, the desperate context prompted pilots to use the tactic of ramming: Lieutenant Mikhail Goram rammed a Ju 88 bomber with his propeller and then managed to gain control of his damaged fighter and land safely. For his bravery, Goram received the Order of Lenin. The air base of the 434th IAP was repeatedly attacked by the enemy. For the first month of combat, the 434th IAP recorded a loss of sixteen aircraft. With these losses, the air regiment was reinforced with new LaGG-3 aircraft, equipped with ShKAS machine guns. The month of October also offered a context for some memorable aerial triumphs, mostly against Ju 88 bombers, although at this stage, such air victories were minimal and occasional in nature.[86]

A fateful turn came with the air regiment's close association with Vasiliy Stalin, the son of the Soviet ruler and then an inspector in the VVS. His aim was to transform the 434th into an elite fighter unit. Owing to his patronage, the 434th welcomed into its ranks some of the most talented and aggressive pilots. A privileged son of the Soviet political elite, the young Stalin was not alone in his enthusiasm for aviation: Timur Frunze, the son of a hero in the Russian Civil War and a key organizer of the Red Army, chose the air force for his military career. Two other sons of the Soviet elite, Leonid Khrushchev and Vladimir Mikoyan, would die in air combat; Stepan and Aleksey Mikoyan were also airmen. Vasiliy Stalin's stepbrother, Yakov Stalin, was captured in the opening days of the war and would die as a prisoner of war.[87]

If Vasiliy Stalin acquired a deserved reputation for heavy drinking and erratic personal behavior, he did possess an aptitude for flying and won no small measure of respect among the airmen of the 434th IAP. He earned his pilot's wings from the famous flight school at Kacha in March 1940 and subsequently recruited a number of its graduates and instructors. Further advanced training for squadron commanders followed at Lipetsk in January–May 1941. His appointment as director of the Inspectorate of the VVS took place the following September. At the conclusion of the Stalingrad campaign, he achieved the rank of colonel. As a pilot, the young son of Stalin had trained in the prewar I-15bis fighter and then made the transition to the late-model Yak-1 and LaGG-3 fighters.[88] His tireless efforts to promote the 434th IAP as a special unit began in earnest in the spring of 1942. The goal was to field an air unit on a par with the best in the *Luftwaffe*. His role as inspector brought him into personal contact with many of the most talented pilots and the latest technological breakthroughs. Accordingly, he displayed a keen interest in transferring these assets to the elite 434th.

As the battle for Stalingrad approached, the 434th IAP experienced rapid growth.[89] It was staffed with a remarkable cadre of experienced pilots, many of them transferred from other air units. They all shared the common traits of combat experience and proven skills as military pilots. Command of the 434th passed to Major Ivan I. Kleshchev, a talented twenty-four-year-old pilot who had flown in the prewar air skirmishes against the Japanese at Khalkin Gol in the Far East. A core group of battle-hardened pilots joined Kleshchev: Captain Semyon P. Korzinkov, Lieutenant Ivan I. Izbinskiy, Lieutenant Mikhail A. Goram, and Lieutenant Vladimir A. Orekhov. Even with this stellar group of pilots, Kleshchev remained a standout, a man widely respected for his personal bravery, aggressive flying style, and manifest skills as a leader. He joined the special 434th in May 1942 and was always at the cutting edge of sorties, especially in the summer months of 1942, when the air regiments shifted to operations around Stalingrad. He won the Gold Star, Hero of the Soviet Union, for his exploits: archival records indicate that Kleshchev downed sixteen enemy aircraft and another fifteen in group actions.[90] He died while attempting to land in a snowstorm on December 31, 1942. At the time, Kleshchev had flown 380 sorties.[91]

During defensive operations against the German forces advancing on Stalingrad, the 434th IAP scored a number of air victories, but its air action was scattered in nature. There were frequent shifts in locale in response to enemy advances on the ground. As in the past, the pilots of the 434th targeted enemy bombers, but they were increasingly involved in intense air battles with escorting *Luftwaffe* fighters—often the newly deployed Messerschmitt Bf 109G types. Losses in Soviet aircraft and crews remained high in this period, with the *Luftwaffe* still enjoying air supremacy over the front. Flying the Yak-7b in air operations against the *Luftwaffe* proved to be a morale builder, however. The advanced Yak fighters—a total of thirty-two aircraft—were deployed in three squadrons. The veteran pilots of the 434th IAP preferred the Yak design to the MiG-3 and the LaGG-3. The sleek Yak-7b was powered by the 1,180-horsepower M-105PF engine and armed with 20mm cannon and a large-caliber machine gun. Pilots noticed that the new fighter was more difficult to control than the Yak-1, but this negative attribute was overshadowed by the Yak-7b's demonstrated superiority in horizontal speed, maneuverability, and powerful armament.[92] For the 434th IAP, the blend of experienced combat pilots and improved aircraft technology signaled the drive by the VVS—always slow and incremental—to gain parity with the *Luftwaffe*.

Even in the midst of these desperate days, air personnel of the 434th found time to study and redefine their approach to air tactics. The *Luftwaffe*'s superiority in combat was related, in part, to tactics and not necessarily to advanced aircraft designs (this perceived arena of advantage would soon be challenged). The flexible use of two-aircraft formations, consisting of an element leader and a wingman, had impressed frontline VVS pilots. Slowly, as in the West, this pattern would be copied, first on an informal basis and then as an official rule. The 434th IAP embraced the concept that altitude was a decisive factor in air combat. The regiment, by chance, had acquired two flyable Bf 109s as "trophies." These captured enemy fighters were highly prized for their technical data and insights into actual performance in terms of speed, maneuverability, and flight controls. The acquired data proved invaluable to 434th IAP pilots, as did the opportunity to see up close the vaunted German fighter they encountered in the skies over Stalingrad.[93]

One persistent problem for the 434th IAP—and for all other frontline air units at Stalingrad—was the dearth of airfields. The vast landscape west of the Volga River and beyond was essentially flat and devoid of forests, making improvised airstrips difficult to conceal from marauding reconnaissance aircraft and highly vulnerable to attack once they were spotted. Moreover, it proved to be very difficult to maintain essential logistical support for all forward airfields. By necessity, both ground crews and combat pilots were often compelled to live in extremely primitive conditions. On July 15, the 434th moved to

Gumrak, a permanent air facility located 37 miles (60 kilometers) west of Stalingrad. They shared the air base with the 150th BAP. Both units were attached to the newly organized 8th Air Army, which possessed some 300 aircraft of various types and vintages.[94] At Gumrak, the 434th IAP flew numerous sorties to provide cover for infantry and as escorts for bomber missions. Eventually, the Gumrak air base had to be abandoned with the German Sixth Army's advance to Stalingrad. Once it was encircled by the Red Army during counteroffensive operations, Gumrak became the German Sixth Army's vital link to the outside world.

In this defensive stage, the 434th IAP challenged the *Luftwaffe* in a variety of contexts. There were efforts to down Ju 87 Stukas and to engage in air combat with escorting German fighters. One day, July 26, proved to be a momentous interlude for air combat, provided by the pilots of the 434th IAP. There were eleven separate air battles that day with marauding enemy fighters and bombers in the region of Kalach. Chronicles of the 434th record a banner day, with thirty-four enemy aircraft downed.[95] Vasiliy Stalin was at Gumrak with his elite regiment, but he did not participate in any air actions. The feats of the 434th IAP caught the attention of a reporter from *Krasnaya zvesda,* who chronicled the July air battles. Major Kleshchev emerged in this context as one of the VVS's most heralded fighter pilots. Yet there were also grievous losses to report—a significant attrition in aircraft and airmen to the powerful *Luftwaffe,* which continued to maintain a lethal presence in the skies around Stalingrad. Records indicate that no fewer than sixteen of the most experienced and accomplished fighter pilots were killed in air combat in September alone, a list that included Vladimir Mikoyan, the son of powerful Soviet leader A. I. Mikoyan. In the defensive Stalingrad campaign, lasting from July 13 to October 3, 1942, the 434th IAP flew a total of 1,479 combat sorties against the enemy and claimed 138 enemy aircraft destroyed.[96] The celebrated air unit achieved special status on November 22, 1942, when it was designated the 32nd GIAP by the People's Commissar of Defense. The air regiment was then posted to the Kalinin *Front,* where it participated in myriad offensives, culminating in the conquest of Berlin in 1945.[97]

The prolonged struggle at Stalingrad also offered an arena for VVS ground attack units to perfect their tactics and develop a more efficient mechanism for command and control. As early as May 1942, the

VVS air assets in the Stalingrad had been reinforced with two ground attack regiments (243rd and 266th ShAPs). Other shifts followed as part of a timely and hurried redeployment to the Southwestern *Front*, including seven fighter regiments and several bomber units. The aim at this point was to gather sufficient airpower to strike forward *Luftwaffe* airfields. Among the ground attack units was the battle-hardened 7th GShAP (*Gvardeyskiy Shturmovoy Aviatsionnyy Polk*, or Guards ground attack air regiment) of the 230th ShAD. At the forward edge of the ground assault were the Il-2 Shturmoviks, soon to be the signature warplane for the Soviet Air Force. These *Shturmoviki* routinely hit their targets at extremely low altitudes, with repeated assaults at 300 to 500 feet (100 to 150 meters). The Il-2 aircraft first attacked an airfield near Konstantinovka, then a frontline enemy airfield with ninety aircraft. The Il-2s made a surprise strafing run, and the after-action report recorded a measure of success—twenty-two of the ninety parked aircraft were damaged.[98]

In the weeks that followed, several Il-2 units made repeated attacks on German airfields at the Southwestern *Front*, hitting both bomber and fighter inventory wherever found. In addition, these same ground attack units struck infantry and mechanized units. Tank and motorized convoys, along with bridges and river crossings, were struck in a desperate attempt to slow the advance of the enemy. At this stage of the war, however, Soviet boldness was not matched by any measure of effectiveness. Many lingering defects in VVS tactics and organization compromised combat efficiency. Too often, the Il-2 units operated in small groups, which limited the potential striking power of ground attack aviation. These small clusters of attacking Il-2s were easy to thwart with fighters and antiaircraft fire. There was a tendency, in the face of spirited enemy resistance, for the Il-2s to disperse and act independently, which often increased their vulnerability to German fighters. Pilots opted to attack less valuable targets such as trucks rather than tanks. Flight briefings were often unfocused, and there was a general absence of proper coordination. These complaints were contained in a report that spring by the commander of the Southwestern *Front*. A reorganization of VVS units in the Southwestern *Front* on June 9 placed them under the 8th Air Army of General T. T. Khryukin. This move promised more efficient command and control, but there were still nagging problems outside the scope of any reorganization

Pilots of the 504th ShAP, Kharkov area, end of May 1942. Sitting: deputy squadron commander V. K. Batrakov (killed in action September 15, 1942), G. K. Zotov, F. V. Yanchenko, Gonta, and I. F. Pilipenko. Standing: Ya. N. Lyapin, Koryazhkin, Yu. V. Orlov, I. I. Pstygo, P. I. Malinin, and A. V. Rybin. (From the collection of Dmitriy Karlenko)

scheme. For example, most VVS air units were operating at half strength, which meant that in mid-June, the 8th Air Army could deploy only twenty Il-2s and another eighteen day bombers for ground attack missions.[99]

Yet the 8th Air Army continued to deploy its *Shturmoviki* in an aggressive fashion and frequently against larger enemy formations. However, these sorties were often ineffectual or disastrous. On August 12, a total of thirteen Il-2 Shturmovik aircraft, drawn from the 226th and 228th ShADs and accompanied by just two Yak-1 fighters, launched a predawn raid on an enemy airfield near Oblivskoye. Air intelligence indicated there were 126 aircraft based at this airstrip. Once they reached the targeted base, the Il-2 pilots made a low-level strafing attack on the parked aircraft, a sweep that prompted fire from the startled enemy antiaircraft batteries. The attacking Il-2s managed to avoid enemy fighters and returned home without a loss. This high-risk sortie was largely ineffectual, becoming a sort of harassment raid at best. Not all raids, however, were so fortunate. Later, Il-2 aircraft drawn from the 686th ShAP (escorted by twelve Yak-1s and five LaGG-3 fighters) made another raid on nearby *Luftwaffe* airstrips at Olkhovskoye and Podolkhovskoye. This sortie had been detected in advance by the enemy, which opened intense defensive fire as the *Shturmoviki* approached. As the Soviet pilots attempted to make a second sweep, they were attacked by thirty Messerschmitt Bf 109 fighters. In the maelstrom of air combat that followed, a number of Soviet pilots were killed, wounded, or forced down. Even though some damage was inflicted on the enemy, this encounter revealed the dangers and the enormous pressure faced by ground attack pilots at this stage of the war.[100]

There were persistent weaknesses endemic to the VVS ground attack units in the summer of 1942. With the constant movement and rebasing, it was difficult to gain authoritative reconnaissance data on the enemy. With each passing day, or even over the course of hours, the *Luftwaffe*'s deployment could change. When enemy airfields proved to be problematic targets, an effort was made to attack tanks and mechanized units. Effective communications between the 8th Air Army headquarters and operational units also remained a daunting challenge, a factor that led to confusion and even cases of friendly forces coming under attack. On the tactical level, there was a problem of discipline. Typically, the Il-2s attacked in groups of six to eight aircraft—at the time, the equivalent of squadron strength. These ground attack planes approached their targets in echelon formation and, as a rule, made more than one pass—sometimes as many as three passes. With each pass, the ordered formation often disintegrated into a "string" of single aircraft. This spacing robbed the low-flying aircraft of mutually supportive defensive fire. Enemy antiaircraft batteries took delight in firing on these widely separated and vulnerable Il-2 aircraft. Once the first pass was completed, the alerted enemy fighters were quick to become airborne and attack the Il-2s, typically hitting stragglers from below and behind. Sadly for Soviet aircrews at this stage of the war, there were few radio-equipped aircraft. Often, to the disadvantage of ground attack pilots, they found it necessary to engage in air combat as a desperate means of survival, but the slow-moving Il-2 was no match for experienced *Luftwaffe* fighter pilots. Still, there were some Shturmovik pilots who emerged from dogfights the victor. One talented pilot with the 807th ShAP, Sergeant Danilov, claimed a Bf 109 on August 24, 1942; a Ju 88 on the following day; and then, remarkably, a Bf 110 on August 29.[101] Such feats, however, were the exception.

In the intense struggle, Il-2 pilots were also called on to make high-risk sorties against enemy strongholds among the destroyed buildings in the center of Stalingrad. To reduce attrition in aircraft, ground attack missions were flown at dusk or dawn or on moonlit nights. In the final stages of the defensive fight at Stalingrad, from August 28 to November 18, Shturmovik crews flew a total of 406 such missions. Finding enemy airfields and strongholds in such marginal conditions proved difficult, prompting Shturmovik units to employ U-2 biplanes as "pathfinders." These obsolete aircraft dropped flares and incendiary bombs just in advance of a ground attack. In the desperate days of the defense of Stalingrad, the Il-2s were often directed to perform the awkward task of an interceptor, attacking marauding *Luftwaffe* Ju 87 Stukas and He 111 and Ju 88 bombers.[102]

For the counteroffensive at Stalingrad—the bold encirclement of German forces—ground attack units drawn from the 8th, 16th, and 17th Air Armies played a highly visible role. Seven air divisions and two independent air regiments participated, a force that included some 317 operational Il-2s. Close ground support for the advancing Soviet troops became the sole mission in this initial phase of the counteroffensive. Lack of effective coordination between attacking Il-2s and their escorts continued to plague ground attack operations. One attack on Pitomnik airfield on December 10 ended in tragedy: lack of a proper escort resulted in the loss of four of seven attacking Il-2s. The *Luftwaffe* continued to exact a high toll on VVS ground attack units. *Shturmoviki* did manage to score some notable victories in their attacks on German transports and bombers seeking to resupply the besieged Sixth Army. Low-level strafing of arriving and departing German relief aircraft by Il-2s posed a serious problem for the German army at Stalingrad. Some of these sorties were flown without fighter escorts in the most severe weather.[103] Like the 434th IAP and other fighter units, the VVS ground attack crews achieved a mixed record at Stalingrad. With a small inventory of aircraft and inexperienced pilots, frontline air units survived the cruel challenge of the Stalingrad campaign, but not without enormous sacrifice.

The VVS at Stalingrad displayed no lack of aggressiveness in the struggle for air supremacy with the *Luftwaffe*. The Stalingrad campaign, as noted, demonstrated the VVS's impressive ability to adapt to the vagaries of air combat: the cruel attrition in aircraft and crews and the lingering problems in communications, intelligence gathering, and efficient command and control techniques. Geography, weather, and the need for continual rebasing placed enormous strains on logistical entities in the rear areas.

The Soviet use of airpower played a major role in the outcome of the battle at Stalingrad. The Germans made a valiant attempt to repeat the successful Demyansk airlift, but they failed. The consequences were profound. As events proved, the *Luftwaffe* survived Stalingrad, but it emerged from that air war severely weakened overall and with its transport operations in the East crippled. It also lost that elusive factor of *esprit,* the high confidence that animated *Luftwaffe* operations in 1941–1942. The vast German technological edge no longer existed.

The campaign for Stalingrad evolved into both a mobile and a position style of warfare. As the German army advanced toward the Volga River, the communication and logistical challenges intensified, and the geography stretched the *Luftwaffe*'s capacity to provide essential air support and resupply. The intense battles around Stalingrad became a form of position warfare, with limited advances for both sides. This shift influenced the operational goals and effectiveness of both contending air forces. Hitler, who had presided over a series of vast mobile thrusts into Soviet territory, fatefully decided to embrace a form of position warfare. Accordingly, the *Luftwaffe*—even with its vaunted power and mobility—proved inadequate to the task at hand. It embarked on a vain quest to overcome distance, weather, and the still viable Soviet air arm.

For the VVS—in terms of organization and tactics—there was the challenge to exploit the exposed and weakened enemy. Stalingrad provided an occasion—a fiery one—to implement the 1942 reforms. In their larger meaning, the Stalingrad air operations compelled the VVS, for the first time, to organize and coordinate large-scale efforts in support of several *Fronts*. The air blockade was more than a token effort to intercept German transports crossing to the pocket from Morozovskaya and Tatsinskaya airfields; it involved a complex system of fighter interception, ground assault, and bomber sorties in full coordination with ground operations. Four air armies, along with the ADD and elements of the PVO, were committed to the blockade, enhanced by the use of a radio control system. The logistical problems associated with the prolonged Stalingrad conflict placed enormous strain on the Soviets. Ruthless mobilization measures made the difference.

Stalingrad demonstrated the elaborate requirements for the conduct of large-scale air operations: administrative centralization; the creation of large, mobile air armies for rapid deployment; close coordination and liaison with ground forces; and the mobilization of logistical support. For the first time, the VVS command structure administered four air armies and five ADD divisions over a vast area in a five-month air campaign, shifting from strategic defense to a coordinated air offensive and air blockade.

[handwritten margin note: NOVOKOPF IS NOW IN CHARGE.]

For the VVS, the Stalingrad conflict brought honors and recognition. A total of nine air divisions were given the designation "Guards." Seventeen pilots received the highest decoration for bravery, Hero of the Soviet Union. Another 1,000 medals were awarded to VVS personnel for their participation in the air war at Stalingrad. The official Soviet claim was up to 3,000 German combat and transport aircraft downed (1,000 during defensive operations, and 2,000 during offensive operations). This expansive figure stood in contrast to the Germans' admission of the loss of 488 aircraft.[104] Actual Soviet losses were high: 2,000 aircraft lost during the defensive stage, and 2,769 lost during offensive operations.[105] The VVS tally also included 102,392 sorties, of which 67,500 were in the defensive stage and 34,892 in the offensive stage.[106]

Among the experienced air army commanders who emerged from the Stalingrad conflict were Generals S. A. Krasovskiy (17th Air Army), S. I. Rudenko (16th Air Army), T. T. Khryukin (8th Air Army), K. N. Smirnov (2nd Air Army), and A. Ye. Golovanov (ADD). These men, as events proved, became the leadership core for the postwar VVS High Command.

The triumphal mood following the epic victory did not conceal the many and serious weaknesses of the VVS at this juncture of the war. The frontline air units had weathered the storm of Stalingrad and emerged with renewed strength on many levels. Certainly, there was a clearer view among Soviet air commanders, top to bottom, of the correct tactics to employ in air operations; however, the gap between acknowledging this shared consciousness and putting it into actual practice remained large, though narrowing. Failures by VVS fighter pilots to employ vertical maneuver in air combat persisted. Coordination among Soviet air groupings had improved dramatically, but VVS combat pilots displayed much less discipline than the enemy. By this stage in the war, the use of radios had become more common in air operations, but it had not been fully adapted as a standard operational tool. Moreover, advanced technologies in aircraft design and armament were now reshaping the striking power of the Soviet air arm. Yet the transformation was not complete at Stalingrad, notwithstanding the combat successes of certain VVS air units. The optimal use of new technologies, along with improved air tactics, took time. All the new modes of fighting had to be tested in the crucible of battle. The process of change was in motion, but the VVS remained inferior to the *Luftwaffe* in many qualitative measures in the late winter of 1942–1943. The Stalingrad battle had revealed a bloodied but more determined Soviet air arm, a dramatic contrast to the bloated and disoriented victim of Operation Barbarossa.

Among the more experienced VVS air units, there was now a rough parity with the *Luftwaffe*, a fact that would become even more dramatic in the Kuban air battles that soon followed in the spring of 1943. Looking back at the reforms of 1942 under the aegis of Air Commander Novikov, the VVS had emerged as an increasingly mobile and lethal air arm, one bent on perfecting its skills in combined operations with ground forces. The use of the air blockade tactic at Stalingrad had been a real innovation—and a very lethal one. The air armies were ideal for wide-ranging operations on the Eastern Front. Although the air armies were not autonomous—they would continue to be subordinated at times to *Front* commanders—they had established a muscular presence in the war. The growing inventory of aircraft also allowed the *Stavka* to make excellent use of its ever-expanding reserves.

Stalingrad entered historical consciousness as one of the most brutal and decisive battles of the war. For the Soviet Air Force, this difficult air campaign became an intense interlude to inaugurate a series of broad reforms in organization and air tactics that would soon set the stage for a rapid shift in the fortunes of both the VVS and the still formidable *Luftwaffe*.

Chapter Four

Over the Kuban

In April–May 1943, the Kuban River in the North Caucasus became the remote locale for one of the most dramatic air battles in World War II. These fierce air engagements fell chronologically between the German campaigns at Stalingrad and at Kursk. In Western accounts, this two-month air war has been relegated to a sort of historical limbo, being overshadowed by the more dramatic "turning points" at Stalingrad and Kursk. Soviet chronicles of the air war, however, approach the Kuban episode in the same fashion as Americans view the Battle of Midway—a pivotal moment or benchmark in the long path to victory.

In retrospect, the Kuban struggle may seem marginal in the larger scheme of the war. There were no major breakthroughs during or after the conflict by either side. No large army grouping was defeated, enveloped, or captured. The whole affair, at first glance, appears to be simply an interlude of air combat between two epic battles. For the VVS, the air engagement in the North Caucasus became a decisive moment in the quest to gain parity with the *Luftwaffe*. Moreover, the Kuban chapter marked for the Soviets the transition from a defensive to an offensive posture. Here, for the first time, the VVS displayed a rapidly evolving organizational efficiency, ever-shifting air tactics, numerical superiority, and clever employment of its vast air reserves. All these components came together during the Kuban period, culminating two arduous years of development, adaptation, and piecemeal experimentation. As Alexander Pokryshkin, a veteran of these air operations, asserts in his memoirs, the Kuban was used as a proving ground to articulate in theory and demonstrate in practice the isolated "lessons" learned in air combat tactics between 1941 and 1943.[1]

The Kuban bridgehead was formed in the aftermath of Stalingrad and the hasty withdrawal of German forces in the North Caucasus. Roughly coextensive with the Taman peninsula and situated east of the Kerch Strait, the bridgehead became the last German toehold in the Caucasus.[2] There, fifteen divisions of the German Seventeenth Army, along with some Romanian troops, fashioned a network of powerful defensive positions in February–March 1943. The fortified line extended down from the marshy Kuban River delta on the northern shore of the Taman peninsula, through the hill country just east of Krymskaya, to the seaport of Novorossiysk on the Black Sea. A secondary series of strongpoints, the so-called Blue Line, provided further defensive capability against the anticipated Soviet superiority in infantry and tanks in the Krymskaya sector. The Soviets, however, feared that the bridgehead would serve as a staging area for another offensive in the North Caucasus, given the German goal of capturing the oil fields near Baku.[3] Consequently, the Kuban bridgehead had strategic importance, compelling the *Luftwaffe* and the VVS to deploy some of their best air units in the sector.

The Caucasus region possessed a widespread and powerful appeal to those fighting the German invader. At the geographic heart of the Caucasus, the Kuban was located at the approach to the Soviet Republic of Georgia, the birthplace of Joseph Stalin. Scattered across the entire North Caucasus area were more than fifty ethnic groups. This ethnographic patchwork surpassed even the Balkans in diversity. Mountain tribes, Christian or Muslim, often lived in isolation, speaking separate and mutually incomprehensible languages. All these groups lived restively under Soviet rule and displayed varying degrees of loyalty to Moscow during the period of the German invasion. Many mountain tribes openly welcomed the German invaders. To add to Soviet anxiety in 1942–1943, there was the fear of Turkish intervention in the wake of any dramatic reversal of Soviet military fortunes in the Caucasus.

Going back to the sixteenth century, the Caucasus had occupied a special place in the national consciousness. Russians viewed the region with awe and profound attachment. Among all the Russian hinterlands, the Caucasus alone prompted positive images. It was a region of exotic beauty, polyglot cultures, and fierce and independent mountain tribes—a locale of relative freedom beyond the grasp of bureaucratic Russia. During the nineteenth century, the Caucasus had entered Russian literature in the writings of Pushkin, Lermontov, and Tolstoy. Consequently, Russians had deep ties, cultural as well as political, to the Caucasus in the twentieth century—it was an inextricable part of *Rodina*, the Motherland.[4]

The German thrust across the Don toward the Soviet oil fields in the summer of 1942 had forced both sides to conduct air and ground operations in the Caucasus Mountains, a remote and rugged terrain of unusual diversity. At the center of the North Caucasus is the meandering, 563-mile-long (900-kilometer) Kuban River, with its many changing aspects—the rapids near Mount Elbrus as the river descends through narrow, rocky gorges; the long, winding movement through the Stavropol uplands, where the Kuban widens and slows to become a natural inland waterway; and the final passage through the lowland marshes on the northern shore of the Taman peninsula into the Sea of Azov.

The vast and towering Caucasus mountain range, the source of the Kuban River, extends for more than 600 miles (966 kilometers) from the Black Sea to the Caspian Sea. Taller than the Alps, the Caucasus Mountains provided a natural barrier between Europe and Asia on the Soviet Union's southern periphery. On the northern tier of this mountain range—at Maikop, Grozny, and Baku—were vital Soviet oil fields, first developed in the late nineteenth century and once the setting for Stalin's revolutionary work. The Germans sought to control the strategic Caucasus oil reserves and gain access to other crucial raw materials such as iron, copper, and natural gas. Moreover, the German occupation of the Caucasus would deny the Soviet Union a secure and safe supply route for Lend-Lease shipments from Iran.[5] For invader and defender alike, the Caucasian landscape provided few good highways. The formidable topography, always subject to the extremes of weather, compromised mobility and created a logistical nightmare for both sides. An intense struggle for air supremacy unfolded in this rugged, if beautiful, region, a shifting sequence of violent air engagements above a varied terrain of mountains, valleys, rivers, winding roads, towns and cities, and a jagged Black Sea coastline.

THE FIERY SKIES OVER THE NORTH CAUCASUS

Air combat in the Kuban sector fell into three distinct phases, each of which was characterized by fierce and unrelenting struggle. Hostilities commenced on April 4, 1943, when the Soviets launched a counter-offensive in the Kuban region. This ill-fated move quickly stalled in the face of German resistance. Then, on April 17, the Germans set Operation Neptune into motion, an offensive that called for the German Seventeenth Army to capture Myskhako, a small beachhead held by Soviet marines along the coast of the Black Sea. To help counter this move, the Soviets deployed the 4th and 5th Air Armies, along with elements drawn from the 8th and 17th Air Armies, the ADD, and the Black Sea Fleet's air arm. All air operations were coordinated personally by Air Commander Novikov.[6]

The German attackers encountered intense Soviet air and ground resistance in the Kuban region. To neutralize the Soviet defenders, the *Luftwaffe* flew a total of 1,560 sorties on the first day of Operation Neptune, which included 511 sorties by Ju 87 dive-bombers. The VVS managed to respond with 538 sorties.[7] This air initiative of the Germans—as well as the assault on Myskhako—ultimately failed. In the aftermath of the stalled German offensive, on April 29, the Soviet 56th Army launched a flanking maneuver to capture the small coastal town of Anapa, then a key logistical center and staging area for the Myskhako operations. In the second phase, over the village of Krymskaya, the German and Soviet air forces engaged in an intense struggle, with high attrition on both sides. The Soviet ground offensive was stalled, but the VVS displayed a muscular presence in the skies over the Kuban—even in the face of considerable losses in aircraft and aircrews. The third phase began on May 26 with an assault by Soviet infantry and armor on the German fortified positions, the so-called Blue Line. Again, the VVS and the *Luftwaffe* were drawn into an intense struggle to gain air supremacy.

For the *Luftwaffe*, the deployment of air assets to the Kuban was difficult. Aircrews were put under great pressure, and the logistical support for air operations became a daunting task. It was no longer easy to assert and maintain air superiority. *Luftflotte* 4 possessed a mixed array of aircraft types: fighters, bombers, dive-bombers, reconnaissance, and air transports. This powerful air arm included some of the *Luftwaffe*'s most experienced and talented fighter groups, most notably Guenther Rall's III/JG 52, which had moved to the Kerch area in March 1943.[8] Moreover, the *Luftwaffe* introduced some of its latest aircraft during the Kuban air operations: the Messerschmitt Bf 109 G-4,

Two Ju 87 Stukas of 7./St.G. 2 *Immelmann* dive on a Soviet target in the
Kuban area, spring 1943. In June, this unit was transferred to the
Kharkov–Belgorod area in the southern sector of the Kursk salient. The
Luftwaffe made excellent use of the slow-flying and vulnerable Stukas,
which routinely required fighter escorts. (From the collection of Von
Hardesty)

the Hs 129, and some experimental versions of the Ju 87 (Ju 87G) and
the Ju 88 (Ju 88P).

Given the enormity of the Eastern Front and the finite assets available to German air commanders, the *Luftwaffe* did not possess a fixed
strength in any given theater or at any given time. It was not unusual
for *Luftwaffe* air units to fly sorties against multiple fronts in one day.
For example, German bomber units were flying missions over the
Kuban in the morning and then over the Dnieper River area in the afternoon. German airmen were called on to support widely separated
ground forces as a sort of "fire brigade." The ever-shifting air operations of the *Luftwaffe*—flown in a context of diminishing resources—

denied Soviet air intelligence precise figures on the number of enemy aircraft facing them. Consequently, comparisons of *Luftwaffe* and VVS air strength are difficult to reconstruct from 1943 to 1945. Soviet intelligence found it easier to calculate the strength of *Luftwaffe* fighters in a given area because fighter squadrons, with their limited range, were routinely posted close to any theater of action. *Luftwaffe* fighter units were respectable in size at this stage of the war: two groups from JG 3 (II and III/JG 3), and three groups from JG 52 (I, II, and III/JG 52). There were also Slovak and Croatian air units assigned to JG 52. The total number of German fighters amounted to around 180 machines; they were based at Anapa, Gostagayevskaya, Kerch, and Taman.[9] During the previous fall (October–November 1942), a significant number of *Luftwaffe* air units had been withdrawn from the Russian Front to meet the Allied challenge in North Africa and the growing requirements for Reich defense.[10]

The VVS's 4th and 5th Air Armies, now supported by the ever-growing *Stavka* reserves as well as elements of the Black Sea Fleet aviation and PVO air units, assumed the challenging role of neutralizing the *Luftwaffe* in the Kuban. German airpower in the narrow confines of the bridgehead was considerable, a formidable mix of older- and newer-model aircraft, from obsolescent Ju 87 Stuka dive-bombers to late-model Bf 109G fighters. The Soviets brought to the air struggle modern Yak and Lavochkin fighters, Il-2 Shturmovik and Pe-2 bombers, and a significant number of newly acquired Lend-Lease P-39 fighters and A-20 bombers. The Soviets even deployed a small number of Spitfire V fighters, made available by Great Britain to support the Soviet war effort.

The *Stavka* placed a high priority on the unfolding Kuban air operations. To achieve greater centralization in command, the air commander of the *Front*, General K. A. Vershinin, took control of all available air units of the 4th and 5th Air Armies. By April 17, the VVS possessed more than 300 fighters. On April 18, Marshal Zhukov and Air Commander Novikov arrived at the North Caucasus *Front* as *Stavka* representatives. Novikov immediately ordered additional reserves into the theater, a total of 370 fighters. Overall Soviet air strength was increased by 900 aircraft.[11] General Vershinin coordinated and supervised the two air armies led by able subordinate air commanders: General N. F. Naumenko (4th Air Army) and General S.

K. Goryunov (5th Air Army).[12] Associated with the VVS buildup under Vershinin's command were air units drawn from the Black Sea Fleet. Vershinin later described the Kuban air battles as unparalleled in their intensity, sometimes involving thirty to forty fighters aloft in combat at one time.[13] On certain days, up to a hundred air battles took place over the Kuban sector. In the airspace above the village of Abinskaya, where the VVS command post was located, for example, he reported seeing an aircraft fall every ten minutes.[14] The growing ability to mobilize and deploy airpower would be a key factor in sustaining Soviet air operations in the skies over the Kuban.

As the critical air battle loomed, the dramatic transformation of the VVS became clear to frontline pilot and ace Guenther Rall, then attached to the battle-hardened III/JG 52. Rall had reached a forward *Luftwaffe* base at Kerch in March 1943. He now discovered a large inventory of new Soviet fighters and Lend-Lease aircraft, most notably the P-39 Airacobra. "The VVS," he noted, "had also changed their tactics, so it was [a] far more effective air force." Caught up in the vortex of air combat over the Kuban, Rall was surprised and alarmed at the diminished fighting capacity of the *Luftwaffe*: "It was a hopeless situation on the Crimean Peninsula. The cavalry was killing its horses. The ocean was filled with blood. Every thirty minutes we were attacked. We had no supplies, no spare equipment, nothing." Keeping aircraft operational was no small challenge, as Rall recalled, with chief mechanics swarming "like wasps" over damaged planes searching for parts.[15]

For the efficient transition of VVS pilots into combat operations, the 4th Air Army had organized a realistic training program—one forged in the context of battle experience. During March and April, experienced pilots instructed the new arrivals in air combat techniques. The instruction was detailed, practical, and based on a careful analysis of *Luftwaffe* tactics. The VVS adoption of the *para,* a mirror copy of the *Luftwaffe Rotte* formation, had gone a long way in providing Soviet fighter operations with flexibility. Along with the Soviet military in general, the VVS actively emulated the hated but tactically and technologically superior enemy. The battle-experienced *Luftwaffe* remained a formidable adversary in 1943. Although the new models of Soviet fighters and bombers had narrowed the technological gap considerably, air tactics was a persistent problem area for VVS air units, in particular for

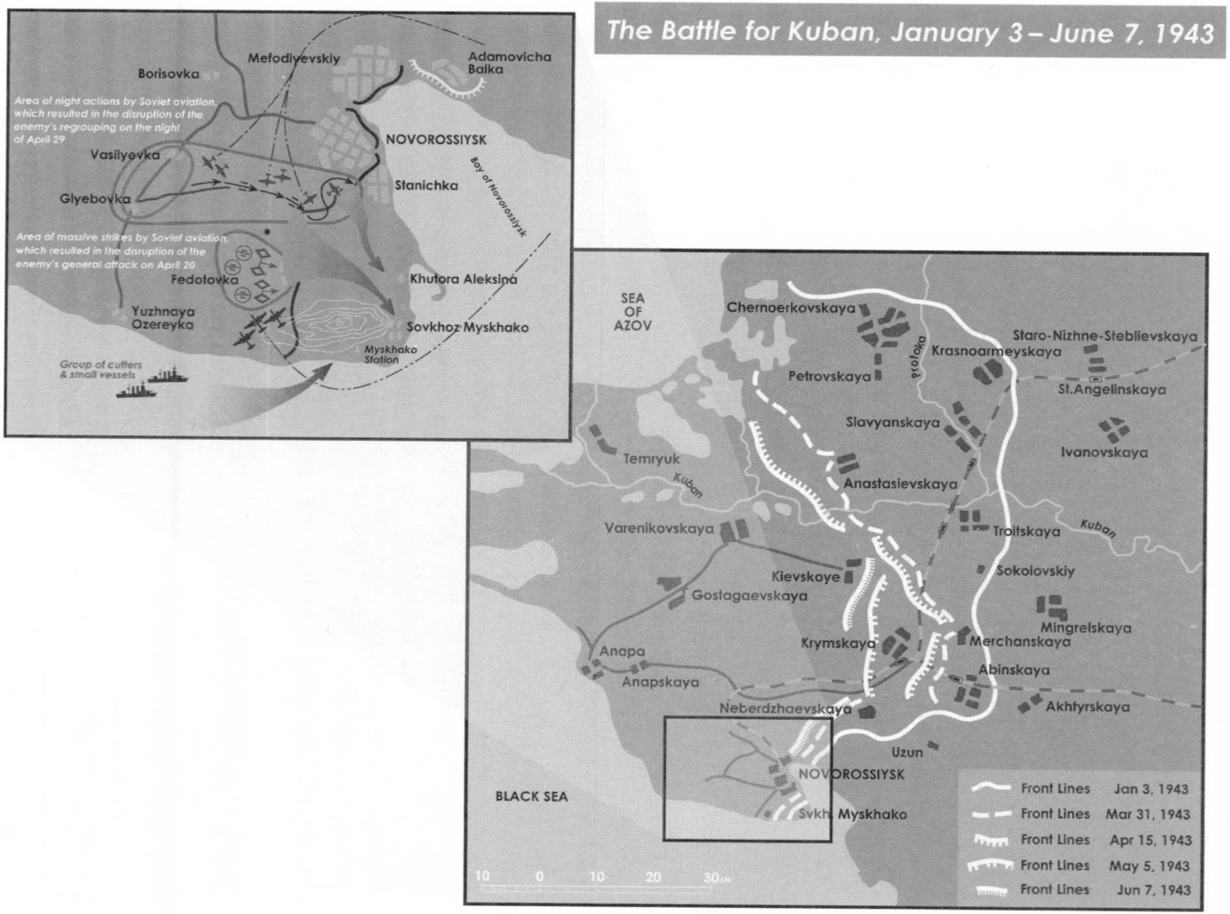

The Battle for Kuban, January 3 – June 7, 1943

Map 5 (Terry Higgins © 2011, adapted from *Dragons on Bird Wings*, vol. 1, Aviaeology 2006)

SEA OF AZOV

Temryuk

Kuban

Staro-Nizhne-Stebliievskaya

St.Angelinskaya

Ivanovskaya

Chernoerkovskaya

Krasnoarmeyskaya

protoka

Slavyanskaya

Petrovskaya

Anastasievskaya

Troitskaya

Kuban

Sokolovskiy

Mingrelskaya

Merchanskaya

Akhtyrskaya

Abinskaya

Varenikovskaya

Kievskoye

Gostagaevskaya

Krymskaya

Uzun

Neberdzhaevskaya

NOVOROSSIYSK

Svkh Myskhako

Anapskaya

Anapa

BLACK SEA

Front Lines	Jan 3, 1943
Front Lines	Mar 31, 1943
Front Lines	Apr 15, 1943
Front Lines	May 5, 1943
Front Lines	Jun 7, 1943

10 0 10 20 30 km

Adamovicha Balka

Borisovka

Metodiyevskiy

NOVOROSSIYSK

Bay of Novorossiysk

Stanichka

Khutora Aleksina

Vasiliyevka

Glyebovka

Yuzhnaya Ozereyka

Fedotovka

Sovkhoz Myskhako

Myskhako Station

Area of night actions by Soviet aviation, which resulted in the disruption of the enemy's regrouping on the night of April 29

Area of massive strikes by Soviet aviation, which resulted in the disruption of the enemy's general attack on April 20

Group of cutters & small vessels

the fighter air arm. The Kuban became a singularly important sphere for the VVS to make the necessary adjustments in air combat tactics, one of the final hurdles on the way to parity with the *Luftwaffe*.

Airfields in the Kuban were few in number and routinely difficult to supply and maintain once they were established. Most were grass airstrips with only rudimentary facilities for maintenance and storage. Logistics across this rugged terrain presented a formidable challenge for both sides. Housing for aircrews and ground personnel remained primitive, often consisting of tents, dugouts, or temporary structures. Battlefield requirements dictated sites away from the few roads that existed in the area. As it turned out, the *Luftwaffe* managed to occupy the few good airfields in the region. Once the Kuban bridgehead was established, the Soviets began to build a new network of airfields, an effort that was hampered by the spring rainy season. Some of these airfields, as the Germans discovered later, turned out to be "dummy" fields. By contrast, the *Luftwaffe* fighters operated from the better, more established airfields, such as Anapa, with bombers flying sorties from rear facilities at Kerch in the Crimea. This relative advantage in air basing was crucial, allowing the *Luftwaffe* to concentrate its forces in a skillful, flexible, and lethal fashion.

The Soviet logistical services faced immense odds, even with the assistance of Lend-Lease materiel and transport. Distance, time, and the extremes of weather presented enormous obstacles. One of the Soviet Union's great achievements in the war with Germany was its ability to mobilize and concentrate massive airpower. Airfield servicing battalions (BAOs), along with other logistical services, met the requirements in an impressive fashion.[16] With the increasing number of aircraft flowing into the VVS inventory, the need for a more effective rear services or logistics command became evident. The institutional basis for an expanded rear services had been in place in the prewar years, but the vagaries of geography and the wartime requirements presented unique challenges. When the VVS air armies were organized in 1942, this new formation of air units required sustained logistical support. In this crucible of combat, a new quasi-independent logistical arm with viable command and control systems slowly took shape. The elements required to support an air army consisted of technical supply, airfield construction, motorized transportation, fuel, and medical service. The overriding priorities became efficiency, discipline, and coordination, although these qualities were never easy to attain in the fluid and demanding context of the war. Yet the goal of perfecting effective rear service organizations commanded the attention of the aviation high command throughout the war.[17]

The BAO became the familiar and ubiquitous organization spearheading the complex logistical work. The BAO was subordinate to the air basing region, or RAB. But in its optimal form, the BAO was a self-contained operation often set up to serve either single- or multiengine air regiments. These logistical specialists routinely handled requests for provisions, ammunition, fuel, spare parts, repairs, and medical aid. A typical BAO possessed its own wheeled transport company. Myriad tasks were performed, from camouflage to airfield maintenance in all weather conditions.

Life for aircrews at the front varied widely, depending on geography and the character of operations. At newly occupied airfields, accommodations were often primitive, with pilots and ground crews sleeping under the wings of their aircraft. Often airmen sought billeting in a nearby village, if available. Sometimes such temporary quarters could be 1 to 2 miles (1.6 to 3.2 kilometers) from the air base. Once they were in place, forward airstrips took on certain creature comforts—tents or permanent quarters for housing, hangars, and storage areas. But as the airmen often complained, the construction of shelters was slow. In addition to a landing strip, the BAO constructed a command post for the regimental commander and two bunkers for thirty-six airmen, one bunker for maintenance personnel, and revetments for the unit's aircraft. In winter conditions, special care was taken to provide warming covers and heating equipment for the aircraft. If a base was occupied for any long stretch of time, it took on a more sophisticated look, with a whole complex of structures, storage facilities, and bunkers for personnel.[18]

Notwithstanding the fact that the *Luftwaffe* exercised the initiative in the early stages of the conflict, German air operations suffered from systemic problems and enormous strains in the wake of the Stalingrad defeat. Southern Ukraine was a vital strategic position for the Germans, and air commanders there came to the cold realization that they possessed limited resources in terms of aircraft and aircrews. By 1943, the overall condition of the *Luftwaffe* in the East had deteriorated sharply. The army's demands for air support during the 1942 offensive operations in the North Caucasus had not been fully met: German air units, often with meager reserves, were asked to cover a vast region—the frontage in the northern Caucasus alone was 800 miles (1,290 kilometers). These immense distances prevented effective operations by fighter aircraft. Increasingly, the *Luftwaffe* assumed a defensive posture, largely restricting its air support to the bridgehead proper. There were occasional offensive thrusts—for example, air raids on the seaport at Tuapse—but there were no attacks or even reconnaissance of other targets farther south along the Black Sea coast, such as the seaport at Batumi. *Luftwaffe* transports continued their yeoman work, flying fuel and supplies to forward units and flying out the wounded. These herculean efforts demonstrated the versatility of the German air arm, but the larger tactical requirements of the *Wehrmacht* were left unfulfilled. Defense, conservation, and improvisation, according to Asher Lee, would dominate *Luftwaffe* operations for the remainder of the war.[19] The Kuban air war revealed in a dramatic fashion the reduced (and declining) operational strength of the *Luftwaffe* in the East.

Myskhako

The first obstacle to German plans to stabilize the Kuban bridgehead perimeter was the Soviet-held beachhead at Myskhako. On February 4, 1943, just two days after the surrender of General Paulus at Stalingrad, a Soviet assault group landed southwest of the German-occupied port of Novorossiysk. Once ashore, the small party established a 19-square-mile (49-square-kilometer) beachhead that was quickly reinforced by troops from the Soviet 18th Army. Called the "Little Land," the Soviet-held enclave became a serious problem for the Germans, threatening the port of Novorossiysk, which secured the right flank of the Kuban bridgehead. The seaborne assault had caught the Germans off guard, and their repeated efforts to overrun Myskhako met with fierce resistance. As long as the Soviet enclave survived, the Germans could not stabilize the right flank of the Kuban bridgehead.

The strategic port of Novorossiysk was situated on the northern shore of the U-shaped Bay of Novorossiysk. In their withdrawal from the northern Caucasus, the Germans had abandoned most of the coastline along the 3-mile-long (4.8-kilometer) bay below the heavily fortified seaport. The Soviet assault group had landed on the German-held northern shore, just southwest of Novorossiysk. This bold move enabled the Soviets to flank Novorossiysk on two sides, penetrate the Kuban bridgehead perimeter at a crucial point, and challenge the Germans for effective control of the bay.

The landing site, situated on the rugged shores at the foot of Mount Myskhako, was a rocky terrain that offered the Soviets many excellent defensive positions. Steep foothills, covered by numerous clusters of woods, provided ideal cover. Once in place, the Soviet defenders were difficult to dislodge, even with sustained bombardment by airpower and artillery; Soviet bunkers had to be taken one at a time. After the initial landing in February, the Germans moved forcefully against the beachhead and cleared several pockets of Soviet resistance. But the reduced beachhead held on, compelling the Germans to break off their attack after heavy losses. The Soviets managed to reinforce the Myskhako beachhead on a regular basis in February–March by sea, mostly at night from the seaport of Gelendzhik.

Earlier, the *Luftwaffe* had flown repeated air strikes against Gelendzhik and the heavy volume of Soviet seaborne reinforcements crossing the Bay of Novorossiysk, with mixed results at best. Increased VVS air activity made such attacks difficult and costly. Nevertheless, these raids applied enough pressure to compel the Soviets to resort to the nighttime reinforcement of Myskhako. During February and March, the Germans assigned a number of *Luftwaffe* flak artillery units to Novorossiysk, and these units, using parachute flares, directed heavy fire from their 88mm guns onto the Soviet traffic crossing the bay at night. Like a magnet, Myskhako drew both sides into fierce combat in April 1943.

The German offensive against Myskhako (Operation Neptune) began on the morning of April 17, 1943, at 0630 hours. Anticipating fierce resistance, the German ground assault moved out only after intense artillery and air preparation. The V Corps (4th Mountain Division and 73rd and 125th Infantry Divisions) was committed to overrunning the entrenched Soviet positions. To assist these elements from the Seventeenth Army, the *Luftwaffe* deployed two fighter groups (with associated Romanian, Slovakian, and Croatian air units). The Croat and Slovak pilots served as part of JG 52; the Romanian

Interrogation of a *Luftwaffe* bomber crew at headquarters of the 216th
SAD, Kuban region, February–March 1943. Seated at the far left is air
division chief of staff Colonel B. A. Abramovich; standing third from the
left is deputy division commander M. N. Volkov. (From the collection of
Valeriy Romanenko)

squadrons were organized separately. Soviet sources described the
April 17 air bombardment at Myskhako as heavy, involving 1,074 airplanes, of which 200 were fighters.[20] This projection of enemy
strength was highly inflated, based on flawed intelligence from the
field. The Soviet bastion, organized in depth, stood like a granite cliff
against wave after wave of German air assaults. The German air assault included both day and night raids designed to destroy the besieged enclave. Watching this large number of Stukas make their
bombing runs, typically from heights of 10,000 feet (3,000 meters),
deeply impressed Rall, who flew fighter escort duty. "This was the last
time," he recalled, "when I observed such an air strike by such a large
number of Stukas, making repeated bombing runs from altitude."[21] Although it could be a devastating air weapon, the Ju 87 was slow, especially in climb-outs after a dive-bombing attack, making it highly
vulnerable to attack by marauding VVS fighters breaking through the

screen of *Luftwaffe* escorts. Myskhako was routinely bombed by Ju 88 bombers, and these German air attacks achieved some measure of success against Soviet artillery positions and troop concentrations. However, the overall stalemate at Myskhako persisted.

To thwart the attack on Myskhako, the VVS deployed nearly 500 combat aircraft, including about 100 bombers, but it faced enormous problems in maintaining an air presence over the battle zone.[22] In addition to being hastily improvised, many of the Soviet airfields were quite remote from the scene. To reach the embattled airspace around Novorossiysk, many VVS air units had to fly over the northwestern spur of the Caucasus Mountains, sometimes from as far back as Krasnodar. By contrast, *Luftwaffe* fighter aircraft reached the battle zone quickly from airfields at Anapa and Gostagayevskaya—a mere 25 to 30 miles (40 to 48 kilometers) away. More important, the German pilots could remain over Myskhako for thirty to forty minutes, as opposed to the brief ten-to-fifteen-minute time frame allotted to VVS fliers. To complicate matters, VVS aircraft frequently encountered fog and low clouds in the mountains.

During this initial phase of Myskhako air operations, the *Luftwaffe* conducted air strikes with little interference from Soviet fighters. Only three Ju 87 Stukas, badly damaged from VVS fighter aircraft, crash-landed after completing their attack runs, and a small number suffered damage from Soviet antiaircraft fire.[23] Compared with these modest *Luftwaffe* losses, the German Seventeenth Army suffered heavy casualties in its abortive ground assault, which yielded an advance of only half a mile (0.8 kilometer). On the second day of the Myskhako offensive, Ju 87s, in attack waves of twenty-five aircraft, flew repeated sorties against the beleaguered Soviet defenses. This daylong operation began at 0445 hours and ended at 1830 hours. The German air units encountered little interference from Soviet fighters and only sporadic antiaircraft fire. The Ju 87s hit varied targets within the Soviet-held sphere—the southern part of Novorossiysk, the railroad bend, the old fort, and the mud baths that had once been part of a Black Sea health spa. Despite the marginal weather conditions—cloudy and overcast—the Germans scored a number of hits on Soviet infantry and artillery positions. These successes, however, were modest. After two days, the Soviets still retained a firm grip on the Myskhako beachhead.[24]

This *Luftwaffe* Ju 87D-3, probably S7 + JH of 1./St.G 3, was downed by Soviet fighters on April 3, 1943, in the Krymskaya area. (From the collection of Valeriy Romanenko)

Mention of the word *Myskhako* prompts an image of fierce determination and heroic sacrifice in Russian historical memory. At Brest, Sevastopol, and Stalingrad, Soviet troops had established a formidable reputation for resistance in the extreme—a willingness, on occasion, to fight to the last man. In retrospect, Soviet historical accounts have portrayed this phenomenon as an expression of the patriotism that animated the Soviet army throughout the war. The VVS mirrored this ferocity and discipline in the aforementioned aerial ramming tactic called the *taran*, which was commonplace in air combat between 1941 and 1943. Taking full advantage of this war-generated nationalism, the Communist Party conducted "party-political" work at all levels of the air force. Party control, though separate from operational command, remained pervasive. The political department of the VVS worked to instill high morale and discipline. Communists were portrayed in postwar histories as selfless and courageous fighters, and the party as an institution was viewed as a special repository of authority and nationalistic fervor.[25] VVS pilots who displayed extraordinary bravery were often given party membership.

When appeals to patriotic duty faltered and the impact of party indoctrination evaporated under the pressures of combat, some political commissars resorted to coercion. At Stalingrad, for example, political officers armed with handguns stood in boats ferrying reinforcements across the Volga, making sure no one broke away from his assigned duty. As a group, VVS personnel were more highly motivated than other components of the Soviet military, but the ever-present political and security functionaries were a sobering reminder of the party's intention to retain firm control. During the Moscow and Stalingrad campaigns, the NKVD had assumed a decisive role, carrying out Stalin's ruthless determination to thwart the German invaders. At Moscow, the NKVD had played a key role in mobilizing the populace, overseeing the defensive network, and punishing any manifestation of defeatism.[26] So-called blocking detachments had stood behind the Soviet armies, ready to neutralize any attempt to retreat. These detachments showed no mercy to individuals or units that displayed a lack of will to resist to the end. A. S. Shcherbakov, a veteran Communist Party functionary, assumed firm leadership of the Red Army's Main Political Directorate and displayed a fervent desire to enforce Stalin's will.[27] The VVS felt the impact of these policies. Many airmen, justly or unjustly accused of infractions and slated for imprisonment, were allowed to continue flying combat missions and were offered one year off their sentences for each enemy aircraft downed.[28]

Myskhako provided an opportunity for an important future leader of the Communist Party, Colonel Leonid I. Brezhnev, to demonstrate his skills in party-political work. Brezhnev headed the political department of the 18th Army during the struggle. His work—exaggerated, in retrospect—centered on maintaining "the high morale, steadfastness, and bravery" of the Myskhako defenders.[29] Like Nikita Khrushchev at Stalingrad, Brezhnev and many other Soviet political leaders forged their future careers during the war.

The massive deployment of Soviet airpower became a vital factor by April 20, the fourth day of the German offensive. On this day, the Germans launched another major effort to overrun the Soviet defenses. On the ground, the Seventeenth Army again suffered heavy losses, forcing it to break off the operation the following day. In the air, the VVS appeared in considerable numbers. The tenacious defense of Myskhako on the ground and the escalating VVS presence above the beachhead stalled the German drive in a decisive fashion. The German Seventeenth Army made no substantial progress after determined and costly assaults. In the air, the *Luftwaffe* employed nearly all its available combat aircraft to turn the tide, attacking infantry and artillery positions, the Soviet headquarters command post, and landing areas along the beachhead. One night mission involved 165 Ju 87s attacking beachhead landing points in dive-bombing runs from 10,000 feet (3,000 meters). The *Luftwaffe* recorded some notable successes as units of *Fliegerkorps* I shot down 91 VVS aircraft, while German fighters operating on the right flank of the Seventeenth Army scored another 56 victories.[30]

On April 20, according to Soviet sources, Myskhako was the scene of a decisive air battle. Although these accounts confirm the intensity of the struggle mirrored in German histories, they present a different chronicle of the events. The Soviet goal was to interrupt and neutralize German offensive operations on the ground and in the air. This Soviet aggressiveness became evident early in the morning of April 20, when 60 VVS bombers, escorted by 30 fighters, struck at German troop concentrations just beyond the periphery of the beachhead. This attack, thanks to careful planning, occurred about thirty minutes before the anticipated German ground assault on Myskhako. After a short interval, another wave of 100 Soviet aircraft struck the German staging area.[31]

To disrupt *Luftwaffe* operations over the entire Kuban bridgehead, a special group of fighter interceptors was organized (in close coordination with aviation units of the Black Sea Fleet) to attack German air traffic flying from airfields near Kerch. And in an effort to further confuse and weaken German air activity, long-range bombers from the ADD were ordered to strike enemy airfields in the Crimea, including the major German base at Sarabuz. This raid, according to one postwar German source, was highly successful, with 100 German aircraft destroyed or damaged.[32] During this phase of the conflict, VVS aircrews were flying as many as three sorties per day.

On April 21, Novikov visited a forward command post, where he was able to observe the intense air combat firsthand. While flying an Il-2 against German targets near Novikov's command post, pilot N. V. Rykhlin and his rear gunner, I. S. Yefremenko—both from the 805th ShAP—discovered the perils of flying ground attack sorties without fighter escorts. In a sudden dive, four German fighters ambushed Rykhlin's Il-2. During the prolonged and unequal battle that followed,

The VVS deployed the Lend-Lease P-39 Airacobras in massive numbers in the Kuban, April 1943. This fighter was highly regarded by Soviet pilots for its powerful armament, maneuverability, and modern radio instrumentation. Friends congratulate Captain V. Drygin (seventeen personal plus eight shared victories) of the 298th IAP on yet another victory. (From the collection of Carl-Fredric Geust via Valeriy Romanenko)

Rykhlin and Yefremenko shot down two of the German fighters. Before the engagement was broken off, Rykhlin was wounded, and his Il-2 was severely crippled. Nevertheless, Rykhlin managed to limp back across the lines to a nearby Soviet airfield and land safely. For their courage, both fliers were given battlefield promotions by Novikov—Rykhlin was promoted to lieutenant, and Yefremenko to junior lieutenant. Later, they were both awarded the Gold Star, Hero of the Soviet Union.[33]

Having seized the initiative at Myskhako, the VVS now attempted to assert local air superiority over the Novorossiysk sector. On April 21–22, the Soviets flew numerous sorties over Myskhako during daylight hours, actively seeking out enemy aircraft. They claimed the destruction of forty-five German aircraft during this period. The number of *Luftwaffe* sorties declined sharply, almost in inverse proportion to VVS sorties: the 1,248 sorties by the *Luftwaffe* on the first day of the offensive were reduced to 281 sorties on April 24.[34] At this juncture, the Germans abandoned their effort to liquidate the Myskhako beachhead, although considerable air and ground action continued sporadically along the northern shore of the Bay of Novorossiysk for several weeks. On April 24, the assault group at Myskhako, reinforced with fresh troops, counterattacked, and by April 30, it had made some gains. According to Soviet sources, the *Luftwaffe* lost 182 combat aircraft in air battles between April 17 and 24, with another 260 damaged or destroyed on the ground. VVS aircraft losses were not specified in Soviet sources beyond the vague statement that they were "considerably less" than German losses.[35]

Whatever the actual figures for the two sides, the Soviets claimed an air victory in the first phase of the fighting over Myskhako. The *Luftwaffe*'s reduced presence after April 20 signaled that the Soviets had achieved a tenuous command of the air. From April 17 to 29, the number of *Luftwaffe* aircraft destroyed or damaged on the airfields approached 260, forcing the withdrawal of aircraft to larger air bases at Saki and Sarabuz.[36]

Krymskaya

In late April, the village of Krymskaya replaced Myskhako as the major arena for the escalating air war over the Kuban. At Krymskaya, located near a railway junction northwest of Novorossiysk, the Soviet 56th Army launched a major ground offensive on April 29. The goal was to establish a breakthrough corridor toward Anapa to the Black Sea coast. The *Stavka* hoped to split the German army groupings in the Taman peninsula and destroy the Kuban bridgehead.

The Soviet offensive began at 0740 hours, following an intense artillery preparation. The Soviet planners anticipated victory, hoping to catch the German defenders off guard again. Having blunted the German effort to take the Myskhako beachhead, the Soviets were confident that the Seventeenth Army was on the defensive, its strength depleted. The VVS demonstrated its growing power and maturing skills as it supported the 56th Army at Krymskaya. On the night before the offensive, units drawn from the 4th Air Army and the ADD flew air preparation missions against the German positions, dropping 210 tons of bombs. The 46th GNBAP (*Gvardeyskiy Nochnoy Bombardiro-vochnyy Aviatsionnyy Polk,* or Guards night bomber air regiment), a female Guards unit under Major Ye. D. Bershanskaya, participated in these night bombing sorties just outside of Krymskaya. Flying U-2s, the women pilots made "precise attacks" against German ground forces.[37]

At 0700 hours on April 29, the VVS 4th Air Army made another massive raid to coincide with the opening of a ground offensive by the 56th Army. For three hours, VVS aircraft—144 bombers, 82 ground attack airplanes, and 265 fighters—pounded the enemy positions. The VVS made 1,268 sorties that day, including 379 night sorties. The Soviet goal was to administer a powerful preparatory air strike in the initial phase and then provide sustained air support for the ground forces advancing on two sides of Krymskaya.[38]

Air units from the *Luftwaffe's Fliegerkorps* I quickly moved to stem the Soviet breakthrough attempt. Bombers, ground attack aircraft, and fighters flew repeated sorties against the advancing Soviet forces. On April 29, the skies over Krymskaya were filled with German and Soviet combat aircraft. In a narrow 15- to 18-mile (24- to 29-kilometer) sector, the *Luftwaffe* engaged the VVS in an intense air struggle, against a backdrop of fierce ground fighting. In the period leading up to May 12, huge air battles became a daily occurrence in this sector—up to forty clashes per day, involving fifty to a hundred aircraft from each side.[39]

Soviet bombers and ground attack aircraft supported the advancing Soviet troops with growing effectiveness. On May 3, 162 aircraft from the 2nd BAK (*Bombardirovochnyy Aviatsionnyy Korpus* or bomber air corps), commanded by Major General V. A. Ushakov, made sustained attacks on German artillery positions. These blows came at intervals of fifteen minutes and were coordinated with Soviet infantry and tank units that had penetrated German defensive positions south of Krymskaya. Simultaneously, Il-2 Shturmoviks from the 2nd Mixed Air Corps, commanded by Major General I. T. Yeremenko, paved the way for Soviet tanks to assist in this breakthrough attempt. During a four-day period, bombers and Shturmoviks completed 2,243 sorties in support of this operation.[40] Such a display of massive air support revealed the growing prowess of VVS tactical airpower. The 4th Air Army concentrated 90 percent of its combat sorties in this 19-mile-long (30-kilometer) zone, part of a 100-mile (160-kilometer) front line. These large-scale air operations established a new benchmark for the VVS in the crucial year of 1943.

Against Soviet airpower at Krymskaya, the *Luftwaffe* scored many successes, or what one German historian called "rich grazing": thirty-two Soviet aircraft downed on April 30, thirty-five on May 3, and another twenty-four on May 7. Despite these air victories (unconfirmed by Soviet sources), the *Luftwaffe* faced overwhelming odds as the VVS deployed massive concentrations of combat aircraft. Both Soviet and German accounts acknowledge that during the first week in May, the VVS, no doubt at considerable expense, achieved air superiority over the Krymskaya sector.[41]

The scale of these air engagements surpassed any previous VVS air operation in the South. From April 29 to May 10, the VVS 4th Air Army, in cooperation with naval air units and the ADD, flew 10,000 sorties. Over half these missions were against German ground positions along the front lines and in the rear. VVS pilots claimed 368 German aircraft.[42] Although the VVS achieved momentary air control over the crucial Krymskaya sector, this difficult and costly achievement did not alter the ground situation: the 56th Army had failed to break through to Anapa and the Black Sea.

A. L. Ivanov of the 57th GIAP flew British Spitfires in the Kuban during April–June 1943. His memoirs suggest that the Spitfire, despite its legendary role in the Battle of Britain, did not perform well on the Eastern Front.[43] "Our English birds," Ivanov lamented, "resemble too closely the Messerschmitt (Bf 109)." This confusion created danger for the Spitfire-equipped 57th Guards. Ivanov himself was shot down twice by other VVS fighter pilots from neighboring air units who mistook him for the enemy. Soviet antiaircraft units showed the same tendency to fire, often with great accuracy, on the Soviet Spitfires. Several expedients were tried to make the Spitfire safer, including changing the unit markings on the fuselage. Ivanov's account of the Spitfire's performance has been challenged in other extant VVS combat records, which suggest that the Spitfire—even if occasionally mistaken for an enemy aircraft—proved to be an effective interceptor in the hands of skilled VVS pilots. In fact, many frontline Soviet pilots looked upon

Spitfire Vb of the 57th GIAP during an aerial battle over the Kuban. Major Osipov's 36th IAP achieved Guards status on February 8, 1943, and was redesignated the 57th GIAP. (From the collection of Gennadiy Petrov via Carl-Fredrick Geust)

the Spitfire as a high-performance aircraft, equal to the *Luftwaffe's* Bf 109 types. Whatever its actual merits, after three months, the VVS withdrew its small number of Spitfires from the combat zones.[44]

The Soviet 56th Army finally captured Krymskaya on May 4, but the German defenders held fast elsewhere. Throughout most of the Soviet offensive at Krymskaya, the VVS challenged the *Luftwaffe* for air superiority with increasing aggressiveness. Generally, VVS aircrews flew twice as many daily sorties as the *Luftwaffe*. With the Soviets' claim of 368 downed German aircraft for the period April 20 to May 10, Vershinin could assert that the *Luftwaffe* was losing an average of 9 bombers and 17 fighters every twenty-four hours. Vershinin did not list Soviet losses, but based on German sources, one can speculate that they were substantial. By May 9–10, however, the *Luftwaffe* once again reasserted itself over the Krymskaya sector, establishing local air superiority. Renewed German control of the air demonstrated that the *Luftwaffe* remained powerful, despite the attrition of its ranks and the obvious gains of the VVS in the Kuban.

Over the Blue Line

On May 26, after a lull of nearly two weeks, the Soviets resumed their ground offensive against the German positions west of Krymskaya. Here, the Germans had constructed the well-fortified "Blue Line," which secured the central sector of the Kuban bridgehead. The Soviet thrust aimed to establish a breakthrough zone between the villages of Kiyevskaya and Moldavanskaya. To spearhead this ambitious ground assault, the *Stavka* deployed the reinforced 56th Army. The recent Krymskaya action had weakened the *Wehrmacht*'s strength in the sector, but the Blue Line afforded the German defenders the advantage of prepared defenses located on a series of elevated points. Also, the *Luftwaffe* was available to intervene if any serious Soviet breakthrough occurred.[45]

Soviet military planners anticipated an aggressive challenge from the *Luftwaffe* and quickly moved substantial reserves to forward airfields adjacent to the Blue Line to reinforce the 4th Air Army. The Soviets constructed an elaborate network of command posts and radio guidance stations to assist in the coordination of air and ground operations against the Blue Line. For the initial stage of the Soviet offensive, the VVS was to play a major role, providing air preparation and intercepting the anticipated *Luftwaffe* response.

The VVS mounted a massive air preparation strike on the morning of May 26, preceded by night bombing raids and an artillery barrage. A total of 338 aircraft (84 bombers, 104 ground attack planes, and 150 fighters) attacked the narrow breakthrough sector.[46] Once this strike was completed, the Soviets launched a powerful armored and infantry thrust against the German lines. The coordinated air and ground assault brought some immediate success, but a determined German counterattack soon stalled the Soviet drive. Soviet tanks often managed to pierce the enemy lines in depth, only to find themselves separated from their infantry support. More than a hundred Soviet tanks were lost on the first day.[47]

The Germans' response in the air was immediate. Their ability to hold the Blue Line depended in large measure on a swift reaction. Within three hours of the start of the offensive, the *Luftwaffe*, by Soviet reckoning, had flown 1,500 sorties. This rapid German counterstroke hit Soviet positions along the front lines and at some airfields as far back as Krasnodar. In the afternoon, the *Luftwaffe* made another raid, flying 600 sorties against the advancing Soviet troops. These alternating Soviet and German raids punctuated the hostilities on May 26.[48] Although Soviet sources are silent on the impact of this concerted *Luftwaffe* action, the Germans had in fact regained local air superiority. Whatever the tally of Soviet losses for May 26, the 4th Air Army had committed a substantial number of its aircraft to the offensive and displayed an unprecedented aggressiveness.

From the first day of the Blue Line offensive, the VVS committed itself once more to a schedule of sustained ground support. The 4th Air Army had demonstrated its skills at tactical air support in the massive air strike on May 26. The coordination of 338 combat aircraft, mostly bombers and Shturmoviks, required no small administrative effort. The air strike, which began at 0630 hours, fell on a narrow breakthrough corridor 4 miles (6.43 kilometers) wide and only 1 mile (1.6 kilometers) deep. Covered by 150 fighters, the strike force approached the target zone in three echelons: the first wave consisted of 84 bombers; the second, 36 Il-2 Shturmoviks; and the third, 49 Il-2 Shturmoviks. The higher-flying bombers served as the cutting edge, hitting the narrow sector with a concentrated blow. The Il-2s followed at nearly treetop level with a series of close-in attacks on the beleaguered German defensive positions.

This phase of the Kuban air war allowed experimentation with new ground attack techniques. For the first time, Il-2 Shturmoviks dropped a smoke screen in advance of the armored and infantry assault. Nineteen Il-2s in two groups flew this maneuver, approaching the target area at an altitude of 30 to 60 feet (10 to 20 meters). The Il-2, with its formidable armor plating, was well suited for such a task, and Shturmovik pilots, already accustomed to the rigors of hedge-hopping sorties over enemy lines, performed their assignment effectively.[49] The smoke screen caught the German defenders by surprise, allowing the Soviet ground forces to pierce the enemy's first line of defense. Before a spirited German counterattack stymied the Soviet advance, a breakthrough corridor of 2 to 3 miles (3.2 to 4.8 kilometers) had been secured. As the VVS 4th Air Army sustained its ground attacks against German frontline positions, Il-2 losses mounted steadily. The airspace over the Blue Line was constricted, and the intensity of the ground fighting compelled both sides to commit airpower on an ever-increasing scale. The *Luftwaffe* fighters remained a powerful foe, always capable of exacting a fearful toll of Soviet aircraft and aircrews. German antiaircraft units were ubiquitous and proficient. Despite these dangers, VVS *Shturmoviki* scored some notable successes in the two-week offensive over the Blue Line. On June 2, Senior Lieutenant N. P. Dedov led thirty-six Il-2s against German artillery and infantry positions near Moldavanskaya. Knowing in advance the powerful enemy fighter and antiaircraft defenses in the area, Dedov experimented with a new technique of ground attack, hoping to reduce losses. With a fighter cover of thirty planes, Dedov directed thirty Il-2s, divided into columns of six, against the predetermined enemy target at an approach altitude of 2,600 feet (800 meters). An interval of 1,300 to 1,600 feet (400 to 500 meters) separated the attacking Shturmoviks. Once over the target area, each column formed into a "closed circle." This tactic allowed each Shturmovik pilot to descend individually in a deep dive toward the enemy position, drop his bombs close in, bank to the left, and then return to the protected environs of the battle circle. Dedov's air strike proved to be quite effective, and losses were minimal. A group of four Bf 109s, according to Soviet records, managed to avoid the closed circle, with its considerable defensive firepower. Later, Vershinin ordered all his 4th Air Army Il-2 units to adopt this tactic as a standard procedure for ground attack.[50]

The *Luftwaffe* also introduced some new tactics, aircraft types, and weapons. This effort represented a German response to the reality of improving Soviet military equipment in 1943 and the increasing threat from Soviet armor and artillery. In 1941, the powerful Soviet T-34 tank had appeared in considerable numbers, along with the "Katyusha" truck-mounted multiple rocket launchers. In the Kuban, and more dramatically at Kursk in July, the Germans faced the formidable challenge of coordinated thrusts by Soviet armor, artillery, and airpower. The Kuban air campaign provided the *Luftwaffe* with a brief interlude to learn a great deal from the VVS, particularly about the potential uses of "obsolete" aircraft. For instance, the Germans organized bomber and later nighttime ground attack harassment raids using He 46C, He 45C, and Ar 66 aircraft. All along the vast Eastern Front, the VVS deployed its own vintage U-2s, some flown by all-female units, to harass the German lines, bomb airfields and communications centers, and maintain links with partisan elements in the German rear areas. The endless expanse of the Russian Front allowed seemingly obsolete airplanes to perform vital combat roles. Unlike on the Western Fronts, the combatants in the Soviet Union found ample opportunities to experiment with myriad forms of tactical air operations.

During the Kuban air battles, Hans-Ulrich Rudel assumed command of a special antitank unit that tested a number of new ground attack techniques and weapons. One of Germany's most decorated pilots, Rudel flew more than 2,500 combat missions during the war, sank the 26,000-ton Soviet battleship *Marat*, and became the acknowledged master of "tank-busting," with more than 500 Soviet tanks claimed. Rudel's special unit studied in detail the silhouette patterns of Soviet tanks and their points of vulnerability, such as the engine, fuel tanks, and ammunition racks.[51] Rudel's antitank command was ordered to the Crimea in the spring of 1943. For the first time, the Germans deployed the Hs 129B equipped with 37mm cannon, a new type of aircraft the Soviets observed with interest.[52] The major adaptations, however, occurred with older models—Ju 88s, Ju 87s, and Bf 110s. All these planes were equipped with larger-caliber antitank weapons, and to pierce the armor plate of Soviet tanks, the high-velocity ammunition was redesigned with tungsten-hardened cores. Rudel preferred the Ju 87D, which was fitted with a 37mm cannon beneath the wings and renamed the Ju 87G. The slow-flying Ju 87 Stuka, already highly vulnerable to Soviet fighters, became even slower and less maneuverable as the Ju 87G variant. To accommodate the increased firepower, the Stuka's dive brakes were removed. Most of Rudel's pilots, despite their commander's élan and confidence, found the Ju 87G difficult to fly and often defenseless against Soviet forces.

Air operations over the Kuban also influenced the development of VVS bomber tactics and deployment. The *Stavka* had decided to place its primary emphasis on tactical airpower. Fighter and ground attack aviation expanded between 1941 and 1943 at an accelerated rate. Yet the VVS adopted a flexible approach in its building of a powerful tactical air force that included the use of light and medium bombers. The Pe-2 provided the VVS with effective bombers that could be used in a variety of air support operations. In addition, Lend-Lease supplied the VVS with A-20 Havocs (dubbed "Bostons" by VVS personnel), allowing the Soviets to expand their bomber inventory in a short time frame.

The VVS 4th Air Army began a systematic policy of attacking German rear areas during the Kuban fighting. These bomber raids paral-

Reserve air regiments are busy preparing crews of American-built Douglas A-20 Boston bombers, coming in quantities via the Persian corridor beginning in April 1942. The flag on the left is the VVS banner. (From the collection of Valeriy Romanenko)

leled a similar aggressiveness in the fighter and ground attack units. VVS bombers hit not only German airfields but also bridges, port and supply installations at Taman and Kerch, seaborne traffic across the Kerch Strait, and German naval bases on the southern coast of the Crimea. Moreover, they struck areas hitherto immune from attack by Soviet airpower. These deep raids executed from April 20 to 28 became a serious problem for the Germans, compelling them to relocate bomber units farther from the front and adopt elaborate air defense measures for rear area installations and communications. Given the finite nature of *Luftwaffe* aircraft inventory at this stage of the war, these countermeasures were costly and time-consuming.[53]

CLOSING THE GAP — SMALL AIR UNIT ACTION

The growing effectiveness of Soviet fighter aviation became evident in small air unit action, typically at the air regiment level. For example, the 812th IAP's air operations over the Kuban embodied all the strengths and weaknesses of Soviet fighter aviation at this stage of the war. The composition of the 812th had been dramatically strengthened in December 1942 with the addition of aircrews from the 534th IAP, then posted in the Far East. Major A. U. Yeremin assumed command of the reconstituted air regiment, which began transition training to Yak-1 fighters. A man with great presence, a powerful bass voice, and a decisive manner, Yeremin led the 812th IAP during the difficult days of April–May 1943, the so-called Kuban Meat Grinder. Yeremin reported to Major General Ye. Ya. Savitskiy, then commander of the 3rd IAK of the 4th Air Army.

The action in the Kuban, by necessity, had been preceded by only a minimal interlude of transition training in the late-model Yak-1 fighters. Consequently, the pilots reached the perilous skies of the Kuban sector with no combat experience. Yet the air regiment possessed considerable flying experience (albeit in older prewar models). The unit was characterized by high morale and a strong sense of cohesion. One pilot in the 812th IAP, Alexander Ivanov, told of their daily life during the worst days of the Kuban operation, when it was common to fly three, four, or even five sorties each day. Ivanov's recollections echo the descriptions of fierce air engagements by Georgiy Golubev and many others. In this baptism of fire, Ivanov observed, they quickly learned the advantages of altitude and speed, how to adapt to new air tactics, and the vulnerabilities of *Luftwaffe* warplanes. It was a time of transition, and Ivanov candidly observed that combat losses in the 812th were persistent, with only 15 to 20 percent of the "combat-capable" pilots surviving the ordeal: "But, as a rule we did not think about our losses; our main goal was to kill the enemy. In the evening, after the sorties, everyone assembled for supper and discussed what happened that day. For us every victory was a celebration. And practically the whole short southern night was spent in discussions. Soon the truck arrived to take us to the airfield. At the airfield, people fell asleep wherever they could until the command was issued to sortie." Ivanov was one of the fortunate pilots who survived the Kuban, learning to be proficient with his Yak-1 fighter.[54]

In January 1943, Colonel Pavel T. Korobkov assumed command of the 265th IAD. The 812th IAP flew under Korobkov, along with the 291st and 402nd Air Regiments, which contained airmen reassigned from the Far East. Korobkov came to the Kuban with considerable experience. He had served in the Spanish Civil War against Franco's air force and against the Japanese at Khalkin Gol. Korobkov's combat experience earned him respect as he and his air division faced the ordeal at Kuban. Given the combat inexperience of his newly assembled air regiments, Korobkov initiated an intense training regimen for all his pilots, telling them, "We have little time and even less gasoline." Given the constraints of time and resources, Korobkov allowed his pilots a mere three demonstration flights in a trainer, urging them to study their new aircraft carefully on the ground and learn all the "idiosyncrasies and advantages the Yak enjoys over the fascist aircraft." After the completion of this improvised and hurried training program, the 265th IAD ferried some Yak-1 fighters from the Stalingrad sector to the front. By March 1943, the 812th IAP had received twenty of its allotted Yak-1 fighters.[55]

The actual deployment to the Kuban began on April 17. Pilots of the 812th flew south, touching down at airfields along the way—at Morshansk, Rossosh, Rostov-on-Don, Tikhoretskaya, and Krasnoarmeyskaya. The last portion of the flight path crossed an area frequented by German fighters. The ground crews and mechanics finally reached the front on transport aircraft. Krasnodar served as the basing area for the entire 265th IAD. The 812th IAP, with its now augmented inventory of twenty-nine Yak-1 fighters, settled into their frontline duties at the Krasnoarmeyskaya airfield. Quickly, the air regiment began to fly patrols consisting of ten to sixteen Yaks. The 812th IAP was now in the war zone and would soon be facing the *Luftwaffe* in a fierce struggle for air supremacy.[56]

Sometimes as many as fifty air skirmishes occurred daily in the skies over Myskhako and Krymskaya. Initially, the 812th IAP made some tactical errors that compromised the effectiveness of its operations. The combat formation of attacking VVS fighters—that is, the echeloning of aircraft by altitude in groups—frequently proved ineffectual. There was a problem of coordination between attacking and cover groups, along with inattentiveness to the optimal use of speed and maneuverability. Often, VVS aircraft in the heat of battle fell into the outmoded tactic of defensive circles, which allowed a smaller number of enemy fighters to attack in a sustained fashion. Radios were still in short supply, and their quality was always unpredictable.

In this initial phase, many pilots still considered radios unnecessary or even a burden. Inexperienced pilots infrequently exploited the sun and clouds for concealment. All too often, Soviet pilots allowed air combat to slip into a vortex of chaotic maneuvers devoid of proper discipline and coordination. During the first three days of the Kuban operations, the 812th IAP and other regiments in the 265th IAD took severe losses. Korobkov—with the active and full support of air corps commander Savitskiy—took great pains to correct these tactical errors as the fierce and relentless air battle over the Kuban unfolded in April–May 1943.[57]

Pilots of the 812th were aware that the *Luftwaffe* had deployed some of its most experienced air units in the Kuban, such as JG 3 *Udet* under Major Wolf-Dietrich Wilcke and JG 52 under Major Dietrich Hrabak. The latter ended the war with 125 air victories. His unit also had within its ranks Guenther Rall, one of the most fabled fighter pilots of the war and the third ranking German ace, who scored 275 air victories in the war. All the German air units—including fighters, bombers, and dive-bombers—brought extensive combat experience to the Kuban. Moreover, they had already faced VVS aircraft in all possible flying scenarios and were aware of the technical failings and tactical vulnerabilities of their Soviet adversary. The task of achieving parity became a seemingly impossible one for the inexperienced Soviet pilots. But remarkably, this gap was swiftly narrowed. Rall observed that the Kuban became the unanticipated place for Soviet fighter aviation to display great boldness and air combat skill—for the first time and in a sustained and lethal way.[58]

Alexander Tishchenko, a young pilot transferred to the 812th from the Far East, flew in many air sorties beginning on April 20 and extending through the month of May. His exploits and narrow brushes with death offer a glimpse of the lethal character of air combat. On April 20, his first sortie took him to the Myskhako beachhead to seek out attacking German bombers. He flew as part of a group of sixteen Yak-1 fighters ordered to Myskhako–Novorossiysk that day. "Black spots appeared on the horizon," he remembered, "which upon closure turned out to be twelve Ju 88 bombers escorted by six Bf 109s." Tishchenko boldly attacked one bomber, scoring direct hits on the fuselage. The enemy bomber then slowed and began to smoke. Almost instantaneously, Tishchenko's own Yak-1 came under attack from the rear. Now the prey, his Yak-1 absorbed accurate and close-in fire on the fuselage and cockpit area. "I turned my head and grew cold when I saw the yellow nose of the Messerschmitt through the shattered armored glass," Tishchenko reported. "Quickly—instinctively rather than consciously—I turned to the left and opened the canopy. Then I put the Yak in a dive. I heard the whistling and felt the sharp pain from the pressure change. The earth was rushing up to meet me. Carefully I began to bring the wounded aircraft out of the dive. My eyes grew dark and the pressure pushed me back heavily in the seat. Finally, I managed to level the aircraft, but my engine had died." Tishchenko skillfully steered his aircraft into a crash landing, and he was later rescued. He had survived his first day of combat. With time and experience, the bold pilot earned his place as one of the regiment's most effective frontline pilots, eventually receiving the Gold Star, Hero of the Soviet Union.[59]

Another pilot in the 812th, Ivan Fedorov, faced extreme danger in his first encounter with the enemy over the Kuban. His experiences suggest the arbitrary nature of air warfare. On this initial sortie, he spotted three flights of Ju 88s forming a column at around 9,850 feet (3,000 meters). Suddenly, a group of Bf 109s made their appearance:

Several Bf 109s with outboard cannons flashed like shadows and disappeared in the direction of the blinding sun. We could not tell. I understood that they were firing only when I saw the burning aircraft of Ivan Martynenko, wingman of our flight commander. To the right and slightly above, I caught sight of tongues of flame. I turned my head—pieces of burning Yaks, like a fantastic frightening dream, were flying off in various directions and tumbling toward earth. Not far from me, somersaulting slowly, fell a tail section with a red star on it. Who was the pilot? What happened to him?[60]

Fedorov later recorded his first victory by downing a Bf 109. The same boldness that exposed him to repeated danger set the stage for personal triumph:

Moving the throttle to full stop, I pulled the control stick toward me, tracing the flight trajectory of the Messerschmitt. I was closing on him! I felt a sense of excited belief that I would catch him. I even managed to catch a glance of his cockpit. . . . I opened fire on the Messerschmitt when the range closed to fifty meters. The cannon barked continuously, creating a wave of delight in my spirit. And only when a long tongue of flame crawled along the right side of the Messerschmitt did I release the trigger. I closed on him, adjusting my speed and, in order to be completely at ease, took aim and pounded him point-blank with all my weapons. I did not take my finger off the trigger until my weapons went silent. The Messerschmitt burned sill brighter, was shrouded in thick black smoke and, falling into a steep spin, fell to the earth.[61]

Air corps commander Savitskiy's memoirs include an accurate description of the air combat over the Kuban, the world experienced firsthand by Tishchenko and Fedorov in April–May 1943. Savitskiy remembered the air battles over Myskhako and Krymskaya as a series of duels between large numbers of aircraft in a "small three-dimensional space." Air engagements were abrupt and violent, sometimes lasting a long time. No stranger to air combat, Savitskiy remembered: "Downed aircraft fell out of the sky, others departed for their own airfields to refuel and rearm. New groups arrived to replace them. Pilots might fly four or five sorties over the course of several hours, and participate, in essence, in one and the same battle that had begun in the morning. And so it went all day long . . . Junkers and Peshkas (Pe-2s), Messerschmitts and Yaks, Fokkers (Soviet term for Fw 190s), and LaGGs burned, exploded in midair, and fell out of the sky."[62]

One of the most proficient Soviet air units to emerge in the Kuban was the 16th GIAP. This elite group—which had obtained its coveted Guards status on July 3, 1942, for exemplary work in the first year of the war—included some of the Soviets' highest-scoring aces. No less important, the air regiment showcased some of the crucial reforms in air tactics that would soon transform the fighter air arm. The 16th GIAP did much to foster in theory and in practice the modern air tactics deemed necessary to gain parity with the *Luftwaffe*. Even the German pilots took special note of this unit's presence in the skies ove the Kuban, keeping apprised of its sorties by routinely monitoring VVS radio traffic.[63]

Captain P. T. Tarasov of the 812th IAP reports to 3rd IAK commander, Major General Ye. Ya. Savitskiy, on a captured *Luftwaffe* Bf 109G-4 of 7./JG 52. On May 28, 1943, Tarasov forced the German pilot, Herbert Meissler, to land this Bf 109, once flown by celebrated ace Eric Hartmann. Meissler was taken prisoner. (From the collection of Valeriy Romanenko)

Alexander Pokryshkin, one of the most talented group command-ers to emerge in the war, played a prominent role in the development of this remarkable unit. His skills as a fighter pilot were widely her-alded, but one of his major contributions to the war effort was as a group leader. Surrounding Pokryshkin were other "heroes of the Kuban," pilots who, though not members of the 16th GIAP, were des-tined to redeem the tarnished reputation of VVS fighter aviation. For instance, two brothers, Dmitriy and Boris Glinka, scored twenty-one and ten victories, respectively, during this period. Arguably one of the most talented and flamboyant fighter pilots was G. E. Rechkalov, who emerged as the second ranking Soviet ace in World War II and was a two-time recipient of the Gold Star, Hero of the Soviet Union.[64] There were others: Vadim I. Fadeyev, with nineteen victories in the Kuban;[65] N. E. Lavitskiy with fifteen;[66] and P. M. Berestnev with eleven.[67] Each of these elite fighter pilots scored ten or more victories during the two-month Kuban campaign. There were occasions when Pokryshkin and Rechkalov flew in the same *zveno* over the Kuban.[68]

On April 8, the eve of the first day of Kuban air operations, the 16th GIAP reached Krasnodar airfield. The air unit flew into combat the following day. Its Kuban debut, however, proved to be less than impressive, in part due to the eight months of reserve status and the hurried transition training on Lend-Lease P-39 fighters. Over the course of ten days, a total of five pilots and ten aircraft were lost. This awkward beginning in April contrasted sharply with the 16th GIAP's proficiency in May, the second and final month of Kuban air action: the regiment was credited with fifty-five air victories—a tally of forty Messerschmitt Bf 109s, ten Ju 87 Stuka dive-bombers, two Do 215s, two Ju 88s, and one He 111.[69]

The 16th GIAP became associated with the "formula for victory," the so-called new air tactics of *Vysota–skorost–manevr–ogon* (altitude, speed, maneuver, fire). The adaptation to new tactics also involved emulation of the *Luftwaffe*'s practice of deploying fighters in twos and fours, often echeloned by altitude (the so-called Kuban Escalator). Each *para*, following the *Luftwaffe*'s practice, consisted of an element leader and a wingman. "Falcon's Strike" mimicked the *Luftwaffe*'s sudden attacks from above, usually from the side of the sun, while "Pendulum" employed highly effective high-speed patrol tactics over the battlefield. All these changes spelled enhanced flexibility and effectiveness, and the talented airmen of the 16th GIAP quickly scored some dramatic victories in the first month of Kuban operations using these tactics. Guards Captain Pokryshkin, a strong advocate of modern air tactics, downed ten Bf 109s; his fellow pilot Fadeyev downed twelve Bf 109s, and Rechkalov downed seven Bf 109s and one Ju 88. By the end of the month, the entire regiment had participated in 28 air engagements during the course of 289 sorties.[70]

The process of adapting to modern air tactics, however, did not begin with the 16th GIAP, notwithstanding the strong advocacy apparent in this regiment. The actual process was more widespread, spontaneous, and experimental and must be understood within the broader context of VVS reforms in the aftermath of Operation Barbarossa. Evidence of adaptation to new tactics was apparent as early as June 20, 1942, in a "top-secret" directive issued to the air divisions and air regiments of the 8th Air Army. After pointing out certain deficiencies and poor organization in combat operations, the directive endorsed the deployment of fighters in groups of two and four aircraft; echeloned formations; techniques for mutual support, coordination, proper escort, and coverage of Shturmoviks and bombers; vertical maneuver; and full exploitation of altitude. The directive openly acknowledged the superiority of the enemy's air tactics and called for Soviet pilots to study and emulate them.[71]

The reforms were enthusiastically embraced by Pokryshkin, whose name is frequently linked to them. He had grown up in Siberia, and as a youth in the 1930s he became enamored of the aerial feats of Valeriy Chkalov. He made his first solo flight in a U-2 biplane in 1937. In the late 1930s, Pokryshkin flew I-15s and I-16s as a VVS fighter pilot and made the transition to the MiG-3 just prior to the outbreak of war with Germany. Always a serious student of air combat tactics, Pokryshkin was profoundly affected by the disaster that befell the VVS during Operation Barbarossa. At the air academies, at the flight training schools, among flight instructors, and in various manuals and printed instructions, Pokryshkin found a bewildering pattern of outmoded concepts about air combat. His first encounter with the *Luftwaffe* took place on the second day of the war in an area near Yassy. At the time, Pokryshkin was flying a MiG-3, which he skillfully maneuvered and managed to down an enemy airplane after his own had been set aflame. This triumph and narrow escape exposed Pokryshkin's own inadequacies, the technical inferiority of VVS fighter aviation, and the acute need for new air combat tactics.[72]

Pokryshkin's role as a student and teacher of air combat tactics began with that first combat experience. The front lines, he said, made the study of combat tactics a "living necessity, a rule, a law." The requirements at the front differed markedly from the rehearsed skills acquired in flight training. As a senior pilot and squadron commander, he worked with newly assigned pilots, providing a crash course on the realities of air combat with the *Luftwaffe*. Always critical of "academic" or "theoretical" types who taught abstract concepts about flying, Pokryshkin forcefully asserted that combat was the best teacher. He displayed a willingness to learn and, if necessary, to adopt the superior methods of the enemy. Pokryshkin studied air combat in great detail, conversed with fellow pilots on the best tactics, and began the piecemeal adoption of proven techniques. "The effectiveness of every technique, formation, and calculation," according to Pokryshkin, "was tested in fire," and "conclusions rested on the lost lives of our comrades." Adoption of the formula "altitude, speed, maneuver, fire" was not unique to the VVS. Although it had been forged in a context of relative independence, it was not an original idea, and Allied fighter pilots at the time would have found Pokryshkin's "discoveries" to be simplistic and derivative. Indeed, they were, but for the VVS—which had been operating for two years in isolation against the technically and tactically superior *Luftwaffe*—Pokryshkin's formula expressed in words a whole matrix of battle-tested knowledge.[73]

For Pokryshkin, altitude was the primary element because it gave the Soviet fighter pilot a crucial advantage hitherto unexploited: freedom of maneuver, a lofty vantage point to search for the enemy, and the option of selecting the best target. From altitude, the Soviet pilot had the initiative. After a dive on the enemy, the speed acquired in the vertical axis gave the pilot the crucial factor of time—often just a few seconds—to make his attack. Together, altitude and speed translated into a set of flexible options of maneuver in either the vertical or the horizontal axis. Finally, Pokryshkin emphasized the importance of close-in fire on enemy aircraft. Like Erich Hartman and other fighter aces, Pokryshkin stressed the importance of firing at short range. The flying skill and patience required for this self-imposed discipline brought obvious rewards—greater accuracy and concentration of firepower. Behind Pokryshkin's formula was the shift by VVS fighters to the tactic of vertical maneuver. Deployed in *para* formations, VVS fighters in 1943 exhibited a more competent and aggressive posture, attacking from altitude and providing cover for one another. Victories mounted, and losses diminished. In many cases, the technical capabilities of a given aircraft dictated optimal maneuvers. The Bf 109's F and G models had more powerful engines, allowing them to climb to altitude faster than their Soviet counterparts. The LaGG and Yak types flew more effectively at lower altitudes. In addition, there was the problem of the absence of radios in many VVS aircraft. Thus, Soviet pilots in close-in formations had to signal by waving their wings and adopting defensive circles.

Over the Kuban, there was the important transition to the new and unique "transoceanic" fighter, the P-39 Airacobra. The appearance of this American fighter accelerated the process of reform in fighter tactics. With its powerful engine, which made the aircraft an ideal platform to test new air tactics, the Lend-Lease P-39 was capable of operating efficiently at greater altitudes than were the Yaks and LaGG fighters, but it was the Cobra's standard radio equipment and powerful weaponry that proved decisive. By this stage of the war, the VVS fighter command had begun to adapt to the *Luftwaffe's* formations of two and four aircraft—a transition already made by the Royal Air Force (RAF) in the Battle of Britain. The reformers, including Pokryshkin, called for the full exploitation of altitude or vertical maneuver, yet the process of reform moved forward in a piecemeal fashion and cannot be ascribed to one person. Some pilots displayed a certain suspicion toward the reforms; others actively embraced them. Major General Alexander Borman, commander of the 216th SAD that housed Pokryshkin's 16th GIAP, used his position to move the reforms forward, eventually winning the support of the 4th Air Army commander Konstantin Vershinin. It was Vershinin who applied the reforms to an entire air army.[74]

The role of new tactics marked the growing maturity and combat effectiveness of the VVS in 1943. Once embraced, these reforms shaped the VVS's combat role for the rest of the war. VVS air combat tactics in 1942 still possessed a formality, with prescriptions for optimal speeds, altitudes, and almost all flying maneuvers. Yet this highly scripted approach was changing under the pressures of war and the manifest superiority of the *Luftwaffe's* air tactics. Experienced VVS pilots were now given previously unthinkable liberties—the ability to select group composition, optimal formations, methods of engagement, and the most advantageous speed and altitude for a given assignment. The command "Do as I said" was replaced with "Do as I do."[75]

Luftwaffe pilots began to observe a mirror image of their own tactics in the VVS attack formations. Soviet pilots had been trained in the 1930s to fly in a tight horizontal pattern, in groups of three, and according to fixed rules. As with Britain's RAF, there was a belated recognition by the Russians that this type of formation was too inflexible and dangerous when engaged in combat against the *Luftwaffe*. The *Luftwaffe* flew in the *Rotte* and *Schwarm* formations, the former consisting of an element leader with a wingman, and the latter consisting of a "finger four" formation. This kind of organization allowed flexibility and maneuver, with all the advantages of attack and cover roles built into the basic two-man formation. With newer, high-performance aircraft and accumulated combat experience, Soviet fighter units began to break out of the straitjacket of prewar air combat tactics. The *para* and *zveno* formations appeared in 1942–1943 as copies of the *Rotte* and *Schwarm* to fully exploit the impressive maneuverability of Soviet fighter aircraft. The change was gradual and was accomplished in a piecemeal fashion. German pilots reported in 1943 that VVS fighters still formed into defensive circles once they were attacked, but more often than not, this maneuver was merely transitional. Rather than staying in a defensive formation, VVS fighters began to attack as soon as a favorable opportunity presented itself. Experienced Soviet pilots showed considerable initiative and flying skill in reaction to German attacks.[76]

Yet the air engagements over the Kuban, by definition, were chaotic and unpredictable, notwithstanding the emphasis on discipline, coordination, and group action. Georgiy Golubev, Pokryshkin's onetime wingman, recalled the endurance required for the dawn-to-dusk sorties. In the congested airspace above the Krymskaya sector, for example, dogfights arose with chilling suddenness, one following another. Once a pilot entered this deadly environment, he found himself in a confusing vortex of air combat: "the flash of tracers, the rattle of machine gun fire, flak bursts, and the wild intermingling of aircraft at various altitudes." Often, as Golubev observed, a single dogfight extended in an unpredictable fashion: "First a diving Bf 109 would trigger an attack by a Yak, which in turn drew into battle the intended victim's wingman. In a short time a LaGG appeared, quickly followed by a P-39 'Kobra.'" These fighters—at once hunters and hunted—"extended across the blue Kuban sky as if held together by an invisible thread." On the ground, maintenance crews, according to Golubev, worked feverishly to maintain this high level of operational activity. Their role was crucial and included a sequence of duties and gestures that the fighter pilot remembered with appreciation: "They fastened you in the cockpit, started the engine, and shouted parting words of encouragement."[77]

The 16th GIAP became one of the first regiments to make the transition to the Lend-Lease P-39 Airacobra. Both the air regiment and the much-maligned aircraft itself would gain no small amount of fame. Valeriy Romanenko, an expert on the history of the Airacobra in Russian service, writes that "Soviet pilots preferred the Cobra despite some of its shortcomings to any other aircraft received from the Allies, including the Spitfire VB."[78] When the first P-39s reached the Soviet Union in December 1941, both American and British air planners had already deemed the aircraft obsolescent. By 1943, in the North African and Sicilian campaigns, the U.S. Army Air Forces used the P-39 sparingly, largely for escort or coastal patrols. As with all Allied aircraft types shipped under Lend-Lease to the Soviets, there was a host of technical problems; in the case of the P-39, its deficiencies included a tendency to fall into a flat spin and certain engine defects. Yet the aircraft was a durable flying machine, agile, highly maneuverable, and equipped with powerful armament.

At the front, Soviet pilots found the P-39 a strange new aircraft that was, at first glance, a challenge to understand and master. The so-called "transoceanic fighter" came with some atypical features, most notably a tricycle landing gear, a fixed canopy, an engine mounted mid-fuselage, and peculiar automobile-style doors that opened on both sides (with roll-down windows). These doors hinged at the front, with the pilot routinely entering and exiting from the right side. German pilots such as Guenther Rall initially dismissed the unusual design as eccentric, even comical.[79] When Soviet pilots tested the P-39, they found many aspects of the cockpit design unfamiliar. Yet the aircraft possessed modern instrumentation, in particular, standard navigation equipment and well-designed radios. The armor plating offered the pilot considerable protection, with the forward windshield being constructed of bulletproof glass. The P-39's powerful armament—with forward-firing cannon—made it a lethal weapon when flown by an experienced pilot.[80]

THE KUBAN IN RETROSPECT

The intense air war over the Kuban, especially the final phase over the Blue Line, ushered Soviet fighter aviation into a new, more aggressive era. An outstanding group of Soviet fighter aces emerged in the Kuban skies. Gone were the days when Soviet fighters avoided the *Luftwaffe* or, if compelled to fight, found themselves totally ill equipped to contend with the enemy. German evaluations of the VVS in 1943 confirmed the dramatic improvement of Soviet fighter aviation. During the first years of the war, VVS fighter pilots, with a few exceptions, displayed little aggressiveness toward the *Luftwaffe*. The appalling VVS losses during the summer of 1941 conditioned Soviet fighter pilots to feel a profound sense of inferiority, a reflex reinforced by the objective circumstances of poor training, the confusion associated with outmoded tactics, deficiencies in command and control, and the transition to a new generation of fighter aircraft.

By 1943, Alexander Novikov, ably supported by innovative air army commanders, had guided the VVS to a higher level of flying proficiency. *Luftwaffe* fighter pilots and bomber crews could no longer operate freely and count on the passivity of the Soviet Air Force. Over the Kuban, in fact, VVS fighter units employed on a small scale the *Okhotniki*, or free hunter, tactic first used successfully at Stalingrad. Frequently, this meant the deployment of one *para*, always with skilled pilots, to the enemy rear to hit any targets of opportunity. Throughout the war, the VVS emphasized a flexible pattern of air combat formations in its fighter arm to meet shifting combat requirements. Sometimes the Soviet commanders complained that their fighters failed to provide effective support for the army. This became a serious problem in the Kuban, where the *Luftwaffe* conducted many ground attack and bomber raids on Soviet positions at Myskhako, at Krymskaya, and in Blue Line sectors. Soviet fighters displayed poor target selection, and during enemy bombing raids they attacked fighter escorts rather than the bombers. This allowed German bombers to strike their targets with little interference from Soviet interceptors.

Quickly learning their lessons, VVS fighter pilots made every effort to break up the German bomber formations and give the *para* formations an opportunity to attack individual aircraft. Close coordination with command posts on the ground allowed Soviet fighters to meet urgent requests for air support more effectively. Once enemy bombers entered an antiaircraft zone, the VVS fighters withdrew and flew parallel to the flight path of the enemy aircraft. If the enemy bombers approached in elements at different altitudes, the VVS fighters attacked the topmost group. To work in harmony with antiaircraft batteries, VVS pilots were briefed in detail on Soviet gun positions along the front lines. On occasion, VVS fighters executed a closed-circle maneuver to tempt German fighters into a Soviet antiaircraft zone.

Although the Kuban conflict of 1943 ended in a bloody stalemate—broken off after both sides failed to achieve their purposes—it proved to be the largest air combat encounter on the Eastern Front to date. The VVS challenged the *Luftwaffe* for local air superiority on an unprecedented scale. For the first time, the German fighter air arm faced a spirited contest from the VVS, and as German accounts testify, the VVS achieved a measure of air mastery during most phases of the Kuban fighting.

Such an air triumph was accompanied by high attrition in aircraft and personnel. Exact figures have not been published. Soviet accounts of the Kuban air war record 34,921 VVS sorties flown and the destruction of 1,100 German aircraft (800 in air combat), but they remain largely silent on Soviet personnel and aircraft losses.[81] German accounts, however, suggest a significant loss of VVS aircraft during the Kuban operations—as high as 1,300.[82] For latter-day historians, these rival claims are perplexing—they exceed the actual number of aircraft deployed by each side.

By June 7, 1943, the Kuban air engagements drew to a close. Two weeks later, the Military Council of the North Caucasus *Front* claimed victory in the air, noting that the VVS had compelled the *Luftwaffe* to abandon combat operations over the Kuban. On July 7, Air Commander Novikov issued a directive claiming that the VVS had emerged from the engagements with enhanced strength and control of the air. Propaganda aside, the Kuban air battle could not be called a victory in strictly military terms. The stalemate on the ground persisted, with the Red Army failing to achieve its objectives despite massive air support. There had been enormous losses in what had become the "Kuban Meat Grinder." Air superiority remained an elusive goal. The withdrawal of *Luftwaffe* units from the area signaled not a defeat but merely a prudent move to obligations elsewhere. However, one could argue that it was another kind of a victory—a psychological one. For the first time, VVS air units had employed innovative tactics on a large scale and achieved some measured success. These new air tactics were employed by many rank-and-file pilots, not just the most talented and experienced airmen. The Kuban allowed the VVS to employ innovative air tactics on a broad scale—from top to bottom in frontline squadrons, regiments, and divisions. It gave a tremendous boost of confidence to those who tasted success. It also became a stepping-stone for further mastery and advances. Those who weathered this battle became the backbone for a revitalized VVS in the battles to come. Like at Stalingrad, the *Luftwaffe* was capable of achieving local air superiority—but for only a short period. This diminished capability was a dramatic contrast to the formidable role the *Luftwaffe* had played in the summer of 1941.

Both sides now turned their attention to the North, to a salient occupied by the Red Army around the town of Kursk. Here, the Germans planned to launch their third summer offensive in Russia. Soviet intelligence had intercepted the German plans well in advance, and the *Stavka* now prepared to mobilize its air and ground forces to blunt the anticipated German attack and then launch the Soviets' first major summer offensive of the war. These events, already in motion at the time of the Blue Line engagements, quickly shifted the focus away from the Kuban sector.

At age twenty-two, Captain Petr Sgibnev took command of the 2nd GIAP of the air forces of the Northern Fleet. He was regarded as one of the most skilled Soviet Hurricane pilots. At the time of his death in an air accident on May 3, 1943, Sgibnev had been credited with sixteen personal and four shared air victories. He is shown here at Vayenga airfield in September 1942. (From the collection of Valeriy Romanenko)

Letters from home reach this pilot in the cockpit of his MiG-3 fighter aircraft. (From the collection of Von Hardesty)

Polikarpov U-2 (renamed Po-2 after the death of designer N. N. Polikarpov in July 1944) with a 200-pound (100-kilogram) FAB-100 bomb. These versatile aircraft were used extensively in night operations and in the most adverse weather conditions throughout the war. (From the collection of Valeriy Romanenko)

Beginning in March 1942, female volunteers filled the ranks of the army to serve as nurses, armorers, and parachute packers and in various support roles. Here, Junior Sergeants M. N. Gashina, N. P. Bessonova, and V. A. Stasenko are arming a Browning machine gun for a Lend-Lease A-20 medium bomber in the winter of 1943. (From the collection of Valeriy Romanenko)

Camouflage became a routine practice in wide-ranging VVS air operations. Shown here is the shielding of an Il-4 ADD bomber. (From the collection of Von Hardesty)

In August 1944, the 15th "Sevastopolskiy" GBAP of the ADD flew from the Uman airfield in Ukraine. A. Dudakov (in a jeep with the regiment commander) served as squadron commander for this air unit, which was assigned American-built B-25 medium bombers. (From the collection of Aleksandr Dudakov via Oleg Korytov)

Dramatic photograph of two Soviet Il-4 long-range bombers in flight, date and locale unknown. (From the collection of Von Hardesty)

Il-4T torpedo bomber with a 45-36AV torpedo on its way to the target. (From the collection of Oleg Korytov)

This Ju 88 bomber crew celebrates the benchmark of 1,000 sorties flown in the East. For *Luftwaffe* bomber crews, attrition remained high throughout the war. (From the collection of Von Hardesty)

The American P-39 Airacobra proved to be ideally suited for the Eastern Front. It was highly prized by elite Guards units, which flew P-39s against the Luftwaffe with great success. Pictured left to right are Senior Lieutenant N. G. Kuzmin (eight victories) and deputy regiment commander Captain A. A. Yegorov (twenty-five personal plus six shared victories) of the 212th GIAP attached to the 2nd Air Army, 1st Ukrainian *Front,* Germany, 1945. (From the collection of Oleg Korytov)

Aircrews of the 2nd Air Army are given instructions on the ShKAS machine gun installed on a Po-2 night bomber, Ukraine, 1944. (From the collection of Valeriy Romanenko)

This Bell P-63 Kingcobra had the honor of being the 5,000th airplane delivered to the VVS via the ALSIB route. Left to right: Colonel Russel Keillor, Brigadier General Dale Guffney, and Colonel Petr Kiselev at Ladd Field, Alaska, September 10, 1944. (From the collection of Von Hardesty)

Armorer Korneyko of the air forces of the Black Sea Fleet readies a 100-pound (50-kilogram) FAB-50 bomb for installation. The inscription on the bomb reads "A Gift for Hitler." (From the collection of Von Hardesty)

A Soviet ground crew repairs a battle-damaged Il-2 Shturmovik. Keeping combat aircraft operational required no small amount of effort. (From the collection of Valeriy Romanenko)

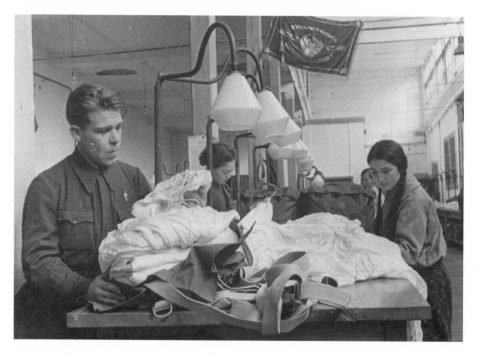

The home front was critical to the war effort. Here, workers prepare a parachute for transfer to the front. (From the collection of Von Hardesty)

This wounded Soviet airman managed to return to his home air base,
where ground crewmen offer assistance, date and locale unknown.
(From the collection of Von Hardesty)

Pilot of a Pe-2 dive-bomber. His flight garb is typical of that worn by VVS
airmen in the war. (From the collection of Von Hardesty)

Yak-1B fighter in flight. (From the collection of Von Hardesty)

Soviet naval aviators stand next to a Lend-Lease flying boat, a PBY-6A Catalina. The Soviet Union received 48 Consolidated PBY-6A Catalinas and 137 Consolidated PBN-1 Nomads. (From the collection of Oleg Korytov)

Lieutenant Yevgeniy Tushkov of the 21st GIAP on the wing of his P-39, which showcases one of his awards—the Order of Glory. He achieved 7 personal victories in 150 sorties and 40 engagements. (From the collection of Aleksey Pekarsh)

A rare relaxed moment for a Pe-2 bomber crew with the air unit's mascot, 1st Ukrainian *Front*, ca. 1944. (From the collection of Von Hardesty)

Highly prized Tu-2 bombers in flight to the target. (From the collection of Valeriy Romanenko)

At the Central Aerodrome in Moscow, the interned American B-29 "General H. H. Arnold Special" is disassembled piece by piece to copy its parts. This clandestine work set the stage for the production of the Tu-4 strategic bomber, which made its debut in 1947. (From the collection of Von Hardesty)

Three-time recipients of the highest Soviet award, Hero of the Soviet Union. Left to right: Colonel A. I. Pokryshkin, Marshal G. K. Zhukov, and Major I. N. Kozhedub. (From the collection of Valeriy Romanenko)

Air Marshal Aleksandr Novikov, the highly talented and energetic VVS air commander from 1942 to 1945. (From the collection of Von Hardesty)

Colonel General (as of August 1944, Marshal of Aviation) S. A. Khudyakov, whose wartime duties included VVS chief of staff and deputy VVS commander. In December 1945, he was accused of treason and arrested. He was executed on April 18, 1950, only to be posthumously rehabilitated in 1954. (From the collection of Valeriy Romanenko)

Colonel General M. M. Gromov, commander of the 3rd Air Army (May 1942–May 1943) and the 1st Air Army (May 1943–June 1944). On July 12–14, 1937, Gromov, along with A. B. Yumashev and S. A. Danilin, made a world-record transpolar flight in a single-engine Tupolev ANT-25, covering 6,306 miles (10,148 kilometers) from Moscow to San Jacinto, California. (From the collection of Valeriy Romanenko)

Lieutenant General K. A. Vershinin, commander of the 4th Air Army. From 1946 to 1949, he was VVS commander. (From the collection of Valeriy Romanenko)

Major General I. S. Polbin, commander of the 2nd Guards Bomber Air Corps. A talented air commander, Polbin flew 157 combat missions. He was killed during his last mission on February 11, 1945, in the Breslau area after taking a direct hit by an antiaircraft round. (From the collection of Valeriy Romanenko)

Soviet aircraft designers. Left to right: S. A. Lavochkin, A. N. Tupolev, A. S. Yakovlev, and A. I. Mikoyan. (From the collection of Valeriy Romanenko)

Chapter Five

Kursk

When Hitler and the German High Command planned their third major offensive in the summer of 1943, they targeted the Soviet-held bastion around the small city of Kursk. The salient measured 150 miles (241 kilometers) long and 100 miles (161 kilometers) wide. The fortified Soviet enclave occupied a crucial position some 300 miles (483 kilometers) south of Moscow. It was situated in the middle of the long Eastern Front, then extending from Leningrad southward through Novgorod, Smolensk, and Kharkov to Taganrog on the Sea of Azov. The projected German offensive, code-named Operation Citadel, called for a powerful pincer movement against this exposed Soviet position: the Ninth Army was to advance southward from Orel, while the Fourth Panzer Army was to spearhead a drive northward from the Belgorod–Kharkov sector.

Unlike previous summer campaigns, Operation Citadel, by design, pursued only limited objectives. For the *Wehrmacht* in 1943, there were no planned thrusts deep into Russian territory or grandiose ambitions of toppling the Soviet regime in one decisive offensive. By encircling the Kursk salient, the Germans hoped to knock out a powerful Soviet army grouping, straighten out the forward line to allow better lateral communication, and strengthen the overall strategic position of the German forces in the aftermath of the debacle at Stalingrad. The limited scope of the Kursk offensive mirrored the ever-shrinking capacity of Hitler's war machine: in 1941, the *Wehrmacht* had invaded the Soviet Union on three axes and established a 994-mile (1,600-kilometer) front; by 1942, the offensive to Stalingrad and the North Caucasus engaged the Soviets along a 354-mile (570-kilometer) front; now, at Kursk in the summer of 1943, Germany's armed forces in the East concentrated on a narrow 124-mile (200-kilometer) front.[1] If successful, the offensive would set the stage for a deeper penetration by the

Wehrmacht into the vast region southeast of Stalingrad. Nazi Germany mobilized a large concentration of armor and airpower to assure breakthrough zones north and south of Kursk. Hoping to catch the Russians off balance, Field Marshals Erich von Manstein and Guenther von Kluge, the German army group commanders, had urged an early May date for the offensive, to coincide with the end of the *Rasputitsa,* or rainy season.

In 1943, the widely dispersed German military was thinly spread across myriad fronts. This deployment alone created vulnerability to Soviet counterattack and encirclement. Moreover, the Germans were now engaged in total war with ever-diminishing resources. Intense fighting in North Africa had led to a major retreat and withdrawal by the *Wehrmacht*. This Allied victory set the stage for the invasion of Sicily. Anglo-American bombing missions acquired a new intensity and lethality, with around-the-clock sorties attacking targets in the Third Reich and Nazi-occupied territories. The specter of an Allied invasion in northern Europe haunted German war planners. The attack on the Kursk salient offered a unique opportunity to reverse German military fortunes in the East in advance of an Allied invasion.

The German decision to strike at Kursk, however, was compromised by many delays. Hitler, in fact, decided to postpone Operation Citadel to allow the deployment of the latest Pz. Kpfw V Panther and Pz. Kpfw VI Tiger tanks.[2] This delay would prove to be fateful because it allowed the Soviets ample time to prepare elaborate and echeloned defenses at the Kursk salient. The old blitzkrieg formula of dive-bombers, intense artillery bombardment, and massive blows by advancing tanks with supporting infantry would be tested in a decisive way. As the *Wehrmacht* soon learned, the Soviet defense of the Kursk salient would follow a different script from the one employed in northern France in 1940.

The *Luftwaffe* component earmarked for the Kursk offensive represented about 66 percent of the total German combat aircraft on the Eastern Front.[3] For the summer offensive, selected German air units were transferred from Germany, France, Norway, and other sectors of the Russian Front to forward airfields near Kursk in the spring of 1943. Following an elaborate timetable, these reinforcements arrived in stages prior to July 5, the revised date to launch the summer offensive. Two major *Luftwaffe* concentrations—*Luftflotte* 6 (Orel) and *Luft-*

flotte 4 (Belgorod–Kharkov)—took shape in May and June with a combined strength of around 1,800 aircraft.[4] General Hans Jeschonnek, the talented *Luftwaffe* chief of staff, supervised the gradual buildup of airpower for the Kursk operation. At the start of the offensive, the 1st Air Division and *Fliegerkorps* VIII consisted of 730 and 1,100 aircraft, respectively. The air contingent consisted of 340 single-engine and 55 twin-engine fighters, 400 single-engine dive-bombers, 550 twin-engine bombers, and approximately 180 ground attack planes.[5] The mobilization of such air elements in one sector had the predictable consequence of exposing the northern and southern sectors of the German frontal positions to VVS air attack. For example, there was now only one fighter group in the Leningrad area—II/JG 54. The southern sector was better covered with the deployment of Romanian air units as part of *Fliegerkorps* I and IV. Slovak and Croat pilots were also active in the II/JG 52 group flying in the Crimean–Taman peninsula sector. The deployment of German air units north and south of Kursk required a precise schedule and the construction of new airfields—all to be accomplished without giving away telltale signs of German intentions.

By June 1943, the Soviet partisan movement in the occupied areas had already grown to a formidable size with the capacity to disrupt the tenuous supply lines from Germany to the East. The German rear had become a second front, with countless acts of sabotage by partisans against enemy personnel and supply lines. Logistical problems for the *Luftwaffe* arose at the same time, with considerable efforts expended to overcome both the rigors of geography and partisan warfare. On the eve of Kursk, partisans increased the tempo of incidents; some 841 separate acts were reported, which delivered a significant blow to the overstretched German supply lines. For the *Luftwaffe*, aviation fuel and spare parts were routinely in short supply. All these factors severely limited the extent (and sustainability) of German air operations.[6] A more fundamental consideration, however, was the fact that *Luftflotten* 6 and 4 entered the Kursk air operations without substantial reserves. If Operation Citadel stalled and became a prolonged struggle, the normal attrition in aircraft and crews would quickly and dramatically weaken the *Luftwaffe*'s striking power. Already, German air units found it difficult to assert and maintain local air superiority, even as German ground units demanded increased ground support.

The Soviet High Command approached the Battle of Kursk with measured confidence. There was no ignorance or uncertainty about the enemy's strategic planning. Rudolph Rossler and the "Lucy Ring," having penetrated the higher levels of the German High Command, provided the *Stavka* with accurate intelligence. With this foreknowledge of German intentions, Soviet military planners constructed elaborate and echeloned defensive fortifications within the Kursk salient. Hitler's fateful decision to delay the start of the offensive until July gave Moscow the fortuitous opportunity to thoroughly mobilize its growing air and ground forces to meet the German challenge.

There were two large army groupings at the core of Soviet defenses at Kursk: the Central *Front* under General K. K. Rokossovskiy, and the Voronezh *Front* under General N. F. Vatutin. To the southeast, in reserve, was the Steppe *Front* commanded by General I. S. Konev. Within the bulge proper, the *Stavka* placed two-thirds of its artillery and tanks to blunt the anticipated thrusts north and south of Kursk. Rokossovskiy and Vatutin together commanded a formidable military force: 1.3 million troops, 20,000 guns and mortars, 3,600 tanks and self-propelled guns, and 2,212 combat aircraft.[7] At Kursk, the *Stavka* deployed the largest number of combat aircraft for frontline operations since the summer of 1941. The total strength of the VVS, drawn from the 2nd (Voronezh *Front*), 16th (Central *Front*), and 17th (Southwestern *Front*) Air Armies, stood at 2,650 aircraft of various types; if air units from the PVO and long-range aviation were included, this number swelled to nearly 3,700 aircraft.[8] At the end of the Kursk campaign, there would be a total of six air armies deployed against the enemy. The augmented airpower on the Soviet side reflected the renewed capacity of the relocated aviation factories and the timely shipments of Lend-Lease aircraft.[9] The Soviet aircraft production rate had increased threefold since December 1941, when the aviation factories had resumed production beyond the Ural Mountains. Whereas in 1942 it had taken 20,000 man-hours to manufacture an Il-4 bomber, it now required only 12,500 man-hours.[10]

The refinement of VVS organization and deployment continued unabated in these most perilous times. There were ongoing changes in response to combat experience and the pressures associated with the rapid growth in aircraft inventory, new technologies, and evolving air tactical doctrines. One major change in the second half of 1942 was

Installation of an AM-38 engine in an Il-2 Shturmovik on the production line at Aviation Factory Number 18 in Kuybyshev (now Samara). A total of 36,154 Il-2s of various types were manufactured during the war years. (From the collection of Valeriy Romanenko)

the creation of an air corps organization. Specialized fighter, bomber, and ground attack air corps took shape to assure greater effectiveness. These were not necessarily fixed configurations; there were exceptions to the rule, but they were considered optimal to meet the demands of a highly dynamic situation. Air divisions were usually composed of three to five regiments. Some ground attack divisions— for example, the 224th, 225th, and 291st ShADs—possessed separate attached fighter regiments. Training for eventual transition to a combat zone attained a high priority. The new quantitative edge enjoyed by the VVS allowed the organization of fresh regiments in immediate rear areas. Of the approximately 4,000 aircraft made available in May 1943, a total of 3,133 were assigned to frontal aviation. This rapid pace of augmentation in aircraft continued into June, as evident in the formation of the 7th and 8th IAKs. In July, the VVS command formed the 10th IAK and the 5th and 7th ShAKs (*Shturmovoy Aviatsionnyy Korpus*, or ground attack air corps). By the time of the Kursk struggle, the air corps configuration had been consolidated into a pivotal organizational scheme.[11]

The Soviet war planning dictated an impregnable set of defenses at Kursk. On the eve of the battle, in June 1943, Moscow organized a *levee en masse*—a civilian labor force of 300,000 people—to build a succession of defensive lines to stop the German infantry and tanks. Three fortified lines, positioned at intervals over a distance of 25 miles (40 kilometers), stood ready to meet the full force of the German attack.[12] Three thousand miles (4,828 kilometers) of trench lines, numerous tank traps, and an elaborate system of fortified defensive positions fashioned from wood and earth protected Kursk in echelons along the anticipated breakthrough corridors. More than 400,000 mines were laid. Forward Soviet airfields now bristled with fighter and ground attack aircraft, poised like a coiled spring to challenge the *Luftwaffe* for air superiority and to assist ground forces in the destruction of enemy mechanized units.

If these elaborate defenses failed, General Konev's Steppe *Front* armies stood ready to intervene, along with additional infantry and tank reserves available in the Soviet rear. Once the defensive phase had achieved its purpose and Operation Citadel had been blunted, the *Stavka* planned to break out of the Kursk bastion. In the North, armies of the Western, Bryansk, and Central *Fronts* would overwhelm Orel;

farther south, the Voronezh, Steppe, and Southwestern *Front* forces would advance against Belgorod and Kharkov. As they had at Moscow in 1942, the *Stavka* hoped to roll the Germans back, this time toward Kiev and the Dnieper River, in the first major summer offensive of the war. The counteroffensive at Kursk would signal an end to the long and costly period of defensive warfare.

Soviet air preparations for defense of the Kursk salient began in mid-April 1943 and consisted of two air armies: the 16th under General S. I. Rudenko, attached to the Central *Front* below Orel, and the 2nd under General S. A. Krasovskiy, supporting the Voronezh *Front* in the Belgorod–Kharkov sector. The 17th Air Army of General V. A. Sudets of the Southwestern *Front* had been identified for deployment in defensive operations. Numbering over 2,650 combat aircraft, the 16th, 2nd, and 17th Air Armies boasted 1,062 fighters, 900 ground attack aircraft, 674 bombers, and 14 reconnaissance planes.[13] These robust figures reflected the operational aircraft available to air commanders of the participating air armies. In fact, the VVS now surpassed the *Luftwaffe*'s air strength quantitatively. Moreover, both the 16th and 2nd Air Armies mirrored the technical advances of the VVS now apparent at midwar: frontline fighters such as the sleek Yak-1b and Yak-7b and the radial-engine La-5 were worthy matches to the German Messerschmitt Bf 109G and Fw 190; the redoubtable Il-2 Shturmovik ground attack aircraft, now in mass production in a double-seat version, had been fitted with an advanced and durable AM-38F engine; and the whole inventory of Soviet warplanes included a significant addition of Lend-Lease aircraft, including the A-20 "Boston" twin-engine bomber and the P-39 Airacobra fighter. New arrivals consisted of Yak-9D and T versions, along with the radial-engine La-5FN, but their quantities remained limited.[14]

When compared with German aircraft, the newly arriving Soviet warplanes still embodied certain technical inferiorities, even though this gap had been narrowed dramatically. Given the raw materials at hand, Soviet aircraft often possessed many wood components. Poor-quality assembly resulted from a dearth of skilled laborers. These defects resulted in poor performance, more often than not leading to an unacceptable number of noncombat crashes and accidents. The poor standards of Soviet aircraft production soon prompted the anger of Stalin. When he learned that a significant number of VVS aircraft were ill suited for combat on the eve of the German offensive at Kursk, he called for an emergency meeting of the People's Commissariat of the Aircraft Industry to address the problems in quality control and performance, which included new repair and maintenance brigades being sent to the front.

On June 6, the first maintenance battalion reached the 16th Air Army. It would soon be reinforced by similar technical cadres working feverishly to inspect and service defective combat aircraft at some 12 frontline airfields.[15] These events were part of a larger pattern of preparatory work that included the deployment of airfield servicing battalions (BAOs) to build or renovate 154 airfields in advance of the German offensive.[16] These BAO units, assisted by civilian laborers, also constructed 50 "dummy" airstrips to confuse the enemy. At each airfield, large quantities of munitions and fuel were stockpiled to sustain air operations for fifteen days. Moreover, at this juncture, the transition to modern types of aircraft (Soviet and Lend-Lease) was nearly complete; only night bomber units, equipped with U-2s, flew prewar models in the summer of 1943.[17]

One persistent problem for the VVS in the weeks leading up to Kursk was the absence of properly trained flight crews. This deficiency—a persistent one going back to the prewar days—was now acute. In 1942, the dearth of trained aircrews had prompted the VVS leadership to critically examine flight school curricula and training programs then under way in the reserve units. With expanding air inventories, new air armies and air corps, and the need to adapt to shifting challenges from a still-powerful *Luftwaffe*, Soviet air commanders moved quickly to reform the training programs. Modernization and rigorous new standards were introduced in flight schools and reserve air units. Overarching all these changes was the goal of adapting training to actual combat experience, with a stress on incorporating war-induced lessons into the training regimen. Unforeseen problems in 1943, such as shortages in fuel, compromised the effectiveness of training programs. New pilots often had only minimal frontline training in combat aircraft—some with as little as fifteen to twenty hours, and others with as few as five to eight hours. Selecting commanders for small units also proved difficult in this context, as many pilots lacked extensive combat experience. Bomber crews often lacked proper navigational knowledge, the skill to coordinate missions with fighter escorts, and baseline experience in bombing targets with accuracy. A series of "friendly fire" incidents in May–June, in which VVS bomber crews attacked their own troops, led to formal inquiries and swift demotions of certain personnel. The baseline requirement to monitor compliance with all military orders, particularly new training standards, took on a new and compelling urgency for the VVS air staff.[18]

After-action reports for the 1st BAK of the 2nd Air Army revealed a pattern of poor performance and even accusations of "criminal" behavior for the reckless bombing of its own ground troops. Documents from the 293rd BAD, for example, revealed a whole range of inadequacies, mostly linked to the inferior training program: poor flying technique, inattention to proper radio communications, and lack of coordination with fighter escorts. According to this report, some aircrews were slow to follow orders and displayed a high degree of disorientation in the combat zones. Certain steps were taken to remedy the situation, in particular, the forging of an effective command of bomber units over targeted areas.[19] Since staff training was minimal or nonexistent in some air units, there was no effective way to monitor performance. The proper coordination of air and ground action remained an elusive goal on many occasions.

Though impressive, the Soviet air deployment proved to be less than overwhelming. The VVS certainly failed to make optimal use of its quantitative edge because of the lingering gap with the *Luftwaffe* when it came to qualitative factors such as experienced aircrews, consistent use of modern air tactics, and effective command and control techniques. The Germans' qualitative advantage was most evident in the fighter air arm. As the intense battle unfolded, the key to the ultimate success of the Soviet Air Force would rest with the *Stavka*'s capacity to maintain an effective flow of reinforcements. Stalin had emphasized the creation of massive air reserves in rear areas, along with tank, artillery, and infantry concentrations, that could be thrown into battle at crucial moments. By 1943, the Air Corps of the *Stavka* Reserve had grown into a vast reservoir of airpower, fueling the various air armies with a seemingly endless flow of aircraft and aircrews. On March 29, 1943, Novikov ordered these reserves to be used only along the major axes of offensive operations. He wisely refused to permit his vital air reserves to be dispersed aimlessly into the various air armies.

Such VVS reserve components, by order of the *Stavka*, moved back to the rear once a sector ceased to be an active combat zone.

During the arduous apprenticeship in the first two years of the war, the VVS High Command learned the advantages of centralization and mobility. With the increased tempo of air combat operations in 1943, Novikov acquired additional experience in using reserves to achieve overwhelming local air superiority in key offensive operations. At Kursk, he faced the challenge of orchestrating the various operational air armies: the 2nd, 16th, and 17th in the defensive stage, and the addition of the 1st and 15th Air Armies during offensive operations. Moreover, there was the realization that the VVS could not wait in a defensive posture for the enemy to attack. Launching preemptive air strikes wherever possible in German rear areas to create confusion and slow the flow of reinforcements to the front became an urgent task. For example, on April 22, VVS bombers attacked *Luftwaffe* reconnaissance bases at Orsha and Orsha South, inflicting severe losses and leaving the enemy with only one strategic reconnaissance air unit operational in the Kursk sector.[20]

The intensely fought Kuban air campaign had demonstrated to Novikov and his staff the enormous effort required to coordinate several air armies in joint operations. Along the vast sweep of the Eastern Front, Novikov tightened his administrative control and insisted on effective lateral communication among the staffs of the various air armies. During the Kuban period, he had perfected techniques for adjacent air armies to maintain daily contact with one another. As the VVS approached the Kursk air battle, there was a keen awareness that in the sphere of organization, the period of apprenticeship had passed. For the first time, the VVS could display its newly acquired skills in coordinating major air operations.

At the top, the *Stavka* made a concerted effort to recruit talent for the higher echelon of the air force command structure, promoting capable officers to key administrative and planning positions. In May 1943, General S. A. Khudyakov assumed the post of air force chief of staff. In a subsequent appointment, the talented General F. Ya. Falaleyev became deputy commander of the air force. The Soviet Air Force Military Council expanded its role as the overall planning and mobilization center for Soviet airpower, paying particular attention to improving the training programs for pilots, navigators, and air personnel. To be avoided at all costs were the aerial defeats of earlier campaigns, when hastily trained pilots and aircrews had entered combat, sometimes in units as large as squadrons or regiments, with no practical training. Soviet air planners had learned that pilot training must embody the lessons of combat. Stalingrad had shown the requirements for conducting an effective air blockade, and the Kuban had been the occasion to update fighter combat tactics; now Kursk would offer its own crucible to test the VVS on both defensive and offensive air operations. During 1943, Novikov wisely allowed the curriculum for VVS combat tactics to be rewritten at the front. Once the gulf between operational reality and rear training programs was narrowed, the VVS began to demonstrate improved skills in large offensive operations.

The VVS High Command carefully monitored the German buildup for Operation Citadel. Only certain tactical details of the planned offensive had not been fully disclosed to Soviet intelligence, along with any last-minute changes made by German field commanders. The VVS 4th RAP, for example, had discovered a large concentration of enemy tanks near Orel on May 14, the first real confirmation of Operation Citadel.[21] In time, the systematic use of air reconnaissance revealed the details of the planned German summer offensive: troop groupings, a network of airfields, patterns of aircraft deployment, defensive fortifications, artillery positions, staging areas, and reserves. For the first time, the VVS made full use of aerial photography as an aid to operational planning.

Air intelligence officers closely monitored the movement of *Luftwaffe* air units, especially those deployed adjacent to the frontline sectors. The 16th Air Army took special pains to track segments of enemy infantry and mechanized units in the Orel–Glasunovka and Orel–Bryansk sectors. To achieve more accurate intelligence data, the 454th BAP of the 2nd Air Army intensified its regular intelligence-gathering duties. Similar steps were taken with bomber squadrons of the 244th BAD in the 17th Air Army, where fast Lend-Lease Boston aircraft were deployed for reconnaissance sweeps over enemy territory. On July 1, VVS aircraft spotted a concentration of German tanks, apparently from XLIII Panzer Corps, in the areas of Tomarovka, Zybino, and Borisovka. Upon hearing this alarming news, the command of the Voronezh *Front* ordered a new round of aerial photographs of enemy positions to a depth of 6 miles (10 kilometers). Although this exercise in air intelligence proved useful and timely, VVS intelligence failed to track the precise movements of II SS Panzer Corps, one of the main elements in the forthcoming German offensive at Kursk. This intelligence failure proved to be a negative factor in shaping the course of the defensive battles north of Belgorod.[22]

With five VVS air armies deployed at forward airstrips in and around the Kursk salient, the Soviet battle plan dictated a precise and coordinated application of airpower for the defensive stage. The 17th and 2nd Air Armies shared airfields to allow optimal maneuver. Moreover, they allocated up to 180 aircraft whenever necessary for mutual reinforcement. The actions of the 2nd and 17th Air Armies were coordinated by the *Stavka*.[23] For the first time in the war, the VVS entered a major battle with a solid logistical base. Operation Citadel occurred against a backdrop of overall Soviet military renewal. The earlier combat experiences at Stalingrad and in the Kuban heralded the revived combat capabilities of Soviet airpower. Novikov approached Kursk with confidence, sharing the growing awareness that the pendulum had swung in a dramatic way toward the Soviet side. At the time, however, German military planners saw their recent losses as reversals, not decisive defeats. At Kursk, they planned to reassert the strategic initiative on the Eastern Front. The *Luftwaffe* had suffered serious losses in aircraft and crews in the brutal conflicts of the past year, and these could not be easily replaced. Though weakened, German airpower at Kursk was still considerable, consisting of 552 bombers, 339 single-engine fighters, 55 twin-engine fighters, 176 ground attack planes, 396 dive-bombers, 148 reconnaissance aircraft, and 115 miscellaneous aircraft.[24]

Compared with the *Luftwaffe*, the VVS had more than twice as many fighters and enjoyed superiority in absolute numbers in ground attack planes. Only in day bombers did the *Luftwaffe* hold the advantage.[25] Along with increased mass production, the Soviets' ability to design high-performance combat aircraft was improving. At Kursk, the VVS introduced its La-5FN fighter to match the *Luftwaffe's* new Fw 190. A radial-engine mutation of the ineffectual LaGG-3, the La-5 (and its later iteration, the La-7) quickly achieved rough parity with the Fw 190. Between 6,500 and 13,000 feet (1,980 and 3,960 meters), the Soviets claimed the La-5FN was 25 to 50 miles (40 to 80 kilometers) faster

La-5 fighters ready for a combat sortie, Belgorod area, 1943. (From the collection of Valeriy Romanenko)

than the Fw 190 in horizontal flight—and more maneuverable. In the savage air combat to come over Kursk, the VVS surpassed the *Luftwaffe* in total aircraft by 1.4 to 2.7 times, depending on the phase of the battle and the circumstances.

Major Guenther Rall, now one of Germany's most proficient aces, flew with the III/JG 52 out of a primitive and "crater-pocked" airstrip near Belgorod. He encountered a Soviet La-5 fighter—hitherto unknown to many German airmen—on his first sortie over the Kursk salient. He observed: "It was late afternoon, around 5 o'clock, I was flying on a westerly heading [in] a standard two-ship formation . . . at 19,000 feet (5,800 meters). . . . I saw two spots coming toward us. Behind them was a huge, wide cumulus cloud. . . . It was dazzlingly bright. We approached at full power, and as we got closer and closer, I was able to detect what appeared to be radial engines. . . . I thought they might be the new Focke-Wulf FW 190s with the stubby nose that had arrived on the Russian Front two days earlier. . . . I couldn't see the plane's colors or emblems." As a precaution, Rall climbed to gain height and to secure a better vantage point to identify the approaching mystery planes. Rall then caught the distinctive livery of Soviet fighters—the telltale dark green color and red stars. For the first time, Rall saw the newly deployed La-5 radial-engine fighter at Kursk. However, the German ace found himself dangerously close to his adversaries—a mere 165 feet (50 meters) above the Soviet fighters. Rall acted instinctively, making a steep dive and firing a full burst into the cockpit of one of the La-5s. The maneuver, if effective, closed the range sharply between the two aircraft, forcing Rall to pull up his Bf 109 in an attempt to avoid a collision. That proved impossible, and he smacked violently into the Soviet fighter: "The noise of grinding metal as our aircraft smash[ed] one against the other in mid-air was unbelievably loud. My propeller cut off his right wing. As my speed carried me over him his prop sliced my undercarriage, slashing the fuselage . . . he went into a spin and never recovered, poor guy. . . . I thought the engine was about to break off, so I adjusted the throttle . . . to smooth it out, but nothing worked. I was 13,000 feet (3,960 meters) over Russian territory and needing to land. . . . I made my turns very gently . . . careful to pull no Gs so the aircraft wouldn't break apart." Rall eventually made it back to German-held territory, landing in a field near his base. For Rall and his fellow fighter pilots, the debut of the La-5 came as a surprise—a reality German intelligence had failed to detect and report. Rall recorded in his memoirs that his forward air unit systematically monitored Soviet radio communications, using Russian volunteers to gather technical and operational data; this tool, however, had not disclosed the deployment of the La-5 in the Kursk sector.[26]

Rall's near-fatal sortie was part of a larger series of air strikes by the *Luftwaffe*. German bombers and ground attack aircraft hit Soviet lines of communication, rail junctions, airfields, and supply depots. The first massed air raid on Kursk itself occurred on May 22, when 170 German bombers attempted to knock out the rail terminal. This particular aerial incursion by the *Luftwaffe* did not go unchallenged. According to Soviet accounts, fighter aircraft from the 2nd and 16th Air Armies, along with fighter aircraft from the 101st Fighter Air Division (PVO), intercepted the German bombers on the approaches to Kursk.[27] Again on June 2–3 the *Luftwaffe* made another major effort to destroy the Kursk rail terminal. More than 400 bombers in several waves exceeding 150 aircraft participated in this mission, according to Soviet accounts.[28] The combined day and night bombing raid prompted a spirited reaction by the VVS, along with air elements attached to the Kursk air defense zone. Coming in waves and from different directions, the *Luftwaffe* bombers successfully penetrated the Kursk air defenses and put the rail terminal out of action for twelve hours. Certain Soviet sources list 145 German aircraft downed (104 by VVS fighters and 41 by antiaircraft fire), with a modest loss of 27 Soviet fighters. They note that this massed air raid was an important benchmark, "the last major daytime raid by fascist aviation against Soviet rear facilities."[29]

During this same period, air elements from the 1st, 15th, 16th, 2nd, 17th, and 8th Air Armies participated in one of the largest VVS air raids of the war. Between May 6 and 8, they hit a number of German airfields situated along a 735-mile (1,183-kilometer) sector in the central part of the front opposite Kursk. Novikov aimed to disrupt the German air buildup for Operation Citadel, then in progress.[30] A month later, between June 8 and 10, the VVS again struck at German airfields—this time, the *Luftwaffe* air bases from which strategic bombing raids were being conducted against Soviet war industries at Gorkiy, Saratov, and Yaroslavl.[31] Such massive air raids represented an important milestone, dramatically demonstrating the growing strength and range of VVS operations. At best, however, the VVS bombers only weakened *Luftwaffe* air strength in the offensive zones (in 1943, Soviet bomber units remained the least effective branch of the expanding VVS). Wherever they were attempted, these bold daylight raids on *Luftwaffe* air bases proved costly in VVS aircraft, a fact concealed in Soviet histories of the air war in the East. Such raids were a crucial part of VVS planning.

The Soviets, in fact, achieved greater success against German rail and road communications with their night raids. The rapid increase in night bombing sorties on the eve of Kursk greatly alarmed the German command. In addition to attacking airfields, the *Stavka* deployed ADD night bombers to hit rail centers and supply depots filled with materiel earmarked for Operation Citadel. The *Luftwaffe* countered these attacks by deploying both light and heavy flak units at crucial points. The absence of *Luftwaffe* night fighters meant that VVS aircraft could penetrate the combat zones in large numbers. Among all the Soviet wartime air operations, these persistent and highly effective night bomber units received the least attention.[32]

Crew of a Soviet Pe-8 heavy bomber (serial number 42058) with ASh-82 radial engines, Kratovo airfield, June 1943. When this bomber, belonging to the 746th BAP of the ADD, was shot down on July 21, 1943, half the crew was killed. (From the collection of Valeriy Romanenko)

The VVS now broadened the scope of free-hunting tactics with the *Okhotniki* at Kursk, including for the first time large numbers of Shturmovik pilots. By maintaining a continuous air presence in enemy rear areas during the day—even in the most extreme weather—the *Okhotniki* applied enormous pressure on the *Luftwaffe* and the German antiaircraft crews ordered to protect vital supply and communication lines. In groups of two to four aircraft, the *Okhotniki* roamed over their assigned zones as cunning and mobile predators attacking trains, motorized columns, and infantry. Whenever they discovered a German train, they hit the locomotive first; if they spotted a motorized column, they hit the lead vehicle. The *Okhotniki,* flying in either fighter or ground attack planes, helped fill the acknowledged Soviet void in day bombers, even as they enlarged the scope of air operations. During the two months prior to the Battle of Kursk, these free hunters flew 2,000 sorties. Even so, they did not significantly interrupt the flow of German supplies and reserves. But they did manage to extend Soviet airpower into the German rear and compel the hard-pressed *Luftwaffe* to diffuse its finite resources. Many of the regiments or air elements transferred for work as "hunters" flew their high-risk frontline assignments hurriedly and with minimal training. Most sorties were flown against enemy rail and road convoys. The Soviet command assumed that bombers from ADD would offer the optimal pressure for these targets.[33]

THE KURSK OFFENSIVE UNFOLDS

The script for Operation Citadel called for the German armies to begin their two-pronged drive on Kursk on the morning of July 5. Already alerted to the German plans (if not the precise time and place of the offensive), the Soviets launched a bold predawn raid on five *Luftwaffe* airfields in the vicinity of Kharkov. About 300 combat aircraft (100 Il-2s escorted by 94 fighters in the strike group and another 102 fighters tasked with blocking German airfields) from the 2nd and 17th Air Armies participated in this mission, which sought to catch the enemy bombers at the very moment they were assembling for their opening sorties against the Kursk salient. Soon after the large Soviet bomber formation was airborne, German radar detected their flight path. The *Luftwaffe* command quickly ordered fighters from the Belgorod and Kharkov sectors—JG 3 and JG 52—to intercept the oncoming air armada. Just at daybreak, the Soviet aircraft pierced the German-controlled airspace over Kharkov, where they faced waves of *Luftwaffe* fighters.

The resulting air engagement became one of the most spectacular of the war. More than 120 VVS aircraft, by *Luftwaffe* estimates, were downed. General Hans Jeschonnek, chief of the *Luftwaffe* General Staff, watched the unfolding air battle from a command post of *Fliegerkorps* VIII. German fighter pilots took a fearful toll of the attacking Soviet aircraft above 10,000 feet (3,000 meters). When the Soviet bombers descended to begin their attack runs, German antiaircraft units took their measure, scoring a series of dramatic hits. Only a few Soviet attackers survived the gauntlet of German fighters and ground fire to drop their bombs on the crowded German airfields. German losses were modest. The failure of this preemptive strike in the South allowed the *Luftwaffe* a freer rein to assert local air superiority, if only for a short time.[34]

For many decades, what happened in the skies over Kharkov during the first hours of Operation Citadel remained a rather murky episode in Soviet historical literature. Silence on the abortive Kharkov raid endured until the post-Communist period, when a new generation dealt with the Kursk battle in a more forthright manner.[35] In the end, this more objective approach did not necessarily detract from the larger picture of the VVS gaining greater combat efficiency at the midpoint of the war. This ill-fated raid, in fact, was part of a larger bombing campaign that took place in the three months leading up to the German offense at Kursk. Soviet bombers struck at rail stations and enemy formations at Brest, Gomel, Bryansk, Orel, and other cities. These raids—with more than 10,000 sorties flown—were conducted by air units of the ADD, the long-range bomber command under General A. Ye. Golovanov.[36]

Even as the air battle over Kharkov unfolded on July 5, two German spearheads moved forward on the ground. The opening four days of Operation Citadel sparked intense air combat over the breakthrough corridors. Sometimes as many as 200 to 250 aircraft tangled in fierce air battles. In the southern sector, the *Luftwaffe* mounted 2,387 sorties; farther north in the Orel sector, they flew 2,088 sorties on the opening day in support of the German Ninth Army in an area 25 miles (40 kilometers) wide and 7 miles (11 kilometers) deep.[37]

Air Combat over the Northern Sector

Although the Soviet High Command had learned the general direction of the German offensive, it lacked precise knowledge of when the offensive would begin and the precise locale of the main thrust. In the North, General K. Rokossovskiy shrewdly discerned where, in fact, the enemy would strike. He acted on his best guess and organized the Soviet air and ground defenses. On the eve of the German assault, a German soldier from the 6th Infantry Division of the Thirteenth Army was captured and interrogated. He told his captors that his unit had been ordered to clear mines at the front. Most important, he revealed that the planned German attack would take place at 0300 hours on

July 5. Once alerted, Marshal G. K. Zhukov took this newly secured information seriously and ordered that special measures be taken to stiffen defenses in the zone of attack. These measures, however, proved to be limited in many ways, since darkness precluded adjustments in artillery fire targets and the full use of aircraft to interdict the enemy. At 0230 hours, General S. I. Rudenko took steps to deploy his forward air elements in a more effective way. He ordered one-third of his fighter force to be ready at dawn to intercept the enemy. The remaining fighters were held back, by means of Special Military Order No. 0048, to deal with any contingency or shift in enemy tactics. For example, a total of three groups of forty fighters each were drawn from the 6th IAK to participate in this action on the morning of July 5. Ground attack aircraft and bombers followed at 0600 hours. Rudenko aimed to gain air supremacy, but his schedule of patrols and the number of deployed aircraft suggested hesitation. He justified his measured steps based on the uncertainty about *Luftwaffe* plans.

Under constant pressure from a determined enemy, VVS air units did manage a spirited effort to thwart the German offensive. The first sorties were flown by elements of the 6th IAK, a formation of forty fighters departing in the predawn darkness for the salient. Fighter patrols, each numbering thirty aircraft, quickly followed this first wave. Major V. F. Volkov of the 157th IAP led eighteen Yaks over the salient and engaged twenty-five Ju 88 bombers, escorted by Fw 190s. The German aircraft from III/JG 51 approached the target area in an echeloned formation from 6,500 to 23,000 feet (2,000 to 7,000 meters). In the uneven struggle that followed, the VVS scored some measure of success: regimental records recorded the loss of four fighters and the downing of nine Fw 190s. In another engagement, Captain V. N. Zalevskiy, leading eight Yak fighters, managed to shoot down two enemy bombers, only to fall prey to attacking Fw 190s. His fighter was severely damaged, and Captain Zalevskiy, wounded in the leg, parachuted to safety. In a parallel air battle lasting forty minutes, the VVS lost another five fighters. As the first day of the Kursk battle unfolded, VVS air units failed to gain air supremacy. The air battles were intense, with the VVS enduring significant losses.[38]

Viewed in retrospect, the 16th Air Army command had missed a vital opportunity to concentrate optimal force against German bombers. Moreover, the deployment of fighters in groups of six to eight aircraft

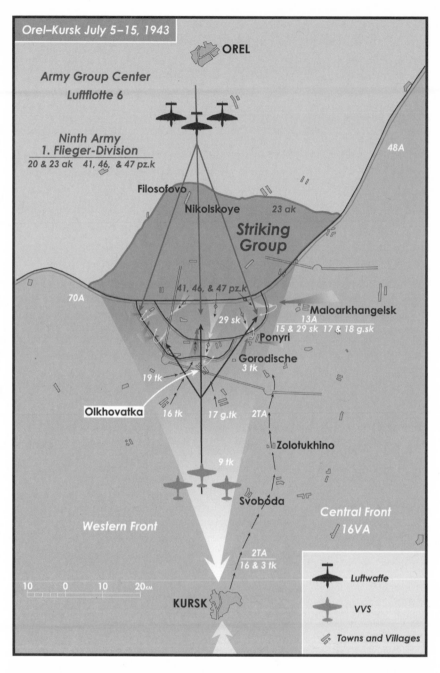

Map 6 (Terry Higgins & Zach Downey-Higgins © 2011 [based on Russian source material supplied by the authors])

proved inadequate to thwart the aerial attacks on the defending ground troops. Once they were over the battle zone, these VVS fighters fell into the gun sights of marauding Fw 190s. The resulting air engagements were intense, with the Germans ultimately gaining mastery of the skies. One tactical victory for the VVS came on the morning of July 5 with a fighter patrol from the 53rd GIAP: Lieutenant P. P. Ratnikov led eight Yak fighters against a group of seventy bombers, shooting down two He 111s and two Ju 88s. Ratnikov attacked the enemy bombers out of the sun at an altitude of approximately 10,500 feet (3,200 meters). That morning, according to Soviet records, the *Luftwaffe* conducted 1,000 sorties, 850 of them by bombers. The Soviet pilots and aircrews, to the frustration of their commanders, displayed a noticeable lack of initiative, preferring, for the most part, to blindly follow orders as opposed to conducting a spirited assault on the enemy.[39]

The hesitation of the VVS pilots allowed the *Luftwaffe* to gain control in the skies above Kursk. This reality made it extremely difficult for the 6th IAK and 1st GIAD (*Gvardeyskaya Istrebitelnaya Aviatsionnaya Diviziya*, or Guards fighter air division) to implement Order No. 0048 to maintain patrols over the battle zone. Records of the 163rd IAP, for example, suggest that because enemy attacks were concentrated on so many targets, it was impossible to dispatch more than four fighters at a time to counter each attacking group, which exceeded the Soviet response by six to eight times. There were other problems beyond enemy harassment, especially the lack of effective command and guidance of VVS fighters from the ground.[40]

The deployment of Il-2 Shturmoviks earned a greater measure of success for the Soviets. Two air units, the 2nd GShAD (*Gvardeyskaya Shturmovaya Aviatsionnaya Diviziya*, or Guards ground attack division) and 299th ShAD, were battle-tested veterans of the Stalingrad campaign. Aiming to disrupt advancing enemy mechanized units in the northern sector, these Shturmovik units attacked at low level and in the face of intense antiaircraft fire, destroying some thirty-one enemy tanks, along with other mobilized transport. The losses suffered by the Shturmovik air units, in particular the 299th ShAD, were huge, but they were a signal that the VVS was ready to challenge the enemy in the air and on the ground.[41] This arena of combat on the first day also saw the renewed deployment of La-5 fighters: sixteen of the new radial-engine fighters from the 486th IAP engaged a formation of thirty Ju 88s with Messerschmitt Bf 110 escorts, losing a total of four aircraft.

The opening day brought many frustrations to the Soviet air planners. The VVS may have lost as many as 98 aircraft by nightfall.[42] During the afternoon, the VVS faced an augmented enemy air presence over the breakthrough corridor, which, according to one account, included 300 German bombers escorted by 100 fighters at one juncture. Against the *Luftwaffe* in this sector, the 16th Air Army flew 1,720 combat sorties (including 1,232 during the day), engaged in 76 group air battles, and, by its own account, scored 106 victories.[43] The air activity at Kursk on the first day of battle suggests that despite its elaborate preparations, the VVS performed sluggishly against the determined *Luftwaffe*. Once the VVS began to respond in force to the challenge of Operation Citadel, there were many tactical errors. VVS fighters on occasion abandoned their primary targets—the German bombers and ground attack planes—to engage enemy fighters. Tactical discipline frequently dissolved in a confusing spiral of overlapping air battles. The communications system failed at certain junctures, allowing German aircraft to deliver effective blows against Soviet defensive positions with no adequate alert or spirited VVS response.[44]

The primary aim of the Soviet fighters was to attack the enemy bombers appearing over the salient in massed formations. As the air battles unfolded, the VVS—as in the case of air units of the 16th Air Army—failed to concentrate their attacks in an optimal way. Moreover, the German fighter escorts, often flown by highly experienced pilots, offered relentless opposition, downing no small number of Soviet aircraft. Air commanders explained the losses as tragic, a reflection that this had been a "baptism" into combat for many young pilots.[45] These same newly arrived pilots often displayed a lack of discipline and proper technique in engaging the enemy. These deficiencies in VVS fighter sorties on the first day caused no small amount of alarm within the air force command. Throughout the first day, Soviet airpower showed little organization and little capacity to direct concentrated air strikes against the *Luftwaffe*, even within the confined airspace over the breakthrough zones. This awkward debut of the VVS on July 5 permitted the *Luftwaffe* to assert temporary air superiority. The German plan was for the *Luftwaffe* to provide full and sustained support to the ground forces moving in a pincer movement from positions north and south of Kursk. Stukas hit the Soviets immediately to the rear of their defensive frontline positions. On that first day, the *Luftwaffe* deployed dive-bombers in five or six sorties to maximize the impact of airpower. German bombers simultaneously assaulted VVS air bases in the Kursk area. VVS air units would not seriously reverse German air superiority over the Kursk salient until July 7.

The first day in the northern sector ended on very unfavorable terms for the Soviets. *Luftflotte* 6 had inflicted heavy losses on defending Soviet air units and Soviet ground troops. Yet the German offensive failed to make any significant advance. The Soviet defenders, though hard-pressed, had not entered the battle without knowledge of the enemy's plans. Lacking the element of surprise, the advancing *Wehrmacht* faced the stiff resistance of the defending 13th and 70th Armies. Aided by massive strikes from ground attack aviation, the Soviets managed to blunt the Germans' forward advance in the North. Once this was stopped, the possibility of a subsequent German breakthrough diminished dramatically after one day of battle.

On July 6, the second day of the battle, the VVS launched a series of concentrated air strikes against German positions. This tactic corrected the opening-day error of dissipating Soviet air assets over the enemy's entire staging area. On Rokossovskiy's Central *Front*, the 16th Air Army, commanded by General Rudenko, made repeated assaults on elements of the German Ninth Army approaching the Olkhovatka ridge, which was defended in depth by the Soviet 13th Army. The 6th SAD, 2nd Guards, and 299th ShAD—a force of 450 airplanes—hit German infantry and tanks in the vicinity of Podolyan and Soborovka.[46] As the VVS applied more pressure on German ground forces, *Front* air commanders moved to a forward command post to assume direct control over air operations. For the first time, there was an efficient, mobile early-warning system in place. Accordingly, VVS units in both defensive zones began to perform their tasks with some discipline and in closer coordination with ground forces. With improved air control and communications, VVS fighters managed to intercept enemy bombers and ground attack planes more promptly. Further, a more organized VVS was able to project Soviet airpower into the German rear areas, frequently compelling the *Luftwaffe* fighters to abandon their ground support role for air defense.[47]

Stalin expressed anger over the VVS's poor performance on the first day, being alarmed that his air force could not quickly gain air supremacy. General Rokossovskiy's reassurances to the *Stavka* that this situation would be reversed allowed for a timely reprieve.[48] The 16th Air Army now faced the daunting task of reversing the complex and threatening situation. Soviet ground forces faced great peril, with the course of the battle still undecided. Shturmovik units and bomber air elements flying Lend-Lease Bostons assumed an aggressive role, flying missions in the face of spirited opposition from enemy fighters and antiaircraft batteries. Losses were high, as evident in combat sorties of the 221st BAD, which lost 10 aircraft. Overhead, VVS fighters renewed their struggle with the *Luftwaffe* for air supremacy, but by the end of the second day, the situation continued to be very difficult, notwithstanding a spirited effort. The 16th Air Army recorded 91 aircraft missing. Whereas on the first day the VVS had lost a substantial number of fighters, on the second day, this grim pattern became evident in the ground attack units at the front. After two days, the 16th Air Army had been reduced by some 190 aircraft.[49] This pattern of attrition was most pronounced in the fighter air arm, where the 6th IAK lost 81 aircraft and 58 pilots. The 1st GIAD reported only 28 serviceable Yak and P-39 fighters. In the face of these grievous losses, Marshal Zhukov ordered the transfer of the 234th IAD, then attached to the Bryansk *Front* as part of the 15th Air Army.

In the past, Soviet historians have routinely marked July 7 as a watershed in the struggle for dominance in the northern sector. On that morning, the German Ninth Army launched an offensive on the heights just north of Olkhovatka and Ponyri, an advance that was vectored along the pathway of the Orel–Kursk railway. It would be in this unfolding battle that the *Wehrmacht* inserted elements of the 4th Panzer Division. After some initial success, the German XLI Panzer Corps faced stubborn resistance by the Soviet 307th Rifle Division. The 16th Air Army provided timely and effective support to the ground troops in this critical battle. General Rudenko dispatched all three bomber divisions in his possession to hit the advancing German panzer units. For Rudenko and the VVS command, the accuracy and impact of these bomber sorties brought some keen satisfaction. VVS air actions were highly concentrated and focused, achieving great tactical success that day.[50]

In this unfolding battle, aircrews from the 229th ShAD flew a total of 120 sorties, attacking German tanks with PTAB 2.5-1.5 bombs.[51] More than 200 enemy tanks had been concentrated to attack Ponyri. Elements of the 431st ShAP, led by Senior Lieutenant D. I. Smirnov, destroyed or damaged 20 tanks in the area of Buzuluk. This triumph set the stage for further air action against German mechanized and tank units: pilots of the 874th ShAP, in sorties over the region of Maloarkhangelsk, reported the destruction of another 40 enemy tanks with the minimal loss of six aircrews. Interestingly, *Luftwaffe* fighters failed to seriously disrupt these massed attacks by the 16th Air Army.[52] Unable to sustain the level of the opening day's air operations, the *Luftwaffe* began to decline sharply in effectiveness. German fighters could achieve momentary air superiority only if they stayed concentrated and aggressive. The ubiquitous VVS squadrons at Kursk maintained a constant air pressure and, by their sheer numbers, asserted a measure of air ascendancy.

For the VVS command, the day of July 8 offered an occasion to act decisively. Fighters were deployed to clear the airspace in advance of bomber and Shturmovik missions. Airmen of the 1st GIAD were at the cutting edge of this tactical move. Hero of the Soviet Union Captain V. N. Makarov of the 1st GIAD led fifteen Yak-1 fighters to secure the airspace over positions held by the 13th Army. They were vectored by radio by Lieutenant Colonel Krupenin, the division commander, and in a span of forty minutes, this group engaged in two air battles. In the first, they dispersed an estimated forty German Bf 110 twin-engine aircraft. No sooner had this engagement taken place than Makarov and his group were ordered to the area around Olkhovatka; his orders were to intercept some fifty *Luftwaffe* aircraft, including a strong contingent of Ju 88 bombers and Ju 87 dive-bombers. The Soviet airmen later reported that they downed five Ju 87s, two Ju 88s, and one Fw 190. Although this claim would not be reflected in surviving German records, the air action itself was important for the VVS command in terms of fashioning more effective control of fighters from the ground. On the fourth day of the battle, the need for VVS support of ground forces had become urgent, as Soviet losses continued to mount. Elements of the 3rd GIAD, drawn from the 15th Air Army of the Bryansk *Front*, took on this difficult task and displayed great effectiveness. The ability to reorient deployed aircraft was a crucial aspect of the evolving VVS command and control techniques.[53] The following day, July 9, the 16th Air Army launched an important air strike against the enemy—a sweep of 150 ground attack aircraft and bombers against the German 9th Panzer Division in the area of Soborovki. German air operations continued, but now in inverse proportion to Soviet air actions. On July 10, the Soviets observed that the German army had been effectively stalled, particularly in its effort to overrun the Olkhovatka ridge in the Orel–Kursk sector.

The VVS command now turned its attention to massed attacks by bombers and ground attack aircraft. This move called upon the 16th Air Army to apply maximum available airpower to blunt the German advance. The Soviet plan pivoted on the fact that German forces— tanks, artillery, and infantry—had been concentrated in a narrow land corridor and, once in place, were vulnerable to a massed air attack. Beginning at around 0530 hours, six groups of Pe-2 aircraft from the 241st and 301st BADs struck the enemy with some success.[54]

At this juncture, the VVS experimented with some innovative tactics. To assure greater success, the air commander of the 16th Air Army called for a fighter sweep in advance of the arrival of the bombers. This cleared the air, if only temporarily, to allow the bombers to execute an effective strike. The tactic worked well. The coordination of fighter escorts with attacking bombers and Shturmoviks posed a serious problem for the German defenders.[55] By July 9, the enemy's capacity to engage in offensive operations had been seriously weakened. More important, this episode demonstrated a key learning curve for Soviet air planners as they forged new tactics.

The following day, July 10, the Soviets repeated the tactic, this time with even greater success. This experience informed future air operations of the 16th Air Army by demonstrating the importance of fighter sweeps in advance of bombing missions. Beginning in the early morning, the Germans renewed their attacks, targeting the sector where the 13th and 70th Armies joined. It is estimated that the *Luftwaffe* flew a total of 1,136 sorties during the course of the day. This increase in sorties resulted from the deployment of twin-engine aircraft and dive-bombers. The *Luftwaffe*'s ability to shift air assets in this timely way demonstrated flexibility in the tactical zone, where it did not enjoy numerical superiority.

The VVS endured heavy losses in the air action over the northern sector as a result of the *Luftwaffe*'s active and determined posture to thwart Soviet operations. By one estimate, the 16th Air Army had to write off some 439 aircraft, or 38 percent of the entire inventory. A total of 391 planes had been lost in air combat or otherwise, a measure of VVS commitment in the northern sector. General Rudenko recorded that in one week he had lost 55 percent of his fighters, 37 percent of his ground attack planes, and 8 percent of his bombers.[56]

During this defensive stage of the Kursk battle, the whole northern sector became an arena for intense air action. Over the first two days, the *Luftwaffe* achieved air supremacy as German airmen managed to neutralize VVS fighter units in the sector. Moreover, German bombers enjoyed relative freedom to carry out their missions. At this juncture, Soviet pilots displayed many of the weaknesses manifest in the past: lack of discipline, poor coordination with ground forces, lack of cohesiveness within squadrons and regiments, and an inefficient command and control infrastructure. In the fighter arm, pilots often failed to demonstrate initiative, along with poor flying technique, which mirrored their lack of experience. These deficiencies would haunt the VVS in the summer of 1943. Newly formed units thrown into the hellfire of aerial battles paid dearly. Heavy losses were endured stoically, even as combat experience allowed for change and adaptation. The full adaptation to combat proved to be a painful and prolonged process—one that was always linked to heavy losses. Kursk offered some bitter lessons. It was not always possible to decree the implementation of change from the "top" in the form of orders or instructions.

For the VVS, the air war in the northern sector had its interludes of triumph and achievement. The 16th Air Army remained a fighting force in a rather hostile and unforgiving environment, demonstrating an ability to handle the blows as well as to quickly understand the new realities of the air war. Starting from the third day of the battle, it switched to massive strikes at the enemy's armor and troop concentrations. *Luftflotte* 6 was unable to efficiently counter such massive concentrations of Soviet bombers and Shturmoviks. From July 7, these air actions started to directly affect events on the ground. The events of July 9 and 10 put an end to the German Ninth Army's hope that Operation Citadel would succeed.

Air Combat over the Southern Sector

On July 5, on the eve of the German offensive at Kursk, the VVS launched a predawn raid in the South, striking *Luftwaffe* airfields in the vicinity of Belgorod and Kharkov. Around 300 combat aircraft from the 2nd and 17th Air Armies participated in this preemptive strike. The aim was to deal a massive blow to German airpower. Among VVS commanders, there was debate on the efficacy of such an operation, and some argued that German mechanized forces should be attacked after the main corridor of advance had been identified. On the initiative of General N. F. Vatutin, commander of the Voronezh *Front*, the raid went forward with the bold assumption that a devastating blow against German airpower would disrupt or slow the advance on Kursk.

Around 100 Shturmovik aircraft, supported by 200 fighters, struck the widely separated enemy airfields. The element of surprise was lost when German radar picked up the incoming Soviet aircraft at a distance of 80 to 93 miles (130 to 150 kilometers). German air defense batteries at the targeted airfields were quickly alerted by radar stations "Freya" and "Wurzburg." These same early-warning techniques were not always available to VVS air commanders at this stage of the war. The *Luftwaffe* then ordered fighters from the JG 3 *Udet* and JG 52 units to intercept the VVS attackers. A spectacular air engagement followed as German fighters—flown by some of the most talented and experienced pilots—challenged the VVS air flotilla. The Germans challenged the Soviet attackers at 10,000 feet (3,000 meters), just before the latter initiated their attack runs. Only a few Soviet aircraft survived the gauntlet of German ground fire and fighter interceptors. Later, the *Luftwaffe* commanders claimed 120 Soviet aircraft downed, which, if true, was a stunning reversal of Soviet military fortunes on the eve of the Kursk battle. These raids on enemy airfields also weakened the VVS's capacity to make ground attack sorties in the near term. Only a few of the Soviet aircrews survived the gauntlet of German fighters and antiaircraft fire. The failure of this preemptive strike in the South allowed the *Luftwaffe* a freer rein to assert local air superiority. A week passed before the VVS could reestablish a strong air presence in the Belgorod–Kharkov sector.[57]

Even as the air battle over Kharkov unfolded on July 5, two German spearheads moved forward on the ground, with close air support by the *Luftwaffe*. The German units spearheading the attack included the Fourth Panzer Army and Army Group Kempf. The opening four days of Operation Citadel sparked fierce air combat over the breakthrough corridors.

The first day of air combat in the southern sector was especially intense for both sides. The stakes were high, and each air force displayed a determination to gain air supremacy over the battle zone. For example, the Germans' *Luftflotte* 4 flew 2,387 sorties on July 5. The VVS 2nd and 17th Air Armies responded with 1,322 and 446 sorties, respectively. General S. A. Krasovskiy ordered about half his sorties flown by fighter aircraft. By contrast, the Germans devoted around 70 percent of their sorties to attack aircraft, in particular dive-bombers.[58]

At around 0500 hours, German artillery opened fire on the Soviet 6th Guards Army. Coincidental to this opening salvo, *Luftwaffe* bombers—in groups of sixty to seventy aircraft—appeared overhead, dropping explosives on the first and second lines of defense. These initial raids were intense, with perhaps as many as 400 sorties in the first hour. By 1100 hours, the II SS Panzer Corps moved forward, covered by elements of *Fliegerkorps* VIII. To challenge the *Luftwaffe* air cover, there were only two groups of VVS fighters from the 5th IAK; they offered spirited resistance, but to no avail. In the air action that followed, the VVS managed to mobilize greater strength and effectiveness. Twenty La-5 fighters from the 41st and 88th GIAPs in the areas of Yakovlevo, Bykovka, and Cherkasskoye attacked twenty Ju 87s and forty to fifty Ju 88s and He 111s. In the midst of this air battle, Senior Lieutenant A. G. Pavlov of the 41st GIAP led ten La-5s against a large group of He 111s and Ju 87s, with some success. The Shturmoviks of the 2nd Air Army were deployed belatedly, around noon, because of heavy losses during their predawn strikes at *Luftwaffe* airfields. The 291st ShAD distinguished itself by scoring some hits on German tank units with its effective PTAB 2.5-1.5 bombs.[59]

During the intense air action over Kursk, Ivan N. Kozhedub, later the Soviet Union's top ace, made his combat debut. Flying in the 240th IAP of General Krasovskiy's 2nd Air Army, Kozhedub had only recently joined this fighter regiment. Before Kursk, he had served as a flight instructor. Coming from a Ukrainian peasant background, the twenty-three-year-old Kozhedub had the requisite humble origins to become an important Soviet war hero. His father had encouraged him

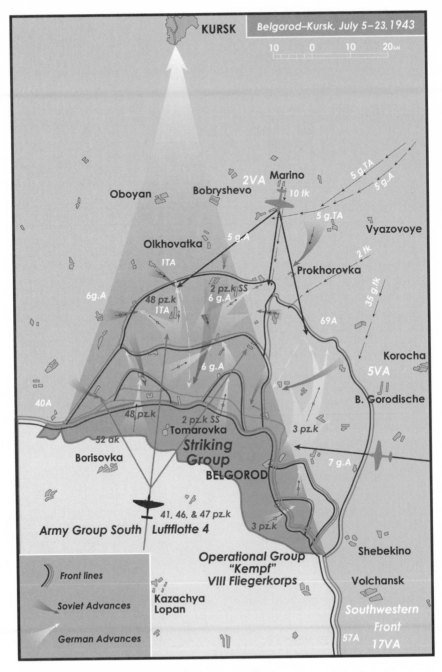

Map 7 (Terry Higgins & Zach Downey-Higgins © 2011 [based on Russian source material supplied by the authors])

to become an engineer, but as a youth, Kozhedub's interest fixed on aviation.

Like Pokryshkin, Kozhedub followed with enthusiasm the prewar aerial feats of Soviet pilots, especially the polar flights of Chkalov. After attending a technical school, Kozhedub received his pilot's license in 1940. On the eve of Barbarossa, he joined the Soviet Air Force and quickly displayed talent as a flier, but his superiors ordered him to serve as a flight instructor during the first year of the war. This duty in a rear area made Kozhedub restive, and after repeated requests, he finally received a combat assignment and joined a fighter unit near Moscow in November 1942. There, Kozhedub made the transition to the new Lavochkin La-5. Like many great aces, Kozhedub's first encounter with the enemy nearly proved fatal. Flying a combat sortie south of Kursk, Kozhedub lost contact with his leader. Alone, he detected a formation of German aircraft and recklessly dived toward them. His sweep, though unexpected, did little damage. Soon two Bf 109s pursued him aggressively, firing accurately and at close range. Kozhedub abruptly brought his damaged La-5 to a lower altitude to elude his pursuers and then flew at treetop level toward the Soviet lines. The damaged La-5—easily mistaken for its rival, the Fw 190—drew sporadic fire from Soviet antiaircraft batteries, which shot away one of its wing tips. Kozhedub landed safely, but the experience dramatically illustrated the dangers of combat with the *Luftwaffe*, where boldness without flying technique usually proved fatal.

During the hectic days of Operation Citadel, Kozhedub repeatedly placed himself in perilous situations, but his quick adaptation to the demands of air combat enabled him to escape death—often by a narrow margin. By the fifth day of Operation Citadel, he had destroyed two Ju 87s and two Bf 109s, receiving at the end of the Kursk hostilities the Order of the Red Banner and a promotion to the command of his own fighter squadron. During the subsequent Soviet campaign to cross the Dnieper River, Kozhedub, in a burst of energy and skill, scored eleven victories in ten days in some of the most bitter air combat of the war. His most impressive display of combat skill came in 1944 over Romania, where he downed eight German planes in one week. He ended the war with sixty-three victories, becoming the top-scoring Allied ace.[60]

The exploits of small air units offer insights into the intense air action in the southern sector. For example, Second Lieutenant A. A.

Dobkevich of the 61st ShAP led a spirited ground attack on German tanks, trucks, and artillery batteries in the area of Butovo. Flying at low altitudes of 1,000 to 2,000 feet (300 to 600 meters), Dobkevich and his fellow airmen made the first and highly effective attack run, a sortie that was followed by the deployment of aircraft from the neighboring 241st and 617th ground attack regiments. Numerous enemy tanks and vehicles were left burning in the aftermath of the raid. Once the German advance had been neutralized, the VVS command made an intense effort to prevent the enemy from reassembling and moving. Certain air units, such as the 617th ShAP, displayed results that were as dramatic as they were effective: a total of 8 sorties on July 5 and the recorded destruction of fifteen enemy tanks and six automobiles. The 29 sorties by the 61st and 617th Shturmovik regiments resulted in a tally of thirty tanks and eighteen other vehicles. The use of PTAB ordnance made a strong impact, creating a wall of fire with fifteen burning tanks. Moreover, it is important to note that a total of 117 Pe-2 bomber aircraft were part of the action. Crews flying the Pe-2s completed a total of 115 sorties on the first day, attacking concentrations of enemy armor and infantry in the areas of Butovo, Zybino, Rakovo, Kazatskoye, Pushkarnoye, and Tamarovka, although losses were significant. Famed Soviet bomber pilot I. S. Polbin, flying a Pe-2, participated in these initial air operations. These episodes offered a mirror on the growing intensity of Soviet ground attack crews.[61]

Yet there were problems with deployment, and tactical misjudgments severely compromised the growing strength and striking power of the VVS. For example, the command of the 2nd Air Army deployed the 302nd IAD of the 4th IAK into the ongoing struggle for air supremacy. On July 5, it was ordered to the front lines to destroy attacking German bombers rather than engage enemy fighters. The results were negligible at best. Moreover, bombers of the 1st BAK lacked the proper cover for any sorties and were forced to stay out of action. The delays endured for nearly a week.

German fighters discovered that they could not cover the entire southern sector in an efficient way. Often, VVS ground attack aircrews made sudden and devastating attacks. Even if the hard-pressed *Luftwaffe* fighter pilots could not consistently interdict attacking Soviet aircraft, they displayed impressive skill in air combat and scored a huge toll in VVS aircraft and crews. Soviet records indicate a total (in both the northern and southern sectors) of 260 VVS aircraft lost on the first day, July 5, and at least 220 of these were downed in air combat.[62] These losses stood in contrast to isolated incidents in which VVS airmen achieved notable victories. One problem identified by commanders was the failure to deploy enough aircraft to achieve a sustained advantage over the aggressive sorties of the *Luftwaffe*. This tactical error was corrected in the days that followed. Losses on both sides were heavy. In the southern sector alone, the VVS lost 159 aircraft on the first day.[63]

Between July 5 and 8, the *Luftwaffe* remained on the offensive. Still, the VVS made plans to engage the enemy in a forceful manner. The command of the Voronezh *Front*, in fact, set July 8 as the day for decisive action. General Vatutin possessed significant reserves to halt the enemy advance. The 2nd Air Army flew in support of the 10th and 2nd Tank Corps, which the *Stavka* had allocated to reinforce Vatutin's armies. In this phase of the battle, a total of 110 Shturmoviks from the 291st ShAD and 1st ShAK were deployed to strike enemy mechanized and infantry groups. Soviet planners hoped for a quick breakthrough in the German positions, but this ambitious goal proved unworkable. The Soviet drive was compromised by extremely poor organization and lack of coordination among the various branches of the ground and air forces. The actions of the *Luftwaffe*'s *Fliegerkorps* VIII played a significant role in thwarting this Soviet counterstroke. Despite the fact that the 2nd Air Army had flown some 957 sorties (more than in preceding days), the whole effort ended in failure.[64]

By July 10, bad weather had set in and persisted for several days, abruptly reducing the number of air operations on both sides. By July 11, the 2nd Air Army had launched only 539 sorties, and of these, only 133 were for ground attack missions. Shturmoviks were flying in small formations—groups of four or six airplanes. Due to the acute shortage of serviceable aircraft, there was no chance of organizing concentrated strikes.[65] On the morning of July 12, all VVS Shturmovik units were still grounded. This exacerbated the problems of the tank corps of General P. A. Rotmistrov's 5th Guards Tank Army, which attacked without air support and with only weak artillery support. Seventy-eight Pe-2s of Polbin's 1st BAK were unable to influence the ground battle. Another fourteen bombers were unable to take off due to the weather. Six bombers were lost, and the rest barely managed to return

Highly decorated airmen stand next to an Il-2 Shturmovik. (From the collection of Valeriy Romanenko)

home at treetop level in conditions of poor visibility. The *Luftwaffe* was also affected by the weather and could master only 654 sorties that day. After 1000 hours the weather improved slightly, allowing 142 sorties of Il-2s over the course of the day.[66]

The results of the fierce battles on July 12 can be viewed as a stalemate. Despite relatively low losses in armor, the German Fourth Panzer Army and Army Group Kempf failed to achieve their tactical goals. At the same time, units of the II SS Panzer Corps inflicted heavy losses on the Soviet 5th Guards Tank Army, which lost 340 (by some accounts, as many as 500) tanks and self-propelled guns on the field at Prokhorovka.[67]

Despite the fierce battle at Prokhorovka, it should not be considered the central event along the Soviet-German Front on July 12. That designation rightfully belongs to the offensive toward Orel by units of the Bryansk *Front* and the left wing of the Western *Front*. The German command started to plug holes in the northern sector and counter possible Soviet advances in Donbas by transferring several fighter and ground attack groups from the southern sector of the salient. The last days of the defensive operations of the Voronezh *Front*, the period July 16 to 23, were characterized by the total air superiority of Soviet aviation. On July 17, units of *Fliegerkorps* VIII managed to get in the air 138 times; this number diminished to 79 the following day. Over the course of defensive battles in the southern sector, the 2nd Air Army of General Krasovskiy lost 371 aircraft. Combined with the losses of the 17th Air Army of General Sudets, the total amounted to around 549 aircraft lost.[68]

During the defensive stage, fighter aircraft provided cover for air strikes by ground attack and bomber aircraft. Efforts to destroy enemy fighters as an active and singular task had to await the end of the defensive period. VVS operations were compromised by the ineffectual command and control of fighter assets. The 2nd Air Army's evaluations of the air action pointed to deficiencies in radio communications and coordination. However, Shturmovik units proved more effective, flying a total of 2,644 sorties. Some air units, such as the air division led by Colonel A. N. Vitruk, proved to be highly effective and exhibited greater skills in organization and combat technique. Losses in this division remained rather high, however, with some 100 Il-2 aircraft lost in one month and another 97 taken out of action for repairs.[69]

The largest blunder made by the command of the 2nd Air Army was the decision to concentrate the entire fighter contingent to provide cover for ground forces, which meant the lack of a fighter escort for the only VVS bomber unit of the *Front*. No less important, the attacking VVS strike force was unable to drop an optimal amount of bombs and explosives on the enemy. The VVS managed to unload 1,244 tons of bombs (including PTAB), while the *Luftwaffe* managed to drop approximately 7,000 tons. Because fighter aviation was engaged in defensive operations, covering certain areas and providing escorts, it was not actively engaged in search-and-destroy tactics, which contributed to the failure to achieve air supremacy during defensive operations. Significant weaknesses existed in the command and control of fighter units. Only when division- or corps-level air commanders were present at vectoring radio stations was some level of success achieved. Otherwise, even large units failed to accomplish their objectives without proper control over the radio. These shortcomings were noted by air commanders, and during offensive operations, air activities became marginally more concentrated and focused.[70]

One example of how the VVS command learned from its recent experience was Novikov's directive of July 7, 1943, issued in the midst of intense fighting during defensive operations at Kursk. He noted the many positive structural and organizational changes in the VVS; then he analyzed the many significant shortcomings in air combat that had become apparent. Combat missions were frequently vague, without specific goals to be achieved. This resulted in a reduced sense of responsibility among air commanders at all levels. Aviators were more concerned with flying a sortie than accomplishing a mission. Operational planning was also far from ideal. Novikov mentioned a lack of creative approaches and a tendency to use standard means and methods (e.g., the same altitudes, directions, and attack methods). There was lack of prestrike reconnaissance of targets and their air defenses. Radio vectoring was actively deployed in all air armies but did not satisfy the requirements of modern aerial combat. The radio network was not wide enough, and its personnel did not possess the necessary qualifications. Fighter units rarely engaged in "free hunting" over enemy territory or the destruction of enemy aircraft during their approach to the front lines. The rigid linking of patrolling fighters to specific areas prevented Soviet pilots from active offensive air engagement. Unit commanders were advised to pay close attention to flying pairs' cohesiveness and coordination during combat. These pairs had to be permanent, which, according to Novikov, would increase the wingmen's responsibility for the actions of their leaders. He also called for the ability to create numerical superiority by implementing a tactic similar to one used by the *Luftwaffe*—that is, radio calls for reinforcements during engagements. Another innovation suggested by Novikov in this directive was the development of "free hunter" tactics using the best pilots. The directive called for increased initiative among division and regiment commanders, providing them with greater flexibility in the planning of combat operations. Such operations required thorough planning and should not be treated as ad hoc measures. The directive paid special attention to the utilization of compact formations and the increased self-defense of strike groups due to the high density of defensive fire, as well as coordination with fighter escorts and antiaircraft artillery.

THE SOVIET COUNTEROFFENSIVE,
JULY – AUGUST 1943

The formidable challenge of halting Operation Citadel proved successful. Even more surprising for the German High Command was the Soviets' ability to launch a powerful counterattack that led in the near term to the liberation of Orel and Kharkov and set the stage in late 1943 for the liberation of a vast swath of Ukraine, the industrial heartland of the Donbas, and eastern Belorussia. The counteroffensive called on the *Stavka* to engage in detailed planning and allocation of resources. It would be in this crucible of conflict that command and control techniques were to be tested and further perfected. For the VVS, participation in a massive offensive operation offered a context to organize and deploy its ever-growing cadres of trained air personnel and inventory of military aircraft.

The *Stavka* gave the formidable VVS armada of five air armies a prominent role in the counteroffensive at Kursk: establish air control over the targeted battle zones, offer cover to advancing Soviet troops and armored units, and provide sustained air support along the breakthrough corridors. The plan called for concentrated air strikes in cooperation with ground forces, to be followed by graduated air sorties into the enemy's rear areas.[71]

To blunt the menacing specter of the VVS, the *Luftwaffe* exercised tight stewardship over its waning air strength. Such control dictated the application of airpower only in the decisive combat sectors and abandoning, for the most part, the crucial Soviet rear areas. The *Luftwaffe* faced the unrelenting task of supporting the hard-pressed German frontline troops. These wide-ranging assignments nearly exhausted its remaining operational strength. No diversified, large-scale air operations typical of 1941 could be sustained for any length of time, given the reduced inventory of operational aircraft and air crews. Moreover, the loss rate was particularly high in the contested airspace over the front lines, ample logistical support was rarely in place, and the low serviceability of many air units now reached alarming proportions. At Kursk, the Germans reinforced their air strength by transferring air assets from *Luftflotte* 4 to *Luftflotte* 6, primarily bomber and ground attack aircraft. This transfer of aircraft and crews severely weakened German airpower at Belgorod, allowing the VVS to gain air superiority

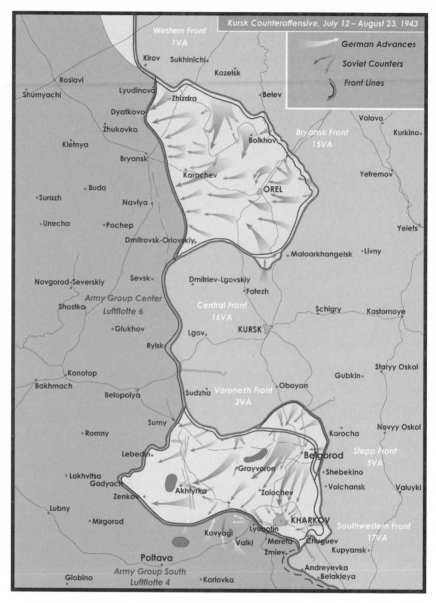

Map 8 (Terry Higgins & Zach Downey-Higgins © 2011 [based on Russian source material supplied by the authors])

in the southern sector. As the battle unfolded in both its defensive and offensive phases, the Soviets regarded German dive-bombing aircraft as the most threatening in a tactical sense. Consequently, the VVS took pains, especially in the counteroffensive, to strike German forward airfields to minimize the threat of bombers and dive-bombers.

Even as the *Luftwaffe* husbanded its finite resources at Kursk, the VVS increased its operational range. Soviet airpower began to operate routinely as far as 15 miles (24 kilometers) into the German rear. Such combat sorties hit German supply routes, storage areas, and airfields. The VVS's night bombing also increased dramatically at Kursk, presenting another serious problem for the hard-pressed German air defense units. The *Luftwaffe* continued to maintain technical superiority over the VVS, but the impact of superior Soviet numbers was evident. Persistent attacks by the Soviets made an impression, and with each passing month, the improvement in VVS air tactics became clearer. German observers found these VVS ground attack units especially hard-hitting and effective.[72]

Prior to the start of the counteroffensive, the 1st and 15th Air Armies had been attached to the Western and Bryansk *Fronts*, with an operational inventory of 1,322 and 995 aircraft, respectively. This force was reinforced with around 300 bombers from long-range aviation units. In quantitative terms, VVS air assets in the Orel axis reached 3,300 combat aircraft and outnumbered the *Luftwaffe*'s 630 to 650 operational aircraft approximately fivefold.[73]

At dawn on July 12, the Soviet ground forces began their advance with a salvo of intense fire from 4,000 guns and mortars on targeted enemy positions. Once ordered into action, three VVS air armies attacked German-occupied Orel, and an air assault approached the targeted enemy defenses from three sides: the 1st Air Army of the Western *Front* under the command of Lieutenant General M. M. Gromov, the 15th Air Army of the Bryansk *Front* headed by General Lieutenant N. F. Naumenko, and elements of the 16th Air Army of the Central *Front* led by its overall commander General S. I. Rudenko. From the Air Corps of the *Stavka* Reserve, selected air units moved to frontline airfields to augment Soviet air strength. The 1st Air Army, for example, expanded its operational strength with the addition of the 2nd Bomber, 2nd Ground Attack, and 8th Fighter Air Corps units. The other participating air armies received similar reinforcements. Only in day bombers did the VVS display a numerical inferiority to the *Luft-waffe* in the Orel sector. These timely reinforcements made the *Luft-waffe*'s position extremely difficult just as German troops in the Orel sector faced the dangers of encirclement.[74]

At Orel, the VVS assumed a combat role consistent with its augmented size and capability. In the preliminary phases, the VVS made full use of its air reconnaissance squadrons, which by 1943 had achieved a new level of maturity. Prior to the actual launching of the offensive, the VVS directed its air activity into the enemy's rear areas with steady blows from night bombers. Coordination and communication with partisan units reached a new level of efficiency at Kursk. The objectives set for the 1st and 15th Air Armies were defined within a combined arms context: to provide direct support to the advancing ground troops, to provide cover once a breakthrough corridor had been established, and to protect the steady flow of armor into the enemy rear areas. To augment the VVS striking power, elements of long-range aviation (ADD) under Colonel General A. Ye. Golovanov were deployed. A total of six ADD air corps (the 1st, 2nd, 3rd, and 4th Guards, and the 5th and 7th) were ordered to conduct operations on the two nights before the attack, with 600 sorties planned for each night. Around 400 of these sorties were assigned to hit targets facing the Soviet 3rd and 63rd Armies, and another 200 were set to take place along the breakthrough corridors of the 61st and 11th Guards Armies. The aim of light night bomber aviation (U-2 units) was to exhaust frontline enemy defenses in advance of the counteroffensive.[75]

Luftflotte 6 stood poised to face any challenge from the increasingly lethal and effective Soviet air arm. On the ground, the entrenched German defenses around Orel were also keyed and ready to thwart all VVS air attacks. Once launched, the VVS air operations proved to be aggressive. The weight of the air assault fell on narrow breakthrough corridors of the Soviet offensive. The German defenders conceded ground slowly at Orel, and only after considerable Soviet effort and sacrifice. Along the Bryansk breakthrough sector, the *Luftwaffe* opposition turned out to be aggressive, even in the face of overwhelming VVS numbers. At Bolkhovsk, north of Orel, the VVS played an important role, helping the Western and Bryansk *Front* armies break the stubborn German ground opposition. The VVS maintained considerable pressure on the German defenders by deploying bombers in

Il-4 bombers of long-range aviation (ADD) in flight to the target. (From the collection of Dmitriy Karlenko)

waves of pinpoint attacks. These bombing missions began on July 11, at the moment ADD and bomber units from the 15th Air Army hit German defenses near Novosil (east of Orel). Another attack followed on July 12, which included bomber and ground attack aircraft. As the bomber and ground attack sorties increased in tempo in the weeks leading up to the fall of Orel, the VVS achieved smoother coordination with other components of the Soviet armed forces. Along the breakthrough corridors, Soviet accounts described a devastating combination of air and ground forces hurled against the retreating Germans.

For the intense struggle that ensued during the counteroffensive, the VVS attempted to coordinate air and mechanized units. Prior to the action, joint exercises had been organized, allowing aircrews to interact with ground troops and tank units. For example, the 231st and 224th ShADs worked with the 1st and 5th Tank Corps to perfect their skills in combined arms tactics. VVS air commanders at the front were intent on improving their techniques of guidance and control. One of the persistent problems in the past had been the inability of VVS air units to operate in a mode of high efficiency over time.

There were also key directives for the fighter air arm. The counteroffensive demanded the optimal use of air assets. The 1st and 15th

Air Armies faced the daunting task of achieving the narrow—if traditional—objective of local air supremacy. Attainment of this sort of dominance over the battlefield, of course, had set the stage for the *Luftwaffe*'s great success earlier in the war. A heavy workload was assigned to the 15th Air Army to maintain a constant presence over the zone of advance during the counteroffensive. No fewer than 15 to 20 fighters were to be deployed over the battlefield at any time, with a total of 110 fighters provided to cover the ground troops.

To reinforce this massive assault, the 15th Air Army ordered a raid of eighty-nine Il-4 medium bombers from the 113th BAD. These bombers, flying at low altitudes, became an important tactical weapon, dropping more than 500 high-explosive and 3,000 fragmentation bombs. The bold bomber mission faced only modest resistance from the *Luftwaffe*, but there were losses. Two bombers were downed, even with close escort from fighters of the 66th GIAP. The enemy also managed to down two fighters from this same escort unit. Two other attacking bombers did not return to the base, having been lost in a midair collision. Mixed into the action on this first day were aircraft of the 308th ShAD, operating at low altitude and using smoke screens to assist ground troops crossing the river Zusha. The Shturmoviks served as a cutting edge, with infantry following behind them.[76] As the first day unfolded, the air and ground struggle grew more intense and bloody.

The German defensive lines held, notwithstanding the massive blows. At noon, air combat increased dramatically. In response, the VVS sent to the front as many aircraft as could be mustered. From the airfields of the 1st GIAK (*Gvardeyskiy Istrebitelnyy Aviatsionnyy Korpus*, or Guards fighter air corps), waves of fighters departed for the combat zone. This spirited effort to assert and maintain air supremacy initially proved ineffectual. Yakovlev and Lavochkin fighters, operating in small groups of six to eight aircraft, could not seize control of the embattled airspace. Aggressive Fw 190 and Bf 109 fighters offered stubborn resistance. On occasion, Shturmovik sorties achieved modest results, as in the case of the 3rd and 225th ShADs, which lost nine Il-2s on this first day. Yet in the midst of this highly fluid and often unforgiving battle scene, there were isolated triumphs—individual victories by fighter pilots; attacks by Shturmoviks on key German positions, including several hits on the *Wehrmacht* headquarters at Kishkino; and harassment raids by *Okhotniki* in German rear areas.

Part of the tactical advantage achieved by the *Luftwaffe* was the fact that it was able to fly more combat sorties; for example, the 15th Air Army completed 686 sorties, versus 1,111 by the enemy. However, the Germans had achieved this advantage with great effort.[77]

In the days that followed, the Soviets pressed forward with Operation Kutuzov to capture Orel. As part of the offensive, the VVS now operated with greater efficiency and success. On the ground, Soviet forces advanced deeply into German defensive lines, approaching the Orel–Bryansk railroad and emerging on the left bank of the Oka River. By August 5, the 3rd Guards Army entered Orel proper, and by August 18, elements of the Bryansk *Front* also reached the besieged city. Simultaneously, Soviet forces broke through and reached the enemy rear, forcing the Germans to deploy reserves from the Kharkov area— now highly vulnerable as the target of the next Soviet offensive. The counteroffensive at Orel gave evidence to the *Stavka*'s growing skills in planning and executing offensive operations.[78]

At Orel, VVS ground attack units demonstrated extraordinary aggressiveness. One example was the 3rd ShAK, which deployed 113 Il-2 Shturmoviks to complete a total of 141 missions. In the area of Bogdanovo, an element of 25 Shturmoviks from the 225th ShAD offered sustained and effective support for the ground forces as they breached the German defenses. This breakthrough expanded to about 6 miles (10 kilometers), which set the stage for the 3rd Guards Tank Army to advance.[79] Sometimes the action was more personal, if equally dramatic. On July 21, fighter pilot Lieutenant D. G. Trushkin of the 66th GIAP engaged four German aircraft in a dogfight near Zybino. In the chaotic swirl of air combat, Trushkin managed to damage one Bf 109 flown by Hans Paulmann of 7/JG 52. The German pilot decided to parachute to safety in this emergency, but he was over Soviet-held territory. Upon landing, Paulmann was captured by soldiers of the 235th Rifle Division. Meanwhile, Trushkin had to make a forced landing when he faced his own emergency—he had run out of fuel. As the story goes, Trushkin landed near the captive Paulmann as he was being taken to the rear. The two air warriors met and chatted briefly. For his feat—saving the life of his commander and shooting down an enemy aircraft—Trushkin received the Order of the Red Banner, which was awarded to him by Air Commander Novikov.[80]

During this phase of the Orel air operations, the VVS took pains to target enemy communications lines, striking roads and railways wherever possible. To sustain the pressure, night raids by bombers were ordered, again hitting vulnerable targets near the front or in the rear areas. There were even occasions when VVS aircraft struck *Luftwaffe* airfields, a mission that long-range aviation carried out in bad weather and against formidable antiaircraft defenses.

Even with the high attrition in aircraft and crews, the VVS persisted in its daily sorties throughout July and into early August. One example was the severely weakened 3rd ShAK, which on August 1 could muster only seventy-five sorties for the whole day. In this case, the pilots reported the destruction of 9 tanks and 30 vehicles. The neighboring 225th ShAD, reporting for the period August 1–6, claimed the destruction of 63 enemy tanks and 400 vehicles near Orel. By the same token, Soviet records reveal that the *Luftwaffe* managed to sustain daily operations consisting of 1,250 to 1,653 sorties.[81] Whatever the precise figures for sorties flown and targets hit in late July and early August, the air war around Orel was intense and unrelenting for both sides. One clear indicator of the imminent Soviet triumph was the fact that on August 3, the Germans began to destroy hangars and buildings at their major airfield at Orel, making the facility inoperable. For the Soviets, this was the harbinger of a massive German retreat from the embattled Orel sector.

Among the many lessons learned at Orel was the importance of mobilizing sufficient air units to reach the front at critical times. This was a matter of both deployment and tactics. Against a still formidable *Luftwaffe*, the VVS faced the daunting task of achieving air supremacy in a combat zone and at the same time offering essential and timely air support for the advancing ground troops. The VVS needed significant improvements in the organization of combat work, training and initiative among command and flight personnel, and the focused use of aviation at the main sectors. Even with the ultimate victory at Orel, it was apparent that wherever the VVS asserted control of the air, this triumph proved to be short-lived. Another shortcoming was the critical ability to block enemy transportation to the front. One factor that favored the *Luftwaffe* in this prolonged air campaign was the central location of its airfields. In contrast, VVS air units reached the zone of operations from several places, all of which were distant from the front lines. Losses for the VVS at Orel from July 12 to August 18 amounted to 996 aircraft, a substantial blow to its combat effectiveness. German losses were 3.5 to 3.8 times less, which reflected the qualitative and quantitative correlation between the VVS and the *Luftwaffe* in the summer of 1943.[82]

THE STRUGGLE FOR KHARKOV — OPERATION RUMYANTSEV

In the South, the Soviet counteroffensive aimed to liberate the city of Kharkov and set into motion a drive to regain the entire Ukraine. Kharkov had been a hotly contested city from the outset of the war, and it would change hands more than once. In the immediate aftermath of Stalingrad, on March 14, the Germans had retaken Kharkov, which set the stage for the reconquest of Belgorod four days later. This forward movement of the *Wehrmacht*, which achieved a temporary restabilization of the front for the Germans, was halted by the spring thaw. Ironically, this would turn out to be the last major military triumph for Nazi Germany in the East. For the Soviet Union, Operation Rumyantsev achieved a reconquest of Kharkov.

Operation Rumyantsev aimed to use the forces of the Voronezh and Steppe *Fronts* to penetrate the five lines of German defenses between Kursk and Kharkov. The 1st Tank and 5th Guards Tank Armies were assigned the task of spearheading the offensive from the North. A secondary force of the 27th and 40th Armies, supported by four tank corps, would help establish the breakthrough. Further support for the drive to the embattled city would follow later from the East and Southeast. The assault on the German defenses began on August 3. Again, as at Orel in the preceding weeks, the German defenders proved to be stubborn and resourceful. Though weakened, the *Luftwaffe* still deployed a formidable air flotilla to brunt the attacking ground forces and challenge the VVS for control of the skies. The ensuing battle, with all its intensity, continued to the end of August. The city of Kharkov fell to the Soviets on August 28, bringing Operation Rumyantsev to a triumphal conclusion.

On the eve of the August battles, the Soviet 2nd and 5th Air Armies were reinforced with 753 and 769 aircraft, respectively. The 2nd Air Army made use of radios to improve the command and control of air operations. At the division and corps levels, commanders received briefings to ensure the best integration of air units flying different types of warplanes. Detailed steps were taken to enhance control; for example, two additional radio stations were set up to vector fighters in the 10th IAK. Unlike the July operations, the majority of divisional and corps command posts were moved much closer to the front line. Both air armies implemented a plan for ground attack aviation to operate in front of the artillery, a necessary move to suppress targets outside the range of artillery units. Bomber crews hit important enemy defensive concentrations and artillery positions. Shturmoviks and bombers were used in massive concentrations. The concentration of aviation along the breakthrough corridors was unprecedented. In the 2nd Air Army, efforts were made to forge close links between air unit commanders and the ground forces; for example, air sorties of the 291st ShAD were integrated with the 6th Guards Army, and those of the 5th ShAK were integrated with the 5th Guards Army.[83] Special attention was paid to the air support of tank armies. Radio stations were set up to achieve this coordination. For all these air operations, the VVS command endorsed the key principle of centralization, especially during the critical breakthrough phases of the Soviet counteroffensive.

The VVS in Operation Rumyantsev demonstrated a newfound confidence and resourcefulness. The augmented strength of the participating air armies contrasted sharply with the diminished power of the *Luftwaffe*. Yet the aircrews of the *Luftwaffe* were asked to fly numerous sorties to maintain an effective air presence in the Kharkov sector. Guenther Rall, who narrowly survived a midair collision on the opening day of the Kursk offensive, scored his 200th air victory on August 29, just as the Soviets gained control of Kharkov. "It wasn't difficult to notch up high scores," Rall later observed. "We often went on five, six, or seven missions in a single day." For Rall, the Kharkov campaign meant flying the first sortie at dawn, followed by numerous sorties during the day, as needed. There were frequent landings to refuel and rearm. Each mission brought its own risks and dangers.[84] Even for a talented pilot such as Rall, the possibility of survival, in his mind, was more a result of good fortune than mere flying skill. Rall also observed the growing demands within the *Wehrmacht* for the *Luftwaffe* to provide effective air support, a task made more difficult by the reversals at Stalingrad and Kursk.[85]

Hauptmann RALL

Guenther Rall became one of the *Luftwaffe*'s most proficient aces and flew on several fronts, including over the Kuban and at Kursk. He survived the war with 275 victories and later served with the postwar *Luftwaffe*. (From the collection of Von Hardesty)

By contrast, the VVS emerged in 1943 with renewed strength and confidence—even in the face of lingering problems in tactical operations and substantial losses. The reasons for this trend were multiple. The muscular aircraft inventory allowed the air armies to endure a high rate of attrition and still sustain a high level of operational strength. For example, the 2nd and 5th Air Armies performed well, notwithstanding huge losses in aircraft and aircrews in July. The process of integrating air operations with the movements of infantry and mechanized forces reached a new level of refinement. Radios were increasingly used for the command and control of operational aircraft. This sort of management of air assets gave the VVS enormous striking power—even against a formidable *Luftwaffe*.

With the success of the Kharkov campaign, the Germans' summer offensive was dramatically reversed. Now the VVS was poised to participate in operations that would set the stage for the liberation of Ukraine.

A TURNING POINT

In the Soviet counteroffensive at Kursk, the VVS had executed its first large-scale "air offensive." Seeking dominance in the air and launching massed ground attack sorties against the enemy now became the script for combined arms warfare. For the Soviets, there was a deliberate and highly successful effort to concentrate airpower at key junctures in both the defensive and offensive stages of the Kursk campaign. During the counteroffensive, VVS fighters provided the protective canopy for advancing infantry and mechanized forces or participated as the cutting edge along the main avenues of attack. VVS Shturmovik units flew low-level ground missions, hitting German positions just beyond the range of Soviet artillery. The Soviet tactical bomber force hit both frontline targets and enemy formations in the rear. The constant strafing, bombing, and rocket barrages—often at low altitude—created confusion and prevented the enemy from making the necessary counterstrikes to halt a breakthrough by Soviet troops. Ground attack units also moved with designated tank formations as they broke into the enemy's rear area. Shturmoviks assisted the advance on the ground, protected the flanks, and, at Kursk, played a major role in the destruction of enemy tanks and armored vehicles.

At Orel and Kharkov, the VVS air armies demonstrated the growing lethality of the air offensive mode of attack. For the first time, the VVS High Command put the air offensive concept into operational practice on a large scale—and with increased sophistication. Wherever Soviet troops advanced, the VVS appeared in strength, attacking enemy tanks, artillery, and defensive positions. Along the attack corridors and in depth behind the enemy lines, Soviet bombers and ground attack aircraft swept down on their targets. Overhead, VVS fighter squadrons, providing protective canopy, aggressively challenged the *Luftwaffe* for local air superiority. When Soviet forces penetrated the enemy's tactical defense zone, the VVS, always deployed along the cutting edge, provided cover for tanks and infantry, suppressed enemy artillery, and attempted to isolate forward German troops from their reserves. Such sustained air operations at Kursk were costly in both men and machines. The VVS effort, though exacting in terms of attrition, achieved the strategic initiative in the air.

The intense struggle for control of the air continued after the dra-

Aircrew from the 617th ShAP (as of April 5, 1944, the 167th GShAP) poses with their Shturmovik aircraft, August 1943. Pictured are pilot Lieutenant V. P. Aleksukhin (left) and gunner A. D. Gatayunov (right). Their aircraft bears the name of legendary eighteenth-century Russian military commander Aleksandr Suvorov. (From the collection of Valeriy Romanenko)

matic Soviet victories at Orel and Kharkov. In the wake of the Kursk triumph, three VVS air formations, the 16th, 2nd, and 5th Air Armies, supported the operations of the Central, Voronezh, and Steppe *Fronts* in the general Soviet offensive to cross the Dnieper River and capture Kiev. From late August to December 1943, the VVS assisted the army in a series of fast-moving drives to outflank the enemy, establish river bridgeheads, and destroy pockets of resistance.

The 16th Air Army, supporting the Central *Front*, would engage in a number of fierce duels with the *Luftwaffe* as the year closed. At Nezhin, at the Desna River, and at the Dnieper north of Kiev, VVS units from the 16th Air Army provided support for advancing Soviet troops.

Farther south, the VVS performed a similar role, often without established airfields or sure logistical support. Even as these air operations unfolded, the 17th and 8th Air Armies participated in the

Commander of the 202nd BAD briefs a Pe-2 aircrew. The Pe-2 became the principal Soviet frontal bomber, with 11,247 built during the war. (From the collection of Valeriy Romanenko)

concurrent Soviet drive to liberate the Donbas below Kursk. At Taganrog, Shturmovik air units played a pivotal role in breaking through German defenses. Moreover, VVS air elements became an important weapon in harassing retreating German columns.

When Soviet troops successfully crossed the right (western) bank of the Dnieper River at several points in October, German air attacks increased in tempo. The VVS again faced the challenge of maintaining control of the air—in this case, over the Dnieper bridgeheads. During this period, Lieutenant K. A. Yevstigneyev, squadron commander of the 240th IAP, displayed his skills in the contested airspace over the Dnieper, shooting down twelve enemy aircraft in nine air battles. Yevstigneyev, a two-time recipient of the Gold Star, Hero of the Soviet Union, ended the war as the fourth-ranking VVS ace, with fifty-two personal and three shared victories.[86]

The liberation of Kiev on November 6 and the subsequent consolidation of the Soviet bridgehead on the Dnieper River provided a triumphal conclusion to the epic Battle of Kursk. The ability of the VVS

A coterie of highly skilled fighter pilots from the 240th IAP (as of July 2, 1944, the 178th GIAP) of the 2nd Air Army. Left to right, with their wartime air victories (personal + shared): Yu. A. Lyubenyuk (11 + 1), A. S. Amelin (17), and K. A. Yevstigneyev (52 + 3). (From the collection of Valeriy Romanenko)

to maintain active operations in the general offensive following the intense Kursk fighting clearly indicated the maturing operational skills of the air armies, the ability of the *Stavka* and air force planners to mobilize and deploy airpower effectively, and the capacity of rear services to sustain air operations over vast distances. This experience, of course, would be important for the final period of the war beginning in 1944.

Among all the factors contributing to the Soviet success at the Dnieper was the VVS's decided numerical advantage over the *Luftwaffe*. With this vast quantitative edge, sometimes as much as ten to one, the VVS could choose the time to assert air superiority. German air personnel learned the grim truth: the VVS in 1943 had acquired a new competence born of battle experience and upgraded air tactics. After Kursk, the *Luftwaffe* no longer possessed the means to win any sustained air battle with the Soviets. However, German airpower—if properly applied—could make a powerful impact on ground operations or even gain temporary air dominance over a battle zone. The *Luftwaffe* had been severely weakened, but it remained a powerful and dangerous foe.

For Soviet historiography, the epic battle at Kursk concluded the second period of the Great Patriotic War. From the launching of the Soviet counteroffensive at Stalingrad on November 19, 1942, to the end of December 1943, the Soviet Union fought and seized the strategic initiative from the Germans. The VVS, with its expanding inventory of aircraft and new combat tactics, flew with renewed confidence against the technologically superior enemy. As each month passed, the VVS asserted its increasing numerical superiority, compelling the *Luftwaffe* to go over to the defensive after Kursk.

Along with a display of its maturing operational art at Kursk, the VVS leadership forged a more efficient pattern of coordination with the army. Most of these dramatic improvements grew out of Air Commander Novikov's reorganization of 1942. He had stressed centralization and the close interaction of airpower and ground forces, and at Kursk, this imperative dominated Soviet Air Force operational planning. *Front* commanders met with air army staffs to establish unified procedures. VVS air corps and air division commanders assumed positions at the command posts of ground forces to achieve more effective air-ground interaction during battle. Air reconnaissance now played a crucial role in supplying essential information on the enemy's deployment and movement. The increased scope of air force operations in 1943, implemented to meet the shifting defensive and offensive requirements of the Soviet army, called for the constant perfection of operational planning skills.

Squadrons of VVS fighter aircraft flew over the Kursk battle zones with greater discipline, providing cover and assuming the additional tactical role of fighter-bombers. It was a slow process of refinement forged in combat. Improving combat discipline was achieved with the broad use of radio control. And such changes reflected a pattern of constant refinement of technique on the Soviet side. VVS command posts, which were now being integrated into the larger army network of communication, became a vital factor, calling VVS fighters into action quickly to meet the shifting requirements of the front.

Always intent on learning lessons, the VVS High Command did not let the Battle of Kursk pass without adapting the rich experience to air operations planning. In December 1943, the VVS Military Council convened a special meeting of military district air force commanders, commanders of reserve air brigades, and representatives from the frontline air armies. They met to consider how to improve training in the reserve air regiments. Out of this conclave, a series of new combat training courses for fighter, ground attack, and bomber aviation was developed. The conference helped forge a training procedure that would meet the demands of offensive air operations in 1944.

One practical expression of this approach came during December, when the 17th Air Army, then committed to the projected campaign to liberate the right bank of Ukraine, held a conference of air division, regiment, squadron, and flight commanders to discuss the need to improve air combat skills for offensive operations. General V. A. Sudets, commander of the 17th Air Army, joined with General R. Ya. Malinovskiy, the *Front* commander, and the two *Stavka* liaison representatives (Marshal Vasilevskiy and General Falaleyev) to plan for the new offensive. Already at work in the frontal air armies were personnel from the Main Directorate of Combat Training for Frontal Aviation (established in January 1943 and headed by General D. F. Kondratyuk), who conducted lectures, war games, group exercises, and demonstration flights on various aspects of individual and group tactics. Together, these programs were narrowing the qualitative gap with the better-trained *Luftwaffe*.[87] The VVS command did not conceal the existence of some serious shortcomings, many associated with the rapid expansion of the air force and the compelling need to achieve a high level of professionalism in all operations. Time was required to correct these deficiencies.

At the end of the Battle of Kursk, the VVS possessed a decided numerical superiority over the *Luftwaffe*, an edge that would be magnified in the last year and a half of the war. The coming campaign to liberate Soviet territory and drive toward Berlin would reveal how well the VVS had improved the quality of its equipment, tactics, and training. Deficiencies in organization and tactics would continue to beset the Soviet air arm, but a corner had been turned.

Chapter Six

At Full Stride

The year 1944 signaled the final phase of the Great Patriotic War (January 1, 1944–May 9, 1945). Deployed at the cutting edge of a series of dramatic war-ending offensive operations, the Soviet Air Force achieved a remarkable new level of maturity. Even with the extraordinary losses of 1941, the Soviet military managed to rebound in 1942–1943 at Moscow, Stalingrad, and Kursk. Each bloody triumph displayed the growing capacity of the Soviet Union to wage war. Behind the impressive reversal in military fortunes was the expansion of the transplanted Soviet war industries, which by 1944 had achieved a formidable level of productivity. The Soviet Union, like the United States, had forged the tools for total war.

The Soviet Union's fighting strength in January 1944 totaled 6,165,000 men, 88,900 guns and mortars, 2,167 rocket launchers, nearly 5,000 tanks and self-propelled guns, and 9,239 aircraft.[1] Among these categories, the air arm had exhibited a remarkable capacity for recovery. At this juncture of the war, the VVS had grown to a size nearly equal to its prewar deployment. For Soviet air commanders, there was renewed confidence with the realization that the VVS had achieved rough parity with the *Luftwaffe* in both technical and tactical strength. No longer the "paper tiger," the VVS now participated in massive offensive operations with highly flexible air armies as a key component in the emerging Soviet concept of combined arms warfare. Moreover, the strategic initiative in the air had shifted to the Soviet Union, although the *Luftwaffe* still possessed residual strength and the ability to challenge, on occasion, the growing might of Soviet airpower. The VVS entered the final stage of the war with high morale and an array of modern aircraft and sophisticated weaponry.

The Soviet Union found itself poised to reclaim its lost territories and begin the arduous march to Berlin. At the onset of 1944, the Germans still occupied Estonia, Latvia, Lithuania, most of Belorussia, Moldavia, a large slice of Ukraine, and the Crimea. Germany still deployed 4,906,000 men on the Eastern Front, along with a substantial arsenal of 54,000 guns and mortars, 5,400 tanks and assault guns, and about 3,000 aircraft.[2] In the air, the *Luftwaffe* could muster, on occasion, 1,000 sorties per day.[3] The *Luftwaffe* survived as a fighting force in Russia in large part because of Soviet air doctrine, which dictated that the VVS operate as an integral part of an air-ground force. If the VVS had been released for extensive and sustained operations as an independent air arm, the attrition in German aircraft might have been higher.[4]

By September 1943, the Anglo-American strategic bombing campaign had placed enormous pressure on Nazi Germany's industrial and urban centers, forcing the withdrawal of a significant number of *Luftwaffe* air units from the East for Reich defense duties. In 1944, the *Luftwaffe* possessed about half its 1941 strength to combat the VVS, but it bravely fought to maintain an effective air presence. Wherever possible, the Soviets shrewdly applied pressure at shifting points on the retreating *Wehrmacht*. German air units found themselves stretched to the limit. Constant movement, high attrition, meager reinforcements, and the growing effectiveness of VVS air operations forced the *Luftwaffe* to abandon any goal of air superiority and seek instead to plug holes wherever possible. As a result, *Luftwaffe* commanders exercised a careful stewardship over their finite and ever-diminishing resources: the critical tasks were to preserve essential equipment and parts, adapt bombers as air transports to supply encircled German troops, and keep a small but viable fighter arm over active battle zones for air cover.

For the *Luftwaffe*, the steady attrition meant not only a decline in operational aircraft but also, and more important, the loss of highly trained pilots and aircrews. These human resources could not be replaced. Such a small cluster of fighters could not meet even the minimum requirements of the German army. Soviet aircraft production for 1943 totaled 28,984 combat planes, mostly fighters and ground attack aircraft, and it grew to 32,649 in 1944.[5] The sobering reality facing the *Luftwaffe* can best be illustrated by the fact that the VVS air armies received 4,560 high-performance, late-model Yak-3s alone from 1944 to 1945. During the entire war, more than 35,000 Yak fighters and more than 22,000 Lavochkin fighters entered service in the frontal air armies, the navy, and PVO units.[6] Against such an air armada, the

Luftwaffe committed its core of highly skilled flight personnel and excellent aircraft, but in 1944, these were finite.

In the aftermath of Kursk, the Soviets drove across the Dnieper River and liberated Kiev, the ancient capital of Russia, on November 6, 1943. The Soviets' winter campaign of 1944 quickly followed on the other successes of this remarkable year, in which the Red Army advanced 808 miles (1,300 kilometers) in the South alone. In the prolonged struggle for Ukraine, the VVS played an active role, particularly during the Korsun–Shevchenkovskiy operation of January–February 1944, which ended with the Soviets reaching the borders of Romania. To the north, the Soviets lifted the siege of Leningrad in January and pushed the German Army Group North back into the Baltic region. The Crimea fell to advancing Soviet forces in April and May. Again, the VVS assumed the crucial tasks of establishing air superiority over the breakthrough zones and providing air support for the ground forces.

The summer and fall campaign of 1944 opened with the Soviet offensive in Belorussia against the German Army Group Center. The massive and overwhelming Belorussian campaign destroyed in short order the German pocket containing a force of more than 300,000 men. This dramatic Soviet victory followed the Normandy invasion and set the stage for driving the Germans out of Poland. During July–August 1944, the Red Army expelled the Germans from most of the Baltic area. In the South, two campaigns—the Lvov–Sandomir operation (July 13–August 29) and the Yassy–Kishinev operation (August–September)—catapulted Soviet forces into Romania, Bulgaria, Poland, and Czechoslovakia. By autumn, Soviet troops had reached Hungary and Yugoslavia. At the end of 1944, only a small portion of Latvia still remained in German hands. For the first time in this prolonged struggle, the Soviet army was poised to strike a blow at German territory.[7]

The Finnish sector became another arena for the Soviets to assert their growing air might in June 1944. The *Stavka* ordered the 13th Air Army, naval aviation from the Red Banner Baltic Fleet, the 2nd Guards Air Corps PVO, and elements of the ADD (long-range aviation) to make a coordinated blow against Finnish defenses in the Karelian peninsula.

The Finnish air force had been supplied with many German-designed aircraft, which only added to its striking power. The Finns launched their so-called Continuation War in 1941 (coinciding, by design, with Operation Barbarossa) to regain the territory lost in the Win-

Flight commander A. S. Dodonov briefs aircrews before a combat sortie. This is likely Dodonov's Pe-8 (serial number 42057), 25th GBAP ADD, January 1944. (From the collection of Von Hardesty)

ter War of 1939–1940. Soviet air operations fit into the larger scheme of the Leningrad *Front* to shatter enemy defenses northwest of Leningrad and capture Vyborg Air Commander Novikov, who arrived on June 6, served as the *Stavka* representative and supervised the joint air operations of the Leningrad and Karelian *Fronts*. Even with the large number of aircraft earmarked for the Belorussian offensive, he had an air flotilla of 1,390 planes (1,296 serviceable): 237 bombers (222 serviceable), 438 ground attack aircraft (412 serviceable), and 715 fighters (662 serviceable). Naval aviation contributed another 494 aircraft.[8]

Over Finland, as elsewhere along the front, Soviet air units flew the latest bombers (Tu-2s, Il-4s, Pe-2s, and A-20 "Bostons"); updated versions of the Il-2 Shturmovik; and Yak-9, La-5, and P-39 Airacobra fighters. Beginning on June 9, 215 VVS bombers flying in long columns hit enemy targets from 3,300 to 9,900 feet (1,000 to 3000 meters). Shturmoviks followed in divisional strength to maintain constant pressure on enemy defenses, railroad and communication centers, and reserves. By June 20, the Soviets had taken Vyborg.[9]

Late-model Il-2 with a distinctive increased wing sweep. This aircraft was attached to the 15th GShAP of the 13th Air Army of the Leningrad *Front* in the summer of 1944. (From the collection of Gennadiy Petrov via Carl-Fredrick Geust)

On the eve of the Yalta Conference (February 4–11, 1945), the Soviets launched their decisive Vistula–Oder operation. This powerful offensive began on January 12 and was followed one day later by the Soviet drive on East Prussia, another bitterly contested campaign destined to last until April 25. The final storming of Berlin began on April 16, when Marshal Zhukov's 1st Belorussian *Front*, joined by Marshal Konev's 1st Ukrainian *Front* and Marshal Rokossovskiy's 2nd Belorussian *Front*, attacked from three sides. Soviet troops met American troops at the Elbe River on April 25 and captured the *Reichstag* on April 30, 1945. As the width of the Eastern Front shrank with each Soviet offensive, the concentration of Soviet airpower became overwhelming.

THE KORSUN–SHEVCHENKOVSKIY OPERATION

In January 1944, the 1st and 2nd Ukrainian *Fronts* inaugurated two major offensive operations that succeeded in recapturing the Soviet cities of Kirovograd, Zhitomir, and Berdichev, along with a dramatic assault on enemy groupings in the Korsun–Shevchenkovskiy area. Although the initial phase of the offensive proved highly successful, German forces still occupied one particular area that now protruded deeply into the expanded Soviet positions. In fact, this rump salient threatened the flanks of two Soviet *Fronts* and presented a formidable barrier to further Soviet advances. Therefore, the Soviet command began preparations for a new offensive to capture this enemy-held territory. At dawn on January 24, the 2nd Ukrainian *Front* renewed its march westward, an offensive that coincided, two days later, with a similar move by the 1st Ukrainian *Front*. By February 3, the advancing Soviets had encircled a substantial German force in the exposed salient—a total of ten divisions and one brigade consisting of 80,000 men, 1,600 guns and mortars, and up to 230 tanks and self-propelled guns.[10] To defend the salient, the Germans deployed most of the air assets of *Luftflotte* 4, which meant there was no effective air support for their troops at the Nikopol bridgehead. The German air contingent consisted of up to 450 warplanes, which included around 120 fighters and 120 to 130 dive-bombers. No fewer than 100 transports were deployed to provide relief to the surrounded troops.[11]

The Soviets simultaneously endeavored to prevent any breakout of the trapped German force and blunt any efforts by the enemy to establish an escape corridor. On February 11, a series of intense battles took place on the outer ring of the pocket. The German forces' counterstroke came within 6 to 7 miles (10 to 12 kilometers) of their trapped comrades. However, the Soviets were able to halt the German relief effort.[12] The Soviet command reacted swiftly by moving reserves to the threatened sector. These efforts were significantly hampered by rising temperatures, which made the roads impassable. This situation also critically affected the ability to supply ground troops with fuel and ordnance. Supply was therefore turned over to aviation. Due to the absence of air transport planes, supply duties were assigned to the 326th NBAD (*Nochnaya Bombardirovochnaya Aviatsionnaya Diviziya*, or night bomber air division), equipped with U-2s. From February 8 to 16, the division flew 822 sorties and delivered 49 tons of fuel and 65 tons of ordnance, which was not enough to improve the situation significantly. However, delivering more using the light U-2s was impossible in those conditions. At the same time, the Germans used significant quantities of transport and bomber aircraft and were able to deliver the necessary supplies to provide stiff resistance for sixteen days and evacuate 3,000 wounded. Soviet fighters managed to shoot down a considerable number of these transports but were not able to paralyze the relief effort.

On February 14, Air Commander Novikov, on orders from Stalin, arrived at the headquarters of the 1st Ukrainian *Front* to mobilize all possible air assets to thwart enemy tanks and mechanized forces. However, this tactical move proved difficult when poor weather grounded most aircraft. For example, elements of the 291st ShAD faced blizzard conditions and could not reach their designated target zone. On the following day, four Il-2s, carrying half their routine bomb loads, attempted to strike enemy tanks. Only three of them reached the target, causing minimal damage to the enemy and failing to delay the German advance. Novikov found a nonstandard solution and assigned U-2s of the 208th NBAD to the strike mission. Each U-2 was equipped with cassettes carrying up to 250 PTAB bombs. On the morning of February 15, ninety-one U-2s attacked German tank columns. The U-2s proved to be better suited for actions in adverse weather than were Il-2 Shturmoviks. At noon, another sixty-three U-2s repeated the strike. Numerous tanks were reported destroyed and damaged.[13]

For the Korsun–Shevchenkovskiy operation, the VVS organized an air blockade modeled on the Stalingrad experience of the previous year. Novikov organized four zones to interdict the German transports supplying the encircled troops. General S. A. Krasovskiy of the 2nd Air Army worked with General S. G. Korol, commander of the 9th IAK PVO, to deploy the maximum number of fighters to destroy the oncoming German transports. VVS ground attack units struck at enemy forward airfields at Uman, Vinnitsa, and Novo–Ukrainka.[14] The 5th Air Army also deployed its available strength for direct air support of Soviet ground troops attempting to liquidate the German pocket.

The air blockade of the Korsun–Shevchenkovskiy pocket became an effective tactic. Between January 31 and February 15, for example, the VVS recorded 257 air victories, including 31 downed German transport aircraft. For the entire period of the air blockade, the Soviets, by their own reckoning, destroyed 457 German aircraft in the air and at the staging airfields for the airlift. These figures appear to be exaggerated, given the *Luftwaffe*'s reduced aircraft inventory in 1944.

Whatever the actual German losses, the level of VVS air activity remained high during this period. Moreover, the Soviet air blockade played an important role in the ultimate destruction of the Korsun–Shevchenkovskiy pocket by denying the trapped Germans the requisite materiel to hold out.

According to Soviet records, this victory yielded more than 18,000 German prisoners and 55,000 enemy dead and wounded.[15] The German effort at resupply had been pursued in severe weather, and fog and snow kept most of the German planes grounded during the initial phase of the airlift. *Luftwaffe* losses, according to one Western account, totaled forty-four aircraft during the first five days of the airlift. On February 9, the Germans established an improvised airstrip within the pocket, allowing German transports to carry anywhere from 100 to 185 tons of ammunition daily.[16] If true, these figures suggest that the Germans succeeded in escaping a reenactment of Stalingrad on a minor scale. By contrast, Soviet sources remain silent about the successful breakout of more than 30,000 German troops on February 16. Their narrow escape required the painful abandonment of most of their wounded and equipment, a testament to the ever-diminishing capacity of the retreating *Wehrmacht* to stabilize the front.[17]

The Korsun–Shevchenkovskiy air operations occupied a prominent place in VVS offensive actions in 1944. Once again, the burgeoning Soviet airpower demonstrated its ability, even in difficult winter conditions, to organize an air blockade of encircled German forces. At the conclusion of this phase of the winter campaign, the Presidium of the Supreme Soviet of the USSR awarded Alexander Novikov the highest rank in military aviation—Chief Marshal of Aviation. By February 1944, Novikov had established an exemplary record as an air commander. The ability of the VVS to seize the offensive in 1944 rested in large measure on his effective leadership. Many Soviet aviators were awarded medals and promoted at this time.

Once the weather improved on February 26, German fighters assumed a much more aggressive posture. Taking advantage of mistakes made by Soviet Airacobra patrol groups, *Luftwaffe* aces claimed seventeen victories, demonstrating yet again their tactical mastery and providing a reminder that any lapse in vigilance could be very costly.[18] However, with the approach of spring, the VVS gave the *Luftwaffe* no reprieve. The 2nd, 5th, 17th, and 8th Air Armies flew more than

Horrors of war—an advance group of Soviet naval aviators inspects captured Khersones airfield in Sevastopol, May 1944. This was the last *Luftwaffe* airfield in the Crimea. (From the collection of Valeriy Romanenko)

70,000 sorties in the quest to liberate the western Ukraine. The VVS claimed 1,467 German aircraft destroyed in the first three months of 1944.[19] The sustained character of these operations, however, stretched the VVS resupply capacity to the limit, regardless of their real or imagined impact on the *Luftwaffe*. Also, there were obvious signs of strain among VVS air personnel and ground crews.

By mid-April, the Red Army reached the Dniester River and liberated Odessa. At this time, VVS air operations slowed as the *Stavka* shifted its attention to the Crimea. Throughout the spring of 1944, Hitler refused to order the evacuation of the Crimea, where the German Seventeenth Army and the *Luftwaffe's Fliegerkorps* I now found themselves in a perilous situation. The Soviet campaign to isolate the Germans there had begun the previous fall, when the 4th Ukrainian *Front* had occupied the Perekop isthmus and blocked the escape route north into Ukraine. Earlier, the Germans had evacuated the Kuban bridgehead, the site of dramatic air battles during the spring of 1943, for more defensible positions on the Crimean side of the Kerch Strait.

Destroyed Fw 190F at Sarabuz airfield in the Crimea, 1944. Bomb racks are visible under the wing. (From the collection of Valeriy Romanenko)

The VVS 8th and 4th Air Armies applied considerable pressure on the Germans during the winter of 1943–1944. The 8th Air Army alone flew more than 30,000 sorties against enemy defenses and shipping in the Black Sea.[20] The final Soviet campaign in the Crimea began on April 8. Over the next week, the Soviets advanced from the Perekop isthmus and the Kerch Strait toward the Sevastopol fortress on the southwestern coast of the peninsula. The Soviet offensive moved forward rapidly as a result of the German decision to evacuate the Crimea. By May 12, the Germans had removed more than 150,000 troops, but at the cost of their equipment and an estimated loss of 80,000 men.

Throughout the Crimean campaign, the VVS faced modest air opposition from the *Luftwaffe*, a sharp contrast to the intense Kuban air battles of the previous year. General F. Ya. Falalayev served as the *Stavka* representative to coordinate the air units of the 8th and 4th Air Armies, the Black Sea Fleet, ADD, and PVO. He worked closely with Generals T. T. Khryukin and K. A. Vershinin, commanders of the 8th and 4th Air Armies, respectively, to administer a joint operation of more than 35,000 sorties. The Germans' determined defense of the Crimea in 1943 gave way to retreat in 1944, and with the collapse of enemy power there, the *Stavka* planned for its next major summer offensive.

THE FIERY SKIES OVER ROMANIA

In May–June 1944, the skies over northern Romania became an arena for one of the most intense air battles of the war. This would also be one of the last major air campaigns of the *Luftwaffe* to regain a measure of air supremacy in the East. Over the Romanian town of Yassy and the surrounding region, Axis and Soviet airmen engaged in a series of intense and violent encounters. Some of the most celebrated aces on both sides participated in this bloody battle. Gerd Barkhorn, the *Luftwaffe* ace who would end the war with 301 air victories, nearly lost his life over Yassy while attempting to score his 277th victory; some of the most talented surviving German pilots in the East joined him. Like Barkhorn, talented VVS ace Nikolai Gulayev, who would end the war with 57 personal and 5 shared air victories,[21] narrowly escaped death; he was seriously wounded in air combat but managed with great effort to return and safely land at his forward air base.[22] The redoubtable Alexander Pokryshkin also took part in the Yassy air battle, assuming a prominent leadership role. He was joined by other stellar Soviet pilots, including high-ranking aces Ivan Kozhedub and Grigoriy Rechkalov. Yassy was an intense and monumental struggle for both air forces, but ironically, it is one of the least chronicled air battles of World War II.[23]

The story of Yassy can be traced back to the immediate aftermath of the Korsun–Shevchenkovskiy offensive in the winter of 1944. Linked to this offensive was a broader campaign, launched on the 2nd Ukrainian *Front*, to move beyond the prewar boundaries deep into Romania. Beginning in March, Soviet forces moved 125 to 155 miles (200 to 250 kilometers) to the west and southwest. The stakes were high for Nazi Germany at this juncture: the need to keep Romania in the war as an ally, to sustain control of Romanian oil fields, and to prevent a Soviet offensive from spilling over into Hungary and Germany proper. The active role assumed by the *Luftwaffe* in this sector reflected the German High Command's priority of keeping the advancing Red Army at bay. Some of the *Luftwaffe*'s most experienced and proficient air units were thrown into the vortex of battle to strengthen the defense of this strategic arena. Access to the rich oil fields at Ploesti became a compelling wartime priority.

The opening air action over Yassy began on April 28 when the *Luft-*

waffe flew some 807 sorties against Soviet frontline positions around the Romanian town. The following day, the tempo accelerated with another 1,181 sorties. These initial raids were largely ground attack sorties, hitting both advancing Soviet infantry and mechanized units and targets of opportunity in rear areas in close proximity to the front lines. The air assault continued with great intensity, totaling over 4,000 sorties in the first week of May. By contrast, the Soviet 5th Air Army mustered only 1,970 sorties in this same time frame.[24] Interestingly, the Germans deployed not only their advanced Fw 190F-8 aircraft, a lethal adaptation of the Fw 190 radial-engine fighter for low-level sorties, but also the obsolescent Ju 87 Stuka dive-bomber, which still possessed a certain utility on the Eastern Front. Despite being slow and extremely vulnerable to Soviet fighters, the Stuka remained a powerful air weapon in the hands of an experienced crew. Typically, the *Luftwaffe* deployed attack groups of up to thirty to forty aircraft.

For the Soviet High Command, the enemy's aerial assault created a tactical situation fraught with dire implications and even the prospect of the temporary loss of air supremacy. By mid-May, the relentless German air operations prompted fears that the Red Army might be temporarily stalled or even forced to assume a defensive posture. In reaction to the deepening threat, the VVS reinforced forward airfields and took immediate steps to increase the number of operational airfields in the Romanian sector of the front. In this same period, a total of ninety active (and dummy) airfields were constructed. Typically, VVS fighters were deployed about 19 miles (30 kilometers) from the front, Shturmovik air units at 20 miles (32 kilometers), and bombers farther back at 81 miles (130 kilometers). The 5th Air Army attempted to enlarge the scope of its own air operations as a countermove, even as steps were taken to improve the logistics situation. At the end of May, some VVS air units were hampered by the absence of proper aviation fuel for the Allison engines that powered the Lend-Lease P-39 Airacobras.[25]

At this juncture in the war, new technological upgrades were beginning to shape the course of Soviet air operations. The 5th Air Army, for example, made dramatic strides in fitting its forward air units with proper equipment. Radios were now a familiar part of aircraft instrumentation, if not yet universally standard. The delivery of Lend-Lease aircraft only accelerated the transition. For the Romanian operations, a series of radio stations were set up, and radio beacons and modern techniques for air navigation were adopted. For low-flying Shturmovik air units, such changes resulted in more precise deployment and routing to targets, allowing greater surprise and impact with near dead-reckoning vectors to selected targets. Soviet air operations at this stage of the war also benefited from the use of the *Redut* radar system, although the broad use of radar remained problematic because the VVS still lacked properly trained specialists. There were other, less dramatic technical advances, such as the use of oxygen to allow aircraft to operate at higher altitudes. Yet the oxygen equipment presented the same persistent logistical problems experienced with other critical items such as replacement tires, engines, and spare parts—a situation aggravated by constant movement and the enormity of the active front. With the augmentation in VVS air units, many of which were fresh and inexperienced, there were also constant problems with discipline and coordination.

The short time frame of May 28 to June 8 offered forward VVS air units the opportunity to challenge and reverse the *Luftwaffe* air offensive. The initial step was to order a preemptive strike on German airfields at Roman and Khushi. To destroy the German air assets in place, the 5th Air Army deployed the 1st GShAK (*Gvardeyskiy Shturmovoy Aviatsionnyy Korpus*, or Guards ground attack air corps) and the 2nd ShAK, with air cover from the 7th IAK. Launched on May 28, the attack attempted to destroy around 200 German aircraft at these two airfields. Even though the attacking VVS aircraft observed strict radio silence, the enemy's radar warning system proved to be efficient. The element of surprise was compromised, but the raid's impact was significant: the Soviets recorded some thirty-five *Luftwaffe* aircraft destroyed or damaged.[26]

The tempo of German air operations intensified in the days that followed. The *Luftwaffe* ordered substantial numbers of Bf 109s, Fw 190s, and Ju 87s to attack Soviet infantry and mechanized units. On May 30, for example, German air units flew some 2,082 sorties against 2nd Ukrainian *Front* positions. By contrast, the VVS answered this massive air assault with only 703 sorties flown. Typically, groups of twenty to thirty German Fw 190s (bottom cover) and Bf 109s (top cover), often flying in echeloned formations as low as 2,000 to 2,500 feet (600 to 760 meters), provided a protective escort for the always vulnerable Ju 87 dive-bombers. Intense air battles unfolded as VVS fighters challenged this enemy air assault, and Soviet pilots scored some aerial triumphs against the seasoned *Luftwaffe* airmen. For example, Captain K. A. Yevstigneyev of the 240th IAP scored a total of ten air victories over northern Romania. Barkhorn later recalled the aggressive style and talents of certain VVS air units, most notably Pokryshkin's own 16th GIAP, which included noted aces A. Ivashko, N. Trofimov, K. Sukhov, G. Rechkalov, and A. Klubov. The VVS, however, paid a high price in downed aircraft: thirty-three Yak fighters of various types, twelve La-5s, sixty-five P-39 Airacobras, eight Pe-2s, and twenty-eight Il-2 Shturmoviks. German accounts list seventy-eight downed *Luftwaffe* airplanes.[27]

In the vortex of air battles above Yassy, some expert VVS pilots were hard-pressed, facing sudden life-threatening air attacks by the disciplined fighter units of the *Luftwaffe*. At this juncture of the war, attrition had compromised the Germans' capacity to wrestle air dominance from the VVS in any sustained way. On May 30, however, the air corridor above the Soviet 27th and 52nd Armies witnessed a display of German aggressiveness in a targeted tactical zone. Soviet pilot F. F. Archipenko of the 129th GIAP recorded a vivid example of how the enemy could execute a well-timed attack with devastating results. While on patrol that day, Archipenko spotted a group of six to eight Fw 190s in pursuit of a Soviet fighter pilot at the controls of a P-39. As the distance narrowed, one of the attacking German fighters made a tight turn and fired at close range on the Airacobra, with devastating results. Archipenko saw the VVS aircraft literally disintegrate with well-placed volleys into the fuselage, cabin, engine, tail, and control surfaces. The attack was sudden, with no avenue of escape for the doomed Soviet pilot. For VVS airmen, the skies above Yassy were filled with deadly peril.

The German airmen continued to disrupt VVS air sorties, especially when there were lapses in coordination and combat discipline. One incident even tarnished the reputation of Captain Grigoriy Rechkalov, one the most celebrated fighter pilots in the VVS. On May 31, German Bf 109s broke up an attacking group of fighters led by Rechkalov and his top cover led by Captain A. F. Klubov. In the foray, the Soviets lost five aircraft. The whole affair suggested a lack of vigilance, and the angry air division commander, Alexander Pokryshkin, complained of Rechkalov's "loss of control" and "absence of initiative." As a consequence, Rechkalov was temporarily removed from his regiment command role. This episode demonstrated that even one of the most celebrated VVS airmen could be compromised by aggressive *Luftwaffe* air tactics. This late in the war, though, the VVS was less tolerant of ineffectual air sorties.

There were unexpected dangers awaiting even the most aggressive and talented Soviet fighter pilots, such as Captain K. A. Yevstigneyev. While flying above the Yassy sector, he led a four-fighter attack on a group of low-flying Junkers (Ju 87s). Suddenly, from altitude, Yevstigneyev faced the guns of ten diving Bf 109 fighters. The enemy fighters were able to split Yevstigneyev's group and then apply pressure in a pincer movement. At this moment, however, Lieutenant V. F. Mudretsov made a counterattack, which prompted the German fighters to withdraw. Again, the attack had been well executed, making full use of surprise and altitude to disrupt the VVS formation. Too often, these isolated enemy attacks took a toll in unit commanders, as in the case of the 438th IAP's Major V. V. Sokolov.[28]

For many German pilots such as Major H. Frank, commander of the II/*Schlahgeschwader* (SG) 2, who was shot down and badly wounded, these tactical triumphs against the VVS over Yassy did not negate the reality of an army in retreat. Moreover, the Yassy operations became an occasion for the VVS to commit some of its most experienced and talented pilots. Pokryshkin's fabled 9th GIAD was active in the Yassy sector, and his *Pokryshkintsy* were not unknown to the *Luftwaffe*. As noted earlier, Barkhorn was wounded in the Yassy air fighting, a reminder that even the most skilled and resourceful of German aces were not immune from danger. The indomitable Hans Ulrich Rudel, the famed *Luftwaffe* Stuka pilot, described in his memoirs a harrowing encounter with VVS fighter pilots in the Yassy sector. On one sortie, alone except for his wingman, Rudel faced an onslaught of twenty P-39 fighters. Taking evasive action by flying low, Rudel discovered that escape was not easy. His rear gunner had been eliminated. Rudel attempted to maneuver as his aircraft was hit repeatedly by accurate fire from the circling Airacobras. One Soviet fighter made a frontal attack, forcing Rudel to dive into a ravine at extreme low altitude. The passage was so narrow that he nearly crashed. Somehow, the German pilot managed to evade his determined foes. Rudel returned to base exhausted in a bullet-ridden aircraft.[29] Often, Soviet fighter pilots pursued German aircraft in their own territory. Lieutenant V. S. Petukhov of the 16th GIAP chased an Fw 190 in a "merry-go-round" manner around a church until the Fw dropped to the ground due to a lack of fuel. Only by luck did Petukhov escape from this encounter unscathed. These individual exploits mirrored the routine perils faced by pilots on both sides.

For the Soviets, there was a reliance on certain tried and true air combat tactics. The VVS deployed twelve to sixteen aircraft in echeloned formations to provide greater mobility and a quick response to *Luftwaffe* sorties. Moreover, "free hunters," or *Okhotniki,* flew in formations of two aircraft across the front lines in the quest for targets of opportunity. These talented and experienced pilots were a threat to all *Luftwaffe* aircraft, since they could strike suddenly and with great effectiveness. Even biplanes such as the U-2 were thrown into the mix, making night harassment raids, often as many as twenty to twenty-four per night, and hitting German airfields and forward positions. Wherever possible, VVS fighter pilots attempted to break through German fighter cover and give chase to the Ju 87 dive-bombers attacking Soviet forward positions. Rudel reported how aggressively the VVS used the Lend-Lease P-39, which proved to be an effective interceptor. On June 1, for example, twelve P-39s from the 100th GIAP boldly engaged a formation of fifty attacking Ju 87s. As these air battles unfolded, the VVS displayed increased skill at fighter cover, the use of radio ciphers and radar, and the deployment of reserves.[30]

Luftwaffe tactics followed a certain pattern. For example, it became routine for groups of twelve to twenty Fw 190s to execute sudden and devastating raids, which were often facilitated by an ineffectual Soviet warning system. The enemy dove and dropped bombs from altitudes of 6,000 to 7,500 feet (2,000 to 2,500 meters). These same Fw 190s assumed cover for the second wave of slow-flying Stukas and were reluctant to engage in aerial battles with their opponents. This role was better executed by the agile Bf 109 fighters, which flew less disciplined sorties and were always alert to targets of opportunity. According to 7th IAK commander General A. V. Utin, these marauding Messerschmitts created a persistent threat everywhere.[31] Many of the German fighter pilots in this sector were aces, and some had acquired formidable reputations: the aforementioned Barkhorn, F. Oblesser,

Erich Hartman, and W. Wolfrum, among others. These fighter pilots displayed great skill in attacking VVS aircraft around Yassy, diving from altitude and exploiting sun and clouds for tactical advantage. As a consequence, VVS pilots adjusted their own tactics in response, most notably raising their patrol altitudes. This led to problems for Il-2s flying at lower levels: Fw 190s routinely attacked from below and Bf 109s from above—a sandwiching maneuver that often led to success. The Soviet fighters drawn to higher altitudes were capable of protecting the Shturmoviks from the top, but this left them vulnerable to occasional and devastating blows from below.

The *Luftwaffe's* combat effectiveness over Yassy and surrounding areas reached its apogee on June 2. On that day, German pilots and aircrews flew a total of 1,347 sorties. From this point onward, German sorties tapered off dramatically. Three days later, the 5th Air Army reached a tipping point in this intense and unforgiving air combat saga, flying a total of 927 sorties to the enemy's 777. The *Luftwaffe* had lost the advantage, and the VVS, now in command, pressed for air supremacy in the skies over Yassy. By June 8, the 5th Air Army alone had flown 5,751 sorties. This pattern would only intensify in the summer of 1944 as the VVS gained firm control of the skies. Never again would the *Luftwaffe* be able to launch such a major air offensive in the East. Defense of the Reich, with finite and ever-diminishing resources, became the fate of the once vaunted German air arm.[32]

Memoirs by surviving German pilots have left many detailed and vivid accounts of air combat in the skies over Yassy. Most of these recollections note the growing alarm over enhanced VVS skills, particularly the effort to engage the *Luftwaffe* at all altitudes. German ace Helmut Lipfert of II/JG 52 described the air battles that unfolded on June 3. "We soon learned," Lipfert recorded in his diary, "that there were Russians in the combat zone who could fly as well as we."

My wingman and I carefully approached the front at 7,500 feet (2,500 meters), being alert to the presence of Il-2s reported in the area. Suddenly, we sighted them, flying 3,000 feet (1,000 meters) below us. As a precaution, I looked around one more time before attacking the Il-2s and spotted two enemy Airacobras with their distinctive red noses coming at us from out of the sun. I quickly instructed my wingman to stay close. I waited and acted as if I had not noticed the approaching fighters. When the Russians were in firing range, we made a tight turn. The two Airacobras shot past as they were unable to turn with us. The Russian pilots, however, did not abandon the fight. They pulled up and came down at us again. They made one attack after another, forcing us to a lower altitude. Soon the two enemy aircraft became four. Now in the face of these alternating attacks, we were denied any opportunity to fire. My wingman was even hit several times. I then rammed the throttle forward, pulled the stick back into my stomach and spun down from 3,000 feet (1,000 meters) to almost ground level. I pulled out and raced away to the southwest. I saw an aircraft at my seven o'clock position—to my relief, it was my wingman's "109." He had stayed rigidly behind me and had even emulated my spin. I decided not to let the Russians catch us so easily a second time, so we climbed quickly to around 13,500 feet (4,500 meters). But even at this higher altitude several Airacobras jumped us from above and gave us a scare. . . . On the third sortie we climbed to 18,000 feet (6,000 meters); I had never encountered Russian aircraft at a higher altitude. But once again we failed to even reach the front. All I saw were Airacobras above. We were forced to flee the area. Now I had really had enough, and following a steep Split-S I made [for] my home with my wingman as fast as I could. I was furious when I landed. Never before had the Russians simply not allowed me to get into attack position.[33]

Over Yassy and the entire northern Romanian sector, the VVS displayed its muscular reserves in a timely and effective way. This reservoir of air assets mirrored the vast expansion of the Soviet air armies. By contrast, the *Luftwaffe* had to contend with high attrition and only sporadic reinforcements of machines and personnel. This use of reserves by the VVS, in retrospect, was a fateful harbinger. In 1942, a typical air army consisted of 300 to 400 aircraft, depending on deployment and operational status. By midwar, this average had increased to 650 to 1,000 aircraft. And for the final air offensives of the 1944–1945 campaign, the typical air army fielded 1,800 to 2,500 aircraft. Critical battles such as the final assault on Berlin saw the deployment of more than 3,000 aircraft. Improved command and control techniques and air tactics allowed the VVS to operate in myriad settings and weather conditions. Evident in the skies over Yassy in the spring and early summer of 1944 were telltale signs of the maturation of Soviet airpower in the crucible of the Eastern Front, a dress rehearsal for the final drive to Berlin.[34]

The intense air struggle over Yassy became the last time the *Luftwaffe* asserted and maintained local air supremacy over the battlefield—in this case, under the pressures of a major Soviet offensive. At Kursk, such operations in a key battle zone assured dominance for a week; at Yassy, by contrast, control of the air—always tentative— endured for just two days. In both cases—at Kursk and at Yassy—the German commanders implemented impeccable command and control, and the pilots endured heavy workloads. The *Luftwaffe* maneuvered its resources, bringing airfields close to the battle lines at critical moments. The VVS did not have such an advantage. For example, the 9th GIAD was based at Stefanesthti airfield, 38.5 miles (62 kilometers) from the front lines, while the airfield of the 104th IAP at Kheneshti was nearly 50 miles (80 kilometers) away. It took at least half an hour to get to the battle zone.

On average, every serviceable German airplane made three sorties per day during the first three days of the operation. In contrast, only six of ten Soviet airplanes were launched, and the crews of only a few air units made two sorties a day during the same time frame. This allowed the *Luftwaffe* to achieve numerical superiority and conduct aerial battles with a significant advantage. Even after Soviet patrols were increased to twelve to fourteen fighters in the beginning of June, they had to cover an area that was targeted by twenty-two to twenty-four Ju 87s, accompanied by a pair of Bf 109s and a four-ship formation of Fw 190s. The Germans were also masterful in reinforcing their patrols in the air. Chief of staff of the 5th Air Army, General N. P. Seleznev, noted that credit should be given to the Germans for their skillful coordination of all types of aviation and the ability to boost their presence over the battlefield, which had also been observed in 1943. In addition, he noted that the Germans had demonstrated optimal use of radios for air-to-air and air-to-ground communications.

Although the VVS aircrews made preemptive air strikes at German airfields, they were unable to impose their will on the enemy. Passive tactics of constant patrols put the Soviet fighters at a clear disadvantage and gave the initiative to the enemy. The Germans were able to choose where and how to get to their targets. Soviet aviators bitterly referred to their own actions as "achieving air supremacy following the schedule." General I. D. Podgornyy, commander of the 4th IAK, was one of the air commanders who attempted to implement modern fighter tactics. He noted that permanent patrols were resource-intensive and involved the disproportionate use of engine hours and fuel. Much higher efficiency could be achieved by employing the intercept technique, particularly with the aid of radar and the actions of the *Okhotniki*. The experience gained by Podgornyy's pilots in the fall of 1943 over Dnieper bridgeheads showed that the use of such tactics resulted in more enemy planes destroyed, and the enemy was more often denied the achievement of its objectives. Podgornyy bitterly concluded that inefficient patrol methods had to be continued to bring moral satisfaction to ground troops, especially the infantry, which felt more confident with the presence of its own fighters over the battle-field.[35]

By the spring and summer of 1944, the composition of the VVS had become more heterogeneous. Along with experienced officers who commanded squadrons and regiments, there were many newly minted pilots who lacked combat experience. The former were dangerous opponents to any *jagdflieger* (German fighter pilots), which was demonstrated during the intense aerial battle over Yassy. In terms of tactical preparedness, piloting skills, and accuracy of fire—all of which combine to define a fighter pilot—there was little difference between the leading aces of the opposing sides. The Germans, though, were much more proficient in the conduct of air combat in large groups. Only in 1948 did the VVS conduct air combat exercises in regimental or larger formations against columns of bombers.

THE BELORUSSIAN CAMPAIGN

The Anglo-American landings at Normandy on June 6, 1944, signaled the long-awaited second front against Nazi Germany. This pivotal event, a massive escalation of Allied pressure in the West (albeit a belated effort from the Soviet perspective), marked a turning point in the war. No less spectacular was the Soviet offensive in Belorussia in June–July, which crushed Army Group Center, liberated the last vestiges of German-occupied Soviet territory, and paved the way for the invasion of Poland and the conquest of Berlin. This massive application of Soviet power in the Belorussian campaign, according to General Rudenko, demonstrated the enlarged role of the VVS in the major army offensive during the third period of the war. The Belorussian air offensive, in both its preparatory and its attack phases, revealed the VVS at full stride—5,683 operational aircraft from five air armies, supplemented by 1,000 bombers drawn from eight ADD bomber air corps.[36]

Code-named Operation Bagration, after a Russian national hero in the war against Napoleon, the Soviet summer offensive had an ambitious aim: to annihilate Field Marshal Ernst Busch's Army Group Center. In June 1944, Army Group Center occupied a salient, more or less coextensive with Belorussia, that extended eastward along the upper reaches of the Dnieper River toward Moscow. This bulge covered a vast area with a 650-mile (1,200-kilometer) front, a region of marshy lowlands, forests, and lakes situated between the Baltic states and Ukraine. The area had remained under German occupation since 1941. However, Soviet offensives north and south of the salient in 1943 left the flanks of Army Group Center dangerously exposed. The German High Command, anticipating a Soviet summer offensive in the South, had stripped Busch of a significant amount of his infantry, tanks, and artillery, a move that made the Germans' position in the center extremely vulnerable. On the eve of the Soviet attack, Army Group Center consisted of approximately 400,000 men.

Operation Bagration became the most carefully planned Soviet offensive in the war. The *Stavka* had elaborated a blueprint for a two-phase offensive in mid-May that called for the extensive use of airpower in both phases. Novikov himself played a prominent role in the *Stavka* planning sessions held on May 22–23 with Marshals Zhukov and Vasilevskiy and the participating *Front* commanders. The first phase of the Belorussian offensive, scheduled to begin on June 22, called for four Soviet *Fronts* to break through the German-held salient at six points. With overwhelming forces concentrated on the narrow breakthrough sectors, the Soviets planned to envelop Army Group Center. Partisan activity, already a serious challenge to German forces in Belorussia, would move into high gear concurrently, destroying vital supplies and creating havoc in the enemy rear. Once

German opposition had been crushed, the second phase, set to start on July 15, would carry the Soviet drive westward into Poland, the Baltic states, and East Prussia.[37]

According to Earl Ziemke, Operation Bagration proved to be a worthy Soviet counterpart to Operation Barbarossa, which had been launched on the same date three years earlier. "In executing the breakthrough," he wrote, "the Russians showed elegance in their tactical conceptions, economy of force, and control that did not fall short of the Germans' own performance in the early war years."[38] Airpower played a crucial role, hitting German positions with overwhelming firepower. The VVS assigned 1,733 ground attack airplanes from five air armies.[39] The depleted ranks of the *Luftwaffe*, now critically short of personnel and aircraft replacements, could not muster even token resistance on June 22, a situation made worse by shortages in aviation fuel.[40]

The lethal power of the VVS air offensive in Belorussia can be understood only if examined against the backdrop of the Soviet aviation industry. During the first six months of 1944, Soviet aircraft production made a phenomenal leap, allowing the *Stavka* to assign 5,000 combat aircraft to its frontal air armies, the ADD, the naval air arm, and the PVO.[41] By June 1, 1944, Soviet airpower (including the ADD and naval aviation) consisted of 18,709 planes.[42] Total production for the first half of 1944 reached 16,000 airplanes; this permitted the VVS to fully replenish its air armies, which had suffered high attrition during the winter months.[43]

Soviets records suggest that *Luftflotte* 6, then deployed at airfields at Minsk, Baranovichi, and Bobruysk, possessed 1,342 aircraft on the eve of the offensive.[44] German figures closely correspond to this estimate, recording 1,269 aircraft assigned to *Luftflotte* 6, including 398 bombers, 137 fighters, 152 ground attack planes, and 142 reconnaissance aircraft.[45] Although German aircraft production had increased in 1944, the *Luftwaffe*'s replacement capacity could not keep pace with the Soviets'. Against the growing VVS juggernaut, the *Luftwaffe* in the Eastern Front found itself outnumbered almost six to one in operational combat aircraft.[46]

On the eve of Operation Bagration, Novikov again sought to improve the effectiveness of VVS air operations. In a directive to all frontal air armies in early June 1944, he summarized the results of the

winter air operations, pointing out shortcomings and ordering correc-
tive measures to be taken by division commanders. He reaffirmed in
his directive the tactical character of VVS air operations: the various
air staffs were to work diligently to improve the interaction of aviation
with tank and mechanized formations. In July, Novikov ordered all
fighter division commanders and their air staffs to tighten up radio air
control procedures, an area of persistent difficulties. Air control for
both fighters and ground attack aircraft became more problematic in
1943–1944 with the expanded inventory of aircraft and the aggressive
posture assumed by the VVS. Novikov found that his stress on centralized control of air operations had been too rigidly applied, to the point
where the VVS lost flexibility and the capacity to respond quickly.
Consequently, he prohibited air army commanders from controlling
the actions of individual groups of VVS aircraft; instead, they were to
give general instructions to the various air corps and division commanders, who would then direct the frontline sorties as circumstances
dictated.

Overall, VVS air operations in the 1st and 3rd Belorussian *Fronts* reflected the principle of centralization, which was now the normative
pattern. Yet air commanders occasionally permitted some decentralization of command to allow rapid shifts in deployment and operations. Often there were urgent calls for air support to assist advancing
ground forces. To respond in a timely and effective way, the VVS embraced the key principle of mobility on the tactical and operational
levels. To achieve this end, there was the need to allow local commanders some degree of initiative. Such concessions did not compromise the overriding notion of centralization of airpower, however. Air
army commanders retained their ability to oversee the unfolding pattern as air assets were targeted and retargeted. The Belorussian campaign offered new avenues to exercise flexibility in the application of
airpower.[47]

Novikov also ordered the air army chiefs of staff to visit their subordinate staffs in a systematic fashion to sharpen overall control and
efficient interaction. As reinforcements arrived at frontline airfields,
Novikov himself, along with *Stavka* air liaison officers such as General
Falaleyev, visited the headquarters of the various *Front* commanders
to plan and coordinate air operations. Such activities were administrative as well. Novikov oversaw the construction of seventy new air-

fields to accommodate the ten VVS air corps and eight air divisions sent to the Belorussian axis in the first half of June.[48]

Planning for the Belorussian air operations, which included mobilization, basing, command and control, and logistical support, required considerable effort. Novikov's centralized structure made these time-consuming tasks much easier for the various air armies. Marshal Zhukov, representing the *Stavka,* arrived at the front on June 5. His overall leadership, along with that of Marshal Vasilevskiy, encouraged the effective use of the combined arms concept. Zhukov worked with Novikov and other air commanders, such as Golovanov, Rudenko, and Vershinin, in planning the operations for frontal aviation and the ADD. At one point, the tough-minded Zhukov required the commander of the 1st Belorussian *Front* and his army subordinates to rehearse the forthcoming offensive in a remote forest. There, in a scaled-down simulation, the army, division, and regiment commanders acted out the script for the offensive, working out the details of interaction and answering Zhukov's questions. Zhukov took particular pains to involve the various air commanders in these elaborate preparations. Novikov suggested, and Zhukov approved, the idea of massive bombing sweeps by the ADD in the preparatory phases of Operation Bagration. For ten days leading up to the offensive, VVS bomber units attacked the various enemy airfields, flying a total of 1,472 sorties.[49]

Night bombing missions by women pilots, flying the open-cockpit U-2 biplanes, also applied pressure on enemy positions opposite the Soviet 2nd Belorussian *Front.* The 46th GNBAP, commanded by Major Ye. D. Bershanskaya, illustrated the willingness of the Soviet military to allow women to engage in actual combat. This air regiment engaged in numerous night bombing sorties; they were flown at extremely low altitudes and often through a gauntlet of enemy antiaircraft fire, always a high risk. Other women became prominent war heroines, such as Colonel V. S. Grizodubova, Hero of the Soviet Union and commander of the 31st GBAP (*Gvardeyskiy Bombardirovochnyy Aviatsionnyy Polk,* or Guards bomber air regiment), and Major Marina Raskova, a prewar long-distance aviator who was killed in action and later buried in the Kremlin wall. There was also a female ace, Lilya Litvyak, who flew with the 7th IAP and, before her death in 1943, downed seven German planes (four personal and three shared).[50] German airmen were always surprised to encounter VVS women pilots in active combat roles. One *Luftwaffe* pilot, Major D. B. Meyer, remembered being attacked near Orel by a group of Yak fighters. During the ensuing air duel, the jettisoned canopy of Meyer's fighter struck the propeller of one of the pursuing Yaks, forcing it to crash. Upon landing, Meyer found that his dead adversary was a woman—without rank insignia or parachute. On another occasion, over the Gulf of Finland on May 5, 1943, the *Luftwaffe* downed a Lend-Lease A-20 Boston and discovered that the three-member crew included one woman—a gunner. The use of women in the Soviet armed forces, occasionally in active combat roles, came as a surprise to the German military.[51]

Although the pilots of Major Bershanskaya's regiment acquired fame for their work in the Belorussian campaign, they were not the only women in active or auxiliary military service. In the Soviet army's medical service, women constituted 41 percent of the doctors, 43 percent of the medical assistants, and 100 percent of the nurses. In the Moscow PVO force, 30.5 percent of the personnel were women. Women also served as liaison pilots to the partisans, always a vital combat assignment; snipers (as at Stalingrad); tank crew members; administrative support workers; and, of course, laborers in the war plants. A total of eighty-six women were awarded the Gold Star, Hero of the Soviet Union.[52]

For the Belorussian operations, the *Stavka* assigned air armies to the following *Fronts:* the 3rd Air Army to the 1st Baltic *Front*, the 1st Air Army to the 3rd Belorussian *Front*, the 4th Air Army to the 2nd Belorussian *Front*, and the 16th Air Army to the 1st Belorussian *Front* (see Table 2). This core component was reinforced by the timely arrival of reserve air units. Just prior to the offensive, over a period of ten to fifteen days, the 1st and 16th Air Armies received a substantial number of reserves. For example, the 1st Air Army commander welcomed three air corps and one division of fighters, for a total of 864 aircraft. In addition, the 1st received 280 ground attack aircraft, 272 bombers, and 90 ADD bombers. Following this pattern, the 16th Air Army was reinforced with two fighter corps of 480 planes, along with 270 ground attack aircraft, 190 bombers, and a mixed air unit of some 107 aircraft. Consequently, these two air armies entered the Belorussian campaign with an augmented strength of 2,553 warplanes of various types. The *Luftwaffe* at this stage of the war could not match such a muscular display of airpower.[53]

Table 2. Serviceable VVS Air Army Aircraft by the Beginning of Operation Bagration, June 1944

Aircraft Type	3rd Air Army	1st Air Army	4th Air Army	16th Air Army	Total
Fighter	399	984	193	952	2,528
Bomber					
Day	—	340	—	297	637
Night	79	80	121	155	435
Shturmovik	371	530	196	636	1,733
Reconnaissance	36	30	18	—	84
Total	885	1,964	528	2,040	5,417

The VVS's numerical superiority over the *Luftwaffe* now exceeded four to one—a decisive advantage that routinely assured air superiority to the Soviet side. At the cutting edge of VVS operations were the fighters and ground attack aircraft. In these categories, the VVS possessed overwhelming numbers. For the Germans, there were additional problems associated with fighting a defensive war. The *Luftwaffe* had concentrated the bulk of its force to face the 1st and 3rd Belorussian *Fronts*. This move was complicated by the fact that there were few airfields available or properly situated to conduct effective air operations. Consequently, German air units were deployed in a haphazard fashion and at great depth—distances of 62 to 93 miles (100 to 150 kilometers).

On June 23, Soviet night bombers began systematic sorties against German defensive positions and troop concentrations. In this operation, air units of the 1st Baltic *Front* and the 3rd and 2nd Belorussian *Fronts* flew a total of 1,087 sorties, which amounted to a continuous assault on the enemy defenses. At dawn on June 23, just two hours in advance of the launch of ground operations, groups of Shturmoviks and bombers, a force varying from 30 to 100 aircraft, made coordinated blows on the main enemy concentrations. The VVS aircraft focused on striking German command centers and communication links, in a concerted effort to disrupt the enemy's ability to act. Fighter aviation provided cover for the advancing ground troops in large groups of twenty to fifty aircraft. *Luftwaffe* aircraft proved to be weak and disoriented, appearing only in small numbers and opting not to engage in air combat. By contrast, German air units were more active along the axis of the 1st Belorussian *Front*, but this initiative was blunted by the VVS patrols intent on denying the enemy easy access to the field of battle. On the morning of June 24, the weather deteriorated and limited all air action on both sides, especially bomber sorties flown by air units attached to the 1st Belorussian *Front*. Even in this context, Shturmoviks and fighters, flying in formations of four to eight aircraft, were able to target enemy artillery positions.[54]

The Soviets unleashed the Belorussian campaign over a three-day period in a series of bold offensives that had immediate and devastating results. Advancing Soviet forces attacked the German northern flank on June 22, the central sector on June 23, and the southern area of the German salient just above the Pripyat Marshes on June 24. Each of these attacks fell on Army Group Center, much like successive tidal waves crashing on a beach; they were overwhelming in their effect, forcing the German units to fall back in confusion. Soviet airpower, applied on the cutting edge of the offensive, had a powerful impact. Never before had Soviet aircraft appeared in such numbers and force. General I. Kh. Bagramyan's 1st Baltic *Front* and General I. D. Chernyakhovskiy's 3rd Belorussian *Front*—supported by the 3rd and 1st Air Armies—pushed forward rapidly, shattering Colonel General Georg-Hans Reinhardt's Third Panzer Army and isolating German-held Vitebsk.

By June 25, the German LIII Corps, under Major General Friedrich Gollwitzer, had been encircled at Vitebsk. During the next two days, LIII Corps fought desperately to free itself from the Soviet pincers. VVS units flew repeated sorties against the encircled enemy troops in coordination with Soviet ground forces—a steady application of pressure that forced Gollwitzer to surrender on June 27. For this phase of the operation, the 3rd and 1st Air Armies had a total of 2,881 aircraft.

In the center, General G. F. Zakharov's 2nd Belorussian *Front* moved forward against German defensive positions along the line east of the Dnieper River between Orsha and Mogilev. Here, the veteran 4th Air Army under General Vershinin deployed some 528 aircraft, attacking enemy artillery positions and strafing retreating infantry and mechanized units. This phase of the Soviet offensive proved to be very effective. With their Orsha and Mogilev lines shattered, the Germans retreated westward toward the Berezina River. Near the city of Berezino, the VVS attacked vulnerable German river crossings with elements of the 4th and 16th Air Armies. Between June 28 and 30, the VVS flew 3,000 sorties in a systematic effort to halt the German retreat. Waves of *Shturmoviki* executed low-level strikes at German troops who had clustered on the east bank of the Berezina River. The pressure from these air armies continued unabated from June 29 to July 3. All these coordinated attacks slowed the enemy's withdrawal across the river toward Minsk. Behind the elaborate Soviet air operations was the goal of a pincer movement to close at Minsk. In the center, the VVS established local air superiority quickly, which enabled Soviet aviation to hamper the German withdrawal. By late June, the Germans were fighting desperately to prevent their encirclement at Minsk.[55] The Belorussian offensive in the center witnessed the successful coordination of three strike forces: Soviet tank formations encircled a large concentration of German troops (German Fourth Army) east of Minsk by advancing from the north and the south, infantry assaulted the German frontline positions, and the VVS blocked the enemy's retreat to Minsk.

The bulk of VVS aircraft assisted the advancing tank, cavalry, and mechanized units, often hitting retreating columns of enemy troops. On the first day of the offensive, the VVS carried out more than 4,000 sorties and sorties on the second and third days exceeded 7,000. The great bulk of these sorties struck enemy convoys of tanks, along with mechanized and horse-drawn vehicles. The aim was to apply constant pressure and to deny the retreating enemy the opportunity to form new defensive lines.

To the south, General Rokossovskiy led a two-pronged attack by the 1st Belorussian *Front* against Bobruysk, a heavily fortified German position protecting Army Group Center along the Berezina River above the Pripyat Marshes. Here, Lieutenant General Hans Jordan's powerful Ninth Army occupied both sides of the river. In response, Novikov deployed the 16th Air Army, a force of 2,096 aircraft under General Rudenko, to support Rokossovskiy's assault. The 6th Air Army, under General F. P. Polynin, reinforced Rudenko's air armada with 178 planes.[56] Because the Soviets anticipated powerful German resistance in the Bobruysk sector, the *Stavka* delayed Rokossovskiy's main attack until June 24 to allow ADD units to participate fully in the opening strikes and then shift their power southward in time to assist in the drive on Bobruysk.

The Bobruysk operation allowed the VVS to apply the full fury of an air offensive in both the preparatory and attack phases. More than 300 bombers participated in the night preparatory air strikes. After the artillery barrage on the morning of June 24, VVS bombers and ground attack planes made two massed attacks on German defensive positions. With more than 3,200 sorties completed on the first day, the VVS appeared like a locust storm over the narrow Bobruysk breakthrough zones. Valery Grossman, a Soviet reporter, observed that "the sky was in tumult" as the 16th Air Army attacked enemy fortified positions, "with the rhythmic roaring of the dive bombers, the hard, metallic voices of the attack planes, the piercing whine of Yakovlev fighters. Fields and meadows were splashed with the darting outlines of hundreds of planes."[57] Once the enemy defensive lines had been penetrated by Soviet ground forces, the VVS air units shifted their focus to sustained attacks on the retreating enemy. Systematic strikes by large air groups hit mechanized convoys and troop concentrations. Air commanders vectored VVS aircraft to attack railroad stations, river crossings, and highways—any place the enemy moved and attempted to regroup. The tactic proved to be very effective, creating no small amount of confusion and disorientation within the ranks of the retreating enemy. The 16th Air Army flew sorties against the German forces moving toward Bobruysk, an intense two-day period of air action (June 24–25). Air reconnaissance alerted the Soviet pilots to a large column of cars, carts, and assorted vehicles on a road in the Bobruysk sector, and multiple attacks were made on the exposed German troops as they made their hasty retreat. Wherever possible, the VVS ground attack aircraft attempted to stop and seal off the retreat of convoys on main highways and at river crossings. These air operations were continuous and had a devastating impact on the enemy. The work of the 16th Air Army prevented the enemy from regrouping and in turn aided Soviet efforts to encircle a large German force near Bobruysk.[58]

Once the enemy lines had been penetrated, the VVS assumed tactics of pursuit and harassment. Soviet airmen unleashed a series of powerful blows on the retreating columns of troops and vehicles. As the pressure increased, the enemy became disoriented, with large numbers of troops and vehicles concentrated in narrow roads and retreat arteries. One dramatic example was the air sorties of the 16th Air

Soviet Il-2 Shturmoviks in flight. (From the collection of Valeriy Romanenko)

Army in the Bobruysk sector. Between June 24 and 26, the enemy was forced into disorderly retreat, escaping on various roads leading out of the city. VVS air reconnaissance crews actively monitored the columns of German troops and mechanized units. Groups of VVS bombers repeatedly struck the main force at Titovka, about 4 miles (6 kilometers) east of Bobruysk. Ground attack aircraft were also active, hitting the enemy at a Berezina River crossing. The whole operation reflected the optimal, coordinated use of VVS reconnaissance and attack aviation. As a result of the uninterrupted air strikes at roads and river crossings, the enemy was denied retreat options, and favorable conditions were created for encirclement of the large German grouping.[59]

Despite fierce German opposition, the Soviets surrounded Bobruysk on June 27, trapping elements of the Ninth Army. Some 30,000 troops managed to breach the Soviet ring of encirclement on June 29, but the entire southern sector of Army Group Center had been ripped open. Once the town of Bobruysk fell, Soviet mechanized units continued to advance from two sides on Minsk. On July 3, the forces of Marshal Rokossovskiy[60] and General Chernyakhovskiy closed the pincer west of Minsk. Throughout this offensive, the VVS maintained an aggressive posture, attacking along the breakthrough corridors and applying pressure on the German rear areas. VVS bombers and Shturmoviks struck repeatedly at the enemy on crowded highways and bridges, at airfields, and at supply depots. Soviet aviation strafed enemy reserves moving forward. With its defenses breached at six points, Army Group Center had been shattered, forcing the *Wehrmacht* into a chaotic retreat—a catastrophe of major proportions that could not be reversed by Hitler's appointment of Field Marshal Walther Model on June 28.

By July 4, the Soviet Belorussian offensive had achieved its essential objective: Army Group Center had been crushed and no longer functioned as a viable entity. The German High Command had lost nearly 300,000 men in less than two weeks. As a component in this dramatic victory, the VVS flew 153,545 sorties from June 22 to August 29.[61] Over Belorussia, Soviet tactical airpower flew into combat on an unprecedented scale, giving the VVS absolute air superiority during the entire offensive.

In retrospect, the VVS triumph reflected a blend of converging strengths born of defeat in 1941 and refined over the course of a brutal war. By 1944, the reforms pursued by Novikov and other air commanders had reached fruition. The emerging air force organization had achieved optimal efficiency, allowing sustained air offensives against the enemy. The air armies had been augmented in size and striking power on the eve of a major offensive in a coordinated fashion. Once deployed for action, this massive concentration of airpower quickly dominated the skies. This pattern of reform and renewal affirmed the principle that the air force is an integral part of combined arms warfare. The VVS's transformation could be measured in both quantitative and qualitative terms. The war-induced stress on proper training—training that was keyed to technical changes and battle experience—was evident in the VVS organization and leadership, aircrews, and support entities. That the VVS was now a powerful and effective tactical air arm had been dramatically confirmed on the battlefield.

The Belorussian campaign revealed a variety of new capabilities on the Soviet side. Prior to the launching of the major offensive, the VVS successfully concealed the buildup in air assets. To enhance the element of surprise, aerial reconnaissance carefully and systematically mapped the deployment of enemy forces. Such critical data shaped military planning. Such a spirited program of aerial reconnaissance assisted the VVS's preparatory work for the great offensive, but it also helped refine planning for the ground forces—infantry, tanks, and artillery—as they plotted key targets and breakthrough corridors. The VVS forged an effective series of sorties to fulfill the critical task of ground control. This effort was carried out in full coordination with the ground commanders. During the breakthrough phase, the VVS air units were restricted to the narrow task of providing air support. In this sense, they were attached to the leading edge of the Soviet advance. Such a precise focus proved highly effective. All types of VVS aircraft were mobilized. The weight and concentration of Soviet airpower precluded any sustained effort by the *Luftwaffe* to brunt an offensive once it was in motion. At no time in the war had the VVS displayed such striking power and flexibility in offensive operations.

The VVS also pursued the goal of deploying large air formations in the main axis of a breakthrough operation. In this formidable exercise in combined arms warfare, the Soviets were able to fly countless sorties with a variety of aircraft types. These aircraft offered continual support for the mobile units of the Red Army for the entire duration of the operation. Large reserves were also available to the air army commanders, to be employed as reinforcements whenever necessary. Concentrated air strikes by large groups of VVS aircraft along breakthrough corridors and over the battlefield greatly assisted the ground forces as they advanced into the enemy rear areas.[62]

Among the important Soviet innovations during Operation Bagration was the skillful use of the ADD, the Soviet long-range bombers. Air Marshal A. E. Golovanov and his deputy, General N. S. Skripko, played a vital part in planning the Belorussian air operations. The tactical employment of long-range bombers—in actuality, a force consisting largely of medium bombers (Il-4s, B-25 Mitchells, some A-20 Bostons, and Li-2s converted for night bombing)—represented a shrewd stewardship of the growing ADD inventory. These aircraft had little range and lacked the striking power to operate as genuine strategic bombers. Moreover, Soviet air doctrine had abandoned any notion of strategic bombing prior to the war in favor of building a strong tactical air arm. Golovanov's ADD units (later reorganized as the 18th Air Army) provided a powerful striking force in the breakthrough zones

Mounting of a two-ton high-explosive FAB-2000 bomb on a Pe-8 heavy bomber. (From the collection of Valeriy Romanenko)

and against the immediate German rear areas during Operation Bagration. By 1944, day and night bombing of German rear installations had become commonplace, and in Soviet offensive operations, VVS and ADD bombers assumed an enlarged role in blunting German withdrawal movements.[63]

For individual Soviet pilots, there were frequent opportunities to engage in air combat duels with their *Luftwaffe* counterparts. Fighter pilot G. Lobov, later a lieutenant general in the VVS and recipient of the Gold Star, Hero of the Soviet Union, found the return to the skies over Belorussia in the summer of 1944 a matter of personal vindication. Lobov's fighter regiment had endured bitter defeat during Operation Barbarossa. Now, three years later, Lobov returned to the same area flying a modern La-5 fighter—first over the Vitebsk and Orsha sectors, providing escort for bombers and ground attack planes, and then in fighter sweeps against various targets of opportunity during the German withdrawal. Over Bogushevsk, Lobov escorted bombers in a series of air strikes. Before the attack, VVS fighters cleared the target zone of enemy aircraft. The main force of bombers followed in groups of nine, with a *para* of fighters proceeding to either side of each bomber column (the fighter *para* alternated to the left and right with successive groups). Above, and 1 to 2 miles (1.6 to 3.2 kilometers) to the rear, a larger group of fighters provided cover, Lobov reported.

On one "free hunt" mission near Orsha on June 23, Lobov flew his La-5 in a *para* formation against four Fw 190s. The combat that followed involved alternating upward and downward spirals. Lobov's *para* claimed two victories. Knowing that the Fw 190 was superior to the La-5 in dives, and that the reverse was true in climbing speed, the Germans willingly accepted combat in tight turns, according to Lobov, and if the engagement proved disappointing, they quickly withdrew with a roll and steep bank. Lobov and others avoided combat during diving maneuvers, if possible, and strove instead to catch the Fw 190s at the moment they recovered from a dive.

Lobov and his fellow fighter pilots learned to increase the distances and intervals between pairs, a technique forged through combat experience. "The 'stacks' used in aerial combat in the Kuban were altered slightly. Because the main enemy forces acted from low altitudes up to 9,900 feet (3,000 meters), and the combat qualities of our aircraft enabled us to conduct combat successfully even without an initial altitude advantage over the enemy, we began to concentrate our forces at altitudes up to 13,000 feet (4,000 meters). This immediately increased the number of encounters with fascist aircraft."[64] During the Belorussian air operations, VVS fighters also expanded their sorties against enemy ground targets. Some VVS fighters were equipped with bomb racks and armed with two bombs. These changes required new training.

By the end of August 1944, the Soviet offensive in Belorussia had ended: Army Group Center had been crushed, Belorussia had been liberated, and Soviet troops had marched 373 miles (690 kilometers) westward, reaching Lithuania and Poland. From July to November 1944, the Soviet army cleared Moldavia, captured the Ploesti oil fields and Bucharest, and invaded Bulgaria; in the North, troops swept through the Baltic states and reached the Vistula River at Warsaw. The rapidity of the Soviet advance during this period again stretched the capacity of the various VVS air armies to keep pace. Logistical support became an acute problem. On July 23, the 16th Air Army, which had participated in the Bobruysk–Minsk fighting in support of Rokossovskiy's 1st Belorussian *Front*, found itself with just enough fuel for one refueling of its operational aircraft. The rapid push forward did not always provide adequate airfields for the redeployment of VVS units.

NEW ALLIES AND NEW CHALLENGES

With the impressive air triumphs in Belorussia, the *Stavka* moved to expand VVS air operations and make them more international in scope. This new internationalism took two forms: the expansion of foreign volunteer air regiments to include nationalities that would soon fall under the domination of the Soviet army—Poles, Czechs, Romanians, and Bulgarians—and an awkward collaboration with the Americans in so-called "shuttle raids." Neither of these experiments grew out of any pressing combat requirements of the Russo-German War: the VVS did not lack pilots or aircraft in 1944, and the *Stavka* was confident that victory over Nazi Germany was merely a matter of time. Soviet motivations, always opaque and self-serving, grew out of political considerations in eastern Europe on the eve of "liberation" and a reluctant acquiescence to an important ally's repeated requests for assistance in the strategic bombing campaign against Germany.

The use of foreign pilots originated in 1942 when the Normandie Fighter Air Regiment was organized.[65] This regiment, consisting of French volunteers, participated in air battles at Kursk and later in the Belorussian and East Prussian campaigns. Although some of the *Luftwaffe* pilots considered the French unit a minor irritant at best, Soviet propaganda organs portrayed its combat role in heroic terms and as an expression of international solidarity against "fascist aggression." Several French aces received the Gold Star, Hero of the Soviet Union, and the unit was renamed the Normandie–Nieman regiment in October 1944, in recognition of its contribution in covering Soviet troops crossing the Nieman River.

The Normandie regiment flew a total of 5,240 sorties, fought 900 air battles, and scored 273 confirmed victories in the course of the war on the Eastern Front.[66] Soon the French fliers were not alone. As early as July 1944, Polish pilots were recruited to fight along with Soviet aircrews. As the Soviet army approached Poland, new Polish units took shape—the 1st Warsaw Fighter Air Regiment, equipped with Yak-1s,

Rene Challe (eight victories) and Maurice Challe (ten personal plus five shared victories; missing in action March 27, 1945) of the Normandie-Nieman French regiment with a Yak-9T fighter. (From the collection of Von Hardesty)

and the 2nd Krakow Night Bomber Air Regiment, flying Po-2s. By the end of the year, Polish regiments were numerous enough to organize into divisions—the Polish 4th Mixed Air Division, consisting of the 1st Fighter, 2nd Light Bomber, and 3rd Ground Attack Regiments.[67] Such efforts persisted into 1945, when the Polish 1st Mixed Air Corps, consisting of fighter, bomber, and ground attack divisions, took form under the command of General F. A. Agaltsov. From these Soviet-equipped air units a new "Polish Air Force" emerged in 1945. The Soviet-created Polish air arm flew more than 5,000 sorties from August 1944 to the end of the war.

Other eastern European nationalities soon found themselves participating in expanded Soviet air operations. Czech pilots were organized into a fighter air regiment in July 1944, a unit later expanded into the 1st Mixed Air Division. Like the Poles, the Czechs initially flew with VVS air units. Typically, Czech units flew combat missions over their homeland once the Soviet army had advanced to Czechoslovakia. The Romanians, erstwhile allies of Germany, withdrew from the Axis and joined an alliance with the Soviet Union in 1944. Accordingly, the Soviets organized the Romanian 1st Air Corps to assist the 2nd Ukrainian *Front* in its conquest of Bucharest and the Soviet advance into Transylvania. To assist Tito's partisans in Yugoslavia, the VVS first assigned a special air group, under the command of General A. N. Vitruk, that included the 10th GShAD and the 236th IAD. In 1945, the Yugoslav 1st Fighter Air Regiment and the 2nd Ground Attack Air Regiment were formed for the final campaign to liberate Yugoslavia. No less important was the recruitment of a token number of Bulgarian pilots in September 1944 to fly with the 17th Air Army in support of the 3rd Ukrainian *Front*'s invasion of Bulgaria.

In 1944, cooperation between the Soviets and the Army Air Forces of the United States proved to be highly difficult, notwithstanding the proclaimed "Grand Alliance" against Nazi Germany. For the Soviet Union, the compelling pressure to work jointly with such a powerful ally did not fit smoothly into Soviet plans, especially in 1944, when military collaboration brought few rewards. By contrast, the desperate military context of 1941 had prompted the Soviets to appeal for the Western Allies' direct involvement on the Eastern Front. Now there was little interest in or tangible benefit from pursuing such a course of action. Moreover, the presence of American military units on Russian soil created problems that were at once military, political, and diplomatic. In 1943, the United States had first made overtures to the Soviet Union, asking permission for American bombers to use Russian bases as an eastern terminus for bombing raids conducted from Great Britain and Italy. Further discussions at the Tehran Conference gave the American proposal an important impetus. The United States planned to conduct "shuttle" bombing missions from widely separated bases in the European theater. Called Operation Frantic, this scheme would bring the entire matrix of German war industries within range of Allied strategic bombing. Moreover, such a move on the part of the Allies, it was argued by the Americans, would compel the Germans to spread their fighter defenses even thinner. In addition, from the American perspective, shuttle bombing might reduce the strain already evident in U.S.-Soviet relations by providing a concrete avenue for military cooperation in their common struggle. The Soviets displayed little enthusiasm for such a joint project, but the desire to retain Lend-Lease aid—the crucial shipments of aircraft, weaponry, and raw materials—compelled the Soviets to accede to Operation Frantic, if reluctantly. Stalin approved the plan in February 1944.

By April 1944, the specifics of the proposed shuttle bombing had been negotiated with the Russians. In an April 28 report by Major General F. L. Anderson, deputy commanding general for operations, to the commanding general of the 15th Air Force, the operational plans were outlined. Three air bases (not six, as originally requested) were made available to the Americans at Poltava, Mirgorod, and Piryatin. The 15th Air Force planned for 800 bomber sorties per month, with supervising personnel, supplies, and equipment to be dispatched over the time frame of April–May 1944. For selected aircraft maintenance, the Americans planned to use Russian personnel as airplane and engine mechanics, assistant crew chiefs, sheet-metal workers, fabric workers, and propeller specialists. In theory, the plan appeared workable; it was a way for the Soviet Union to make a vital contribution to the strategic bombing campaign against Nazi Germany.

General Anderson promised an ample supply of high-explosive bombs, incendiary bombs, and ordnance for air operations covering thirty days. Elaborate signal services were required, as well as 12,000 tons of pierced steel planks to reinforce the runways, portable housing and storage buildings, and a 100-bed field hospital.[68] The Soviets, according to Anderson, would supply part of the ordnance (high-explosive bombs and .50-caliber ammunition), deploy 400 support personnel, and complete construction of the runways and airfield facilities under the supervision of American engineers.[69] From the Soviet side, Novikov organized a special section (later an air force directorate) under General A. V. Nikitin, the VVS deputy commander, to coordinate combat activities with all Allied air units on Soviet soil. The 169th Special Air Base took shape to assist the American air group at Poltava. To provide air cover for an estimated 360 B-17 and B-24 bombers, the VVS assigned the 210th IAD (PVO). Each of the three American airfields was assigned individual air defense units. The first shuttle raid took place on June 2, 1944, when a group of 750 aircraft from Italy struck targets in Germany. Following the bombing mission, some 128 B-17 bombers, escorted by 64 P-51 Mustangs, flew to the

Lieutenant General Ira C. Eaker, commander in chief of the
Mediterranean Allied Air Forces, talks to an American fighter pilot after
the first shuttle raid, which was flown from Italy to Ukraine. Looking on
is Major General A. R. Perminov (center), the local Soviet air
commander for the Poltava–Mirgorod air bases. (Courtesy of U.S. Air
Force via Von Hardesty)

Poltava airfield complex. Lieutenant General Ira Eaker commanded
this first group to fly into Soviet territory. According to General Nikitin,
the American aircrews received a warm welcome upon their arrival.
Other raids followed on June 6 and 11. Operation Frantic appeared to
be off to a good start.

On June 21, on the eve of Operation Bagration and the third anniversary of Operation Barbarossa, the U.S. 8th Air Force conducted a
shuttle raid with Berlin as the primary target. It would end in disaster.
After bombing their targets in the German capital, the B-17s and P-51
escorts flew on to Poltava. While en route, the American strike force
was monitored the entire time by a German Ju 88 reconnaissance
plane. At sunset, another German reconnaissance airplane, an He

177, flew boldly over Poltava, photographing the American B-17 bombers now lined up neatly on the crowded airfield. After studying these photographs at Minsk, *Luftwaffe* Colonel Wilhelm Antrup quickly ordered eighty Ju 88s and He 111s from *Fliegerkorps* IV to strike shortly after midnight. Against a backdrop of illumination flares, the *Luftwaffe* bombers made repeated sweeps of the Poltava and Mirgorod airfields. During the ninety-minute raid, no VVS night fighters rose to challenge the attacking *Luftwaffe* aircraft. Soviet antiaircraft batteries also failed to provide a spirited defense of the American airfields, firing only sporadically and inaccurately at the roaming German aircraft. On the ground, American personnel observed the unfolding tragedy with alarm and frustration. The "Damage and Casualty Summary" issued by the Eastern Command, U.S. Army Air Forces, listed forty-seven B-17s destroyed or damaged beyond repair, plus the loss of ordnance and 200,000 gallons of high-octane fuel. This dramatic *Luftwaffe* strike seriously compromised the shuttle bombing operation for weeks.[70] For the Germans, the Poltava raid was a much-needed boost in morale during a year of military reversals. Karl Stein, then a *Luftwaffe* ground attack pilot ferrying a new airplane to Vitebsk, arrived at the Minsk airfield just as Antrup's bombers returned from Poltava. "Not since Barbarossa," one bomber crew member told him ecstatically, "have we done so well. It reminded me of the old days."[71]

One 8th Air Force escort pilot, Benjamin S. Kelsey, observed the raid from a slit trench, after he and other airmen had been removed from their barracks at bayonet point by Soviet guards just as the German raid commenced. Kelsey's recollections of the raid and his perspective on what happened represented the American viewpoint at the time and for many decades to follow. He and the others were strongly encouraged not to comment on the raid or the controversy that followed. Yet Kelsey and other Americans at Poltava blamed the Soviet authorities for allowing the raid to assume such catastrophic proportions. Upon landing at Poltava, Kelsey had requested permission to intercept and shoot down the marauding German reconnaissance aircraft, but his request was denied, allowing the enemy to gain intelligence on the deployment of the American bombers. This charge—even in the context of muted criticism of the Soviet ally— would be widely accepted within the ranks of the American military. The shuttle flights continued, but only after Lieutenant General Carl

Spaatz ordered American officers to abstain from criticizing the Soviet air defenses at Poltava.

Among all the American airmen at Poltava, Kelsey possessed a unique understanding of the Soviet Union and its military. And few enjoyed his status within the leadership of the Army Air Forces. His reputation had been shaped in the prewar years as a military pilot. Kelsey had flown as Jimmy Doolittle's "safety pilot" on the famous "blind flight" of 1929. Moreover, he had served as a test pilot for a number of American fighter designs, including the XP-38, in the prewar years. Unknown to his Soviet hosts, Kelsey had also been a major technical adviser on the design of the Lend-Lease P-39 Airacobra. He had served in a similar role for the P-51 Mustang and test-flew two models of the RAF Spitfire for the Army Air Forces. Between May and June 1940, in fact, Kelsey had been sent to Europe as a roving assistant air attaché to gather intelligence on the air forces of the European powers. His travels took him to Moscow, where he met with the staff of the American embassy and was feted by the Soviet military establishment, which included a performance of the Bolshoy ballet. Seeing the vast terrain of the country, he told his superiors that any future invasion of Soviet Russia by Germany would evoke a new kind of war, one in which large envelopment tactics would define the conflict—a series of huge offensive and counteroffensives operations would be necessary. The German invasion of France in May 1940, in his opinion, should not be the model for any future war in the hinterlands of Russia.[72]

What Kelsey experienced at Poltava in June 1944, however, did not necessarily equip him to perceive the larger context of the German raid and its aftermath. From his narrow vantage point of a slit trench, he felt his anger was justified, prompting him to criticize the inaction of the Soviets. There was substantial truth in this criticism, and it added fuel to the growing tension between the two wartime allies. But the actions and inactions on the Soviet side mirrored a more complex set of circumstances. For the Americans there, the failure of VVS "night fighters" to appear suggested gross incompetence.[73] The Soviet commander, General A. R. Perminov, explained to astonished American officers that the VVS fighters had been ordered to attack enemy airfields. This explanation seemed ludicrous to American personnel, who had watched German bombers in the bright light of marker flares pound the base for nearly two hours. Washington's commitment to Operation Frantic, however, compelled the Americans connected with the shuttle raids to remain silent about the incident. The use of the Poltava airfield complex continued into September 1944.

The Poltava incident has remained clouded in mystery and controversy. Until recently, little was known of Soviet actions in the face of the attack. One Soviet pilot, Lieutenant N. M. Fadeyev of the 802nd IAP PVO, was grounded after he called for destruction of the enemy reconnaissance plane reported by Kelsey. This fact alone suggests that many Soviet airmen shared Kelsey's alarm and advocated action.[74] Hindering the Soviet response was the fact that the local PVO air defense command was not under General Perminov's direct control. This confusing context of overlapping authority was revealed in recently published documents from the KGB archives on the Poltava affair. These documents, which represent an internal assessment by the NKVD (forerunner of the KGB) of the controversial episode, shed some light on Soviet actions during and after the fateful raid. As it turned out, Perminov's mandate did not include defense of the shuttle air bases; he had been given the narrow mandate of providing communication links with the Americans and supervising certain logistical services. Air defense of the base was in the hands of Soviet PVO units not under Perminov's direct command. Consequently, there was poor coordination among the three participants—the American airmen, Perminov's base command, and the PVO air units. The KGB document suggests that there was minimal daily contact and no real contingency planning for an enemy air attack. The document also records an inability to forge common ground and achieve a genuine context for collaboration. In addition, the document echoes an older claim that the Americans had been asked to disperse their aircraft at Poltava, a request the American commanders either ignored or refused. The KGB report suggests that General Perminov could have prevailed on this point if he had been more insistent, taking the matter to the U.S. Military Mission in Moscow if necessary. The archival source states that on June 21, the PVO air command detected the enemy reconnaissance plane thirty to forty minutes after the B-17s landed. Artillery fire against the intruder was ineffectual, and although fighters were scrambled, it came too late—some fifteen minutes after the German plane had departed. When the German bombing raid commenced, antiaircraft artillery fire was ineffectual; small-caliber guns were the only defensive weapons in place at the air base.[75] In retrospect, both American eyewitnesses and newly declassified Russian archival records confirm the poor coordination of Soviet defenses, which allowed the *Luftwaffe* to score a major tactical victory.

For the VVS, however, Operation Frantic played only a marginal role in the war: the shuttle bombing raids were outside the scope of Soviet air operations. Yet it did have diplomatic implications, as noted. For the Americans, of course, there was a substantial loss of aircraft and prestige. The German air triumph at the Poltava and Mirgorod airfields, by one Soviet account, resulted in the destruction of forty-four American B-17s, two C-47s, and one P-38 Lightning. Damaged were twenty-five B-17s, fifteen Soviet Yak-9s, six Yak-7s, one Hurricane, and three U-2 aircraft. Three hundred sixty tons of aviation fuel were burned, and 2,000 bombs were destroyed. One American was killed and fifteen wounded; Soviet losses stood at thirty-one killed and eighty-eight wounded.[76]

In the aftermath of this disaster, General John R. Dean of the U.S. Military Mission in Moscow offered to transfer one squadron (fifteen to sixteen aircraft) of P-61 night interceptors equipped with on-board radar as well as large-caliber antiaircraft artillery equipped with radar-controlled guidance equipment. The Soviet engineering and flight personnel would be thoroughly familiarized with this new equipment. Dean also requested an additional four to five airfields for the dispersal and maneuver of forces and asked to increase the number of aircraft based on Soviet territory by up to 250 for the duration of winter. The number of American personnel on Soviet soil would have increased by 3,000 to 3,500. Generals Vorozheykin and Nikitin reported to Stalin and endorsed this plan, but Stalin refused.[77]

One curious episode, again viewed from the Soviet perspective, took place on June 5, 1944, shortly before the Poltava disaster. Air Commander Novikov, on the eve of his departure from Moscow to supervise the aforementioned VVS air raids on Finland, met with U.S. Ambassador W. Averell Harriman. Earlier, Novikov asserted, Harriman had promised the VVS a contingent of B-29 heavy bombers. Novikov admired the reported speed and payload of the B-29, and he was anxious to use the aircraft to bomb Finnish defenses in the distant Karelian peninsula. At their meeting, however, Harriman told Novikov that the United States would not supply the "promised" B-29s. Implicit in Novikov's reference to Harriman's alleged promise was the Soviet expectation in June 1944 that shuttle bombers—in this case, the most advanced American long-range bomber—would be used against enemy targets on the Eastern Front.[78]

ON TO BERLIN, JANUARY–MAY 1945

The year 1945 found Nazi Germany at the edge of total collapse. The Belorussian offensive of the previous summer had destroyed Army Group Center and now served as a harbinger of the denouement of the Nazi regime itself. The subsequent Lvov–Sandomir offensive pushed the Germans out of Ukraine. Finland dropped out of the war, and the Soviet invasion of the Balkans in August–September 1944 prompted similar moves by Romania and Bulgaria. As reversal followed reversal, the Germans evacuated Greece and Yugoslavia. By the end of 1944, Soviet troops had reached Hungary as far west as Lake Balaton.

Even as Soviet forces advanced from the East to the Vistula River and from the Balkans into Hungary, Hitler unleashed the Ardennes offensive against the British and Americans in December 1944. But rather than weakening the Anglo-American drive and freeing Germany for a renewed offensive against the Soviet armies in the East, the Ardennes drive recklessly consumed the limited reservoir of German fighting strength. An effort in early January to retake Budapest only deepened the crisis. All these events placed Germany in a position of strategic weakness in 1945. The great Soviet offensives would follow, first the Vistula–Oder operation, and finally the capture of Berlin.

The air equation in 1945 now strongly favored the Soviet Union. The *Luftwaffe* had 1,680 serviceable aircraft (610 fighters) in the East by January 1, 1945, covering a broad front from the Baltic to Czechoslovakia.[79] Facing the Soviet army at the Vistula was *Luftflotte* 6, which in November 1944 consisted of 1,377 aircraft, including 182 fighters.[80] These air resources were inadequate to meet the anticipated Soviet offensive in the Vistula–Oder sector facing Berlin. At this late date in the war, the *Luftwaffe* confronted the problem of acute fuel shortages, a consequence of the loss of Romanian oil fields and Anglo-American bombing of German refineries. Whatever residual punch the *Luftwaffe* could muster in 1945 came through improvisation, desperate effort, and the maximal use of existing resources.

Adolf Galland, then commanding *Luftwaffe* fighter operations, found a context of unreality at Hitler's headquarters. During one visit, Galland recalled, Hitler sat at a table before a large-scale map of Russia. As aides looked on, he moved battalions around in a manner inconsistent with their actual deployment and possibility for maneuver. Some units were, in reality, as far as 250 miles (463 kilometers) from where they appeared on Hitler's map. Everyone realized the "planning" bore no resemblance to actual conditions at the front, but no one spoke or attempted to correct the Führer. The whole meeting assumed the character of game playing—chilling, unreal, and foreboding in its implications. Galland had been assigned to various posts in the West over the course of the war, but he had observed the gradual transformation of Soviet airpower. "The technical quality of the Soviet Air Force," Galland later observed, "[had] improved considerably, and by the end of the war Soviet personnel and equipment was roughly equal to the *Luftwaffe*." As did most *Luftwaffe* fliers, Galland praised the Il-2 Shturmovik as a singularly effective warplane.[81]

In contrast to the German situation, the VVS possessed an unprecedented combat strength of 13,936 aircraft by January 1, 1945.[82] It had the strategic initiative in the air, which allowed maximal maneuver, and it had a breathtaking capacity to replace losses in aircraft and aircrews. Ten VVS air armies now challenged the *Luftwaffe*. The Soviet aviation industry had increased production by 15.6 percent in 1944. This meant VVS operational units possessed 13,936 combat aircraft and flew the newest types, including the Yak-3 and La-7 fighters and even some late-model Il-10 Shturmoviks.

With the end of the war near, the VVS would not engage in any strategic bombing campaigns, although Konigsberg, Budapest, and Berlin were hit by Soviet bombers in a systematic fashion. Soviet historians, in retrospect, exaggerated the VVS's wartime strategic aviation operations. VVS bomber units in 1944–1945 continued to be used mainly in tactical and operational roles. One of the postwar tasks for the Soviet Union would be the design and production of heavy bombers for its strategic air arm, which in January 1945 existed more on paper than in reality. In the crucial category of operational fighters and ground attack planes, however, the VVS showed a dramatic up-surge between January 1, 1944, and January 1, 1945: fighters increased from 3,926 to 5,810, and ground attack aircraft from 2,413 to 4,171.[83]

The Vistula–Oder operation commenced on January 12 with a major assault on German defenses spearheaded by the 1st Ukrainian *Front* of Marshal I. S. Konev. The offensive was launched from the Sandomir bridgehead. Stalin had originally planned to unleash the Vistula–Oder offensive on January 20, but he moved the date up to January 12 to counter the German pressure in the Ardennes.[84] Two days later, a second assault by forces of the 1st Belorussian *Front* under Marshal G. K. Zhukov began from the Magnushev and Pulavy bridgeheads. These major offensive thrusts were coordinated with actions by the 2nd Belorussian *Front* on the left and the 4th Ukrainian *Front* on the right. By the beginning of February, the Soviets had advanced some 270 miles (500 kilometers), occupied Krakow, and encircled a large concentration of German troops at Poznan. On the fifth day of the operation, Warsaw fell. After twenty-three days of intensive fighting in extreme weather, the Soviet juggernaut captured strategic bridgeheads on the Oder River and was now a mere 32 to 38 miles (60 to 70 kilometers) from Berlin.

The 16th Air Army, attached to the 1st Belorussian *Front*, and the 2nd Air Army, attached to the 1st Ukrainian *Front*, flew in support of this massive offensive operation. The Soviets enjoyed a decisive superiority in personnel and equipment. Each major assault on enemy positions was preceded by a powerful artillery barrage. The Soviets had some 250 to 300 guns concentrated in the space of little more than half a mile (1 kilometer). The presence of large mobile reserves ensured a rapid forward movement once the enemy lines had been penetrated. Beginning the advance on a frontage of 45 miles (73 kilometers), the Soviets were soon operating along a 310-mile (500-kilometer) front. The daily advance averaged 16 miles (25 kilometers); on some days, the infantry's forward movement reached 28 miles (45 kilometers), and tank and mechanized formations advanced a dramatic 43 miles (69 kilometers). Never before in the war had such massive penetrations of the enemy defenses been achieved.

By crossing to the Oder River, the Red Army planned to move into Germany directly from Poland and set the stage for the climactic assault on Berlin. The *Stavka* assigned Marshal Zhukov as overall commander to spearhead the strategic offensive. With elements from his own 1st Belorussian *Front* and Konev's 1st Ukrainian *Front*, Zhukov advanced on the enemy with fifteen combined arms armies, four tank armies, two air armies, five separate tank corps, one mechanized corps, and three cavalry corps; overall, he had 2.2 million men, 33,500 guns and mortars, up to 7,500 tanks and self-propelled guns, and 5,000 aircraft. The main forces were concentrated on the left bank of Vistula River, on a front of 298 miles (480 kilometers) with three bridgeheads. They were opposed by the enemy's 560,000 men, 5,000 guns and mortars, 1,220 tanks and self-propelled guns, and 630 combat aircraft. The German defenses consisted of a powerful fortification system of seven defensive lines echeloned at 186 to 310 miles (300 to 500 kilometers).[85] The *Stavka* deployed two air armies to support the advancing ground troops—the 16th Air Army commanded by General Rudenko, and the 2nd Air Army led by General Krasovskiy. Rudenko's 16th, consisting of 2,490 combat aircraft, provided air support for Zhukov's main drive along the Warsaw–Berlin axis. The 2nd Air Army had an almost equal number of airplanes: 2,630.[86]

According to Soviet sources, the VVS took pains to conceal the huge air armada earmarked for the Vistula–Oder operation. Air units flew in stages to their forward positions, with elaborate precautions taken to keep their numbers and location concealed. Within the sector of the 16th Air Army, Soviet laborers skillfully constructed fifty-five "dummy" airfields with 818 full-scale models of Soviet aircraft. To add authenticity, the VVS maintained flights into and out of these dummy installations. The VVS was successful in attracting German air strikes to these bogus airfields, while their carefully camouflaged operational airfields were spared.[87] Such meticulous preparations extended to air reconnaissance, and VVS aircrews photographed the German defenses in great depth. Few crucial points escaped Soviet air reconnaissance; it revealed enemy defensive lines, antitank ditches, river crossings, airfields, artillery positions, and the deployment of reserves.[88]

The Soviet advance in the Vistula–Oder offensive took shape in the southern sector, where Marshal Konev's 1st Ukrainian *Front* moved to Krakow and German Silesia. Konev's operation was followed on January 14 by Zhukov's 1st Belorussian *Front*. During the 2nd Air Army's operations in support of the 4th and 3rd Guards Tank Armies, more than 400 Shturmoviks and bombers, flying in groups, continuously hit

Two of the leading Soviet Airacobra aces—Colonel Aleksandr
Pokryshkin (fifty-two victories, with forty on the Airacobra) and Major
Dmitriy Glinka (fifty victories, with thirty-nine on the Airacobra). (From
the collection of Valeriy Romanenko)

enemy defensive positions. These air support units gave valuable assistance to the tank spearheads by attacking German reserves moving
forward to blunt the Soviet breakthrough. Bad weather, however, prevented any large-scale application of Soviet airpower in this sector until January 16. The German Fourth Panzer Army found itself woefully
incapable of resisting the massive onslaught of Soviet infantry, artillery, and tanks. The 2nd Air Army's contribution of 4,000 sorties on
January 16–17 only accelerated a Soviet combined arms operation
that was well on its way to victory.[89] Konev's troops found VVS air
cover helpful at the Mysa, Pilica, and Warta river crossings. Krakow
fell on January 19, and by the end of the month, the 1st Ukrainian
Front had advanced across the Oder into Silesia.

On January 14, Zhukov moved forward north and south of Warsaw,
one day after Soviet troops had launched an assault on the enemy in
East Prussia. As with Konev's operation, bad weather on the opening
day precluded any large-scale Soviet air operations. The 6th ShAK, fly-

ing in support of the 2nd Guards Tank Army, managed only 272 sorties; the 2nd and 11th GShADs flew a mere 345 sorties in support of the 1st Guards Tank Army. No *Luftwaffe* opposition appeared on the first day, according to the Soviets, because of the severe weather. For those VVS pilots who ventured out, the weather became a constant threat, with snowstorms, low clouds, and minimal visibility. Only the most experienced VVS squadrons flew these dangerous missions, which were conducted at altitudes of only 160 to 650 feet (50 to 200 meters). On the second day, the VVS faced similar weather conditions, but Soviet pilots flew 181 sorties, mostly by Shturmovik air units and elements of the *Okhotniki*.[90]

By January 16, the weather had improved sufficiently to allow the 16th Air Army to participate fully in the ground offensive now under way. The third day, Rudenko's air units registered a total of 3,431 sorties in support of the advancing Soviet troops.[91] With the acceleration in VVS air operations, the Soviets could apply greater pressure on the retreating Germans at bridges and river crossings and along rail and road arteries. The roaming VVS air units played a key role in this phase of the campaign by supplying a constant stream of reconnaissance information on the enemy's withdrawal. With this information, the various VVS command posts could more intelligently direct Shturmoviks in hot pursuit of the enemy. The improved weather allowed the *Luftwaffe* to challenge the VVS once again. Air combat took place along the entire sweep of the Soviet advance. The Soviets claimed eighteen victories in twenty-two air battles. The 176th GIAP was one of the elite VVS air units, a stellar group of fighter pilots that included top Soviet ace Major Kozhedub.[92]

At the time of the Soviet assault on Warsaw, the 16th Air Army assigned the Polish 4th Mixed Air Division to assist in the capture of the city. This division flew a reported 400 missions against the German defenders.[93] Even as these events unfolded, the 16th Air Army airlifted a large quantity of mortars, antitank rifles, automatic weapons, ammunition, food, and medicines to "the patriots of the Warsaw underground."[94] Such a gesture of support to the Polish underground appeared to flow from political rather than military realities. When the Poles had desperately required resupply in the summer of 1944, during the Warsaw uprising, the VVS had failed to appear. At that time, the Red Army had advanced to the Vistula River. General Bor (Tadeusz Komorowski) of the Home Army ordered the Polish underground forces in Warsaw to rise up against the Germans on August 1, 1944. For more than two months, the Poles fought alone and heroically before being compelled to surrender on October 9 to an overwhelming German force.

The besieged Polish forces bitterly complained that during this entire uprising, the VVS air units on the east bank of the Vistula had made no effort to intervene on behalf of the Home Army. Meeting only occasional Soviet antiaircraft fire, German Ju 87 Stukas operated freely over the Polish-held sections of Warsaw, making pinpoint dives at forty-five-degree angles against buildings (and sometimes rooms) occupied by the Polish insurgents. The belated appearance of VVS air support in January 1945 coincided with arrival of the Red Army—not with Polish national aspirations. Warsaw was now in ruins, and the Home Army had been crushed. The Soviet-sponsored Lublin government then assumed political authority over the war-shattered Polish capital.

The fall of Warsaw on January 17 led to additional victories as the Red Army moved across Poland to Germany: Lodz on January 19, Poznan on January 25 (surrendering on February 23), and crossing the German border on January 29. By the beginning of February, these advances by Zhukov's 1st Belorussian *Front* had cleared most of central and western Poland of German forces. Now Soviet armies occupied positions on the Oder, only 38 miles (61 kilometers) from Berlin. The speed of these ground movements, as much as 15 to 20 miles (24 to 32 kilometers) per day, created enormous logistical problems for the Soviets. The rapid movement westward toward the Oder made air basing a challenge for the advancing Soviet air armies. The retreating Germans had taken steps to destroy runways and hangars on existing airfields that were still under their control. Moreover, a sudden thaw turned airstrips into arteries of mud. Given these conditions, the VVS commanders were compelled to base aircraft as far back as 124 miles (200 kilometers). This move meant that the advancing tank and infantry units were denied adequate and prompt air cover—being compromised by the limited radius for air sorties.[95] By contrast, *Luftwaffe* air units, which were operating out of more permanent airfields with hard-surface runways, used the critical days of early February to execute a series of air operations aimed to gain local air superiority. Soviet records reveal that on certain days the enemy flew between 2,000 and 3,000 sorties, targeting Soviet bridgeheads in the Kustrin sector. Soviet records also reveal the asymmetry of the air action—the *Luftwaffe* flew a total of 13,950 sorties in ten days over the 1st Belorussian *Front*, compared with a total of 1,530 by VVS aircraft, which were hindered by the absence of suitable airfields.[96] In time, the VVS would once again assume control of the skies, but these events demonstrated the residual strength of the *Luftwaffe*.

When it could not keep up with the rapid pace of the ground forces, the VVS improvised by using German autobahns as temporary airstrips, an emergency measure already adopted by the hard-pressed *Luftwaffe*. The construction of new airfields or the renovation of old ones required time and considerable effort. Frequently, the rapid advance of the Red Army placed these airfields too far back of the front lines to be effective operational bases. The freeways provided ideal airstrips for Soviet fighter units. Colonel Pokryshkin, then commander of the 9th GIAD, was the first to utilize German freeways during the Vistula–Oder offensive.[97] During the entire drive to the Oder River, from January 12 to February 3, the 16th and 2nd Air Armies flew 25,400 sorties, conducted 214 aerial battles, and claimed 209 enemy aircraft.[98]

While the Vistula–Oder offensive unfolded, the Soviet armed forces concluded another hard-fought campaign: the conquest of East Prussia.[99] Concurrent VVS air operations over Konigsberg served as a dress rehearsal for the assault on Berlin. The VVS 1st and 4th Air Armies, commanded by Generals Khryukin and Vershinin, deployed 1,504 and 1,593 aircraft, respectively, for the East Prussian sector.[100] The *Luftwaffe*, according to Soviet sources, had around 775 aircraft from *Luftflotte* 6.[101] The VVS took the same pains to conceal the East Prussian air buildup as it had along the Vistula, building dummy airfields and taking extraordinary steps to achieve camouflage and deception. For the dummy airfields, the VVS built models of 100 ground attack planes and 60 fighters. Radio stations simulating the work of an air army headquarters, a ground attack air corps, and three bomber divisions began operating in the vicinity of the dummy airstrips on the eve of the offensive.

On the morning of January 13, 1945, the 3rd Belorussian *Front* went on the offensive, to be followed the next day by troops of the 2nd Belorussian *Front*. Just prior to the assault, the 1st Air Army con-

During the Berlin offensive, the VVS found itself short of landing strips close to the front lines, so it quickly took advantage of German highway system. The 9th GIAD, commanded by Colonel A. I. Pokryshkin, was the first to adopt this method. This P-39 Airacobra is taking off from the highway toward Berlin. (From the collection of Von Hardesty)

ducted a series of preparatory strikes against the German defenses. By January 15, the two air armies, operating in joint strikes, filled the airspace over Konigsberg and its environs with 1,320 combat aircraft.[102] As in the Vistula–Oder operation, the VVS command planned to use bombers for tactical air support. On the fourth day, for example, 342 Soviet bombers made a massed air strike against German defenses in support of the 2nd Tank Corps. After the tanks had advanced on the ground to the next line of German defenses, the VVS sent another 284 bombers to assist in the second assault. Air support for the tank corps came from five bomber divisions, three ground attack divisions, and one fighter air division. Between January 19 and February 9, the VVS claimed that the 4th Air Army flew 8,130 sorties and the 1st Air Army flew 9,740 sorties, helping Soviet troops storm German fortified positions and surround Konigsberg on three sides.[103]

The importance attached to the East Prussian campaign, representing the first German territory captured by the Red Army, was evident when Air Commander Novikov arrived at the headquarters of the 3rd Belorussian *Front* on February 23 to personally command the VVS air armies over East Prussia. Soon the German garrison of Konigsberg, defined by Hitler in 1945 as a fortress city, became a formidable defensive grouping, blocking the *Stavka*'s goal of quickly liquidating enemy resistance in East Prussia. The assault on Konigsberg unfolded as a carefully planned combined arms operation. Artillery and aviation, in particular, helped destroy both the Germans' will and their capacity to resist.

The VVS placed a heavy stress on bombing, as evident in the breakdown of operational aircraft at this juncture in the war: 1,124 bombers accounted for nearly half the aircraft deployed against Konigsberg. The Soviets utilized airpower in the interest of ground operations, while the Baltic Fleet air arm attempted to block German sea traffic in and out of the city. For the first time in the war, Soviet naval aviation, from the Red Banner Baltic Fleet (commanded by General M. I. Samokhin), participated with the VVS in an offensive. More important, the VVS command acquired additional experience in administrating large concentrations of combat aircraft in diverse operational roles over a narrow sector of the front.[104]

Soviet bombers over Konigsberg encountered fierce resistance from the Germans, who were now defending their homeland. VVS operational plans, worked out at 1st Air Army headquarters, called for two days of preparatory air strikes, beginning on April 1, 1945. These strikes called for 5,316 sorties to drop 2,620 tons of bombs on defensive strongpoints around the city and the surviving *Luftwaffe* airfields.[105] During this final phase of the war, the VVS aimed to destroy "fascist aviation" on an entire front, not merely to subdue German air resistance as part of a Soviet army offensive.

On the first day of the operation, the VVS scheduled 539 aircraft (406 Tu-2 and Pe-2 bombers with 133 fighter-bombers) to make a concentrated attack on German positions. Once the bomber sweep had been completed, a second attack by Shturmoviks would follow in close support of advancing tanks and infantry. Three fighter divisions (the 129th, 240th, and 330th), with supplementary air units from the 11th IAK, were assigned to Konigsberg for fighter cover duty over the battle zone. Other fighter air units were deployed in a larger airspace to intercept any enemy fighters. As events unfolded, the VVS flew more than 4,000 sorties on the first day alone, one of the strongest air strikes yet organized. In subsequent days, six ground attack divisions flew against fortress Konigsberg.[106] Captain Leonid Levin of the 136th GShAP, flying an Il-2, described the challenge his air unit faced at Konigsberg: "A square was drawn on the map. Here is my regiment and here is your regiment, and no one on the ground better move a muscle! If anything was left alive—it was a mark against you! No awards, nothing. We were attacking targets as well as terrain."[107]

Fighter aviation, along with Soviet bomber units, found itself charged with enlarged responsibility for ground attack missions. The entire 130th IAD of Colonel F. I. Shinkarenko flew the specially equipped Yak-9B fighter-bombers with a bomb capacity of 880 pounds (400 kilograms). The large number of VVS aircraft operating over a narrow battle zone required all divisions to fly in assigned corridors and at defined altitudes. Three days before the offensive, the air reconnaissance command had prepared detailed photographs of Konigsberg, along with large-scale maps and diagrams outlining specific targets. Forward command posts with portable radios again played an important role in guiding VVS ground attack aircraft to frontline targets.

A powerful VVS air assault on Konigsberg came on April 7–8, after poor weather had dramatically reduced the number of VVS sorties. This raid coincided with penetration of the city's defenses by Soviet troops and involved the first massed daytime raid by the 18th Air Army. More than 500 VVS bombers, escorted by 108 fighters, struck the forts of Konigsberg for about an hour, leaving, according to one Soviet commentator, "the city engulfed in smoke." The VVS 18th Air Army dropped 550 tons of explosives on the German fortress-city on April 7; after four days, the total was 4,440 tons.[108]

The East Prussian campaign became an occasion for the VVS to demonstrate its improved skills in coordinating several air armies, long-range aviation, and naval aviation. Soviet air historians are quick to point out that the VVS was vital in bringing about the swift and decisive defeat of the enemy in East Prussia. Konigsberg fell to four Soviet armies on April 9, 1945.[109] Within a week, Marshal Zhukov's 1st Belorussian *Front*, then situated along the Oder River in the center of the shortened Eastern Front, launched the final assault on Berlin. The Soviet sweep through Pomerania, along with Konev's drive through Upper and Lower Silesia, placed Soviet forces east and south of Berlin.

Now the German capital awaited the final assault. Stalin's decision to permit Zhukov's armies to storm the symbol of Nazi power meant an important air support role for Rudenko's veteran 16th Air Army. As a spearhead, the 16th was reinforced with the Air Corps of the *Stavka* Reserve to reach an unprecedented level of 3,188 combat aircraft (3,033 serviceable).[110] When the aviation of the 4th Air Army (2nd Belorussian *Front*), 2nd Air Army (1st Ukrainian *Front*), 18th Air Army (long-range bombers), and the recently deployed Polish air arm was added, Soviet airpower for the final Berlin offensive achieved the muscular level of 7,500 combat planes.[111] All the wartime momentum of the resurgent Soviet Air Force came to a peak over Berlin—its vast numbers, improved operational skills, and immense tactical firepower.

The Red Army's steady and difficult advance into the ruined precincts of the German capital coincided with the VVS's success in clearing the skies of the last vestiges of the once-powerful *Luftwaffe*. On the leading edge of the Soviet advance, Shturmoviks made low-level attacks on German tanks and crumbling defenses. Soviet bombers—now free to cross German airspace at will—hit exposed tactical installations within the Berlin defense perimeter. The average density of Soviet aviation along the front line was nearly 50 combat aircraft per mile (1.6 kilometers), and it exceeded 200 aircraft within the breakthrough zone of the 5th Shock Army and the 8th Guards Army of the 1st Belorussian *Front*.[112]

In retrospect, most Soviet accounts of the VVS in the Berlin operation focus on its enhanced organizational and operational skills rather than the impressive number of combat aircraft flown. No previous Soviet offensive involved the number of aircraft deployed on three *Fronts* at Berlin, and the task of forging them, unit by unit, into a coordinated, effective air arm required considerable skill. The air operations at Berlin evolved out of careful preparation and attention to detail, mobilization, and timing. Novikov was at the front, working with the commanders to assure VVS participation in the entire sweep of the offensive to capture Berlin. The VVS faced the challenge of meeting a diverse set of goals—achieving air superiority, effectively supporting the ground forces in breakthrough operations, providing reconnaissance, providing air cover for river crossings (the Oder, Neisse, and Spree Rivers), and flying combat sorties against enemy re-

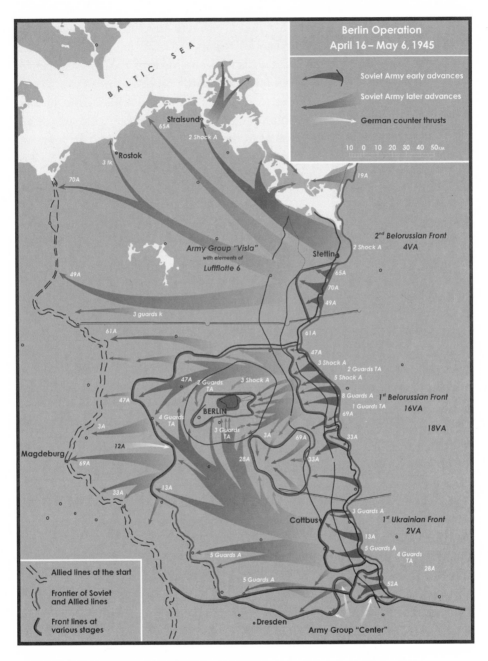

Map 9 (Terry Higgins & Zach Downey-Higgins © 2011 [based on Russian source material supplied by the authors])

serves. The bulk of the aviation of the 16th and 2nd Air Armies (some 75 percent) was ordered to move forward with the tank armies, affirming the operational and tactical character of VVS air action. For the deployment of such a large concentration of air units (209 air regiments in 19 air corps and 65 divisions of the 3 air armies), the VVS organized 23 air base regions (RABs) and 163 air maintenance battalions (BAOs) with large stockpiles of ammunition and fuel.

The *Stavka*, in a directive dated April 1, 1945, called for the 1st Belorussian *Front* to capture Berlin and reach the Elbe River in a twelve- to fifteen-day operation that aimed to divide the enemy defensive forces into pockets of resistance. The main effort was at the Kustrin bridgehead. At this juncture, the advancing Soviets consisted of two tank armies. Air support was provided by the 16th Air Army, which possessed in its strike force twenty-eight air divisions and seven separate air regiments. The formidable air armada deployed 3,000 aircraft—approximately half of them fighters. At no time during the war had an army appeared with such a massive inventory of warplanes.[113]

Soviet sources estimated that *Luftwaffe* air strength in April 1945 stood at 3,300 aircraft, which included all air assets of *Luftflotte* 6 and the Reich defense forces. The 1st Belorussian *Front*, by this reckoning, faced 1,700 aircraft, of which 1,200 were fighters.[114] *Luftwaffe* records from this late stage in the war are fragmentary and unreliable, but one official source cited a figure of 5,072 total aircraft in the *Luftwaffe* on April 13, 1945, with only 3,842 of these serviceable; of this number, 1,648 were single-engine fighters.[115] *Luftflotte* 6 possessed 1,805 total aircraft in April,[116] while the Reich defense forces probably possessed no more than 500 aircraft.[117]

Soviet accounts of the final days of the war suggest the rump German air arm remained formidable, if severely weakened by attrition in airmen and aircraft, the loss of airfields, acute fuel shortages, and the collapse of the command structure. Whatever paper strength the *Luftwaffe* possessed on the eve of the Berlin offensive, it did not necessarily translate into effective air operations. What surprised the Soviets, as well as the Anglo-American air forces, was the *Luftwaffe* airmen's determination to resist to the end. Guenther Rall offers one perspective on the resiliency of the German airmen. In the last weeks of the war, Rall commanded JG 300, and he worked to keep his air unit viable in extreme circumstances. When asked to explain his motives—

at a time he realized the war had been lost—Rall stated that "as long as the Allied air forces bombed Germany," he and many other pilots "felt compelled to defend the country." This mind-set, Rall acknowledged later, was a mixture of youthful bravado, patriotism, and sense of duty. In late April, when a major from the *Luftwaffe*'s General Staff ordered Rall to transfer his surviving group to Prague, he refused. For the young Rall, this was a radical departure from routine, but one justified by the suicidal nature of the order. Returning from his final reconnaissance mission on May 1, Rall gathered his rump air unit and told them the war was over. Rall and his pilots abandoned the airfield at Ainring, near Salzburg, and they eventually surrendered to elements of the advancing American army.[118]

The final assault on Berlin began in the early-morning hours of April 16, 1945, when 150 night bombers from the 16th and 4th Air Armies hit German positions in a coordinated attack with artillery and mortar fire. The Oder River valley became a vortex of artillery fire, explosions, and advancing tanks. A low fog delayed the arrival of the 16th Air Army's major strike force until the afternoon, but by 1500 hours, there were 647 combat aircraft in the air.[119] The appearance of the VVS units sparked a swift response by the *Luftwaffe*, and during the afternoon, a number of air battles raged over the battle zone. Despite the German air resistance, the bulk of the VVS aircraft remained close to the breakthrough corridors, providing air cover and support for Soviet tanks. By the end of the first day, by Soviet estimates, the 16th, 4th, and 18th Air Armies had flown 6,548 combat sorties, mostly against enemy tanks, artillery batteries, and defensive lines. VVS fighter pilots, by their own account, fought 140 air battles, downing 165 *Luftwaffe* planes but losing 87 aircraft of their own.[120]

To the south, Marshal Konev's 1st Ukrainian *Front* moved forward quickly, crossing the Neisse River and penetrating deeply into German defenses. Along the way, Krasovskiy's 2nd Air Army provided substantial air support. During this combined arms operation, the 2nd Air Army delivered concentrated blows by ground attack and bomber aircraft. Out of 3,551 combat sorties recorded on April 16, 1,499 were bomber and ground attack strikes of enemy troops, 102 were strikes at airfields, 687 were for air cover, 988 were for the escort of bombers and Shturmoviks, 163 were for reconnaissance, and 82 were free-hunt sorties.[121] By April 19, Konev's troops had crossed north of Spremberg and

Soviet Pe-2 dive-bombers prepare for takeoff. The aircraft were attached to the 1st Ukrainian *Front,* 1945. (From the collection of Valeriy Romanenko)

threatened Berlin from the south and southwest.

Marshal Zhukov's advance on April 17–19 had been slowed by fierce German resistance—particularly around the Seelow Height—and difficult weather conditions. The *Stavka* ordered the 2nd Belorussian *Front* to go over to the offensive on April 20, a planned Soviet thrust that bypassed Berlin on the north. By April 21, Zhukov's 1st Belorussian *Front* reached Berlin, and German resistance was beginning to collapse under the weight of these successive blows. Soviet troops linked up west of Berlin, just northwest of Potsdam, on April 25. With the Soviet armies encircling the German capital, the *Luftwaffe* lost most of its airfields, and German air sorties lessened dramatically.

On the night of April 26, 563 bombers of the 18th Air Army, flying from western Poland, struck Berlin in a massive raid. As Soviet tank formations captured German airfields, the VVS immediately moved to occupy them, as it did at Tempelhof airport on April 28. VVS air units, drawn largely from the 16th, 2nd, and 18th Air Armies, concentrated much of their striking power for this final push. Bombers of the 18th

Air Army, according to the Soviets, played a significant role in the Berlin operation, flying a total of 91,000 sorties in support of the three *Fronts*. In these last hours, the Soviets acknowledged the loss of 527 aircraft to air combat and antiaircraft batteries. At the same time, the VVS claimed the destruction of 1,132 enemy planes.[122]

The VVS now operated as a unified force, capable of mobilizing huge numbers of aircraft and working efficiently with the infantry and mechanized units on the ground. During the final phases of the war, the enemy's defenses had coalesced into a smaller area with greater concentration—reinforced by a mood of desperation to halt the Soviet advance. The density of enemy troops, by one account, had increased three- to fourfold on the approaches to Berlin. Accordingly, the VVS demonstrated an impressive capacity to concentrate its striking power; for example, the number of Il-2s deployed to the front lines increased dramatically—about six to seven times for each kilometer (0.62 mile)—reaching thirty to thirty-five aircraft (and in some cases up to sixty to eighty aircraft) per kilometer of the front.[123] Such impressive densities allowed the confident suppression of enemy targets. This, in turn, allowed the ground forces to increase their penetration of the enemy's tactical defenses to 5 to 9 miles (8 to 15 kilometers) per day. This prevented the Germans from fending off Red Army blows by deploying tactical and operational reserves and shifting troops from less threatened axes.[124]

At this juncture, the VVS High Command took satisfaction in the fact that its air armies had accomplished all their major goals for the Berlin campaign. These same air operations had been plagued by unfavorable weather conditions, which in turn had forced changes in plans and tactics. The number of sorties flown at Berlin surpassed all previous records for the entire war. During the first stage of the operation (April 16–21), the enemy fiercely resisted the advance of Soviet ground forces. Therefore, aviation adjusted its tactics to provide support for infantry and mobile units in their efforts to pierce the enemy's defenses. During the second stage of the campaign (April 22–25), VVS air units helped the advancing ground forces encircle the German capital. This became an exercise in combined arms warfare, one in which the VVS played a vital role. Soviet night and day bombers, along with Shturmoviks, systematically bombed and strafed targets in the center of Berlin and its outskirts, where the enemy made a final stand. For

Pilot V. D. Beletskiy and his P-39 Airacobra, Gleiwitz (Glivitze) airfield, Poland, 1945. (From the collection of Thomas Salazar)

example, between 1300 and 1400 hours on April 25, the 16th Air Army made a massive strike using 899 aircraft (413 bombers and 486 fighters); this assault was repeated at 1830 to 1930 hours with a force of 590 aircraft (267 bombers and 323 fighters). These strikes were quite effective and aided ground forces during street-to-street fighting in Berlin. Fighters of the 3rd IAK, tasked with free-hunting sorties, fended off opposition from the *Luftwaffe* and covered their own bomber and Shturmovik units as well as the ground troops.

The third stage of the Berlin campaign (April 26–May 8) saw the German resistance collapse with the advance of the 1st Belorussian *Front* to the Elbe River, leading to Germany's capitulation. In this dramatic final phase of the war, the VVS participated in a series of coordinated operations with infantry and mechanized units. VVS air units made special efforts to block the takeoff and landing of enemy aircraft,

The demise of the *Luftwaffe* is vividly portrayed. (From the collection of Von Hardesty)

seen as an effective way to prevent the evacuation of the German leadership from the center of Berlin. Aviation was also tasked to hit individual targets with pinpoint attacks by dive-bombers. The massive deployment of VVS air assets and their uninterrupted influence on the enemy became a signature feature of Soviet airpower during the Berlin operation.[125]

To coordinate the deployment and movement of large air assets, the VVS engaged in detailed planning and insisted on the strict execution of all air operations. Even though aviation units were subordinated to ground commanders to provide coordinated close air support, air army commanders had enough flexibility to concentrate air assets and retarget them to achieve maximal efficiency in combined arms operations. No less important, well-established communications (with the deployment of both wired and wireless equipment) played a crucial role in this critical campaign to capture Berlin. For the first time,

Destroyed Fw 190 on top of the wreck of a Ju 52 is inspected by Soviet airmen. This image is reminiscent of German photographs from the summer of 1941 showing destroyed VVS aircraft, but now the fortunes are reversed. (From the collection of Porfiriy Ovsyannikov via Oleg Korytov.)

there was centralized control of radar stations, which allowed unprecedented situational awareness and greatly facilitated command and control.[126] Finally, air reconnaissance played an important role before and during the Berlin operation. For example, a special reconnaissance squadron reporting directly to the 2nd Air Army commander was deployed at an airstrip 1 to 2 miles (2 to 3 kilometers) from the air army command post. Because the air army command post was located with the *Front*'s command post, the *Front* and air army commanders were always able to assign reconnaissance tasks and receive results in twenty to twenty-five minutes. This ability was invaluable in coordinating aviation activities with fast-advancing mobile ground units and frequently served to verify intelligence data provided by other sources.[127]

Hitler committed suicide on April 30, and German resistance in the ruined capital quickly collapsed as Soviet troops advanced, street

Yak-3 of the 303rd IAD at Tappau airfield in East Prussia, 1945. The Yak-3 was the lightest and most agile VVS fighter during the war. (From the collection of Valeriy Romanenko)

by street, toward the Reichstag and the chancellery. On May 1, fighter pilots of the 2nd Air Army dropped red banners by parachute over the Reichstag, which had fallen to troops of the 3rd Shock Army the previous evening. General Helmuth Weidling, commander of the Berlin garrison, surrendered to Soviet General V. I. Chuikov. On May 9, 1945, representatives of Germany signed the document formalizing an unconditional surrender to the Allies.

The Soviet triumph represented vindication for the VVS, the first victim in the long Russo-German War. The long and tortuous path to victory had seen Soviet airpower renewed in terms of organization, combat effectiveness, and leadership. All these factors were evident in the final and dramatic Berlin campaign—that concluding chapter when the VVS was truly at "full stride." The air force forged a new role as a vital component in combined arms warfare, a doctrine that would be enshrined in Soviet military planning in the decades that followed. Behind the victory, of course, was the aviation industry, which had been relocated and refitted for total war. The improbable defeat of the *Luftwaffe* also signaled the fact that the VVS had gained technical parity with the enemy. Certainly, the VVS had marshaled a quantitative edge in the final year of the war, but it had become apparent that the *Luftwaffe*'s qualitative edge in technology and tactics had also been narrowed, if not eliminated.

The Soviet Air Force had made the transition from defeat in Operation Barbarossa to a dramatic air triumph in the skies over Berlin.

Chapter Seven

Triumph and Vulnerability

Napoleon once remarked that the "most dangerous moment comes with victory." This observation is apt for the plight of Soviet airpower in 1945. At the dramatic outset of the war, the *Luftwaffe* targeted forward Soviet air bases as its first victim. These predawn raids became one of the most devastating preemptive air strikes in history. Few observers in the West gave the VVS any chance of survival in the wake of these unprecedented losses in aircraft. Yet this war-ravaged air arm managed to hang on with surprising resiliency in the pivotal first months of the war, even managing to strike back doggedly, to the surprise and alarm of the German airmen. With time, the Soviet Air Force arose from the ashes phoenix-like to achieve an improbable triumph over the vaunted *Luftwaffe*. On VE Day in 1945, the Soviet air juggernaut possessed an overall inventory of 20,071 warplanes—with no fewer than 7,500 deployed in the decisive Berlin operation alone.[1]

Now at full strength, the muscular and seasoned VVS controlled the entire airspace on the periphery of the Soviet Union—in the Baltic, the Black Sea, and the Far East. No air force had suffered greater losses, endured more hardships, or experienced such a dramatic rebirth. This transformation signaled the advent of Soviet airpower as a formidable component of the post-1945 Soviet military establishment. For the VVS, the difficult war years had fostered rapid modernization and the transition to first-rank status as an airpower. The Soviet Union joined the United States in becoming a true superpower. Accordingly, airpower emerged as a pivotal factor in shaping concepts of national security.

The passage from war to peace, however, brought no small measure of irony. The sudden advent of the nuclear age abruptly recast notions of what a future war might entail. The United States alone possessed this ultimate weapon and the means to deliver it across continents and oceans. Stalin and his military advisers found themselves

During the last months of the war, the VVS obtained several damaged
American B-17 bombers, which were repaired and test-flown. These
aircraft were not used operationally; they were utilized for study and
training purposes when Soviet bomber crews converted to the postwar
Tu-4. (From the collection of Valeriy Romanenko)

haunted by this new and threatening asymmetry in weaponry. Even
with superpower status, there were new perils. Most notably, the triumphal Soviet military lacked a credible strategic bomber force in
1945, not to mention aircraft carriers and atomic bombs.[2]

During World War II, the United States had deployed the Boeing B-
29 Superfortress as its most advanced long-range bomber, a lethal
weapon to deliver both conventional and nuclear bombs in the Pacific
war against Japan. The Soviets had no counterpart to the B-29 in their
aircraft inventory. Developing such a bomber posed a technical challenge of unprecedented scope, a process of adaptation that was
fraught with uncertainty and urgency.

No less vital in reshaping the future trajectory of airpower was a
technological revolution of the first order: jet propulsion. Nazi Germany had pioneered the Me-262, which entered operational service in
1944 and quickly outclassed piston-engine fighters flown by the Allied
air forces. Both the United States and Great Britain managed to deploy
small numbers of jet fighters before the war ended, but these warplanes were not on a par with the German technology and made no
significant impact. The Soviet Union had been experimenting with jet

This American-built B-24 bomber found its way to the 449th BAP. The American unit markings are still visible on the nose and tail sections. This B-24 most likely belonged to the 459th Bomber Group. (From the collection of Oleg Korytov)

engine designs for many years, but given the competing wartime demands, design of a jet-powered aircraft had not been a top priority. Now Stalin and his war planners faced the daunting task of achieving parity with the West in yet another sphere of technology.

Even in the face of these new realities, the Soviet military was not on a war footing in the immediate aftermath of World War II. There was no palpable fear of war with the United States, although tensions continued to mount in the period after the Potsdam conference. Military planners in Washington, however, perceived that any future war would and should make use of atomic bombs: a list of Soviet targets had been prepared by the Joint Chiefs of Staff as early as November 3, 1945.[3] For the Soviets, there was the reality of war exhaustion and the compelling need to consolidate power in those nations in eastern Europe now under Soviet control. In this interregnum before the onset of the Cold War, the Soviet Union joined the United States and Great Britain in a significant program of demobilization. The Red Army reduced its ground forces from 500 to 175 divisions, but the resulting force was reinforced with attention to modern weapons, greater firepower, and mobility.[4]

Air Commander Alexander Novikov emerged as a keynoter for

shaping the postwar reforms in airpower. As the wartime leader of the VVS, he was keenly aware of the shortcomings of the Soviet Air Force. In an insightful letter to Stalin, he argued that the VVS aircraft inventory was outdated and in no way ready to meet the challenge of a modern war. In his opinion, the Soviet long-range bombers, most notably the Il-4, Li-2, and Yer-2, were obsolescent.[5] Moreover, the aviation industry had not provided a single modern multiengine aircraft. When Novikov surveyed the status of tactical aviation, he observed that Soviet aircraft lacked speed and modern equipment, a weakness that would only become more apparent over time. For Novikov, there was the haunting specter of 1941, when the VVS had deployed large numbers of outdated aircraft that were unequal to the task of a modern war. Quantity alone, he argued, would not solve the emerging crisis in national security. Consequently, it was imperative to modernize, to alter the technological character of the aviation sector. In more specific categories, Novikov acknowledged the lack of progress in turbochargers, the absence of radar-equipped night interceptors, and—most critical—the need for an active program to develop jet propulsion technology.[6] Novikov's timely and insightful letter possessed a cruel irony of its own: he had not foreseen the implementation of a new wave of purges. Soon Novikov, his deputies, and key members of the aviation industry found themselves targeted for repression and summarily imprisoned—accused of actions that had led to the VVS's weaknesses in the critical spheres of modernization.[7]

Even with these arbitrary purges, the leadership of the Soviet Union correctly viewed the postwar setting as an occasion for the entire aviation sector to undergo a scientific and technical revolution. This transformation proved to be profound and was the key to the Soviet Union's drive to ensure its place as a major air power. Stalin and his circle of advisers—Vyacheslav Molotov, Lavrentiy Beria, and Georgiy Malenkov—presided over the process of modernization.[8] One overarching goal was the development of nuclear weapons. Success in this realm came in 1949 with the detonation of the Soviet Union's first atomic bomb, followed a few years later with a thermonuclear device. The wider pattern of rapid technological innovation took a variety of forms, engaging a large cadre of engineers and requiring large outlays of economic investment. The process was accelerated by captured German technology and systematic employment of German scientific and engineering talent (by the use of coercion and incentives). Within the VVS and the aviation sector, new voices arose to demand improved quality standards, requiring a more skilled workforce and a revamping of the manufacturing process in aviation and other spheres of weapons experimentation. This priority mirrored the intent of Stalin and the higher leadership in Moscow.[9]

The first move to reshape the VVS turned logically to the development of a new long-range bomber. The dropping of atomic bombs on Hiroshima and Nagasaki demonstrated that strategic bombers could reach an enemy homeland and unleash great destruction. Debates arose on the efficacy of strategic bombing, but few in the Soviet Union questioned the vital role bombers would play in any future war. The practical challenge in 1945 was to gain parity with the United States in this sphere of aviation, which, at the time, was one of the most visible measures of sophistication in airpower. Stalin wisely moved to create a new long-range bomber—one capable of attacking the homeland of any potential enemy. The wartime stress on tactical aviation remained in full effect, and this doctrine became a key component in the postwar commitment to combined arms warfare as a flexible answer to the nuclear threat. In any future war, the Soviets would retain their capability to project powerful armor and mechanized forces into western Europe.

Viewed in the historical context of 1945, the Soviet Union possessed only a minuscule and technologically inferior bomber force. The wartime priority placed on tactical aviation had severely restricted the number and quality of long-range bombers. In fact, the VVS had deployed the four-engine Pe-8 bomber during the war years, but only ninety-one of these aircraft had entered active wartime service.[10] The Pe-8, with its streamlined silhouette, appeared modern in design but lacked the range and performance to be a formidable air weapon. One of the most dramatic uses of the Pe-8 was as a VIP transport: in 1942, Molotov had flown in a Pe-8 from Moscow to Washington for a conference to fashion a wartime protocol for American Lend-Lease aid to the Soviet Union.

In the first half of 1943, Soviet intelligence obtained information on a new American high-altitude, high-speed long-range bomber that later became known as the B-29 Superfortress. A dramatic leap in technology, this American bomber outperformed every strategic bomber then in operational service. With the completion of the Manhattan Project (another program monitored by the Soviets), the Americans possessed the atomic bomb. The combination of the new strategic bomber and the new atomic weaponry was soon deployed against Japan to conclude the war in the Pacific. In the immediate postwar context, the Soviet Union did not possess an adequate delivery vehicle for conventional and atomic bombs; it had no bomber to match the performance of the B-29 Superfortress.

The Soviets began work on a new strategic bomber in September 1943, mobilizing the talents of designers A. N. Tupolev, V. M. Myasischev, and I. F. Nezval. Their separate endeavors suggested a variety of approaches: Tupolev was working on a new indigenous design, the Samolet 64; Nezval focused on an advanced version of the Pe-8; and Myasischev led the DVB 202 project, which paralleled the B-29 design in broad outline. Nezval's design was a minimalist effort at best, with little technical challenge or risk; it represented a stopgap measure to transform the Pe-8 into an effective bomber for the near term. The Tupolev and Myasischev projects, by contrast, required enormous effort and technical sophistication. None of these wartime initiatives, however, came to fruition. The Samolet 64 project faced major difficulties in integrating modern avionics and weapons systems. The Myasischev project never emerged from the formative stage of design and experimentation. As a result, the Soviet Union found itself without a modern, four-engine long-range bomber to match those of the Anglo-American air forces.

In May 1945, Myasischev embraced a new posture, boldly arguing that only by copying the B-29 Superfortress could the Soviet Union close the gap with the United States. He believed that certain aspects of Soviet technology could be adapted—for example, the use of powerful ASh-73TK engines and B-20 20mm guns for defensive armament. Myasischev's letter to the People's Commissariat of Aviation Industry, with an accompanying briefing by A. Ye. Golovanov on the B-29, proved decisive. Stalin was convinced that this was the best option; he ordered that the Superfortress be copied and placed the project on a fast schedule. To lead the complex project, Stalin appointed Tupolev, a man with vast experience and manifest skills as an administrator.[11] The design bureaus of both Myasischev and Nezval were folded into the project under the overall leadership of Tupolev.

Tupolev enjoyed enormous prestige as an aircraft designer, notwithstanding his victimization in the purges of the late 1930s. This bomber project focused narrowly on the goal of replicating the fabled Boeing B-29 Superfortress. Early in the war, Soviet intelligence had gathered data on the American bomber. Confirmation of the bomber's production came during a high-profile visit of Eddie Rickenbacker to the Soviet Union in 1943. Rickenbacker—the famed World War I ace and head of Eastern Air Lines—came to the Soviet Union to inspect the progress of Lend-Lease aid. His willingness to chat candidly about Washington's war planning offered the Soviets a rare chance to obtain details on military aircraft technology. Rickenbacker told his Soviet hosts that the B-29 would soon enter service. This prophecy came true a year later with the launching of the strategic bombing campaign against Japan.

One seemingly logical way for the Soviets to narrow the bomber gap would have been through Lend-Lease aid. But would the Americans share their advanced four-engine aircraft, particularly the B-29 Superfortress? Occasional requests for shipments of long-range bombers were routinely rejected. As it turned out, Lend-Lease aid only narrowly strengthened the tactical airpower of the Soviet Union by shipping only medium-range bombers such as the B-25.[12] Novikov, in fact, made several attempts to secure shipments of B-17 bombers, but his initiatives were rebuffed. There is evidence that Stalin made three formal requests for shipments of the Boeing B-29, which were also refused.[13] Lend-Lease largess supplied the Soviet Union with thousands of tactical aircraft, enormous quantities of raw materials and machine tools for the Soviet aviation industries, and numerous transport aircraft. Despite this generosity, the VVS was denied shipments of cutting-edge four-engine bombers, especially the B-29. For the Americans, of course, the B-29 was one of the most valued weapons in the inventory, a piece of advanced technology not to be shared.

Then fate intervened, setting the stage for the practical implementation of Stalin's order to copy the fabled American bomber. In the summer and fall of 1944, three American B-29s unexpectedly landed in the Far East. These emergency landings caught the local military officials off guard. Expectations on the American side for the return of the aircraft and crews were frustrated. And over time, this unresolved

This Boeing B-29 Superfortress (serial number 42-6256; *Ramp Tramp*) of the 771 BS/462 BG landed at the Tsentralnaya Uglovaya airfield, north of Vladivostok, on July 29, 1944. (From the collection of Konstantin Chirkin)

issue strained relations between Washington and Moscow. One VVS memoirist, a bomber pilot named Vasiliy Reshetnikov, aptly referred to these landings as *dar Bozhiy*, or "a gift from God."[14]

Echoing this sentiment, Stalin soon realized the value of the aircraft and refused to allow their return. His ultimate decision to copy the American bomber—what became one of the most celebrated exercises in technology transfer—would have a profound influence on the evolution of postwar Soviet airpower. Replicating the B-29 proved to be a highly complex process without precedent in terms of scale and technical sophistication. The B-29 possessed many advanced design and construction features with which the Soviet aviation sector was unfamiliar and, at the outset, incapable of reproducing. The crash program, however, was appealing to Stalin since the construction of a Soviet clone of the B-29 offered a swift path to an operational strategic air force. For Tupolev, the project presented a curious blend of opportunity and danger: if successful, he would be catapulted to the forefront of Soviet aircraft designers; if unsuccessful, he might end up in prison or worse.

Tupolev was highly regarded for his long service as a designer and his legendary hard-driving style. He knew the Soviet aviation sector well. Moreover, he possessed an informed understanding of foreign technology and its demands. In the late tsarist period, the youthful Tupolev chose aeronautics as a career field. He was a contemporary of Igor Sikorsky, but unlike Sikorsky, he warmly embraced the Communist revolution. His successes in the interwar years were notable, and he emerged as a talented designer of large aircraft. Many of his multi-engine designs became commercial and military benchmarks in the prewar era. These achievements, however, did not spare Tupolev from repression. He was arrested in 1937 for the alleged crime of being the "head of an anti-Soviet wrecking organization . . . and an agent of French intelligence."[15] After a brief period of imprisonment and brutal interrogation for his "crimes," Tupolev and many in his design bureau were placed in a special NKVD-run workshop. There, he labored on several military aircraft designs, in particular the Tu-2. Life in the prison workshop was an odd mix of internment and good treatment, a welcome exemption from the more severe labor camps of the era. His wartime reassignment to the Samolet 64 project represented a form of rehabilitation. Work on the clone of the B-29 offered an uncertain future for the Soviet designer.[16]

On July 10, 1945, Tupolev began in earnest the replication of the Superfortress. He was allowed to inspect the three interned B-29s now transferred to Izmailovo airfield near Moscow. At once, he clearly understood the daunting task he and his workers faced. Given the size and sophistication of the American strategic bomber, the undertaking would be unprecedented, and there was no guarantee—at least in the near term—that Soviet engineers could fabricate all the necessary components. The contrast in technical sophistication between the purloined B-29 and the typical warplane then being manufactured in Soviet aviation plants was evident. Moreover, the task of technology transfer was challenging. Failure was not an option, as Tupolev and his fellow workers comprehended the high risks associated with the project. One B-29 (serial number 42-6256), nicknamed *Ramp Tramp,* was selected for test-flying and crew training. A second bomber (serial number 42-6365), the *General H. H. Arnold Special,* was targeted for disassembly—component by component. The third bomber (serial number 42-6358), called *Ding How,* remained grounded to serve as a static model. At Moscow's historic Central Aerodrome, Tupolev's engineers and technicians began the complicated task of dismantling the *General H. H. Arnold Special.* Each part had to be cataloged with precise measurements. Even as this laborious activity proceeded, test pilots Mark Gallay and N. A. Ischenko flew demonstration flights with *Ramp Tramp*, mastering the subtle flying characteristics of the American bomber.[17]

Stalin assigned Lavrentiy Beria to serve as overseer of the project. A skilled administrator, Beria's large portfolio also included oversight of the top-secret Soviet atomic bomb program. Stalin's imprimatur and the key link to Beria provided the project with certain advantages in the complex world of Soviet war industries. Tupolev, however, faced a demanding calendar, with just two years to complete the bomber! He realized that he must mobilize a vast cadre of specialists and workers. For the pivotal post of chief deputy, Tupolev wisely named Dmitry S. Markov, a skilled, no-nonsense administrator. Knowing the dangers of working in piecemeal fashion with myriad Soviet factories and research entities, Tupolev and Markov came up with an inspired way to ensure optimal efficiency and integration: they decided on a top-down scheme of administration. A. I. Mikoyan, then deputy chairman of the Council of Ministers, undertook the enormous challenge of coordination. This meant the power of the state—with the implied threat of police sanctions—ensured the timely shipment of components for the new bomber tentatively named B-4. After it was completed and tested, Stalin personally signed the acceptance report and changed the name from B-4 to Tu-4. Tupolev recruited I. M. Sklyanskiy to monitor the timetable, a critical role for this hard-driving engineer. A large exhibit was set up in Moscow to showcase the drawings, actual components, and progress in building the new Tu-4. By means of the exhibit, all participating factories and parts suppliers could record their compliance with the strict deadlines. Tupolev's clever scheme, not just the police threats, added a powerful dynamic to the Tu-4 project.[18]

The beleaguered Tupolev presided over what became one of the most extraordinary programs of retrograde engineering in history. He succeeded in fashioning a close, but not necessarily precise, copy of the legendary B-29. Over the decades, the myth arose that the Tu-4 was an exact replica of the American Superfortress, reflecting a robotic response to Stalin's unambiguous mandate to make a clone. Indeed, Stalin had ordered a precise copy of the B-29, a prudent move to quickly and efficiently achieve a strategic bomber. Soviet technicians were careful to follow Stalin's instructions in detail, more often than not to avoid any charge of laxity or disobedience by the security police who were overseeing their work. Yet the demanding project was never mindless; for expediency, critical compromises were made along the way. What emerged, in the words of L. L. Kerber, was what could be called an analog, rather than a clone.[19]

Among all the sophisticated components of the B-29, one offered a particular challenge to the Soviet engineers: replication of the central station fire control system, or the computerized remote firing system. This system was complex and unique to the Superfortress, and in the minds of many observers, it was beyond the powers of the Soviet engineers to replicate. Yet this task was completed on time and with great effectiveness. I. I. Toropov, a talented and highly innovative engineer, led the team that fashioned the Soviet copy of the computerized firing system. Tupolev decided to install Soviet-made NS-23 cannons on the new Tu-4 bomber. This shift from the American .50-caliber weapons to the 23mm Soviet cannons required significant changes to the control system in terms of weight and ballistics characteristics, and it was one of several technical innovations used on the Tu-4 and subsequent projects.

The B-29 was fitted with four 2,200-horsepower Wright R-3350 engines, the most powerful piston engines ever produced. Finding a suitable Soviet alternative propulsion system became a critical baseline consideration. Here, Tupolev approved the use of an engine design by the talented Arkadiy Shvetsov. This Soviet-made engine was a variant of the M-71 (itself a clone of an earlier Wright engine design). Dubbed the ASh-73TK engine, it was rated at 2,300 horsepower, which represented a marginal improvement on the American Wright R-3350. The Shvetsov engine, however, proved to be inadequate, at least in the initial production run, never matching the performance of the Wright R-3350. Engine overheating and frequent propeller failures plagued the early prototypes. The ASh-73TK design, however, was a sound one, and subsequent refinements by the Shvetsov team eliminated these problems. By employing this alternative aero engine, Tupolev was able to keep the Tu-4 project on schedule.

The first series of Tu-4 bombers was manufactured at Aviation Plant Number 22 in Kazan in early 1947. To achieve an optimal level of serial production, additional plants were opened at Kuybyshev and Voronezh. Three experienced test pilots flew the first operational Tu-4s

Commander of the air forces of the Moscow Military District, Vasiliy Stalin, at the controls of a Tupolev Tu-4. (From the collection of Sergey Isayev)

off the assembly line at Kazan: Nikolay S. Rybko, Mark Gallay, and A. G. Vasilchenko. Early in 1947, Tupolev engaged in a detailed evaluation of the Tu-4's performance—engines, flight controls, and armament. No component of the Tu-4 was spared careful testing and documentation in these acceptance trials. Only two years had passed since the high-priority project had commenced.

The first public display of the Tu-4 took place at Tushino on Aviation Day in August 1947. This highly scripted event caused quite a stir among foreign observers at the air show. Three Tu-4 bombers, followed by a passenger version, made a low flyby at 600 feet (183 meters). Chief Marshal of Aviation Golovanov himself was at the controls of one of the Tu-4s. Military observers from the West assumed that the first three Tu-4s were the interned B-29s acquired by the Soviet Union in 1944. The sudden appearance of the passenger variant, soon to be known as the Tu-70, clearly established that these large multi-engine aircraft were of Soviet origin. The Tu-70 aircraft had been fitted with cannibalized parts from the disassembled *General H. H. Arnold*

The Tu-4 became the VVS's first important strategic bomber in the postwar years. A total of 874 were produced. (From the collection of Ilya Grinberg)

Special to make it airworthy, but those in the grandstand were unaware of this fact. Like a clap of thunder, the Tushino flyby heralded the advent of the Soviets' new strategic bomber force.

Understandably, both American and British air planners were shocked by this extraordinary display. In the tense context of the emerging Cold War, the overflight only added to the alarm in the West. In reality, the newly operational Tu-4 lacked the range to pose any real threat to the United States; it would require a one-way suicide mission to hit Chicago or New York City. Yet in 1952, the perceived threat of the Tu-4 was real. Lieutenant General Thomas D. White, deputy chief of staff for operations for the U. S. Air Force, warned that these Soviet bombers "are capable of making one way attacks on any city in North America. By [aerial] refueling . . . the Soviet bombers could carry out two way operations."[20] The Tu-4 and its jet bomber successors prompted the United States to set up a matrix of defensive systems, most notably the Nike surface-to-air missiles in the 1950s. By the time of the Korean War, the VVS had deployed a total of nine Tu-4 regiments, each with thirty-two bombers. At this juncture, however, the Tu-4—like the B-29 Superfortress—had become largely obsolescent.

The Tu-4 project served as a catalyst for a whole range of technical breakthroughs and the overall modernization of the aviation sector. In a historical context, the development and production of the Tu-4 fertilized the soil for a truly revolutionary event in aviation: develop-

Early Soviet jet fighter, the Mikoyan and Gurevich MiG-9. (From the collection of Sergey Isayev)

ment of the first generation of Soviet jet aircraft, first military and then commercial.[21]

The rapid advance of jet technology signaled yet another and perhaps more enduring technological revolution. The Soviet trajectory of adaptation and experimentation in this critical sphere of technology occurred in several stages. The first was the capture and study of German jet engines. Initially, these German jet engines were married to existing airframe designs for piston-powered aircraft. In time, the acquisition of foreign jet engines allowed important strides forward. Finally, Soviet indigenous designs would appear to power a whole new generation of fighters and bombers.[22] A. M. Lyulka's pioneering work in Soviet jet engine design took place at the Kharkov Aviation Institute in 1937. Unlike Frank Whittle and Hans von Ohain in the West, Lyulka would not be widely remembered for his theoretical endeavors in the prewar years. After a long interruption, Lyulka returned to jet engine development in 1944. Eventually, he would design a workable, if underpowered, axial-flow jet engine.

The wartime debut of the German Me-262 jet signaled the advent of the jet age. The Germans developed the first turbojet aircraft, the

Early Soviet jet fighter, the Yakovlev Yak-15. (From the collection of Sergey Isayev)

Heinkel He 178, in the prewar years. Although the Me-262, with its swept wings, possessed a technological edge, it appeared late in the war and was soon neutralized by the overwhelming power of the Anglo-American air forces. Both the United States and Great Britain produced their own jet fighters—for example, the Bell P-59 and the Gloster Meteor, respectively—but these jets had no significant impact on the air war. Like the British and the Americans, the Soviets worked to overcome the technological gap with the Germans in the first years of the postwar era. It became apparent that Lyulka's earlier work, though innovative, fell short of the advances already achieved by Nazi Germany. Consequently, A. I. Shakhurin, the wartime People's Commissar for the Aviation Industry, proposed copying the Me-262 as the most expedient way to move forward. However, Stalin rejected this proposal in favor of perfecting a new generation of indigenous jet aircraft, which led to the MiG-9 and Yak-15.

The Soviets upgraded the German JUMO-004 and BMW-003 jet engines with their RD-10 and RD-20 series. The development of other jet aircraft during this period suggests the wide-ranging work in this new technology: there was the Su-9, a twin-engine fighter with an early version of an ejection seat; the Su-11, a postwar variant with a Soviet-designed Lyulka TR-1 engine; and plans for the Su-13, powered by a Klimov RD-500, which was a clone of the Rolls Royce Derwent jet engine. Many of these designs were experimental, but they suggest that

Lavochkin La-15 jet fighter in flight. (From the collection of Sergey Isayev)

the major Soviet design bureaus embraced the new jet technology in the immediate postwar era.

The story of Soviet postwar jet engine development would be shaped in a profound way by the acquisition of Rolls Royce Nene and Derwent engines. In 1947, the British government of Clement Atlee approved the sale of these two engines, representing state-of-art jet propulsion technology, to the Soviet Union. Once the twenty-five Nene and thirty Derwent engines arrived, they were divided up among several design bureaus for systematic study. The first reproduction of the Nene was the RD-45 engine. Initially, it was copied and entered production without any modifications. Soon, however, Soviet engineers found ways to upgrade and improve the British engines in their possession. The Soviets were also quick to fit the new jet engines to aircraft; for example, A. S. Yakovlev made extensive use of Derwent engine types to power a series of postwar machines, most notably the Yak-23. The S. A. Lavochkin design bureau adapted both the Nene and Derwent engines to the La-174 aircraft prototypes.[23]

To showcase the VVS's entry into the jet age, the MiG-9 and its sister jet fighter the Yak-15 made a dramatic flyover of Red Square on May Day in 1947. With an engine life of twenty-five hours, this first

On September 21, 1953, Lieutenant No Kum-Sok of the North Korean air force defected in his MiG-15bis to South Korea. This highly prized Soviet-built jet fighter was later tested by the Americans. Eventually, the MiG-15 was transferred to the National Museum of the U.S. Air Force in Dayton, Ohio, where it remains one of the most celebrated aircraft of the Cold War era. (Courtesy of the U.S. Air Force)

generation of jets was transitional at best, but these aircraft provided vital experience in manufacturing, service, and training in jet technology. Soon the Mikoyan and Gurevich design bureau moved forward to supply the VVS with a modern and revolutionary jet fighter. The sleek new fighter, the MiG-15, became a signature aircraft for the jet age. The fresh design had swept wings, a pressurized cabin, and armament consisting of 37mm and 23mm cannons. The streamlined MiG-15 was fast, highly maneuverable, and initially fitted with RD-45F (later VK-1) engines.[24] During the Korean War, the Soviet jet engaged in a series of epic air battles with the U.S. Air Force Sabre—the first air combat between jets. The high-altitude interception of American B-29s by the MiG-15 made a powerful impact on American air operations in Korea. The MiG-15 was produced in nine separate factories in the Soviet Union, along with licensed copies in Poland, Czechoslovakia, and China.

In just a few years, the Soviet Union, whose economy had been devastated by the war, was able to capitalize on advances in rocketry, radar, new materials, and jet propulsion. Soviet engineers skillfully utilized know-how from former allies and enemies and managed to develop parity with the West in critical areas of technology. The VVS entered the new era of the Cold War with global reach.

The phoenix was reborn again.

Appendices

Appendix 1. Characteristics of VVS Western Frontier Military Districts, June 1, 1941

VVS Military District	Types of Aircraft in Inventory	Quantity of Combat Aircraft		Quantity of Aircrews	Crews Ready for Combat Action				Number of Pilots Receiving Conversion Training or Post-Flight School Training	Total Number of Air Divisions	Total Number of Air Regiments
		Total	Unserviceable	Total	Daytime, Simple Weather Conditions	Daytime, Complex Weather Conditions	Nighttime, Simple Weather Conditions	Nighttime, Complex Weather Conditions			
Leningrad	All types	1,288	114	1,296	1,135	323	314	27	161	18	24
	New types: MiG-3, LaGG-3, Yak-1, Pe-2	208	4	1	1						
Baltic Special	All types	1,200	145	787	787	154	126			5	19
	New types: MiG-1, MiG-3, Pe-2, Il-2	156	12								
Western Special	All types	1,658	205	1,702	1,289	285	242	17	574	6	30
	New types: MiG-1, MiG-3, Yak-1, Pe-2, Yak-2, Yak-4	347	39	225	64	4	4		161		

Kiev Special	All types	1,901	227	1,682	1,547	508	359	237	10	32
	New types: MiG-3, Yak-1, Pe-2, Il-2, Yak-2, Yak-4	425	34	212	100			112		
Odessa	All types	962	164	827	699	21	21	205	3	16
	New types: MiG-3, Pe-2	222	9	152	44			108		
Total for five frontier military districts	All types	7,009	855	6,294	5,457	1,291	1,062	1,177	42	121
	New types: MiG-1, MiG-3, LaGG-3, Yak-1, Pe-2, Il-2, Yak-2, Yak-4	1,358	98	590	209	4	4	381		
Long-range aviation[a]	All types	1,333	318	928	928	223	112	23	9	29
	New types: TB-7	9	4	12	12					
Total for five frontier military districts and long-range aviation	All types	8,342[b]	1,173	7,222	6,385	1,514	1,174	1,200	51	150
	New types: MiG-1, MiG-3, LaGG-3, Yak-1, Pe-2, Il-2, Yak-2, Yak-4, TB-7	1,367	102	602	221	4	4	381		

Source: Archive of the Ministry of Defense, fond 35, opis 107559, delo 5 (tom 1), listy 116–153, 170–207, as quoted in V. G. Nikiforov, ed., *Sovetskaya aviatsiya v Velikoy Otechestvennoy voyne 1941–1945 gg v tsifrakh* (Moscow: Glavnyy Shtab VVS, GU VVS SSSR, 1962).

a. Aviation of High Command. Only those units based at the territory or in proximity to the western frontier military districts.

b. Not including aircraft and crews of auxiliary units.

Appendix 2. Number of Sorties Performed by Soviet Aviation during the Great Patriotic War, 1941–1945

Branches of Aviation	1941 (from June 22)		1942		1943		1944		1945 (until May 9)		Total	
	Sorties	%	Sorties	%	Sorties	%	Sorties	%	Sorties	%	Total	%
VVS	269,565	58.70	571,130	66.98	677,857	76.56	817,064	82.28	569,162	92.13	2,904,778	76.28
Long-range aviation	20,741	4.52	39,692	4.65	74,956	8.47	64,284	6.47	20,115	3.26	219,788	5.77
Fighter aviation of PVO Strany	90,991	19.81	106,417	12.48	40,604	4.59	29,715	2.99	1,733	0.28	269,460	7.08
Naval aviation	75,999	16.55	107,339	12.59	74,876	8.46	69,975	7.05	22,571	3.65	350,760	9.21
Civil aviation	1,925	0.42	28,113	3.30	17,123	1.93	12,012	1.21	4,177	0.68	63,350	1.66
Total	459,221	100	852,691	100	885,416	100	993,050	100	617,758	100	3,808,136	100

Source: Operativnoe upravlenie GSh VVS, inventory number 71, pp. 1–40; Shtaba DA, inventory number 2491, listy 2–15; Voyska protivovozdushnoy oborony strany v Velikoy Otechestvennoy voyne 1941–1945 gg, vol. 2, 160; Arkhiv VMF, delo 21651, listy 4–13; Arkhiv GVF, fond 4/s, opis 17, delo 362, listy 78–86, as quoted in V. G. Nikiforov, ed., Sovetskaya aviatsiya v Velikoy Otechestvennoy voyne 1941–1945 gg v tsifrakh (Moscow: Glavnyy Shtab VVS, GU VVS SSSR, 1962)

Appendix 3. Number and Type of VVS Combat Sorties in Eight of the Most Significant Operations of 1941–1945

Number	Operation	Total Combat Sorties	Strikes at Enemy Troops and Equipment	Strikes at Railroad Infrastructure	Sorties for Air Superiority						Reconnaissance Missions	Strikes at River Crossings	Strikes at Naval Traffic	Special and Other Missions
					Total	At Airfields	Cover Missions	Escort Missions	Intercept Missions	Free-Hunt Missions				
1	Battle of Moscow (Oct 2, 1941–Mar 2, 1942)	94,490	45,580	7,780[a]	33,366	2,403	25,948	3,788	1,227		7,764			
	Defensive battle (Oct 2–Dec 4, 1941)	35,105	18,685	1,822	10,351	593	71,90	1,458	1,110		4,247			
	Counteroffensive (Dec 5–30, 1941)	10,150	4,716	427	3,579	130	3,009	354	86		1,428			
	General offensive (Jan 1–Mar 1, 1942)	49,235	22,179	5,531	19,436	1,680	15,749	1,976	31		2,089			
2	Battle of Stalingrad (Jul 12, 1942–Feb 2, 1943)	10,2392	47,555	2,394	40,536	6,538	18,350	12,186	3,462[b]		8,182	307		3,418
	Defensive battle (Oct 2–Nov 18, 1942)	67,500	32,176	1,463	26,677	2,062	14,588	8,307	1,720		5,140	307		1,737

(continued)

Appendix 3. Continued

Number	Operation	Total Combat Sorties	Strikes at Enemy Troops and Equipment	Strikes at Railroad Infrastructure	Sorties for Air Superiority						Reconnaissance Missions	Strikes at River Crossings	Strikes at Naval Traffic	Special and Other Missions
					Total	At Airfields	Cover Missions	Escort Missions	Intercept Missions	Free-Hunt Missions				
3	Counteroffensive (Nov 19, 1942–Feb 2, 1943)	34,892	15,379	931	13,859	4,476	3,762	3,879	1,742		3,042			1,681
	Kuban air operations (Apr 4–Jun 10, 1943)	34,921	14,600		15,276	1,685	7,683	4,974	645	289	2,404		2,560	81
4	Battle of Kursk (Jul 5–Aug 18, 1943) Defensive operation	107,433	61,590	6,989	33,045	1,213	16,584	12,106	2,916	226	5,809			
	(Jul 5–12, 1943)c Counteroffensive	28,161	14,023	547	12,257	319	4,695	5,915	1,270	58	1,334			
	(Jul 12–Aug 18, 1943) Counteroffensive	79,272	47,567	6,442	20,788	894	11,889	6,191	1,646	168	4,475			
5	Belorussian offensive operation (Jun 23–Aug 29, 1944)	153,545	54,134	12,025	64,484	992	26,148	33,628	517	3,199	19,487	1,262		2,153

	Operation													
6	Lvov–Sandomir offensive operation (Jul 13–Aug 29, 1944)	48,274	20,655	948	22,066	239	10,477	10,353	230	767	4,328	241		36
7	Berlin operation (Apr 16–May 8, 1945)	91,384	45,981		39,082	396	17,156	20,066		1,464	5,713			608
8	Defeat of Japanese troops in Far East (Aug 9–Sep 2, 1945)	14,531	2,557d	1,782	4,617	94	2,487	2,036			3,475		735	1,365
Total:	Sorties	646,970	292,652	31,918	252,472	13,560	124,833	99,137	8,997	5,945	57,162	1,810	3,295	7,661
	Percentage	100	45.2	4.9	39.0	2.1	19.3	15.3	1.4	0.9	8.8	0.3	0.5	1.2

Source: V. G. Nikiforov, ed., *Sovetskaya aviatsiya v Velikoy Otechestvennoy voyne 1941–1945 gg v tsifrakh* (Moscow: Glavnyy Shtab VVS, GU VVS SSSR, 1962).

a. Including river crossings, storage facilities, and other missions.

b. Including free-hunt missions.

c. Including ADD and aviation of the PVO.

d. Including fortifications.

Appendix 4. Quantity and Composition of Frontal Aviation at Important Periods of the Great Patriotic War, 1941–1945

Period	Aviation Type				Total Combat Aircraft
	Bomber	Ground Attack	Fighter	Reconnaissance and Artillery Spotting	
Beginning of Great Patriotic War (Jun 22, 1941)	2,212 31.0%	317 4.4%	4,226 59.2%	378 5.3%	7,133 100%
	360	18	1,022	48	1,448
Second period of summer–fall 1941 campaign (Jul 10, 1941)	774 30.8%	128 5.1%	1,532 60.9%	82 3.3%	2,516 100%
	181	29	335	24	569
Third period of summer–fall 1941 campaign (Oct 1, 1941)	508 29.6%	180 10.5%	948 55.2%	80 4.7%	1,716 100%
	209	144	535	44	932
Before Soviet counteroffensive at Moscow (Dec 5, 1941)	590 32.3%	164 9.0%	1,010 55.2%	65 3.6%	1,829 100%
	172	144	564	51	931
Beginning of summer–fall 1942 campaign (May 1, 1942)	1,756 43.5%	435 10.8%	1,757 43.5%	90 2.2%	4,038 100%
	303	412	1,064	41	1,820
Second period of war: winter 1942–1943 campaign (Nov 19, 1942)	1,848 34.6%	1,664 31.2%	1,646 30.9%	177 3.3%	5,335 100%
	652	1,644	1,337	115	3,748

Date										
Beginning of summer–fall 1943 campaign (Jul 1, 1943)	2,014	22.8%	2,817	31.9%	3,690	41.8%	305	3.5%	8,826	100%
	1,149		2,815		3,391		296		7,651	
Third period of war: winter 1944 campaign (Jan 1, 1944)	2,900	31.4%	2,413	26.1%	3,926	42.5%	–		9,239	100%
	–		–		–		–		–	
Beginning of summer–fall 1944 campaign (Jun 1, 1944)	3,146	24.7%	3,797	29.8%	5,815	45.6%	–		12,758	100%
	–		–		–		–		–	
Beginning of 1945 campaign in Europe (Jan 1, 1945)	3,220	23.1%	4,171	29.9%	5,810	41.7%	735	5.3%	13,936	100%
	2,152		4,171		5,810		735		12,868	
End of Great Patriotic War (May 10, 1945)	2,977	21.9%	3,585	26.3%	6,267	46.0%	791	5.8%	13,620	100%
	1,986		3,585		6,267		711		12,549	
Beginning of war with Japan (Aug 9, 1945; 9th, 10th, and 12th Air Armies)	706	21.4%	543	16.5%	1,871	56.8%	173	5.3%	3,293	100%
	679		543		1,871		173		3,266	

Source: Based on V. G. Nikiforov, ed., *Sovetskaya aviatsiya v Velikoy Otechestvennoy voyne 1941–1945 gg v tsifrakh* (Moscow: Glavnyy Shtab VVS, GU VVS SSSR, 1962).

Note: For each date, the first row gives the total number of combat aircraft and the percentage of aviation it represents. The second row gives the number of new aircraft types.

Appendix 5. Deliveries of Aircraft and Engines to the VVS from the Aviation Industry, 1941–1945

Aircraft and Engine Type	1941 Planned	1941 Actual	1942 Planned	1942 Actual	1943 Planned	1943 Actual	1944 Planned	1944 Actual	1945 Planned	1945 Actual	Total Planned	Total Actual
Combat aircraft												
Bomber	4,591	3,754	3,484	3,508	3,868	3,919	4,317	4,058	2,849	2,638	19,109	17,877
Shturmovik (Il-2 and Il-10)	2,318	1,542	7,974	8,191	10,821	10,773	10,732	10,719	5,937	6,015	37,782	37,240
Fighter	8,417	7,220	9,824	9,643	14,052	14,292	17,398	17,872	10,423	10,575	60,114	59,602
Total combat aircraft	15,326	12,516	21,282	21,342	28,741	28,984	32,447	32,649	19,209	19,228	117,005	114,719
Noncombat aircraft												
Transport	275	257	559	466	1,209	1,198	1,497	1,495	1,431	1,181	4,971	4,597
Light and training	2,585	3,101	3,339	3,432	4,094	4,559	6,154	6,008	6,100	5,695	22,272	22,795
Total noncombat aircraft	2,860	3,358	3,898	3,898	5,303	5,757	7,651	7,503	7,531	6,876	27,243	27,392
Total combat and noncombat aircraft	18,186	15,874	25,180	25,240	34,044	34,741	40,098	40,152	26,740	26,104	144,248	142,111
Engines												
Total	37,359	27,916	39,187	37,821	49,585	48,489	54,297	51,939	43,470	40,164	223,898	206,329
Refurbished	6,232	4,588	2,764	3,088	5,022	6,251	4,286	4,416	6,710	7,220	25,014	25,563

Source: Data from Department of Mobilizational Planning of GSh VVS, delo 103, list 1–22, 39–40, as quoted in V. G. Nikiforov, ed., *Sovetskaya aviatsiya v Velikoy Otechestvennoy voyne 1941-1945 gg v tsifrakh* (Moscow: Glavnyy Shtab VVS, GU VVS SSSR, 1962)

Appendix 6. Deliveries of Foreign Aircraft to the USSR, 1941–1945

Aircraft Type	Year of Delivery	Quantity Received under Lend-Lease[a]	Non–Lend-Lease Deliveries[b]	Total Received
Fighter				
Hawker "Hurricane" II	1941–1944	2,634	238	2,872
Supermarine Spitfire PR.IV	1942–1944	—	10	10
Supermarine Spitfire V	1943	150	—	150
Supermarine Spitfire IX and XVI	1944–1945	1,187	—	1,187
Curtiss P-40 Tomahawk	1941–1942	199	48	247
Curtiss P-40E, K, M, and N	1941–1944	1,887[c]	—	1,887
Airacobra Mk.I	1942–1943	211[c]	—	211
Bell P-39D-2, K, L, M, N, and Q Airacobra	1944–1945	4,741[c]	—	4,741
"Mustang" Mk.I	1942	—	4	4
Bell P-63 Kingcobra	1944–1945	2,400	—	2,400
Republic P-47D Thunderbolt	1943–1945	195	—	195
Total fighters		13,604	300	13,904
Bomber				
Douglas A-20 Boston (all models)	1942–1945	2,771[c]	—	2,771
NA B-25B, C, D, G, and J	1941–1945	856	5[d]	861[e]
Handley Page Hampden TB.I	1942	—	20	20
Consolidated B-24D Liberator	1943	—	1[f]	1
Total bombers		3,627	26	3653
Other aircraft				
Curtiss O-52 Owl	1941–1942	19	—	19
Douglas C-47	1942–1945	709	—	709
NA AT-6C and G	1942–1945	84	—	84
AW Albemarle A.W.41	1943	12	—	12
Consolidated PBN-1 Nomad	1944–1945	137	—	137
Consolidated PBY-6A Catalina	1945	48	—	48
Vought-Sikorsky OS2U-3 Kingfisher	1944	2[g]	—	2
Total other aircraft		1,011	—	1,011

(continued)

Aircraft Type	Year of Delivery	Quantity Received under Lend-Lease[a]	Non–Lend-Lease Deliveries[b]	Total Received
Total number of aircraft received	1941–1945	18,242	326	18,568
Aircraft received for familiarization				
Curtiss C-46A Commando	1945			1
DH Mosquito B.IV	1944			1
Short Stirling B.III	1945			1
Hawker Typhoon Mk.IB	1945			1

Source: This table was compiled with the assistance of Valeriy Romanenko, based on his doctoral dissertation: "Lend-Lease Aircraft 1941–1945 (Investigation of Monuments Aspect)" (Center for Protection and Investigation of Monuments of the National Academy of Sciences of Ukraine and Ukrainian Society of Protection of Historical and Cultural Monuments, Kyiv, 2009).

a. Includes aircraft received by the Soviet Purchasing Commission directly in the Soviet territory (Murmansk and Archangel), as well as in Fairbanks and Nome, Alaska, and Abadan, Iran.

b. Pre–Lend-Lease purchases, direct transfers at theaters, and those received as gifts.

c. This number is taken from official documents and requires further validation by calculating the number of aircraft actually received.

d. These five B-25Bs were purchased by the USSR in October 1941.

e. In addition, twelve U.S. Army Air Force aircraft made forced landings in the Far East and were interned. They were repaired and put into service by the VVS (including one B-25B from the Doolittle raid).

f. This aircraft was damaged during takeoff from one of the ALSIB airfields; after repairs, it was transferred to the USSR.

g. These aircraft were part of the battleship Milwaukee inventory. They were returned to the U.S. Navy with the ship in 1947.

APPENDIX 7. THE AIR ARMIES, 1942-1945

The air armies provided the Soviet Air Force (VVS) with a highly mobile air strike force. The Supreme High Command (the *Stavka*) created a total of eighteen air armies—seventeen from frontal aviation, and one (the 18th Air Army) from long-range bomber aviation. Except for isolated special units, the air armies became coextensive with Soviet frontal aviation for the period 1942-1945. Highly centralized and carefully coordinated with the ground forces, the VVS air armies served as an effective tactical air weapon in both defensive and offensive operations.

Each *Front* possessed its own operational air army. During major offensives, particularly in the last stages of the war, the *Stavka* frequently assigned more than one air army to an active *Front*. Throughout the war, the Air Corps of the *Stavka* Reserve systematically reinforced the various air armies to meet the shifting combat requirements. On occasion, the *Stavka* subordinated one air army to a neighboring one to achieve a concentration of air strength for a combined arms operation. Through the air armies, the Soviet High Command achieved swift deployment of airpower, mobility, and unified command.

Between 1942 and 1945, the average size of an air army grew dramatically. Beginning with a modest aggregate of around 200 aircraft in 1942, it reached approximately 1,000 aircraft by 1943; for the final Soviet offensives in 1944-1945, it achieved the unprecedented level of 2,000 to 2,500 aircraft. Such an augmentation in airpower allowed the Soviet military to assert overwhelming air supremacy at crucial points and times.

1st Air Army

Formed: May 5, 1942. Five air divisions attached to the Western *Front* served as the nucleus for the new air army. Later, the 1st Air Army expanded to thirteen air divisions: 201st, 202nd, 203rd, 234th, and 235th IADs (fighter air divisions); 204th and 213th (night) BADs (bomber air divisions); 215th SAD (mixed air division); and 214th, 224th, 231st, 232nd, and 233rd ShADs (ground attack air divisions). From April 24, 1944, the 1st Air Army was part of the 3rd Belorussian *Front*. By the end of the war, it had 1,501 aircraft.

Combat Path: Participated in a series of air operations from Moscow to Konigsberg. Initially assigned to support the Western *Front* near Moscow, the 1st Air Army went on to assist the Soviet army in the Rzhev–Sychevka and Rzhev–Vyazma offensive (1943), the campaign around Smolensk (winter 1943–1944), and the Belorussian and East Prussian campaigns during the concluding phases of the war. At Vitebsk, Orsha, and the Berezina and Nieman River crossings, the 1st Air Army played a significant role. The Normandie-Nieman regiment, a group of French volunteer pilots, served with this air army.

Total Sorties: 290,000

Command: Lieutenant General T. F. Kutsevalov, May–June 1942; Major General S. A. Khudyakov, June 1942– May 1943; Lieutenant General M. M. Gromov, May 1943–July 1944; Colonel General T. T. Khryukin, July 1944–end of war

2nd Air Army

Formed: May 1942, from air units of the Bryansk *Front*. It had eight air divisions—205th, 206th, and 207th IADs; 208th (night) and 223rd (short range) BADs; and 225th, 226th, and 227th ShADs—and two separate air regiments. Later in the war, more units were included. During the Berlin operation, the 2nd Air Army was one of the largest in the VVS, with 2,004 aircraft in its inventory.

Combat Path: The 2nd Air Army flew diverse combat missions from Voronezh in 1942 to Berlin and Prague in 1945. During the Soviet counteroffensive at Stalingrad in November 1942, the 2nd Air Army provided air support for the Southwestern *Front*. Later, it joined with the 8th, 16th, and 17th Air Armies to execute the successful air blockade at Stalingrad. At Kursk, the 2nd Air Army flew more than 15,000 combat sorties in support of the Voronezh *Front* (later renamed the 1st Ukrainian *Front*), followed by air operations in support of the Soviet drive to cross the Dnieper River. During the final phases of the war, the 2nd participated in a number of difficult undertakings: the Korsun–Shevchenkovskiy and Lvov–Sandomir operations of 1944, and the campaigns in Czechoslovakia and Berlin in 1945.

Total Sorties: 300,000

Command: Major General S. A. Krasovskiy, May–October 1942; Major General K. N. Smirnov, October 1942–March 1943; Colonel General S. A. Krasovskiy, March 1943–end of war

3rd Air Army

Formed: May 1942. Organized with air elements of the Kalinin *Front*, consisting of five air divisions: 209th, 210th, and 256th IADs; 212th ShAD; and 211th BAD. It ended the war with 659 aircraft.

Combat Path: The 3rd Air Army first entered combat in July 1942 in the Rzhev sector west of Moscow. In February 1943, it applied air pressure on trapped German army units at Demyansk. Later in the same year, the 3rd Air Army participated in the campaign to capture Smolensk. Attached to the 1st Baltic *Front* in 1944, the 3rd Air Army took part in the Belorussian and Baltic campaigns. In 1945, operationally subordinated to the 1st Air Army, it flew numerous sorties in support of the East Prussian offensive, concluding the war on the Leningrad *Front* in joint operation with the 15th Air Army. The 3rd Air Army provided sustained air support and liaison with partisan units in Belorussian and Baltic areas.

Total Sorties: 200,000

Command: Lieutenant General M. M. Gromov, May 1942–May 1943; Colonel General N. F. Papivin, May 1943–end of war

4th Air Army

Formed: May 1942, based on frontal aviation of the Southern *Front*. Its initial air strength consisted of six air divisions—216th, 217th, and 229th IADs; 218th (night) and 219th BADs; and 230th ShAD—and seven air regiments. By the end of the war, it had an inventory of 1,351 aircraft.

Combat Path: The 4th Air Army, particularly its fighter air units, established an impressive combat record in the Caucasus in 1942. After participating in defensive operations in the Donbas and North Caucasus, the 4th Air Army went on to engage in the intense air battles over Krasnodar, Kerch, and the Kuban in 1943. Once the Crimea was cleared of enemy troops in the spring of 1944, the 4th Air Army moved north to join the 2nd Belorussian *Front* in June–July 1944 for the Belorussian offensive. In January 1945, the 4th Air Army supported the Soviet drive into East Prussia, followed by air operations over the Oder River and at Berlin.

Total Sorties: 300,000

Command: Major General K. A. Vershinin, May–September 1942; Major General N. F. Naumenko, September 1942–April 1943; Colonel General K. A. Vershinin, May 1943–end of war

5th Air Army

Formed: May 1942, based on the North Caucasus *Front*. Its composition at outset included five air divisions—236th, 237th, and 265th IADs; 132nd BAD; and 238th ShAD—and separate air regiments.

Combat Path: The 5th Air Army entered combat in June 1942, providing air support for retreating Soviet forces in the North Caucasus. With the 4th Air Army, it participated in the crucial Kuban air operations in the spring of 1943. At the time of Kursk, the 5th Air Army of the Steppe *Front* (later the 2nd Ukrainian *Front*) engaged in Soviet offensive operations in the Belgorod–Kharkov sector. During the winter of 1943–1944, it flew in support of the Dnieper River crossings and the capture of Kiev. Subsequent operations followed a path across Ukraine into Romania, Hungary, Czechoslovakia, and Austria. By the end of the war, it had 971 aircraft.

Total sorties: 180,000

Command: Colonel General S. K. Goryunov, June 1942–end of war

6th Air Army

Formed: June 1942. Organized with the frontal air units of the Northwestern *Front*, it was composed of five air divisions—239th and 240th IADs; 241st and 242nd (night) BADs; and 243rd ShAD—seven mixed air regiments, and three separate air squadrons.

Combat Path: The 6th Air Army was relatively inactive in the first months of its existence. In 1943, however, it assisted in the air blockade of the Demyansk pocket and participated with an air group mobilized to support the Kalinin *Front*. In November 1943, it was withdrawn into the *Stavka* Reserve, and selected air units were transferred to the 15th Air Army. In February 1944, the 6th Air Army reentered active status in support of the 2nd Belorussian *Front*; it was reassigned in April to the 1st Belorussian *Front* under the overall command of the 16th Air Army. During the summer of 1944, the 6th participated in the Belorussian offensive. Subsequent operations included the Soviet drive into Poland and the Vistula River crossing. It was withdrawn into the *Stavka* Reserve again in September 1944. Command of the 6th Air Army served as the basis for the new, Soviet-sponsored Polish Air Force.

Total Sorties: 120,000

Command: Major General D. F. Kondratyuk, June 1942–January 1943; Colonel General F. P. Polynin, January 1943–September 1944

7th Air Army

Formed: November 1942, Karelian *Front*. Initially, it consisted of four air divisions—258th and 259th IADs; 260th ShAD; and 261st BAD—and a number of separate regiments and squadrons.

Combat Path: Wartime air operations were largely restricted to the Karelian *Front*, although air units from the 7th Air Army participated in joint operations with the naval air arm of the Northern Fleet. In the summer of 1944, the 7th Air Army provided air cover for Soviet troops crossing the Svir River. In October 1944, it covered troops of the 14th Army in their offensive in the Petsamo–Kirkenes sector. By the end of 1944, the 7th Air Army entered the *Stavka* Reserve.

Total Sorties: 60,000

Command: Colonel General I. M. Sokolov, November 1942–end of war

8th Air Army

Formed: June 1942. Organized on the Southwestern *Front* with an initial air strength of ten air divisions—206th, 220th, 235th, 268th, and 269th

IADs; 270th, 271st, and 272nd BADs; and 226th and 228th ShADs—as well as seven separate squadrons, a transport air detachment, and a special air group of the civil air fleet.

Combat Path: The 8th Air Army first entered combat in the summer of 1942, providing air cover in the defensive battles around Poltava and Stalingrad. Once the Soviet counteroffensive at Stalingrad began in November 1942, the 8th Air Army assumed a leading role in the Soviet air blockade of the encircled German Sixth Army. After the Stalingrad air operations, the 8th Air Army supported Soviet offensives of the Southern *Front* (later the 4th Ukrainian *Front*) at Rostov, in the Donbas, and across the Dnieper River in 1943. During 1944, the 8th again played a major role in the South, assisting both the 1st and 4th Ukrainian *Fronts* in wide-ranging air operations from the Crimea to the Carpathian Mountains. The 8th Air Army also participated in the crucial Lvov–Sandomir operation in July–August 1944. In the final Soviet offensives of 1945, the 8th Air Army provided air support for the Soviet army's drive through southern Poland and Czechoslovakia, culminating in the capture of Prague. By the end of the war, its strength was 590 aircraft.

Total Sorties: 220,000

Command: Colonel General T. T. Khryukin, June 1942–July 1944; Lieutenant General V. N. Zhdanov, August 1944–end of war

9th Air Army

Formed: August 1942, based on air units of the 1st, 25th, and 35th Armies of the Far East *Front*. Seven air divisions formed the air army: 32nd, 249th, and 250th IADs; 33rd and 34th BADs; and 251st and 252nd ShADs.

Combat Path: Up to August 1945, the 9th Air Army helped secure the airspace of the Soviet Far East. For the assault in August 1945 on the Japanese Kwantung Army, the 9th Air Army assisted the Soviet 1st Far East *Front*. Reinforced with the 19th BAK from long-range aviation, the 9th Air Army hit the enemy rear at Harbin and other key points. It also aided Soviet airborne troops in landings at major Manchurian cities such as Changchun, Mukden, and Harbin. It ended the war with 1,057 aircraft.

Total Sorties: 4,400

Command: Major General A. S. Senatorov, August 1942–September 1944; Major General V. A. Vinogradov, September 1944–June 1945; Colonel General I. M. Sokolov, June 1945–December 1946

10th Air Army

Formed: August 1942, based on the air force of the 25th Army of the Far East *Front*. It had a total of five air divisions: 29th IAD; 53rd, 83rd, and 254th BADs; and 253rd ShAD.

Combat Path: In the war with Japan, the 10th Air Army was attached to the 2nd Far East *Front*. During this campaign, the 10th devoted most of its resources to the Soviet 15th Army and the Red Banner Amur River Flotilla. By the end of the war, it had 1,294 aircraft.

Total Sorties: 3,297

Command: Major General V. A. Vinogradov, August 1942–September 1944; Colonel D. Ya. Slobozhan, September 1944–May 1945; Colonel General P. F. Zhigarev, May 1945–April 1946

11th Air Army

Formed: August 1942. Based on air units of the 2nd Red Banner Army of the Far East, the 11th Air Army consisted of three air divisions: 96th IAD, 82nd BAD, and 206th SAD.

Combat Path: The 11th Air Army secured the airspace of the Soviet Far East. On December 20, 1944, the *Stavka* reorganized the 11th Air Army into the 18th Mixed Air Corps. For the war with Japan, this air corps entered the 10th Air Army.

Command: Major General V. N. Bibikov

12th Air Army

Formed: August 1942. The 12th was attached to the Trans-Baikal *Front* with a strength of five air divisions: 245th and 246th IADs, 30th and 247th BADs, and 248th ShAD.

Combat Path: Up to August 1945, the 12th Air Army helped secure the border in the Far East and prepare pilots for combat. For the war with Japan, the 12th Air Army possessed thirteen air divisions. Along with its air support role for the advancing Soviet troops in Manchuria, the 12th Air Army flew joint missions with the naval air arm of the Pacific Fleet, landed assault troops at crucial points such as Changchun and Mukden, and airlifted supplies to the 6th Tank Army. Its combat strength by the end of the war was 1,095 aircraft.

Total Sorties: 5,000

Command: Lieutenant General T. F. Kutsevalov, August 1942–June 1945; Marshal of Aviation S. A. Khudyakov, June–September 1945

13th Air Army

Formed: November 1942, Leningrad *Front*. The 13th consisted of three air divisions: 275th IAD, 276th BAD, and 277th ShAD.

Combat Path: The 13th Air Army first participated with the 67th Army of the Leningrad *Front* in January 1943, flying a total of 2,000 sorties in an effort to break the siege of Leningrad. At the beginning of 1944, the 13th

Air Army played an active role in the Soviet offensive that lifted the Leningrad siege. During 1944, air units of the 13th assisted in the capture of Vyborg and, to the south, supported Soviet troops in their drive toward Tallinn. The 13th Air Army ended its active combat role by clearing Estonia of enemy forces in November 1944.

Total Sorties: 120,000

Command: Colonel General S. D. Rybalchenko

14th Air Army

Formed: July 1942. Organized with the aviation of the Volkhov *Front*, the 14th had four air divisions: 278th and 279th IADs, 280th BAD, and 281st ShAD.

Combat Path: The 14th Air Army participated in the 1943 winter offensive by the Volkhov *Front* in the Leningrad sector. A year later, it flew against German defensive positions in the Leningrad–Novgorod sector, part of an offensive effort that lifted the siege of Leningrad. In February 1944, it assisted troops of the Leningrad Front in the Pskov offensive operation and then entered the *Stavka* Reserve. In April 1944, the 14th joined the 3rd Baltic *Front* in the Pskov sector. In the fall of 1944, the 14th Air Army assisted in clearing enemy forces from the Baltic (Tartu and Riga operations). At the end of 1944, it reentered the *Stavka* Reserve, and its air units were reassigned to other air armies.

Total Sorties: 80,000

Command: Lieutenant General I. P. Zhuravlev

15th Air Army

Formed: July 1942. The 15th was organized with three air divisions of the Bryansk *Front*—286th IAD, 284th BAD, and 225th ShAD—and three separate air regiments.

Combat Path: The 15th Air Army first entered combat in the defensive fighting around Voronezh in the fall of 1942. During the following winter (1942–1943), it supported the troops of the Bryansk *Front*. The 15th Air Army participated in the crucial Battle of Kursk in the summer of 1943. In October 1943, it moved to the 2nd Baltic *Front* at Vitebsk to conduct air operations against Army Group North. In 1944, it played an active role in the Soviet drive into Latvia, culminating in the capture of Riga. The 15th ended its combat activity in support of the Leningrad *Front* in April 1945 with a strength of 1,094 aircraft.

Total Sorties: 170,000

Command: Major General I. G. Pyatykhin, July 1942–May 1943; Colonel General N. F. Naumenko, May 1943–end of war

16th Air Army

Formed: August 1942. At the outset, the 16th consisted of four air divisions—220th and 283rd IADs and 228th and 291st ShADs—and two separate air regiments.

Combat Path: The 16th, destined to be one of the major VVS air armies, began its operational life on September 4, 1942, in defense of the Stalingrad *Front*. It then participated in the counteroffensive and air blockade at Stalingrad in the winter of 1942–1943 (Don *Front*). Switched to the Central Front in spring 1943, the 16th contributed 56,350 combat sorties in the crucial Battle of Kursk. In the winter of 1943–1944, it assumed a pivotal role in the liberation of Ukraine and eastern portions of Belorussia. Attached to the 1st Belorussian *Front* in the summer of 1944, the veteran 16th Air Army contributed major blows toward the destruction of Army Group Center, particularly in the Bobruysk and Minsk sectors. For the second half of 1944, units of this air army operated in eastern Poland. The *Stavka* deployed the 16th Air Army in several major operations in 1945, again with the 1st Belorussian *Front*: the Warsaw–Poznan operations in January–February, the East Pomeranian operations in February–March, and the culminating assault on Berlin in April–May. For the Berlin operations, the 16th Air Army possessed 2,618 aircraft (eight air corps, plus separate air divisions and regiments).

Total Sorties: 280,000

Command: Major General P. S. Stepanov, August–September 1942; Colonel General S. I. Rudenko, September 1942–end of war

17th Air Army

Formed: November 1942, based on frontal aviation of the Southwestern *Front*. Initially, the 17th consisted of the 282nd and 288th IADs, 221st and 262nd (night) BADs, and 208th and 637th ShADs.

Combat Path: The 17th Air Army first entered combat at Stalingrad in November 1942, supporting the Soviet counteroffensive to encircle the German Sixth Army. It then participated in the air blockade of the encircled enemy troops. After Stalingrad, the 17th Air Army supported the Southwestern *Front* in its offensive to reoccupy the Donbas. In July, it took part in the defensive battles at Kursk in support of the Voronezh *Front*. Once the Soviet counteroffensive began at Kursk, the 17th moved south, concentrating its air strength around Kharkov in late August 1943. From this sector, it moved westward across the southern Ukraine in the fall of 1943. During the winter of 1943–1944, units of this air army played a major role in the Soviet drive to liberate Ukraine. Other important air campaigns followed in late 1944 and continued to the end of the war: the Yassy–Kishinev operation, the invasion of Hungary, the capture of Vienna, and concluding air operations within the 3rd Ukrainian *Front* in Czechoslovakia, with an inventory of 1,108 aircraft.

Total Sorties: 200,000

Command: Lieutenant General S. A. Krasovskiy, November 1942–March 1943; Colonel General V. A. Sudets, March 1943–end of war

18th Air Army

Formed: December 1944, as successor to long-range aviation (ADD). A total of five bomber air corps (BAKs) made up the 18th Air Army—1st Guards Smolenskiy, 2nd Guards Bryanskiy, 3rd Guards Stalingradskiy, 4th Guards Gomelskiy, and 19th BAK—along with four separate BADs. Together, these units amounted to twenty-two air divisions. Administration remained in Moscow; the command post moved to Brest toward the end of the war.

Combat Path: The 18th Air Army, according to Soviet accounts, established an active combat role in the final campaigns of the war—first in the Vistula–Oder offensive, and subsequently in East Prussia and at Berlin. Its bombing missions were coordinated with Soviet frontal aviation, hitting enemy cities, strongpoints, communications, and reserves. During the storming of Konigsberg (April 7, 1945), the 18th Air Army launched a daytime raid by 516 bombers to assist troops of the 3rd Belorussian *Front*. A subsequent raid on the Oder River defenses consisted of 743 bombers. The 19th BAK participated in the campaign against the Japanese Kwantung Army in August 1945.

Total Sorties: 19,164 (13,368 night) for the period January 1–May 8, 1945

Command: Chief Marshal of Aviation A. Ye. Golovanov

Appendix 8. Top Fifty Soviet Aces

Number	Name	Personal Victories	Shared Victories	Sorties	Engagements	Hero of the Soviet Union (HSU) Awarded for Victories/Sorties/ Engagements by Date	Year of Birth	Unit	Date of Death
1.	Kozhedub, Ivan Nikitovich	64	0	330	120	HSU: 20/146 by Oct 1943 2nd HSU: 48/256 by mid-1944 3rd HSU: 60/326 by end of war	1920	240th IAP/ 178th GIAP/ 176th GIAP	Aug 8,1991
2.	Rechkalov, Grigoriy Andreevich	61	4	450+	122	HSU: 12+2/194/54 by May 1943 2nd HSU: 48+6/415/112 by Jun 1944	1920	55th IAP/ 16th (56+6) GIAP/ 9th GIAD	Dec 22, 1990
3.	Gulaev, Nikolay Dmitrievich	55	5	250	69	HSU: 13+5/95 2nd HSU: 42+3/125/42 by Jul 1944	1918	423rd IAP/ 487th IAP/ 27th IAP/ 129th GIAP	Sep 27, 1985
4.	Yevstigneev, Kirill Alekseevich	52	3	283	113	HSU: 23+3/144 by Nov 1943 2nd HSU: +20/83 by Feb 1944	1917	240th IAP/ 178th GIAP	Aug 29, 1996
5.	Glinka, Dmitriy Borisovich	50	0	~300	~100	HSU: 15/146 by Apr 1943 2nd HSU: 29/183/62	1917	45th IAP/ 100th GIAP	Mar 1, 1979
6.	Skomorokhov, Nikolay Mikhaylovich	46	8	600	143	HSU: 25+8/483/44 by Jan 1944 2nd HSU: 35/520/119 by Mar 1945	1920	164th IAP/ 31st IAP	Oct 21, 1994 (killed in car accident)

Name					HSU details	Born	Units	Died
7. Pokryshkin, Aleksandr Ivanovich	46	6	650 +	156	HSU: 13 + 6/454/54 by Apr 1943 2nd HSU: 30/455 by Jul 1943 3rd HSU: 53/550/137 by May 1944	1913	55th IAP/16th GIAP 9th GIAD	Nov 13, 1985
8. Koldunov, Aleksandr Ivanovich	46	1	412	96	HSU: 15 + 1/233/45 by May 1944 2nd HSU: 46/412/96 by end of war	1923	866th IAP	Jun 7, 1992
9. Vorozheykin, Arseniy Vasilyevich	45	1	300 +		HSU: 19/78/32 2nd HSU: 11/28/1	1912	728th IAP 32nd IAP4 Chief Directorate of frontal aviation of VVS	May 23, 2001
10. Popkov, Vitaliy Ivanovich	41	1	475	117	HSU: 17/168/45 by Aug 1943 2nd HSU: 36 + 1/425/83 by Feb 1945	1922	5th GIAP	Feb 6, 2010
11. Morgunov, Sergey Nikolaevich	41	0	350	96	HSU: 22/234/68 by Sep 1944	1918	15th IAP	Jul 19, 1946 (killed in air accident)
12. Krasnov, Nikolay Fedorovich	40	1	400 +	≈ 100	HSU: 31/275/85 by Dec 1943	1914	402nd IAP 116th IAP 31st IAP 530th IAP	Jan 29, 1945 (killed in air accident)
13. Pivovarov, Mikhail Yevdokimovich	40	1	350		HSU: 21/269/69 by Feb 1945	1919	402nd IAP	May 15, 1949

(continued)

Appendix 8. Continued

Number	Name	Personal Victories	Shared Victories	Sorties	Engagements	Hero of the Soviet Union (HSU) Awarded for Victories/Sorties/ Engagements by Date	Year of Birth	Unit	Date of Death
14.	Serov, Vladimir Georgievich	39	6	~300	104	HSU: 20 + 6/203/53 by Apr 1944	1922	159th IAP	Jun 26, 1944 (killed in action)
15.	Luganskiy, Sergey Danilovich	37	5	390		HSU: 18 + 1/221 by Aug 1943 2nd HSU: 31 + 1 by Dec 1943	1918	271st IAP 270th IAP/ 152nd GIAP	Jan 16, 1977
16.	Kamozin, Pavel Mikhaylovich	36	13	188	63	HSU: 12/82/23 by Mar 1943 2nd HSU: 29 + 13/131/56 by Jul 1944	1917	246th IAP 269th IAP 66th IAP 101st GIAP	Nov 24, 1983
17.	Lavrinenkov, Vladimir Dmitrievich	35	11	448	134	HSU: 16 + 11/422/78 by Feb 1943 2nd HSU: no data	1919	630th IAP 753rd IAP 4th IAP 9th GIAP	Jan 14, 1988
18.	Babak, Ivan Ilyich	35	5	330	103	HSU: 18 + 4 by Sep 1943	1919	45th IAP/ 100th GIAP 16th GIAP	Jun 24, 2001
19.	Chubukov, Fedor Mikhaylovich	35	5	340 +	~100	HSU: 17 + 5/296/52 by May 1944	1920	154th IAP/ 29th GIAP	—

Name					Details	Born	Units	Death
20. Smirnov, Aleksey Semenovich	35	0	306	71	HSU: 13/412/39 by Aug 1943; 2nd HSU: 31+1/496 by Sep 1944	1917	153rd IAP/28th GIAP	Aug 7, 1987
21. Fedorov, Ivan Vasilyevich	35	0	404	107	HSU: 24/285/62 by Aug 1944	1920	812nd IAP	Aug 28, 2000
22. Gnido, Petr Andreyevich	34	7 or 6	406	80	HSU: 14+7/206/43 by Apr 1943	1919	248th IAP/13th IAP/111th GIAP	Mar 17, 2006
23. Alelyukhin, Aleksey Vasilyevich	34	6	601	123	HSU: 11+6/265/65; 2nd HSU: 26/410/114 by Nov 1943	1920	69th IAP/9th GIAP	Oct 29, 1990
24. Zaytsev, Vasiliy Aleksandrovich	34	0	427	163	HSU: 12/115/16 by Jan 1942; 2nd HSU: +22/299 by Aug 1943	1911	129th IAP/5th GIAP/207th IAD/1st GSAK/2nd GIAK	May 19, 1961
25. Amet-khan, Sultan	33	19	603	152	HSU: 11+19 by Aug 1943; 2nd HSU: 30+19/603/150 by end of war	1920	4th IAP/9th GIAP	Feb 1, 1971 (killed in air accident)
26. Komelkov, Mikhail Sergeevich	33	7	321	75	HSU: 32+7/421/75 by end of war	1922	298th IAP/104th GIAP	Apr 25, 2003
27. Novichkov, Stepan Matveevich	33	1	277	51	HSU: 24/173 by Jan 1944	1921	436th IAP/67th GIAP	Jul 20, 1992
28. Borovykh, Andrey Egorovich	32	14	475	113	HSU: 12+14/441 by Jun 1943; 2nd HSU: 31+14/473 by Dec 1944	1921	728th IAP/157th IAP	Nov 17, 1989 (killed in accident)

(continued)

Appendix 8. Continued

Number	Name	Personal Victories	Shared Victories	Sorties	Engagements	Hero of the Soviet Union (HSU) Awarded for Victories/Sorties/Engagements by Date	Year of Birth	Unit	Date of Death
29.	Zelenov, Nikolay Andrianovich	32	10	606	117	HSU: 9+8/482/47 by Jul 1942	1917	127th IAP 154th IAP/ 29th GIAP 14th GIAP	Jun 29, 1944 (killed in air accident)
30.	Kirilyuk, Viktor Vasilyevich	32	8	510	129	HSU: 22+9/448/95 by 1945	1921	164th IAP 31st IAP	Sep 27, 1988
31.	Stepanenko, Ivan Nikiforovich	32	8	414	118	HSU: 14/232 2nd HSU: 32/395 by Feb 1945	1920	4th IAP	2005
32.	Klubov, Aleksandr Fedorovich	31	16	457	95	HSU: 14+19/410/84 by Sep 1943 2nd HSU: 31+19/457/95	1918	10th IAP 84th-A IAP 16th GIAP	Nov 1, 1944 (killed in air accident)
33.	Ryazanov, Aleksey Konstantinovich	31	16	509	97	HSU: 16+16/400/67 by May 1943 2nd HSU: 31+16/509/97 by Feb 1945736th IAP	1920	28th IAP 4th IAP	Aug 1, 1992
34.	Novikov, Konstantin Afanasyevich	31	10	~500		HSU: 10+6/200 by Feb 1943	1919	805th IAP 862nd IAP 131st IAP/ 40th GIAP	Jan 9, 1958

					HSU	Birth	Units	Death
35. Laveykin, Ivan Pavlovich	31	~600			HSU: 24/498/106 by Jul 1943	1921	129th IAP/5th GIAP Inspection of VVS	Dec 2, 1986
36. Arkhipenko, Fedor Fedorovich	30	14	467	102	HSU: 30+14/467/102 by May 1945	1921	17th IAP 508th IAP 129th GIAP	—
37. Likhobabin, Ivan Dmitrievich	30 or 32	9 or 5	224	57	HSU: 17+9/276/45 by Apr 1944	1916	402nd IAP 485th IAP/72nd GIAP	Apr 26, 1994
38. Mudrov, Mikhail Ivanovich	30	7	420		HSU: —	1919	3rd GIAP	Jan 27, 1944 (missing in action)
39. Kulagin, Andrey Mikhaylovich	30	5	762	153	HSU: 22+4/420/106 by Feb 1944	1921	249th IAP/163rd GIAP	Aug 9, 1980
40. Tarasov, Pavel Timofeevich	30	3			HSU: 22+3/235/81 by Dec 1943	1914	15th IAP 812th IAP 274th IAP 265th IAD	Jul 29, 1944 (killed in air accident)
41. Glinkin, Sergey Grigoryevich	30	1	254	75	HSU: 19/148/45 by Nov 1943	1921	5th GIAP	Nov 25, 2003
42. Dyachkov, Aleksandr Alekseevich	30	1	251	54	HSU: 27+1/217/54 by Mar 1945	1923	297th IAP/179th GIAP 177th GIAP 179th GIAP	Mar 31, 1945 (killed in air accident)

(continued)

Appendix 8. Continued

Number	Name	Personal Victories	Shared Victories	Sorties	Engagements	Hero of the Soviet Union (HSU) Awarded for Victories/Sorties/ Engagements by Date	Year of Birth	Unit	Date of Death
43.	Golovachev, Pavel Yakovlevich	30	0	385+	125+	HSU: 17/225/92 by Nov 1943 2nd HSU: 26/485 by Mar 1945	1917	168th IAP 69th IAP/ 9th GIAP 900th IAP	Jul 2, 1972
44.	Dolgarev, Pavel Mikhaylovich	29	7	223	56	HSU: 21 + 7/1502/1942 by Feb 1945	1923	116th IAP	Jun 28, 1994
45.	Merkulov, Vladimir Ivanovich	29	4	321		HSU: 19 + 4/195/82 by Apr 1944	1922	43rd IAP 15th IAP	Nov 26, 2003
46.	Romanenko, Ivan Ivanovich	29	3	188	61	HSU: 16 + 1/85/23 by Jul 1943	1918	774th IAP	Jun 8, 1978
47.	Leonovich, Ivan Semenovich	29	1	340	50	HSU: 26/340/50 by Nov 1944	1920	29th GIAP	Jan 13, 1946 (killed in car accident)
48.	Markov, Vasiliy Vasilyevich	29	0	369	88	HSU: 20/225/67 by Oct 1943	1919	116 thIAP 148th IAP	–
49.	Sachkov, Mikhail Ivanovich	29	0	309		HSU: 19/152/39 by Apr 1944	1918	728th IAP	Feb 12, 1973
50.	Artamonov, Nikolay Semenovich	28	9	254	55	HSU: 18 + 8/165/42 by Mar 1944	1920	297th IAP 193rd IAP/ 177th GIAP	Mar 26, 1945 (killed by antiaircraft artillery)

Source: This table was compiled with assistance from Michael Bykov, based on M. Bykov, *Sovetskye asy 1941–1945. Pobedy Stalinskih sokolov* (Moscow: Yauza, Eksmo, 2008).

Note: Victories were determined from records of the Central Archive of the Ministry of Defense of Russian Federation (Tsentralnyy Arkhiv Ministerstva Oborony, or TsAMO), using documents from regiments and divisions such as operational summaries and combat reports, journals of combat activities, and records of downed enemy aircraft. Postwar memoirs and wartime propaganda material from newspapers and other media were not considered. Therefore, it is important to note that some of the iconic scores that were widely publicized (such as Pokryshkin's fifty-nine victories or Kozhedub's sixty-two) are not supported by archival documents. In some cases, victories cited in award nominations are not substantiated by the above-mentioned documents.

NOTES

Introduction

1. David M. Glantz, "The Soviet-German War 1941–1945: Myths and Realities: A Survey Essay" (paper presented at the Twentieth Anniversary Distinguished Lecture, Strom Thurmond Institute of Government and Public Affairs, Clemson University, Clemson, SC, October 11, 2001), 4–5.

2. Von Hardesty, *Red Phoenix: The Rise of Soviet Air Power, 1941–1945* (Washington, DC: Smithsonian Institution Press, 1982 and 1990).

Chapter One. An Arduous Beginning

1. I. V. Timokhovich, *Operativnoye iskusstvo Sovetskikh VVS v Velikoy Otechestvennoy voyne* (Moscow: Voyenizdat, 1976), 21–22.

2. Tsentralnyy Arkhiv Ministerstva Oborony Rossiyskoy Federatsii (TsAMO RF), fond 208, opis 2683, delo 47, list 44; M. N. Kozhevnikov, *Komandovaniye i shtab VVS Sovetskoy Armii v Velikoy Otechestvennoy Voyne, 1941–1945 gg.* (Moscow: Nauka, 1977), 37.

3. Robert Jackson, *The Red Falcons: The Soviet Air Force in Action, 1916–1969* (London: Clifton Books, 1970), 92.

4. Olaf Groehler, *Geschichte des Luftkriegs 1910 bis 1980* (Berlin: Militarverlag d. DDR (VEB), 1981), 294; Manfred Griehl, *German Bombers over Russia (Luftwaffe at War)* (London: Greenhill Books, 2000), 5.

5. John Toland, *Adolf Hitler* (New York: Ballantine Books, 1976), 924.

6. Timokhovich, *Operativnoye iskusstvo*, 26.

7. M. Timin, "Otvetnyy udar: Deystviya Sovetskoy bombardirovochnoy aviatsii 22 iyunya 1941 goda," *Aviapark* 2 (2010): 38.

8. Ibid., 31.

9. Herman Plocher, *The German Air Force versus Russia, 1941*, USAF Historical Study no. 153 (New York: Arno Press, 1965), 41–42.

10. Aleksey Isayev, *Neizvestnyy 1941: Ostanovlenniy blitskrig* (Moscow: Yauza, Eksmo, 2010), 123.

11. V. P. Nelasov, A. A. Kudryatsev, A. S. Yakushevskiy, et al., *1941 god-Uroki i vyvody* (Moscow: Voyenizdat, 1992), 148.

12. As quoted in Bundesarchiv, Freiburg GQM, 6. Abt., RI 2/1185.

13. G. F. Krivosheyev, ed., *Grif sekretnosti snyat: Poteri Vooruzhennykh Sil SSSR v voynakh, boyevykh deystviyakh i voyennykh konfliktakh: Statisticheskoye issledovaniye* (Moscow: Voyenizdat, 1993), 368.

14. Williamson Murray, *The Luftwaffe, 1933–1945: Strategy for Defeat* (London: Brassey's, 1996), 82.

15. Barry A. Leach, *German Strategy against Russia, 1939–1941* (Oxford: Clarendon Press, 1973), 193, 202.

16. Calculation based on TsAMO RF, f. 35, op. 107559, d. 6, ll. 4–6, 40–82, quoted in Dmitriy Khazanov, *1941 — Gorkiye uroki: Voyna v vozdukhe* (Moscow: Yauza, Eksmo, 2006), 157. For German losses, see BA/MA RL21II/1177 "Flugzeugunfaelle und Verluste bei den (fliegende) Verbaenden," quoted in ibid., 57.

17. Toland, *Adolf Hitler,* 888–889.

18. John Erickson, *The Road to Stalingrad* (New York: Harper and Row, 1975), 8.

19. Leach, *German Strategy,* 193.

20. Erickson, *Road to Stalingrad,* 65.

21. John Erickson, "The Soviet Responses to Surprise Attack: Three Directives, 22 June, 1941," *Soviet Studies* 23, 4 (April 1972): 537.

22. Ibid., 533–534.

23. Ibid.

24. Ibid., 540; Kozhevnikov, *Komandovaniye i shtab VVS,* 39.

25. Erickson, "Soviet Responses," 548.

26. Miroslav Morozov, "Porazheniye letom 1941 goda bylo zakonomernym," in *1941 Velikaya Otechestvennaya Katastrofa. Itogi diskussii* (Moscow: Eksmo, Yauza, 2009), 291–292.

27. Ibid., 294.

28. Ibid.

29. Ibid.

30. Kozhevnikov, *Komandovaniye i shtab VVS,* 34.

31. Morozov, "Porazheniye letom 1941," 303–305.

32. Ibid., 307.

33. Kozhevnikov, *Komandovaniye i shtab VVS,* 36.

34. *Sbornik boevykh dokumentov Velikoy Otechestvennoy Voyny, Vypusk 35* (Moscow: Voyennoye izdatelstvo Ministerstva Oborony, 1955), 127–131; Aleksandr Medved, "Sovetskaya razvedyvatelnaya aviatsiya v nachalnyy period voyny," *Aviatsiya* 8 (2000): 20.

35. *Sbornik boevykh dokumentov Velikoy Otechestvennoy Voiny, Vypusk 34* (Moscow: Voyennoye izdatelstvo Ministerstva Oborony, 1953), 179–186.

36. *Sbornik boevykh dokumentov Velikoy Otechestvennoy Voyny, Vypusk 36* (Moscow: Voyennoye izdatelstvo Ministerstva Oborony, 1958), 109–126.

37. *Sbornik boevykh dokumentov, Vypusk 35,* 127–131.

38. Ibid.

39. Ibid.

40. *Sbornik boevykh dokumentov, Vypusk 34,* 179–186.

41. V. G. Nikiforov, ed., *Sovetskaya aviatsiya v Velikoy Otechestvennoy voyne 1941–1945 gg v tsifrakh* (Moscow: Glavnyy Shtab VVS, GU VVS SSSR, 1962), 7, 69, 81.

42. Rossiiskiy Gosydarstvennyy Voyennyy Arkhiv, f. 9, op. 39, d. 98, l. 163, quoted in M. I. Meltyukhov, *Tragediya 1941. Prichiny katastrofy* (Moscow: Yauza, Eksmo, 2008), 7.

43. Rossiyskiy Gosudarstvennyy Voennyy Archiv, f. 9, op. 39, d. 98, ll. 263–264, quoted in Meltyukov, *Tragediya 1941,* 8.

44. Timin, "Otvetnyy udar," 25–26.

45. Igor Kislov in *Bug v ogne* (Minsk, Belarus, 1965), 108–110, available at

http://militera.lib.ru/memo/russian/sb_bug_v_ogne/index.html (accessed September 11, 2010).

46. Ibid.

47. *Kratkaya istoriya 123 IAP/27 gvardeyskogo istrebitelnogo aviatsionnogo Vyborgskogo polka, Leningradskogo gvardeyskogo istrebitelnogo aviatsionnogo korpusa,* TsAMO, fond 27 gv. IAP, opis 483464s, delo 1.

48. Web page on Ivan Ivanovich Ivanov, http://aeroram.narod.ru/win/taran.htm (accessed September 11, 2010).

49. Ibid.

50. Sergey Kuznetsov, *Yak-1: Nash luchshiy istrebitel 1941 goda* (Moscow: Yauza, Eksmo, 2010), 105.

51. ShVAK is the abbreviation for *Shpitalnogo, Vladimirova aviatsionnaya krupnokalibernaya,* a large-caliber aviation cannon designed by Shpitalnyy and Vladimirov; ShKAS is the abbreviation for *Shpitalnogo, Komarnitskogo aviatsionnyy skorostrelnyy,* a rapid-firing aviation machine gun designed by Shpitalnyy and Komarnitskiy.

52. *Kratkaya istoriya 123 IAP.*

53. *Sbornik boevykh dokumentov, Vypusk 34,* 179–186.

54. Ibid., 8.

55. Ibid., 12.

56. Ibid., 11.

57. Nikiforov, *Sovetskaya aviatsiya v tsifrakh,* 45.

58. Ibid.

59. *Sbornik boevykh dokumentov, Vypusk 34,* 179–186.

60. Murray, *Luftwaffe 1933–1945,* 81–85.

61. *Sbornik boevykh dokumentov, Vypusk 35,* 127–131.

62. Ibid. According to Nelasov et al., *1941 god-Uroki i vyvody,* 149, the losses mounted to 738 aircraft.

63. A. Medved, D. Khazanov, and M. Maslov, *Istrebitel MiG-3* (Moscow: Rusavia, 2003), 132–134.

64. A. A. Novikov, *V nebe Leningrada: Zapiski komanduyuschego aviatsiey* (Moscow: Nauka, 1970), 50–51.

65. V. A. Zolotarev, ed., *Russkiy Arkhiv. Velikaya Otechestvennaya, tom 5(1). Stavka VGK. Dokumenty i materialy 1941 god* (Moscow: Terra, 1996), 21.

66. Novikov, *V nebe Leningrada,* 51; Khazanov, *1941—Gorkiye uroki,* 182.

67. Khazanov, *1941—Gorkiye uroki,* 184–186.

68. Ibid.

69. Nikiforov, *Sovetskaya aviatsiya v tsifrakh,* 9.

70. Nelasov et al., *1941 god-Uroki i vyvody,* 149.

71. Aleksey Isayev, *Ot Dubno do Rostova* (Moscow: AST, Transitkniga, 2004), 128.

72. *Sbornik boevykh dokumentov, Vypusk 36,* 109–126.

73. Isayev, *Ot Dubno do Rostova,* 125–126.

74. Ibid., 126–127.

75. *Sbornik boevykh documentov, Vypusk 36,* 109–126.

76. R. Grams, *Die 14 Panzer-Division 1940–1945. Herausgegeben im Auftrag der Traditionsgemeinschaft der 14. Panzer-Division* (Bad Nauheim: Verlag Hans-Henning Podzun, 1957), 23–24, as quoted in Isayev, *Ot Dubno do Rostova,* 130.

77. Nelasov et al., *1941 god-Uroki i vyvody*, 149.

78. Nikiforov, *Sovetskaya aviatsiya v tsifrakh*, 7.

79. Nelasov et al., *1941 god-Uroki i vyvody*, 36.

80. V. A. Zolotarev, ed., *Russkiy Arkhiv: Velikaya Otechestvennaya, tom 12 (1-2), Nakanune voyny. Materialy soveschaniya vysshego rukovodyashchego sostava RKKA 23-31 dekabrya 1940g.* (Moscow: Terra, 1993), 173–208.

81. Isayev, *Ot Dubno do Rostova*, 100–103.

82. *Spravochnik po boevomu i chislennomu sostavu chastey i soyedineniy Voyenno-Vozdushnykh Sil Sovetskoy Armii (1941–1945 gg.)*, TsAMO, inv. no. 962, as quoted in V. Romanenko, "Porivnyalniy analiz boyovogo skladu Radyanskoi ta Nimeckoi aviatsii u 1941 roci," *Voyenna istoriya* 5 (2009): 85–89.

83. Nelasov et al., *1941god-Uroki i vyvody*, 35.

84. Ibid., 36.

85. Nikifiorov, *Sovetskaya aviatsiya v tsifrakh*, 9.

86. Nelasov et al., *1941 god-Uroki i vyvody*, 36.

87. Ibid.

88. Ibid., 149.

89. By October 1941, a total of 118 aircraft factories (part of a network of 139 plants responsible for 75 percent of aircraft output) were on the move. Due to the loss of aluminum production, the output of color metals was reduced in December 1941 by 430 percent compared with June. In November 1941, Soviet aircraft production dropped to 448 aircraft. See Romanenko, "Porivnyalniy analiz," 85–89.

Chapter Two. The Air Battle for Moscow

1. Andrew Brookes, *Air War over Russia* (Hersham, UK: Ian Allen, 2003), 70.

2. Ibid.

3. Richard Muller, *The German Air War in Russia* (Baltimore: Nautical and Aviation Publishing Company of America, 1992), 54.

4. Rodric Braithwaite, *Moscow 1941: A City and Its People at War* (New York: Vintage Books, 2006), 176–177; Dmtriy Khazanov, *Neizvestnaya bitva v nebe Moskvy 1941–1942gg. Oboronitelnyy period* (Moscow: Tehnika–Molodezhi, 1999), 10–12, 18.

5. Andrew Nagorski, *The Greatest Battle: Stalin, Hitler, and the Desperate Struggle for Moscow that Changed the Course of World War II* (New York: Simon and Schuster, 2007), 220. According to Glantz, Red Army casualties (killed, missing, or captured) totaled 2,993,803. See David M. Glantz, "The Soviet-German War 1941–1945: Myths and Realities: A Survey Essay" (paper presented at the Twentieth Anniversary Distinguished Lecture, Strom Thurmond Institute of Government and Public Affairs, Clemson University, Clemson, SC, October 11, 2001).

6. Khazanov, *Neizvestnaya bitva. Oboronitelnyy period*, 5, 7.

7. Braithwaite, *Moscow 1941*, 169; Khazanov, *Neizvestnaya bitva. Oboronitelnyy period*, 5, 7.

8. Braithwaite, *Moscow 1941*, 169.

9. Ibid., 167.

10. Khazanov, *Neizvestnaya bitva. Oboronitelnyy period*, 7.

11. Braithwaite, *Moscow 1941*, 169.

12. Nagorski, *Greatest Battle*, 186.

13. Khazanov, *Neizvestnaya bitva. Oboronitelnyy period*, 7.

14. Ibid., 9.

15. Ibid., 12.

16. Margaret Bourke-White, *Shooting the Russian War* (New York: Simon and Schuster, 1943), 197–199.

17. Khazanov, *Neizvestnaya bitva. Oboronitelnyy period*, 20.

18. Ibid.

19. Quoted in Nagorski, *Greatest Battle*, 189.

20. Ibid.

21. Braithwaite, *Moscow 1941*, 175.

22. Nagorski, *Greatest Battle*, 186.

23. David M. Glantz and Jonathan M. House, *When Titans Clashed: How the Red Army Stopped Hitler* (Lawrence: University Press of Kansas, 1995), 71–72.

24. Aleksey Isayev, *Kotly 41-go. Istoriya VOV, kotoruyu my ne znali* (Moscow: Yauza, Eksmo, 2005), 213.

25. V. G. Nikiforov, ed., *Sovetskaya aviatsiya v Velikoy Otechestvennoy voyne 1941–1945 gg v tsifrakh* (Moscow: Glavnyy Shtab VVS, GU VVS SSSR, 1962), 47.

26. Ibid., 69, 72.

27. Isayev, *Kotly 41-go*, 210.

28. Nikiforov, *Sovetskaya aviatsiya v tsifrakh*, 47, 69, 72.

29. Khazanov, *Neizvestnaya bitva. Oboronitelnyy period*, 32.

30. Williamson Murray, *The Luftwaffe, 1933–1945: Strategy for Defeat* (London: Brassey's, 1996), 84.

31. Khazanov, *Neizvestnaya bitva. Oboronitelnyy period*, 35.

32. A. G. Fedorov, *Aviatsiya v bitve pod Moskvoy* (Moscow: Nauka, 1975), 98–99.

33. Alexander Boyd, *The Soviet Air Force since 1918* (London: Macdonald and Jane's 1977), 130; A. G. Pervov, "Manevr aviatsionnymi rezervami stavki VGK," *Voyenno-istoricheskiy zhurnal* 2 (1977): 94–100.

34. Khazanov, *Neizvestnaya bitva. Oboronitelnyy period*, 31.

35. Braithwaite, *Moscow 1941*, 181–182.

36. Fedorov, *Aviatsiya v bitve pod Moskvoy*, 100.

37. Walter Schwabedissen, *The Russian Air Force in the Eyes of German Commanders,* USAF Historical Study no. 175 (New York: Arno Press, 1960), 138–139.

38. Vladimir Ratkin, "Muzhskaya rabota," *Mir Aviatsii* 1 (2000): 22–35.

39. Ibid.

40. Isayev, *Kotly 41-go*, 224.

41. Ibid., 226.

42. Khazanov, *Neizvestnaya bitva. Oboronitelnyy period*, 38.

43. Ibid.

44. Isayev, *Kotly 41-go*, 236.

45. Fedorov, *Aviatsiya v bitve pod Moskvoy*, 104.

46. Ibid., 103.

47. Herman Plocher, *The German Air Force versus Russia, 1941*, USAF Historical Study no. 153 (New York: Arno Press, 1965), 228.

48. M. N. Kozhevnikov, *Komandovaniye i shtab VVS Sovetskoy Armii v Velikoy Otechestvennoy Voyne, 1941–1945 gg.* (Moscow: Nauka, 1977), 60.

49. Ibid., 62; N. Dmitrevskiy, *Zashchitniki neba stolitsy* (Moscow: Voyenizdat, 1962), 13–14.

50. Oleg Rastrenin, "Glavnay udarnaya sila," in *Ya Dralsya na Il-2,* ed. A Drabkin (Moscow: Yauza, Eksmo, 2005), 301–304.

51. Seweryn Bialer, ed., *Stalin and His Generals: Soviet Military Memoirs of World War II* (New York: Pegasus, 1969), 265; Glantz and House, *When Titans Clashed,* 62–67.

52. Alexander Werth, *Russia at War, 1941–1945* (New York: Avon Books, 1964), 238.

53. Nagorski, *Greatest Battle,* 167–193. These battalions were used mostly to construct defensive lines; they underwent basic training, after which they were reorganized into regular army units; see Isayev, *Kotly 41-go,* 270–271.

54. Plocher, *The German Air Force versus Russia,* 233.

55. Ibid., 104–107. For Soviet cold-weather operations, see *Samolet* 1 (1941): 29–30; *Sovetskaya Arktika* 12 (1940): 67–69.

56. Fedorov, *Aviatsiya v bitve pod Moskvoy,* 163–164.

57. Khazanov, *Neizvestnaya bitva. Oboronitelnyy period,* 73.

58. General Halder estimated that total losses as of February 28, 1942, stood at 1,005,000 killed, wounded, and missing. See F. Halder, *Kriegstagebuch. Tägliche Aufzeichnungen des Chefs des Generalstabes des Heeres 1939–1942* (Stuttgart: W. Kohlhammer Verlag, 1962–1964), entry for March 5, 1942. Some 1.5 million troops of various nationalities in the alliance with Nazi Germany had been killed, wounded, or taken prisoner on the Eastern Front, and there were 327,000 Germans dead. See Richard J. Evans, *The Third Reich at War* (New York: Penguin Press, 2009), 407.

59. Albert Seaton, *The Russo-German War 1941–1945* (New York: Praeger Publishers, 1970), 187–188.

60. Asher Lee, *The German Air Force* (New York: Harper and Brothers, 1970), 187–188.

61. Ibid., 115.

62. Ibid., 114.

63. Fedorov, *Aviatsiya v bitve pod Moskvoy,* 137.

64. Dmitriy Khazanov, *Neizvestnaya bitva v nebe Moskvy 1941–1942 gg. Kontrnastupleniye* (Moscow: Tehnika–Molodezhi, 2001), 5.

65. Isayev, *Kotly 41-go,* 239–241, 280.

66. Nikiforov, *Sovetskaya aviatsiya v tsifrakh,* 7.

67. Khazanov, *Neizvestnaya bitva. Kontrnastupleniye,* 11.

68. Harrison E. Salisbury, *The Unknown War* (New York: Bantam Books, 1978), 91.

69. Fedorov, *Aviatsiya v bitve pod Moskvoy,* 196.

70. Nikiforov, *Sovetskaya aviatsiya v tsifrakh,* 48, 69, 72.

71. Werth, *Russia at War,* 257–259.

72. Plocher, *The German Air Force versus Russia,* 239, 243.

73. Fedorov, *Aviatsiya v bitve pod Moskvoy,* 204.

74. Nikiforov, *Sovetskaya aviatsiya v tsifrakh,* 48.

75. Fedorov, *Avitsiya v bitve pod Moskvoy,* 212–213.

76. V. A. Zolotarev, ed., *Russkiy Arkhiv: Velikaya Otechestvennaya, tom 15 (4-1), Bitva pod Moskvoy. Sbornik dokumentov* (Moscow: Terra, 1997), 255–267.

77. Ibid., 270–271.

78. Fedorov, *Aviatsiya v bitve pod Moskvoy*, 202; N. A. Svetlishin, *Voyska PVO strany v Velikoy Otechestvennoy voyne* (Moscow: Nauka, 1979), 56–57.

79. Fedorov, *Aviatsiya v bitve pod Moskvoy*, 216.

80. Svetlishin, *Voyska PVO strany*, 61–62.

81. "Protivovozdushnaya oborona Moskvy," in *Sovetskaya Voennaya Entsiklopediya*, vol. 6, ed. N. V. Ogarkov (Moscow: Voyennoye izdatelstvo Ministerstva Oborony SSSR, 1978), 584.

82. *Osoaviakhim* is short for *Obshchestvo sodeystviya oborone i aviatsionno-khimicheskomu stroitelstvu SSSR*, an institution that existed from 1927 to 1948 and provided training in a number of military skills to Soviet youth. A loose translation would be "Society for Promoting Coordination in Defense and Aviation-Chemical Organization of the USSR."

83. Fedorov, *Aviatsiya v bitve pod Moskvoy*, 198.

84. Ibid., 228.

85. Oleg Rastrenin, *Il-2 Shturmovik Guards Units of World War 2* (Oxford: Osprey Publishing, 2008), 26–28.

86. Zolotarev, *Russkiy Arkhiv: Bitva pod Moskvoy*, 287–292.

87. Khazanov, *Neizvestnaya bitva. Kontrnastupleniye*, 130.

88. Nikiforov, *Sovetskaya aviatsiya v tsifrakh*, 13.

89. Fedorov, *Aviatsiya v bitve pod Moskvoy*, 233–234.

90. Nikiforov, *Sovetskaya aviatsiya v tsifrakh*, 104.

91. Fedorov, *Aviatsiya v bitve pod Moskvoy*, 243.

92. Schwabedissen, *Russian Air Force*, 215, 288.

93. Fedorov, *Aviatsiya v bitve pod Moskvoy*, 243–244.

94. Herman Plocher, *The German Air Force versus Russia, 1942,* USAF Historical Study no. 154 (New York: Arno Press, 1965), 16.

95. Alexander Medved, "Sovetskaya razvedyvatelnaya aviatsiya v nachalnyy period voyny," *Aviatsiya* 8 (2000): 20–35.

96. Khazanov, *Neizvestnaya bitva. Kontrnastupleniye*, 113–115.

97. Plocher, *German Air Force versus Russia, 1942,* 69.

98. Ibid., 75–79.

99. Ibid., 150.

100. Fritz Morzik, *German Air Force Airlift Operations,* USAF Historical Study no. 167 (Maxwell Air Force Base, AL: Air University, 1961), 172.

101. Ibid., 158.

102. F. A. Kostenko, *Korpus krylatoy gvardii* (Moscow: Voyenizdat, 1974), 77–78.

103. I. V. Timokhovich, *Operativnoye iskusstvo Sovetskikh VVS v Velikoy Otechestvennoy Voyne* (Moscow: Voyenizdat, 1976), 174–175.

104. Fedorov, *Aviatsiya v bitve pod Moskvoy*, 275–276.

105. Khazanov, *Neizvestnaya bitva. Kontrnastupleniye*, 130.

Chapter Three. Stalingrad

1. David M. Glantz and Jonathan M House, *When Titans Clashed: How the Red Army Stopped Hitler* (Lawrence: University Press of Kansas, 1995), 129–147.

2. A. G. Pervov, "Sovershenstvovaniye rukovodstva Voyenno-vozdush-nymi silami Krasnoy Armii v predvoyennyy period i v gody Velikoy Otech-estvennoy voyny," *Voyenno-istoricheskiy zhurnal* 1 (2006): 10.

3. G. S. Byushgens, ed., *Samoletostroenie v SSSR 1917–1945 gg.*, vol. 2 (Moscow: TsAGI, 1994), 218–222.

4. R. J. Overy, *The Air War 1939–1945* (London: Europa Publications, 1980), 53–55.

5. Pervov, "Sovershenstvovaniye rukovodstva," 10–13.

6. Ibid., 11.

7. Ibid., 12.

8. Lecture delivered by Adolf Galland on February 5, 1981, at the National Air and Space Museum, Smithsonian Institution.

9. M. N. Kozhevnikov, *Komandovaniye i shtab VVS Sovetskoy Armii v Velikoy Otechestvennoy Voyne, 1941–1945 gg.* (Moscow: Nauka, 1977), 80–82.

10. Prikaz Narodnogo Komissara Oborony Soyuza SSR nomer 056 ot 22 yan-varya 1942 goda, Moskva, http://www.airforce.ru/history/ww2/ww2doc/22011942.htm (accessed September 15, 2010).

11. Kozhevnikov, *Komandovaniye i shtab VVS*, 81. Vasilyev became the section chief in 1943.

12. Richard C. Lukas, *Eagles East: The Army Air Forces and the Soviet Union, 1941–1945* (Tallahassee: Florida State University Press, 1970), 24–25.

13. Vladimir Ratkin, "Li-2 na voyne," *Mir Aviatsii* 4 (1999): 33–39.

14. A. Ye. Golovanov, *Dalnyaya Bombardirovochnaya* (Moscow: Delta NB, 2004), 154.

15. Pervov, "Sovershenstvovaniye rukovodstva," 12.

16. Ibid.

17. N. N. Ostroumov, "Organizatsiya aviatsionnykh rezervov v gody voyny," *Voyenno-istoricheskiy zhurnal* 5 (2005): 36–38.

18. Ibid.

19. S. I. Rudenko, "Birth of the Air Armies," *Aerospace Historian* 22, 2 (June 1975): 73–76.

20. V. G. Nikiforov, ed., *Sovetskaya aviatsiya v Velikoy Otechestvennoy voyne 1941–1945 gg v tsifrakh* (Moscow: Glavnyy Shtab VVS, GU VVS SSSR, 1962), 90–91.

21. The 4th Air Army of the Southern *Front* had 244 serviceable aircraft, the 5th Air Army of the North Caucasian *Front* had 312, and the 8th Air Army of the Southwestern *Front* had 378. The PVO and ADD are not included here. These numbers do not prove the four-to-one ratio. This would be true if we counted only the 8th Air Army. It is due to the concentration of air assets at the breakthrough corridors that the *Luftwaffe* could mount decisive superiority. VVS numbers are from Nikiforov, *Sovetskaya aviatsiya v tsifrakh*, 52–53.

22. Ibid., 73.

23. B. A. Gubin and V. D. Sokolov, *Vosmaya vozdushnaya. Voyenno-istoricheskiy ocherk boyevogo puti 8-oy vozdushnoy armii v gody Velikoy Otechestvennoy Voyny* (Moscow: Voyenizdat, 1980), 23–24.

24. Kozhevnikov, *Komandovaniye i shtab VVS*, 96.

25. Seweryn Bialer, ed., *Stalin and His Generals: Soviet Military Memoirs of World War II* (New York: Pegasus, 1969), 354.

26. Ibid.

27. G. K. Prussakov, A. A. Vasilyev, I. I. Ivanov, F. S. Luchkin, and G. O. Komarov, *16-ya vozdushnaya. Voyenno-istoricheskiy ocherk o boyevom puti 16-oy vosdushnoy armii 1942–1945* (Moscow: Voyenizdat, 1973), 28.

28. Kozhevnikov, *Komandovaniye i shtab VVS*, 109.

29. Aleksandr Yakovlev, *Tsel zhizni* (Moscow: Politizdat, 1973), 332.

30. Prusssakov et al., *l6-ya vozdushnaya*, 11.

31. Ibid., 13–15.

32. Ibid., 31–32.

33. Ibid., 32–33.

34. Ibid., 29.

35. Oleg Rastrenin, *Il-2 Shturmovik Guards Units of World War 2* (Oxford: Osprey Publishing, 2008), 42–43.

36. Alexey Isayev, *Stalingrad. Za Volgoy dlya nas zemli net* (Moscow: Yauza, Eksmo, 2008), 108–109.

37. Gubin and Sokolov, *Vosmaya vozdushnaya*, 50.

38. Rastrenin, *Il-2 Shturmovik Guards Units*, 45.

39. Prussakov et al., *16-ya vozdushnay*, 22.

40. Instrukciya po navedeniyu istrebitelnoy aviatsii na samolety protivnika, http://www.airforce.ru/history/ww2/ww2doc/15091942.htm (accessed September 15, 2010).

41. Nikiforov, *Sovetskaya aviatsiya v tsifrakh*, 54–57.

42. I. V. Timokhovich, *Operativnoye iskusstvo Sovetskikh VVS v Velikoy Otechestvennoy voyne* (Moscow: Voyenizdat, 1976), 35.

43. Chief of Staff of the 8th Air Army, Colonel Seleznev, no. 00295, dated August 18, 1942, http://www.airforce.ru/history/ww2/ww2doc/18081942 .htm (accessed September 15, 2010).

44. Heinrich von Einsiedel, *The Shadow of Stalingrad: Being a Diary of Temptation* (London: Wingate, 1953), 7–8.

45. Ibid., 408.

46. Einsiedel was later recruited to participate in the "Free Germany" committee as a tool of Soviet propaganda.

47. Richard J. Evans, *The Third Reich at War* (New York: Penguin Press, 2009), 409.

48. Nikiforov, *Sovetskaya aviatsiya v tsifrakh*, 54–57, 91.

49. Ibid.

50. S. I. Rudenko, *Krylya Pobedy* (Moscow: Mezdunarodnyye otnosheniya, 1985), 123–124.

51. Nikiforov, *Sovetskaya aviatsiya v tsifrakh*, 54–55; S. I. Rudenko, "Aviatsiya v kontrnastuplenii," *Voyenno-istoricheskiy zhurnal* 11 (1972): 48.

52. *Boyevoy ustav pehoty* (Voyenizdat NKO SSSR, 1942), http://militera.lib .ru/regulations/russr/1942_bup/index.html (accessed September 15, 2010).

53. Nikiforov, *Sovetskaya aviatsiya v tsifrakh*, 54–55; Prussakov et al., *16-ya vozdushnaya*, 44.

54. Prussakov et al., *16-ya vozdushnaya*, 48.

55. Nikiforov, *Sovetskaya aviatsiya v tsifrakh*, 108–110.

56. Prussakov et al., *16-ya vozdushnaya*, 44.

57. Wolfgang Pickert, "The Stalingrad Airlift: An Eyewitness Commentary,"

Aerospace Historian 18 (December 1971): 183–186; Williamson Murray, *The Luftwaffe, 1933–1945: Strategy for Defeat* (London: Brassey's, 1983), 152–156; Glantz, *When Titans Clashed*, 139–140.

58. Fritz Morzik, *German Air Force Air Lift Operations*, USAF Historical Study no. 167 (Maxwell Air Force Base, AL: Air University, 1961), 180.

59. Ibid.

60. Ibid., 184.

61. Ibid., 185.

62. Ibid., 186.

63. William Craig, *Enemy at the Gates: The Battle for Stalingrad* (New York: Reader's Digest Press, 1973), 220.

64. Ibid., 216.

65. Ibid., 216–217.

66. Ibid., 308.

67. Timokhovich, *Operativnoye iskusstvo*, 177.

68. Richard Suchenwirth, *Historical Turning Points in the German Air Force War Effort*, USAF Historical Study no. 189 (Maxwell Air Force Base, AL: Air University, 1959), 104.

69. Rastrenin, *Il-2 Shturmovik Guards Units*, 48.

70. Suchenwirth, *Historical Turning Points*, 104.

71. Gubin and Sokolov, *Vosmaya vozdushnaya*, 105–106.

72. Craig, *Enemy at the Gates*, 280–281.

73. N. M. Skomorokhov et al., *17-ya vozdushnaya armiya v boyakh ot Stalingrada do Veny* (Moscow: Voyenizdat, 1977), 15–16.

74. Morzik, *German Air Force Air Lift Operations*, 191.

75. Rudenko, "Aviatsiya v kontrnastuplenii," 52. Rudenko states that the ring was somewhat smaller, 5 to 6 miles (8 to 9.6 kilometers); see also Timokhovich, *Operativnoye iskusstvo*, 175–179, and Kozhevnikov, *Komandovaniye i shtab VVS*, 112–113.

76. Prussakov et al., *16-ya vozdushnaya*, 51.

77. Rudenko, "Aviatsiya v kontrnastuplenii," 49.

78. Ibid., 59.

79. Ibid., 45, 51; see also A. A. Novikov, *V nebe Leningrada. Zapiski komanduyushchego aviatsiey* (Moscow: Nauka, 1970), 206.

80. Walter Schwabedissen, *The Russian Air Force in the Eyes of German Commanders*, USAF Historical Study no. 175 (New York: Arno Press, 1960), 254–255.

81. Morzik, *German Air Force Air Lift Operations*, 191.

82. Gubin and Sokolov, *Vosmaya vozdushnaya*, 114–116.

83. Rastrenin, *Il-2 Shturmovik Guards Units*, 47.

84. Prussakov et al., *16-ya vozdushnaya*, 58–59.

85. Sergey Isayev, *Stranitsy istorii 32-go gvardeyskogo Vilenskogo ordenov Lenina i Kutuzova III stepeni istrebitelnogo aviatsionnogo polka* (Moscow: Arbor, 2006), 6–7.

86. Ibid., 9.

87. Rodric Braithwaite, *Moscow 1941: A City and Its People at War* (New York: Vintage Books, 2006), 66.

88. Isayev, *Stranitsy istorii 32-go gvardeyskogo polka*, 11.

89. Ibid., 13.

90. M. Bykov, *Sovetskiye asy 1941–1945. Pobedy Stalinskikh sokolov* (Moscow: Yauza, Eksmo, 2008), 231.

91. Isayev, *Stranitsy istorii 32-go gvardeyskogo polka*, 19–22.

92. Ibid., 22.

93. Ibid., 22–23.

94. Ibid., 25.

95. Ibid., 30.

96. Ibid., 43–44, 47–48.

97. Ibid., 48–49.

98. Rastrenin, *Il-2-Shturmovik Guards Units,* 42–50.

99. Ibid., 32.

100. Ibid., 33.

101. Ibid., 43.

102. Ibid., 45.

103. Ibid., 47–48.

104. Skomorokov et al., *17-ya Vozdushnaya armiya,* 31; Kozhevnikov, *Komandovaniye i shtab VVS,* 117–118.

105. V. A. Zolotarev, ed., *Russkiy Arkhiv. Velikaya Otechestvennaya, tom 5(2), Stavka VGK. Dokumenty i materialy 1942 god* (Moscow: Terra, 1996), 18, 25.

106. Nikiforov, *Sovetskaya aviatsiya v tsifrakh,* 13.

Chapter Four. Over the Kuban

1. Alexander Pokryshkin, *Nebo voyny* (Moscow: Voyenizdat, 1975), 244–253. For a more detailed account of the Kuban air action, see Alexander Pokryshkin, *Poznat sebya v boyu* (Moscow: DOSAAF, 1986), 226–352.

2. Herman Plocher, *The German Air Force versus Russia, 1943,* USAF Historical Study no. 155 (New York: Arno Press, 1965), 36–50.

3. Valeriy Romanenko, *Aerokobry nad Kubanyu* (Kiev: SPD Romanenko V. D., 2006), 33.

4. N. Denisov, *Boyevaya slava sovetskoy aviatsii* (Moscow: Voyenizdat, 1953), 145.

5. Romanenko, *Aerokobry nad Kubanyu,* 33.

6. A. A. Grechko, *Bitva za Kavkaz* (Moscow: Voyenizdat, 1967), 321–322; Romanenko, *Aerokobry nad Kubanyu,* 39; Oleg Rastrenin, *Raskolotoye nebo. May–Iyun 1943 g.* (Moscow: Eksmo, Yauza, 2007), 9–10.

7. G. Litvin, "55 let bitve nad Kubanyu," *Aviatsiya i Kosmonavtika* 4 (1998): 1–3; Grechko, *Bitva za Kavkaz,* 322–323.

8. Jill Amadio, *Guenther Rall, a Memoir: Luftwaffe Ace and NATO General* (Santa Ana, CA: Tangemere Productions, 2002), 132.

9. O. Kaminskiy, "Messershmitty nad Kubanyu," *Aviatsiya i Vremya* 5 (2005): 39–44.

10. Asher Lee, *The Soviet Air Force* (London: Duckworth, 1952), 126.

11. The 201st IAD of General A. P. Zhukov and the 3rd IAK of the *Stavka* Reserve (consisting of two divisions) commanded by General Ye. Ya. Savitskiy. On April 20, yet another air division arrived—the 287th IAD; see Litvin, "55 let bitve nad Kubanyu," 1–3, and Grechko, *Bitva za Kavkaz,* 330.

12. Grechko, *Bitva za Kavkaz*, 321.

13. *Sbornik boevykh dokumentov Velikoy Otechestvennoy Voyny, Vypusk 7* (Moscow: Voyennoye izdatelstvo Ministerstva Vooruzhennyh Sil, 1948), 51–54.

14. "4-ya Vozdushnaya armiya v boyah za Rodinu," *Aviatsiya i kosmonavtika* 5 (1965): 9.

15. Amadio, *Guenther Rall,* 132–134.

16. Dmitriy Loza, *Attack of the Airacobras: Soviet Aces, American P-39s & the Air War against Germany* (Lawrence: University Press of Kansas, 2002), 129–139.

17. Ibid., 129.

18. Ibid., 139–142.

19. Lee, *Soviet Air Force*, 127.

20. Grechko, *Bitva za Kavkaz*, 325–326.

21. Guenther Rall, interview with Von Hardesty, 1989.

22. Litvin, "55 let bitve nad Kubanyu," 1–3.

23. Plocher, *German Air Force versus Russia, 1943*, 36.

24. Ibid., 37; see also Loza, *Attack of the Airacobras*, 34–47.

25. Grechko, *Bitva za Kavkaz*, 23, 53.

26. P. A. Sudoplatov, *Raznyye dni taynoy voyny i diplomatii. 1941 god* (Moscow: Olma-Press, 2001), 342–352.

27. David Glantz with Jonathan House, *To the Gates of Stalingrad: Soviet-German Combat Operations, April–August, 1942* (Lawrence: University Press of Kansas, 2009), 264.

28. V. Antipov and I. Utkin, *Dragons on Bird Wings: The Combat History of the 812th Fighter Air Regiment,* vol.1, *Liberation of the Motherland* (Kitchener, ON: Aviaelogy, 2006), 60–61.

29. M. N. Kozhevnikov, *Komandovaniye i shtab VVS Sovetskoy Armii v Velikoy Otechestvennoy Voyne, 1941–1945 gg.* (Moscow: Nauka, 1977), 126.

30. Plocher, *German Air Force versus Russia, 1943,* 37–38.

31. Kozhevnikov, *Komandovaniye i shtab VVS,* 126–127.

32. Plocher, *German Air Force versus Russia, 1943,* 38.

33. Kozhevnikov, *Komandovaniye i shtab VVS,* 127.

34. K. A. Vershinin, *Chetvertaya vozdushnaya* (Moscow: Voyenizdat, 1975), 233.

35. Ibid., 234.

36. Ibid., 234–235.

37. Grechko, *Bitva za Kavkaz*, 233.

38. Ibid., 233–234.

39. *Sbornik boevykh dokumentov, Vypusk 7*, 51–54.

40. Vershinin, *Chetvertaya vozdushnaya*, 240.

41. Plocher, *German Air Force versus Russia, 1943,* 38.

42. Kozhevnikov, *Komandovaniye i shtab VVS*, 129; Grechko, *Bitva za Kavkaz*, 335.

43. A. L. Ivanov, *Skorost, manevr, ogon* (Moscow: DOSAAF, 1974), 192–196.

44. Igor Zlobin, "Spitfires over the Kuban," http://lend-lease.airforce.ru/ english/articles/spit/index.htm (accessed September18, 2010).

45. Plocher, *German Air Force versus Russia, 1943,* 38.

46. Grechko, *Bitva za Kavkaz,* 339.

47. Plocher, *German Air Force versus Russia, 1943,* 39; Grechko, *Bitva za Kavkaz,* 339.

48. Kozhevnikov, *Komandovaniye i shtab VVS,* 130.

49. Vershinin, *Chetvertaya vozdushnaya,* 252.

50. Ibid., 254.

51. Plocher, *German Air Force versus Russia, 1943,* 40.

52. Antipov and Utkin, *Dragons on Bird Wings,* 64.

53. Rastrenin, *Raskolotoye nebo,* 9.

54. Alexandr I. Ivanov, foreword to Antipov and Utkin, *Dragons on Bird Wings,* v.

55. Antipov and Utkin, *Dragons on Bird Wings,* 11.

56. Ibid., 13–14.

57. Ibid., 14–15.

58. Rall interview.

59. Antipov and Utkin, *Dragons on Bird Wings,* 18–19.

60. Ibid., 20–21.

61. Ibid.

62. Ibid., 23–24.

63. Rall interview.

64. M. Bykov, *Sovetskiye asy 1941–1945. Pobedy Stalinskikh sokolov* (Moscow: Yauza, Eksmo, 2008), 112–113, 425–426.

65. Ibid., 515.

66. Ibid., 288.

67. Ibid., 58.

68. Loza, *Attack of the Airacobras,* 48–71.

69. Romanenko, *Aerokobry nad Kubanyu,* 49.

70. Ibid.

71. Chief of Staff of the 8th Air Army, Colonel Seleznev, no. 00295, dated August 18, 1942, http://www.airforce.ru/history/ww2/ww2doc/18081942 .htm (accessed September 15, 2010).

72. Pokryshkin, *Nebo voyny,* 3–36.

73. Ibid., 246–247.

74. Romanenko, *Aerokobry nad Kubanyu,* 33–36.

75. Ibid., 33–34.

76. Walter Schwabedissen, *The Russian Air Force in the Eyes of German Commanders,* USAF Historical Study no. 175 (New York: Arno Press, 1960), 198.

77. G. G. Golubev, *V pare s "sotym"* (Moscow: Voyenizdat, 1978), 90–91.

78. Valery Romanenko, "Early Versions of Airacobra in Soviet Aviation," trans. James F. Gebhardt, in Valery Romanenko, *Aerokobry vstupayut v boy* (Kiev: Aerohobby, 1993). English translation available at http://lend-lease.air-force.ru/english/articles/romanenko/p-39/index.htm (accessed September 18, 2010).

79. Rall interview.

80. Loza, *Attack of the Airacobras,* 20–21; Romanenko, *Aerokobry nad Kubanyu,* 34.

81. V. G. Nikiforov, ed., *Sovetskaya aviatsiya v Velikoy Otechestvennoy voyne 1941–1945 gg v tsifrakh* (Moscow: Glavnyy Shtab VVS, GU VVS SSSR, 1962), 13.

82. Litvin, "55 let bitve nad Kubanyu," 2.

Chapter Five. Kursk

1. Andrew Brookes, *Air War over Russia* (Hersham, UK: Ian Allen, 2003), 124.

2. Herman Plocher, *The German Air Force versus Russia, 1943*, USAF Historical Study no. 155 (New York: Arno Press, 1965), 72–74.

3. V. G. Nikiforov, ed., *Sovetskaya aviatsiya v Velikoy Otechestvennoy voyne 1941–1945 gg v tsifrakh* (Moscow: Glavnyy Shtab VVS, GU VVS SSSR, 1962), 91–92, specifies a total of 2,700 German aircraft in the Eastern Front. For the total number of aircraft engaged in Operation Citadel, see Vitaliy Gorbach, *Nad Ognennoy Dugoy: Sovetskaya aviatsiya v Kurskoy bitve* (Moscow: Yauza, Eksmo, 2007), 474.

4. Gorbach, *Nad Ognennoy Dugoy,* 14.

5. Ibid., 15–16.

6. Plocher, *German Air Force versus Russia, 1943,* 80–81.

7. Gorbach, *Nad Ognennoy Dugoy,* 17.

8. Ibid., 17–18. Plans called for the involvement of 17th Air Army units in defensive operations. The 5th Air Army of the Steppe Military District (renamed the Steppe *Front* on July 9, 1943) was utilized as a reservoir, training air units and transferring them to the 2nd, 16th, and 17th Air Armies.

9. Ibid., 14, 21.

10. Vladimir Kotelnikov, *Il-4. "Vozdushnyye kreysera" Stalina* (Moscow: Yauza, Eksmo, 2009), 91.

11. Gorbach, *Nad Ognennoy Dugoy,* 18–19.

12. Earl F. Ziemke, *Stalingrad to Berlin: The German Defeat in the East*, Army Historical Series (Washington, DC: Office of the Chief of Military History, 1968), 134–135.

13. Brookes, *Air War over Russia,* 127, based on David M. Glantz and Harold S. Orenstein, eds., *The Battle for Kursk 1943: The Soviet General Staff Study* (Portland, OR: Frank Cass Publishers, 1999, 2002), 240; Gorbach, *Nad Ognennoy Dugoy,* 474.

14. Gorbach, *Nad Ognennoy Dugoy,* 21.

15. Ibid., 23.

16. Brookes, *Air War over Russia,* 125.

17. M. N. Kozhevnikov, *Komandovaniye i shtab VVS Sovetskoy Armii v Velikoy Otechestvennoy Voyne, 1941–1945 gg.* (Moscow: Nauka, 1977), 148–149.

18. Gorbach, *Nad Ognennoy Dugoy,* 24–26.

19. Ibid., 26–27.

20. Brookes, *Air War over Russia,* 125, 127.

21. Gorbach, *Nad Ognennoy Dugoy,* 35.

22. Ibid., 38.

23. Ibid., 37.

24. Ibid., 474, Table 1.2, Strength of LW by 5 July 1943.

25. Ibid.

26. Jill Amadio, *Guenther Rall, a Memoir: Luftwaffe Ace and NATO General* (Santa Ana, CA: Tangemere Productions, 2002), 154, 159–160.

27. Kozhevnikov, *Komandovaniye i shtab VVS*, 148–149.

28. Gorbach, *Nad Ognennoy Dugoy*, 32.

29. Kozhevnikov, *Komandovaniye i shtab VVS*, 149.

30. Gorbach, *Nad Ognennoy Dugoy*, 29; O. Rastrenin, *Raskolotoye nebo, May-Iyun 1943 g.* (Moscow: Eksmo, Yauza, 2007), 13.

31. Rastrenin, *Raskolotoye nebo*, 13; Gorbach, *Nad Ognennoy Dugoy*, 33.

32. Gorbach, *Nad Ognennoy Dugoy*, 31–32.

33. Ibid., 30–31.

34. Plocher, *German Air Force versus Russia, 1943*, 84–85; Julius R. Goal, "The Kharkov Massacre," *Air Combat* 7, 4 (July 1979): 75–81.

35. Gorbach, *Nad Ognennoy Dugoy*, 106–115.

36. Ibid., 31–32.

37. I. V. Timokhovich, *Operativnoye iskusstvo Sovetskikh VVS v Velikoy Otechestvennoy voyne* (Moscow: Voyenizdat, 1976), 50; Gorbach, *Nad Ognennoy Dugoy*, 475, 483.

38. Gorbach, *Nad Ognennoy Dugoy*, 44.

39. Ibid., 47–48.

40. Ibid., 49.

41. Ibid., 53.

42. Ibid., 57.

43. Kozhevnikov, *Komandovaniye i shtab VVS*, 152; Gorbach, *Nad Ognennoy Dugoy*, 57.

44. Kozhevnikov, *Komandovaniye i shtab VVS*, 152.

45. Gorbach, *Nad Ognennoy Dugoy*, 57.

46. Kozhevnikov, *Komandovaniye i shtab VVS*, 152. See also G. K. Prussakov, A. A. Vasilyev, I. I. Ivanov, F. S. Luchkin, and G. O. Komarov, *16-ya vozdushnaya. Voyenno-istoricheskiy ocherk o boyevom puti 16-oy vosdushnoy armii 1942–1945* (Moscow: Voyenizdat, 1973), 95.

47. Plocher, *German Air Force versus Russia, 1943*, 86.

48. Gorbach, *Nad Ognennoy Dugoy*, 62.

49. Ibid., 70.

50. Ibid., 70–71.

51. PTAB 2.5-1.5 stands for *Protivotankovaya aviatsionnaya bomba* (antitank air bomb) of 2.5 kilograms, with a 1.5 kilogram shape charge.

52. Gorbach, *Nad Ognennoy Dugoy*, 72. For more on PTAB use by Shturmovik units, see Oleg Rastrenin, *Il-2 Shturmovik Guards Units of World War 2* (Oxford: Osprey Publishing, 2008), 61–66.

53. Gorbach, *Nad Ognennoy Dugoy*, 79.

54. Ibid., 83.

55. Ibid., 84.

56. Ibid., 97.

57. Plocher, *German Air Force versus Russia, 1943*, 84–85; Goal, "Kharkov Massacre," 75–81; Gorbach, *Nad Ognennoy Dugoy*, 114–115.

58. Gorbach, *Nad Ognennoy Dugoy*, 127.

59. Rastrenin, *Il-2 Shturmovik Guards Units*, 61; Gorbach, *Nad Ognennoy Dugoy*, 117–118.

60. M. Bykov, *Sovetskiye asy 1941–1945. Pobedy Stalinskikh sokolov* (Moscow: Yauza, Eksmo, 2008), 240.

61. Gorbach, *Nad Ognennoy Dugoy*, 118–120.

62. Ibid., 126.

63. Ibid., 127.

64. Ibid., 151–152.

65. Ibid., 164.

66. Ibid., 168–169.

67. V. N. Zamulin, *Zasekrechennaya Kurskaya bitva. Sekretnye dokumenty svidetelstvuyut* (Moscow: Yauza, Eksmo, 2007), 772; L. Lopukhovskiy, *Prokhorovka: Bez grifa sekretnosti* (Moscow: Eksmo, Yauza, 2005), 489–491.

68. Gorbach, *Nad Ognennoy Dugoy*, 186.

69. Ibid., 188.

70. Ibid., 186–188.

71. Plocher, *German Air Force versus Russia, 1943,* 82, 86.

72. Ibid., 87.

73. Gorbach, *Nad Ognennoy Dugoy*, 195.

74. I. V. Timokhovich, *Sovetskaya aviatsiya v bitve pod Kurskom* (Moscow: Voyenizdat, 1959), 76.

75. Gorbach, *Nad Ognennoy Dugoy*, 199–200.

76. Ibid., 204.

77. Ibid., 207.

78. David M. Glantz and Jonathan M House, *When Titans Clashed: How the Red Army Stopped Hitler* (Lawrence: University Press of Kansas, 1995), 167–169.

79. Gorbach, *Nad Ognennoy Dugoy*, 263.

80. Ibid., 268.

81. Ibid., 285–287.

82. Ibid., 321.

83. Ibid., 342.

84. Amadio, *Guenther Rall*, 161–162.

85. Guenther Rall, interview with Von Hardesty, 1989.

86. Bykov, *Sovetskiye asy*, 163–164.

87. Kozhevnikov, *Komandovaniye i shtab VVS*, 162–163.

Chapter Six. At Full Stride

1. M. N. Kozhevnikov, *Komandovaniye i shab VVS Sovetskoy Armii v Velikoy Otechestvennoy voyne 1941–1945 gg.* (Moscow: Nauka, 1977), 164; V. G. Nikiforov, ed., *Sovetskaya aviatsiya v Velikoy Otechestvennoy voyne 1941–1945 gg v tsifrakh* (Moscow: Glavnyy Shtab VVS, GU VVS SSSR, 1962), 7.

2. Harriet F. Scott and William F. Scott, *The Armed Forces of the USSR* (Boulder, CO: Westview Press, 1979), 27.

3. On January 1, 1944, the *Luftwaffe* units facing the VVS possessed 2,800 operational aircraft, including 1,596 bombers, 728 fighters, and 476 reconnaissance aircraft. This number had been reduced 1,680 by January 1, 1945. See Nikiforov, *Sovetskaya aviatsiya v tsifrakh*, 94–95. German figures coincide: 2,726 total, of which 2,010 were combat aircraft, including 513 fighters, 609

bombers, and 434 reconnaissance aircraft; see Olaf Groehler, "Starke, Verteil-lung, und der eutschen Luftwaffe im sweiten Weltkrieg," *Militargeschichte* 17 (1978): 322–323, 328 (tables 5, 6, 8).

4. Herman Plocher, *The German Air Force versus Russia, 1943*, USAF His-torical Study no. 155 (New York: Arno Press, 1965), 270.

5. Nikiforov, *Sovetskaya aviatsiya v tsifrakh*, 25.

6. This is the total number of manufactured aircraft, not necessarily the number deployed in operational air units. See G. S. Byushgens, ed., *Samole-tostroyeniye v SSSR 1917–1945 gg.*, vol. 2 (Moscow: TsAGI, 1994), 235.

7. David M. Glantz and Jonathan M. House, *When Titans Clashed: How the Red Army Stopped Hitler* (Lawrence: University Press of Kansas, 1995), 179–194.

8. Nikiforov, *Sovetskaya aviatsiya v tsifrakh*, 70, 84–85.

9. I. G. Inozemtsev, *Pod krylom—Leningrad* (Moscow: Voyenizdat, 1978), 208–233; A. A. Novikov, *V nebe Leningrada* (Moscow: Nauka, 1970), 258–259, 273–303.

10. Ilya Moschanskiy, *Razgrom pod Cherkassami. Korsun-Shevchenkovskaya nastupatelnaya operatsiya 24 yanvarya–17 fevralya 1944 goda* (Moscow: BTV-MN, 2005), 19.

11. Vadim Kolechkin, "Aviatsiya pod Korsun-Shevchenkovskim v fevrale 1944g," *Aviatsiya i Vremya* 5 (2004): 36–37.

12. Moschanskiy, *Razgrom pod Cherkassami*, 36.

13. Vadim Kolechkin, "Aviatsiya pod Korsun-Shevchenkovskim v fevrale 1944g," *Aviatsiya i Vremya* 6 (2004): 34–35.

14. Kolechkin, "Aviatsiya pod Korsun-Shevchenkovskim," 5:39.

15. Kozhevnikov, *Komandovaniye i shtab VVS*, 170–171; Moschanskiy, *Raz-grom pod Cherkassami*, 59. According to recently published studies on air ac-tions at Korsun–Shevchenkovskiy, Soviet victories consisted of 218 airplanes in the air and 163 on the ground; see Kolechkin, "Aviatsiya pod Korsun-Shevchekovskim," 6:37.

16. Earl F. Ziemke, *Stalingrad to Berlin: The German Defeat in the East*, Army Historical Series (Washington, DC: Office of the Chief of Military History, 1968), 231.

17. Ibid., 231–238. Based on Soviet claims, 8,000 to 9,000 escaped the trap. A total of 271 tanks, 32 armored personnel carriers, 110 self-propelled guns, 994 guns, 536 mortars, and 1,689 machine guns were lost. See Moschanskiy, *Razgrom pod Cherkassami*, 56.

18. Kolechkin, "Aviatsiya pod Korsun-Shevchekovskim," 6:37.

19. Kozhevnikov, *Komandovaniye i shtab VVS*, 171.

20. B. A. Gubin and V. D. Kiselev, *Vosmaya vozdushnaya. Voyenno-istorich-eskiy ocherk boyevogo puti 8-oy vozdushnoy armii v gody Velikoy Otechestvennoy voyny* (Moscow: Voyenizdat, 1980), 186.

21. M. Bykov, *Sovetskiye asy 1941–1945. Pobedy Stalinskikh sokolov* (Moscow: Yauza, Eksmo, 2008), 139–140.

22. Dmitriy Khazanov, "Bitva nad Yassami, Proval poslednego nastupleniya Luftwaffe na Vostoke," *Aviamaster* 4 (1999): 18.

23. Ibid., 7–32.

24. Ibid., 10.

25. Ibid., 11.

26. Ibid., 15.

27. Ibid., 17, 26. See also Hans Ulrich Rudel, *Stuka Pilot* (New York: Ballantine Books, 1958, 1966), 138–193.

28. Khazanov, "Bitva nad Yassami," 18.

29. Rudel, *Stuka Pilot*, 135–136.

30. Khazanov, "Bitva nad Yassami," 20–23.

31. Ibid., 17.

32. Ibid., 22–27.

33. Helmut Lipfert and Werner Girbig, *The War Diary of Hauptman Lipfert: JG52 on the Russian Front, 1943–1945* (Atglen, PA: Schiffer Military History, 1993), 114–115.

34. L. Mikryukov and G. Bryukhovskiy, "Opyt boyevogo primeneniya aviatsii pri proryve oborony protivnika," *Voyenno-istoricheskiy zhurnal* 2 (1981): 32.

35. Khazanov, "Bitva nad Yassami," 27.

36. S. I. Rudenko, "Osobennosti boyevykh deystviy aviatsii v Belorusskoy operatsii," *Voyenno-istoricheskiy zhurnal* 2 (1971): 22.

37. Kozhevnikov, *Komandovaniye i shtab VVS*, 173.

38. Ziemke, *Stalingrad to Berlin*, 321.

39. "Aviatsionnoye obespechenie Belorusskoy operatsii," *Sbornik materialov po izucheniyu opyta voiny* 20 (September–October 1945), http://www.almanacwhf.ru/?no=6&art=6 (accessed September 27, 2010).

40. Ziemke, *Stalingrad to Berlin*, 462.

41. Nikiforov, *Sovetskaya aviatsiya v tsifrakh*, 63, 70, 75, 84–85.

42. Ibid.

43. Kozhevnikov, *Komandovaniye i shtab VVS*, 172.

44. Ibid., 175.

45. Groehler, "Starke, Verteillung, und der eutschen Luftwaffe," 325 (table 9).

46. *Luftwaffe* strength in the East was 3,267 combat aircraft according to Groehler, "Starke, Verteillung, und der eutschen Luftwaffe," 328 (table 12).

47. "Aviatsionnoye obespecheniye Belorusskoy operatsii."

48. Kozhevnikov, *Komandovaniye i shtab VVS*, 176–177.

49. Ibid., 178–179.

50. Bykov, *Sovetskiye asy 1941–1945*, 592.

51. See also Oleg Korytov and Konstantin Chirkin, interview with Olga Lisikova, trans. J. F. Gebhardt, November 2007, http://lend-lease.airforce.ru/english/articles/lisikova/index.htm (accessed December 6, 2010), and Vseslav Dyakonov, interview with Lyudmila Popova, May 2000–February 2002, http://www.airforce.ru/history/ww2/popova/index.htm (accessed December 6, 2010).

52. V. Mumantseva, "Sovetskiye zhenshchiny v Velikoy Otechestvennoy voyne 1941–1945 godov," *Voyenno-istoricheskiy zhurnal* 2 (1968): 47–54. See also Reina Pennington, *Wings, Women, and War: Soviet Airwomen in World War II Combat* (Lawrence: University Press of Kansas, 2001).

53. "Aviatsionnoye obespecheniye Belorusskoy operatsii."

54. Ibid.

55. Kozhevnikov, *Komandovaniye i shtab VVS*, 182; G. K. Prussakov, A. A.

Vasilyev, I. I. Ivanov, F. S. Luchkin, and G. O. Komarov, *16-ya vozdushnaya. Voyenno-istoricheskiy ocherk o boyevom puti 16-oy vosdushnoy armii 1942–1945* (Moscow: Voyenizdat, 1973), 157–185.

56. Kozhevnikov, *Komandovaniye i shtab VVS*, 182. The 6th Air Army participated in Operation Bagration during its later stages and assisted the 16th Air Army on the left flank of the front.

57. V. S. Grossman, *With the Red Army in Poland and Byelorussia* (London: Hutchinson and Company, 1945), 10; Antony Beevor and Luba Vinogradova, eds., *A Writer at War: Vasily Grossman with the Red Army 1941–1945* (New York: Pantheon Books, 2005), 270–279.

58. "Aviatsionnoye obespecheniye Belorusskoy operatsii."

59. Ibid.

60. K. K. Rokossovskiy was promoted to marshal on June 29, 1944.

61. Kozhevnikov, *Komandovaniye i shtab VVS*, 184.

62. "Aviatsionnoye obespecheniye Belorusskoy operatsii."

63. Kozhevnikov, *Komandovaniye i shtab VVS*, 166, 175–180.

64. *Aviatsiya i Kosmonavtika* 8 (1964): 22–23.

65. Karl Stein, interview with Von Hardesty, May 1979. Stein flew ground attack missions with the *Luftwaffe* on the Eastern Front in 1944–1945. He stated that German pilots considered the French Normandie regiment to be "very aggressive." Four French volunteer pilots received the coveted Gold Star, Hero of the Soviet Union in the war.

66. http://normandieniemen.free.fr/ (accessed September 27, 2010).

67. Alexander Boyd, *The Soviet Air Force since 1918* (New York: Stein and Day, 1977), 182. Jan Szczepanski, in *Polish Society* (New York: Random House, 1970), 33–42, states that there were 230,000 Polish soldiers in the West and another 380,000 in the underground Home Army.

68. Pierced steel planking was used to construct airfield runways. Each piece was approximately 12 feet long by 1.5 feet wide, with interlocking tabs on the sides and ends. This material was used throughout all theaters during World War II. It was manufactured in the United States and provided to the USSR in enormous quantities through Lend-Lease.

69. "Shuttle Bombing Operations Utilizing Bases in Russia," special report by Major General F. L. Anderson to Commanding General, 15th Air Force, April 28, 1944, 3.

70. Glenn B. Infield, *The Poltava Affair, a Russian Warning: An American Tragedy* (New York: Macmillan, 1973), 141.

71. Stein interview.

72. Brigadier General Benjamin S. Kelsey to Von Hardesty, January 8, 1980. Kelsey's analysis of American aircraft technical development through World War II is found in *The Dragon's Teeth? The Creation of United States Air Power for World War II* (Washington, DC: Smithsonian Institution Press, 1982).

73. Infield, *Poltava Affair*, 171.

74. Oleg Bezverkhniy, "Tiyeyi chervnevoyi nochi 44-go," *Zarya Poltavschiny*, June 23, 2000.

75. P. T. Tronko, ed., *Operation "Frantic": Collected Documents and Materials* (Kyiv: Ridnyy Kray, 1998), 134–136.

76. Ibid., 133.

77. Ibid., 137–138.

78. Novikov, *V nebe Leningrada*, 271–272; A. Orlov and N. Komarov, "Flying Fortresses over the Third Reich," *Soviet Military Review* 7 (July 1975): 51–52.

79. Nikiforov, *Sovetskaya aviatsiya v tsifrakh*, 95.

80. Groehler, "Starke, Verteillung, und der eutschen Luftwaffe," 327 (table 11).

81. Adolf Galland to Von Hardesty, February 10, 1981.

82. Nikiforov, *Sovetskaya aviatsiya v tsifrakh*, 7.

83. Ibid., 61, 64–65.

84. Glantz and House, *When Titans Clashed*, 223, 240.

85. V. A. Zolotarev, ed., *Russkiy Arhiv: Velikaya Otechestvennaya, tom 16, 5(4), Stavka VGK. Dokumenty i materialy 1944–1945 god* (Moscow: Terra, 1999), 21.

86. Nikiforov, *Sovetskaya aviatsiya v tsifrakh*, 64–65.

87. S. Shchukarev, "Aviatsionnaya podderzhka nastupatelnykh deystviy Sukhoputnykh voysk v Vislo-Oderskoy operatsii," *Voyenno-istoricheskiy zhurnal* 5 (2005): 27.

88. Kozhevnikov, *Komandovaniye i shtab VVS*, 196–197.

89. Shchukarev, "Aviatsionnaya podderzhka v Vislo-Oderskoy operatsii," 28.

90. Prussakov et al., *16-ya vozdushnaya*, 262–269.

91. Ibid., 271.

92. Ibid., 270–271.

93. Ibid., 277.

94. Kozhevnikov, *Komandovaniye i shtab VVS*, 198.

95. Shchukarev, "Aviatsionnaya podderzhka v Vislo-Oderskoy operatsii," 29.

96. Prussakov et al., *16-ya vozdushnaya*, 295.

97. Kozhevnikov, *Komandovaniye i shtab VVS*, 198.

98. Shchukarev, "Aviatsionnaya podderzhka v Vislo-Oderskoy operatsii," 30.

99. Kozhevnikov, *Komandovaniye i shtab VVS*, 198–207.

100. Nikiforov, *Sovetskaya aviatsiya v tsifrakh*, 64–65.

101. S. I. Rudenko et al., *Sovetskiye Voenno-Vozdushnyye Sily v Velikoy Otechestvennoy voyne 1941–1945gg.* (Moscow: Voyenizdat, 1968), 350.

102. Ibid., 353.

103. Ibid., 355–356.

104. Kozhevnikov, *Komandovaniye i shtab VVS*, 202–203.

105. Ibid., 204.

106. Ibid.

107. Leonid Levin, interview with Ilya Grinberg, May 2003, http://www.airforce.ru/history/ww2/levin/index.htm (accessed April 18, 2011).

108. Kozhevnikov, *Komandovaniye i shtab VVS*, 207. The 18th Air Army operated only at night prior to this raid; the General Staff granted permission to utilize it during the day.

109. Ibid., 208.

110. Prussakov et al., *16-ya vozdushnaya*, 323.

111. Rudenko et al., *Sovetskiye Voyenno-Vozdushnyye Sily v Velikoy Otechestvennoy voyne*, 389.

112. Kozhevnikov, *Komandovaniye i shtab VVS*, 211.

113. Prussakov et al., *16-ya vozdushnaya*, 323.

114. Ibid.

115. "Luftwaffe Strength and Serviceability Tables, August 1938–April 1945,

Compiled from the Records of VI Abteilung, Quartermaster General's Department of the German Air Ministry," U.S. Air Force Historical Research Agency, 512.621 VII/107.

116. Groehler, "Starke, Verteillung, und der eutschen Luftwaffe," 328 (table 13).

117. Donald Caldwell and Richard Muller, *The Luftwaffe over Germany: Defense of the Reich* (London: Greenhill, 2007), 322.

118. Guenther Rall, interview with Von Hardesty, May 1989; see also Jill Amadio, *Guenther Rall, a Memoir: Luftwaffe Ace and NATO General* (Santa Ana, CA: Tangemere Productions, 2002), 248–251.

119. Prussakov et al., *16-ya vozdushnaya*, 336.

120. Ibid., 339.

121. Obzor Boyevyh Deystviy 2 Vozdshunoy Armii, TsAMO, fond, 236, opis 2673, delo 2742, pp. 13–14.

122. Rudenko et al., *Sovestkie Voyenno-Vozdushnyye Sily v Velikoy Otechestvennoy voyne*, 412.

123. Oleg Rastrenin, "Glavnay udarnaya sila," in *Ya Dralsya na Il-2*, ed. A Drabkin (Moscow: Yauza, Eksmo, 2005), 394.

124. Ibid., 401–402.

125. Doklad zam. Komanduyuschego 16 vozdushnoy armiey General-leytenanta t. Beletskogo "Aviatsionnoye obespecheniye Berlinskoy operatsii" in Stenogrammy Dokladov i Vystupleniy na Nauchnoy Konferentsii po izucheniyu Berlinskoy operatsii voysk 1 Belorusskogo fronta, 9–12 aprelya 1946 g., TsAMO, fond 233, opis 2356, delo 804, pp. 332, 341–349, 366.

126. Ibid., 329.

127. Obzor Boyevyh Deystviy 2 Vozdshunoy Armii, 193.

Chapter Seven. Triumph and Vulnerability

1. V. G. Nikiforov, ed., *Sovetskaya aviatsiya v Velikoy Otechestvennoy Voyne 1941–1945 gg v tsifrakh* (Moscow: Glavnyy Shtab VVS, GU VVS SSSR, 1962), 7, 70–86. The breakdown in categories included 13,620 airplanes in frontal aviation, 1,675 airplanes in the ADD, 3,198 airplanes in the PVO, and 1,578 airplanes in naval aviation, excluding the Pacific Fleet. A total of three air armies—the 9th, 10th, and 12th—with 3,293 airplanes, supplemented by 1,549 airplanes of the Pacific Fleet air arm, were deployed against the Japanese in August 1945.

2. David Holloday, *Stalin and the Bomb: The Soviet Union and Atomic Energy 1939–1954* (New Haven, CT: Yale University Press, 1994), 231–237.

3. Ibid., 227.

4. Ibid., 231.

5. The Li-2 was widely used as a night bomber in the ADD. The dedicated version was called the Li-2NB. See Vyacheslav Kotelnikov, "Ot DC-3 do Li-2," *Mir Aviatsii* 4 (1999): 22–23.

6. "Neizvestnyye stranitsy istorii VVS," *Vestnik Vozdushnogo Flota*, July–August 2002, 36–43.

7. "Akt peredachi VVS," in *VVS Rossii. Neizvestnyye dokumenty* (Moscow: Izdatelskiy dom Vestnik Vozdushnogo Flota, 2005).

8. Asif A. Siddiqi, *The Red Rocket's Glare: Spaceflight and the Soviet Imagination, 1857–1957* (New York: Cambridge University Press, 2010), 242.

9. Ye. I. Podrepniy, "Problema kachestva v otechestvennom samoletostroyenii v pervyye poslevoyennyye gody (1945–1947 gg)," *Vestnik Nizhegorodskogo universiteta im. N. I. Lobachevskogo* (Seriya: Istoriya, 2003,), 1:105–110.

10. Mikhail Maslov, "Drednout," *M-Hobby* 5–6 (1997): 29.

11. Vladimir Rigmant, "Bombardirovshchik Pe-8," *Aviatsiya i Kosmonavtika vchera, segodnya, zavtra* 5–6 (2002): 68–72.

12. Richard C. Lukas, *Eagles East: The Army Air Forces and the Soviet Union, 1941–1945* (Tallahassee: Florida State University Press, 1970), 177, 219.

13. G. Scott Gorman, "The Tu-4: The Travails of Technology Transfer by Imitation," *Air Power History* (spring 1998): 19.

14. Von Hardesty, "Made in the USSR," *Air & Space/Smithsonian Magazine* 15, 6 (March 2001): 68–79. V. Reshetnikov performed 307 sorties with the ADD. From 1969 to 1980, he was a commander of long-range aviation, and from 1980 to 1986, he was deputy commander in chief of the VVS.

15. Vladimir Rigmant, "Bombardirovshchik Tu-2," *Aviatsiya i Kosmonavtika vchera, segodnya, zavtra* 30 (September 1997): 10.

16. L. L. Kerber, *Stalin's Aviation Gulag: A Memoir of Andrei Tupolev and the Purge Era*, ed. Von Hardesty (Washington, DC: Smithsonian Institution Press, 1996), 149–240, 255–279.

17. Hardesty, "Made in the USSR," 68–79.

18. Ibid.

19. Ibid., 76–77; Leonid Kerber and Maksimillian Saukke, "Ne kopiya, a analog," *Krylya Rodiny* 2 (1989): 34. See also Gorman, "The Tu-4," 18–26.

20. Ramsey D. Potts Jr., "The Foundations of Soviet Air Power: A Historical and Managerial Interpretation," *Annals of the American Academy of Political and Social Science* 299 (May 1955): 38–48.

21. Yevgeniy Podrepnyy, *Reaktivnyy proryv Stalina* (Moscow: Yauza, Eksmo, 2008), 19.

22. Ibid., 76. See also Dmitriy A. Sobolev, *Nemetskiy sled v istorii sovetskoy aviatsii: Ob uchastii nemetskikh spetsialistov v razvitii aviastroyeniya v SSSR* (Moscow: RITs Aviantik, 1996), 58–118.

23. Vladimir Kotelnikov and Tony Butler, *Early Russian Jet Engines—The Nene and Derwent in the Soviet Union and the Evolution of the VK-1*, Historical Series no. 33 (Derby, UK: Rolls Royce Heritage Trust, 2002), 68.

24. Ye. Arsenyev and L. Krylov. *Istrebitel MiG-15* (Moscow: ExPrint, 1999), 4–11. The VK-1 engine, with a thrust of 2,700 kilograms, represented a Soviet improvement of the RD-45F Neene-II, with thrust of 2,270 kilograms.

BIBLIOGRAPHY

Amadio, Jill. *Guenther Rall, a Memoir: Luftwaffe Ace and NATO General.* Santa Ana, CA: Tangemere Productions, 2002.

Antipov, V., and I. Utkin. *Dragons on Bird Wings: The Combat History of the 812th Fighter Air Regiment,* vol.1, *Liberation of the Motherland.* Kitchener, ON: Aviaelogy, 2006.

Arsenyev, Ye., and L. Krylov. *Istrebitel MiG-15.* Moscow: ExPrint, 1999.

"Aviatsionnoye obespecheniye Belorusskoy operacii." *Sbornik materialov po izucheniyu opyta voyny* 20 (September–October 1945). http://www.almanac whf.ru/?no = 6&art = 6 (accessed September 27, 2010).

Beevor, Antony, and Luba Vinogradova, eds. *A Writer at War: Vasily Grossman with the Red Army 1941–1945.* New York: Pantheon Books, 2005.

Bergstrom, Christer, Andrey Dikov, and Vlad Antipov. *Black Cross/Red Star. Air War over the Eastern Front,* vol. 3, *Everything for Stalingrad.* Hamilton, MT: Eagle Editions, 2006.

Bergstrom, Christer, and Andrey Mikhailov. *Black Cross/Red Star. The Air War over the Eastern Front,* vol. 1, *Operation Barbarossa, 1941.* Pacifica, CA: Pacifica Military History, 2000.

———. *Black Cross/Red Star. The Air War over the Eastern Front,* vol. 2, *Resurgence. January–June 1942.* Pacifica, CA: Pacifica Military History, 2001.

Bezverkhniy, Oleg. "Tiyeyi chervnevoyi nochi 44-go." *Zarya Poltavschiny,* June 23, 2000.

Bialer, Seweryn, ed. *Stalin and His Generals: Soviet Military Memoirs of World War II.* New York: Pegasus, 1969.

Bourke-White, Margaret. *Shooting the Russian War.* New York: Simon and Schuster, 1943.

Boyd, Alexander. *The Soviet Air Force since 1918.* London: Macdonald and Jane's, 1977.

Braithwaite, Rodric. *Moscow 1941: A City and Its People at War.* New York: Vintage Books, 2006.

Brookes, Andrew. *Air War over Russia.* Hersham, UK: Ian Allen, 2003.

Bykov, M. *Sovetskiye asy 1941–1945. Pobedy Stalinskikh sokolov.* Moscow: Yauza, Eksmo, 2008.

Byushgens, G. S., ed. *Samoletostroyeniye v SSSR 1917–1945 gg.,* vol. 2. Moscow: TsAGI, 1994.

Caldwell, Donald, and Richard Muller. *The Luftwaffe over Germany: Defense of the Reich.* London: Greenhill, 2007.

Craig, William. *Enemy at the Gates: The Battle for Stalingrad.* New York: Reader's Digest Press, 1973.

Denisov, N. *Boyevaya slava sovetskoy aviatsii.* Moscow: Voyenizdat, 1953.

Dmitrevskiy, N. *Zashchitniki neba stolitsy.* Moscow: Voyenizdat,1962.

Doklad zam. Komanduyuschego 16 vozdushnoy armiey General-leytenanta t. Beletskogo "Aviatsionnoye obespecheniye Berlinskoy operatsii." In *Stenogrammy Dokladov i Vystupleniy na Nauchnoy Konferentsii po izucheniyu Berlinskoy operatsii voysk 1 Belorusskogo fronta, 9–12 aprelya 1946 g.* TsAMO, fond 233, opis 2356, delo 804.

Dyakonov, Vseslav. Interview with Lyudmila Popova, May 2000–February 2002. http://www.airforce.ru/history/ww2/popova/index.htm (accessed December 6, 2010).

Einsiedel, Heinrich von. *The Shadow of Stalingrad: Being a Diary of Temptation.* London: Wingate, 1953.

Erickson, John. *The Road to Stalingrad.* New York: Harper and Row, 1975.

———. "The Soviet Responses to Surprise Attack: Three Directives, 22 June, 1941." *Soviet Studies* 23, 4 (April 1972).

Evans, Richard J. *The Third Reich at War.* New York: Penguin Press, 2009.

Fedorov, A. G. *Aviatsiya v bitve pod Moskvoy.* Moscow: Nauka, 1975.

Glantz, David M. "The Soviet-German War 1941–1945: Myths and Realities: A Survey Essay." Paper presented at the Twentieth Anniversary Distinguished Lecture, Strom Thurmond Institute of Government and Public Affairs, Clemson University, Clemson, SC, October 11, 2001.

Glantz, David M., and Jonathan M. House. *When Titans Clashed: How the Red Army Stopped Hitler.* Lawrence: University Press of Kansas, 1995.

Glantz, David M., with Jonathan House. *To the Gates of Stalingrad: Soviet-German Combat Operations, April–August, 1942.* Lawrence: University Press of Kansas, 2009.

Glantz, David M., and Harold S. Orenstein, eds. *The Battle for Kursk 1943: The Soviet General Staff Study.* Portland, OR: Frank Cass Publishers, 1999, 2002.

Goal, Julius R. "The Kharkov Massacre." *Air Combat* 7, 4 (July 1979).

Golovanov, A. Ye. *Dalnyaya Bombardirovochnaya.* Moscow: Delta NB, 2004.

Golubev, G. G. *V pare s "sotym."* Moscow: Voyenizdat, 1978.

Gorbach, Vitaliy. *Nad Ognennoy Dugoy: Sovetskaya aviatsiya v Kurskoy bitve.* Moscow: Yauza, Eksmo, 2007.

Gorman, G. Scott. "The Tu-4: The Travails of Technology Transfer by Imitation." *Air Power History* (spring 1998).

Grams, R. *Die 14 Panzer-Division 1940–1945. Herausgegeben im Auftrag der Traditionsgemeinschaft der 14. Panzer-Division.* Bad Nauheim: Verlag Hans-Henning Podzun, 1957.

Grechko, A. A. *Bitva za Kavkaz.* Moscow: Voyenizdat, 1967.

Griehl, Manfred. *German Bombers over Russia (Luftwaffe at War).* London: Greenhill Books, 2000.

Groehler, Olaf. *Geschichte des Luftkriegs 1910 bis 1980.* Berlin: Militarverlag d. DDR (VEB), 1981.

———. "Starke, Verteillung, und der eutschen Luftwaffe im sweiten Weltkrieg." *Militargeschichte* 17 (1978).

Grossman, V. S. *With the Red Army in Poland and Byelorussia.* London: Hutchinson and Company, 1945.

Gubin, B. A., and V. D. Sokolov. *Vosmaya vozdushnaya. Voyenno-istoricheskiy ocherk boyevogo puti 8-oy vozdushnoj armii v gody Velikoy Otechestvennoy Voyny.* Moscow: Voyenizdat, 1980.

Halder, F. *Kriegstagebuch. Tägliche Aufzeichnungen des Chefs des Generalstabes des Heeres 1939–1942.* Stuttgart: W. Kohlhammer Verlag, 1962–1964.

Hardesty, Von. "Made in the USSR." *Air & Space/Smithsonian Magazine* 15, 6 (March 2001).

———. *Red Phoenix: The Rise of Soviet Air Power, 1941–1945.* Washington, DC: Smithsonian Institution Press, 1982.

Holloday, David. *Stalin and the Bomb: The Soviet Union and Atomic Energy 1939–1954.* New Haven, CT: Yale University Press, 1994.

Infield, Glenn B. *The Poltava Affair, a Russian Warning: An American Tragedy.* New York: Macmillan, 1973.

Inozemtsev, I. G. *Pod krylom—Leningrad.* Moscow: Voyenizdat, 1978.

Isayev, Aleksey. *Kotly 41-go. Istoriya VOV, kotoruyu my ne znali.* Moscow: Yauza, Eksmo, 2005.

———. *Neizvestnyy 1941: Ostanovlennyy blitskrig.* Moscow: Yauza, Eksmo, 2010.

———. *Ot Dubno do Rostova.* Moscow: AST, Transitkniga, 2004.

———. *Stalingrad. Za Volgoy dlya nas zemli net.* Moscow: Yauza, Eksmo, 2008.

Isayev, Sergey. *Stranitsy istorii 32-go gvardeyskogo Vilenskogo ordenov Lenina i Kutuzova III stepeni istrebitelnogo aviatsionnogo polka.* Moscow: Arbor, 2006.

Ivanov A. L. *Skorost, manevr, ogon.* Moscow: DOSAAF, 1974.

Jackson, Robert. *The Red Falcons: The Soviet Air Force in Action, 1916–1969.* London: Clifton Books, 1970.

Kaminskiy, O. "Messershmitty nad Kubanyu." *Aviatsiya i Vremya* 5 (2005).

Kelsey, B. S. *The Dragon's Teeth? The Creation of United States Air Power for World War II.* Washington, DC: Smithsonian Institution Press, 1982.

Kerber, L. L. *Stalin's Aviation Gulag: A Memoir of Andrei Tupolev and the Purge Era*, ed. Von Hardesty. Washington, DC: Smithsonian Institution Press, 1996.

Kerber, Leonid, and Maksimilian Saukke. "Ne kopiya, a analog." *Krylya Rodiny* 2 (1989).

Khazanov, Dmitriy. "Bitva nad Yassami. Proval poslednego nastupleniya Luftwaffe na Vostoke." *Aviamaster* 4 (1999).

———. *Neizvestnaya bitva v nebe Moskvy 1941–1942 gg. Kontrnastupleniye.* Moscow: Tehnika–Molodezhi, 2001.

———. *Neizvestnaya bitva v nebe Moskvy 1941–1942 gg. Oboronitelnyy period.* Moscow: Tehnika–Molodezhi, 1999.

———. *1941—Gorkiye uroki: Voyna v vozdukhe.* Moscow: Yauza, Eksmo, 2006.

Kienko, Dmitriy. *Krylya nad Grodno. Boevye deystviya 127 istrebitelnogo polka.* Grodno, Belarus: Khata, 2009.

———. *Krylya nad Lidoy. Boevye deystviya 122 istrebitelnogo polka 22–23 iyunya 1941g.* Grodno, Belarus: Khata, 2009.

Kolechkin, Vadim. "Aviatsiya pod Korsun-Shevchenkovskim v fevrale 1944g." *Aviatsiya i Vremya* 5 and 6 (2004).

Korytov, Oleg, and Konstantin Chirkin. Interview with Olga Lisikova, trans. J. F. Gebhardt, November 2007. http://lend-lease.airforce.ru/english/articles/lisikova/index.htm (accessed December 6, 2010).

Kostenko, F. A. *Korpus krylatoy gvardii.* Moscow: Voyenizdat, 1974.

Kotelnikov, Vladimir. *Il-4. "Vozdushnyye kreysera" Stalina.* Moscow: Yauza, Eksmo, 2009.

———. "Ot DC03 do Li-2." *Mir Aviatsii* 4 (1999).

Kotelnikov, Vladimir, and Tony Butler. *Early Russian Jet Engines—The Nene and Derwent in the Soviet Union and the Evolution of the VK-1.* Historical Series no. 33. Derby, UK: Rolls Royce Heritage Trust, 2002.

Kozhevnikov, M. N. *Komandovaniye i shtab VVS Sovetskoy Armii v Velikoy Otechestvennoy Voyne, 1941–1945 gg.* Moscow: Nauka, 1977.

Krivosheyev, G. F., ed. *Grif sekretnosti snyat: Poteri Vooruzhennykh Sil SSSR v voynakh, boyevykh deystviyakh i voyennykh konfliktakh: Statisticheskoye issledovaniye.* Moscow: Voyenizdat, 1993.

Kuznetsov, Sergey. *Yak-1: Nash luchshiy istrebitel 1941 goda.* Moscow: Yauza, Eksmo, 2010.

Leach, Barry A. *German Strategy against Russia, 1939–1941.* Oxford: Clarendon Press, 1973.

Lee, Asher. *The German Air Force.* New York: Harper and Brothers, 1970.

———. *The Soviet Air Force.* London: Duckworth, 1952.

Lipfert, Helmut, and Werner Girbig, *The War Diary of Hauptman Lipfert: JG52 on the Russian Front, 1943–1945.* Atglen, PA: Schiffer Military History, 1993.

Litvin, G. "55 let bitve nad Kubanyu." *Aviatsiya i Kosmonavtika* 4 (1998).

Lopukhovskiy, L. *Prokhorovka: Bez grifa sekretnosti.* Moscow: Eksmo, Yauza, 2005.

Loza, Dmitriy. *Attack of the Airacobras: Soviet Aces, American P-39s & the Air War against Germany.* Lawrence: University Press of Kansas, 2002.

Lukas, Richard C. *Eagles East: The Army Air Forces and the Soviet Union, 1941–1945.* Tallahassee: Florida State University Press, 1970.

Maslov, Mikhail. "Drednout." *M-Hobby* 5–6 (1997).

Medved, A., D. Khazanov, and M. Maslov. *Istrebitel MiG-3.* Moscow: Rusavia, 2003.

Medved, Aleksandr. "Sovetskaya razvedyvatelnaya aviatsiya v nachalnyy period voyny." *Aviatsiya* 8 (2000).

Meltyukhov, M. I. *Tragediya 1941. Prichiny katastrofy.* Moscow: Yauza, Eksmo, 2008.

Mikryukov, L., and G. Bryukhovskiy, "Opyt boyevogo primeneniya aviatsii pri proryve oborony protivnika." *Voyenno-istoricheskiy zhurnal* 2 (1981).

Morozov, Miroslav. "Porazheniye letom 1941 goda bylo zakonomernym." In *1941 Velikaya Otechestvennaya Katastrofa. Itogi diskussii.* Moscow: Eksmo, Yauza, 2009.

Morzik, Fritz. *German Air Force Airlift Operations.* USAF Historical Study no. 167. Maxwell Air Force Base, AL: Air University, 1961.

Moschanskiy, Ilya. *Razgrom pod Cherkassami. Korsun-Shevchenkovskaya nastupatelnaya operatsiya 24 yanvarya–17 fevralya 1944 goda.* Moscow: BTV-MN, 2005.

Muller, Richard. *The German Air War in Russia.* Baltimore: Nautical and Aviation Publishing Company of America, 1992.

Mumantseva, V. "Sovetskiye zhenshchiny v Velikoy Otechestvennoy voyne 1941–1945 godov." *Voyenno-istoricheskiy zhurnal* 2 (1968).

Murray, Williamson. *The Luftwaffe, 1933–1945: Strategy for Defeat.* London: Brassey's, 1996.

Nagorski, Andrew. *The Greatest Battle: Stalin, Hitler, and the Desperate Struggle for Moscow that Changed the Course of World War II.* New York: Simon and Schuster, 2007.

"Neizvestnyye stranitsy istorii VVS." *Vestnik Vozdushnogo Flota,* July–August 2002.

Nelasov, V. P., A. A. Kudryavtsev, A. S. Yakushevskiy, et al. *1941 god-Uroki i vyvody.* Moscow: Voyenizdat, 1992.

Nikiforov, V. G., ed. *Sovetskaya aviatsiya v Velikoy Otechestvennoy voyne 1941–1945 gg v tsifrakh.* Moscow: Glavnyy Shtab VVS, GU VVS SSSR, 1962.

Novikov, A. A. *V nebe Leningrada: Zapiski komanduyuschego aviatsiey.* Moscow: Nauka, 1970.

Obzor Boevykh Deystviy 2 Vozdshunoy Armii, TsAMO, fond, 236, opis 2673, delo 2742.

Ogarkov, N. V., ed. *Sovetskaya Voennaya Entsiklopediya,* vol. 6. Moscow: Voyennoye izdatelstvo Ministerstva Oborony SSSR, 1978.

Orlov, A., and N. Komarov. "Flying Fortresses over the Third Reich." *Soviet Military Review* 7 (July 1975).

Ostroumov, N. N. "Organizatsiya aviatsionnykh rezervov v gody voyny." *Voyenno-istoricheskiy zhurnal* 5 (2005).

Overy, R. J. *The Air War 1939–1945.* London: Europa Publications, 1980.

Pennington, Reina. *Wings, Women, and War: Soviet Airwomen in World War II Combat.* Lawrence: University Press of Kansas, 2001.

Pervov, A. G. "Manevr aviatsionnymi rezervami stavki VGK." *Voyenno-istoricheskiy zhurnal* 2 (1977).

———. "Sovershenstvovaniye rukovodstva Voyenno-vozdushnymi silami Krasnoy Armii v predvoyennyy period i v gody Velikoy Otechestvennoy voyny." *Voyenno-istoricheskiy zhurnal* 1 (2006).

Pickert, Wolfgang. "The Stalingrad Airlift: An Eyewitness Commentary." *Aerospace Historian* 18 (December 1971).

Plocher, Herman. *The German Air Force versus Russia, 1941.* USAF Historical Study no. 153. New York: Arno Press, 1965.

———. *The German Air Force versus Russia, 1942.* USAF Historical Study no. 154. New York: Arno Press, 1965.

———. *The German Air Force versus Russia, 1943.* USAF Historical Study no. 155. New York: Arno Press, 1965.

Podrepnyy, Ye. I. "Problema kachestva v otechestvennom samoletostroyenii v pervyye poslevoyennyye gody (1945–1947 gg)." *Vestnik Nizhegorodskogo universiteta im. N. I. Lobachavskogo.* Seriya: Istoriya, 2003, Vypusk 1.

———. *Reaktivnyy proryv Stalina.* Moscow: Yauza, Eksmo, 2008.

Pokryshkin, Alexander. *Nebo voyny.* Moscow: Voyenizdat, 1975.

———. *Poznat sebya v boyu.* Moscow: DOSAAF, 1986.

Potts, Ramsey D., Jr. "The Foundations of Soviet Air Power: A Historical and Managerial Interpretation." *Annals of the American Academy of Political and Social Sciences* 299 (May 1955).

Price, Alfred. *The Last Year of the Luftwaffe: May 1944 to May 1945.* London: Greenhill Books, 2001.

Prussakov, G. K., A. A. Vasilyev, I. I. Ivanov, F. S. Luchkin, and G. O. Komarov. *16-ya vozdushnaya. Voyenno-istoricheskiy ocherk o boyevom puti 16-oy vozdushnoy armii 1942–1945.* Moscow: Voyenizdat, 1973.

Rastrenin, Oleg. "Glavnay udarnaya sila." In *Ya Dralsya na Il-2,* ed. A Drabkin. Moscow: Yauza, Eksmo, 2005.

————. *Il-2 Shturmovik Guards Units of World War 2.* Oxford: Osprey Publishing, 2008.

————. *Raskolotoye nebo. May–Iyun 1943 g.* Moscow: Eksmo, Yauza, 2007.

Ratkin, Vladimir. "Li-2 na voyne." *Mir Aviatsii* 4 (1999).

————. "Muzhskaya rabota." *Mir Aviatsii* 1 (2000).

Records of VI Abteilung, Quartermaster General's Department of the German Air Ministry." U.S. Air Force Historical Research Agency, 512.621 VII/107.

Rigmant, Vladimir. "Bombardirovshchik Pe-8." *Aviatsiya i Kosmonavtika vchera, segodnya, zavtra,* 5–6 (2002).

————. "Bombardirovschik Tu-2." *Aviatsiya i Kosmonavtika vchera, segodnya, zavtra* 30 (September 1997).

Romanenko, Valeriy. *Aerokobry nad Kubanyu.* Kiev: SPD Romanenko V.D., 2006.

————. *Aerokobry vstupayut v boy.* Kiev: Aerohobby, 1993.

————. "Early Versions of Airacobra in Soviet Aviation," trans. James F. Gebhardt. In Valeriy Romanenko, *Aerokobry vstupayut v boy.* Kiev: Aerohobby, 1993. English translation available at http://lend-lease.airforce .ru/english/articles/romanenko/p-39/index.htm (accessed September 18, 2010).

————. "Porivnyalnyy analiz boyovogo skladu Radyanskoi ta Nimeckoi aviatsii u 1941 rotsc." *Voenna istoriya,* 2009.

Rudel, Hans Ulrich. *Stuka Pilot.* New York: Ballantine Books, 1958, 1966.

Rudenko, S. I. "Aviatsiya v kontrnastuplenii." *Voyenno-istoricheskiy zhurnal* 11 (1972).

————. "Birth of the Air Armies." *Aerospace Historian* 22, 2 (June 1975).

————. *Krylya Pobedy.* Moscow: Mezdunarodnyye otnosheniya, 1985.

————. "Osobennosti boyevykh deystviy aviatsii v Belorusskoy operatsii." *Voyenno-istoricheskiy zhurnal* 2 (1971).

Rudenko, S. I., et al. *Sovetskiye Voyenno-Vozdushnyye Sily v Velikoy Otechestvennoy voyne 1941–1945gg.* Moscow: Voyenizdat, 1968.

Salisbury, Harrison E. *The Unknown War.* New York: Bantam Books, 1978.

Sbornik boyevykh dokumentov Velikoy Otechestvennoy Voyny, Vypusk 7. Moscow: Voyennoye izdatelstvo Ministerstva Vooruzhennyh Sil, 1948.

Sbornik boyevykh dokumentov Velikoy Otechestvennoy Voyny, Vypusk 34. Moscow: Voyennoye izdatelstvo Ministerstva Oborony, 1953.

Sbornik boyevykh dokumentov Velikoy Otechestvennoy Voyny, Vypusk 35. Moscow: Voyennoye izdatelstvo Ministerstva Oborony, 1955.

Sbornik boyevykh dokumentov Velikoy Otechestvennoy Voyny, Vypusk 36. Moscow: Voyennoye izdatelstvo Ministerstva Oborony, 1958.

Schwabedissen, Walter. *The Russian Air Force in the Eyes of German Commanders.* USAF Historical Study no. 175. New York: Arno Press, 1960.

Scott, Harriet F., and William F. Scott. *The Armed Forces of the USSR.* Boulder, CO: Westview Press, 1979.

Seaton, Albert. *The Russo-German War 1941–1945.* New York: Praeger Publishers, 1970.

Shchukarev, S. "Aviatsionnaya podderzhka nastupatelnykh deystviy Sukhoputnykh voysk v Vislo-Oderskoy operatsii." *Voyenno-istoricheskiy zhurnal* 5 (2005).

Siddiqi, Asif A. *The Red Rocket's Glare: Spaceflight and the Soviet Imagination, 1857–1957.* New York: Cambridge University Press, 2010.

Skomorokhov, N. M., et al. *17-ya vozdushnaya armiya v boyakh ot Stalingrada do Veny.* Moscow: Voyenizdat, 1977.

Sobolev, Dmitriy A. *Nemetskiy sled v istorii sovetskoy aviatsii: Ob uchastii nemetskikh spetsialistov v razvitii aviastroyeniya v SSSR.* Moscow: RITs Aviantik, 1996.

Spravochnik po boyevomu i chislennomu sostavu chastey i soyedineniy Voyenno-Vozdushnykh Sil Sovetskoy Armii (1941–1945 gg.). TsAMO, inv. no. 962.

Suchenwirth, Richard. *Historical Turning Points in the German Air Force War Effort.* USAF Historical Study no. 189. Maxwell Air Force Base, AL: Air University, 1959.

Sudoplatov, P. A. *Raznyye dni taynoy voyny i diplomatii. 1941 god.* Moscow: Olma-Press, 2001.

Svetlishin, N. A., *Voyska PVO strany v Velikoy Otechestvennoy voyne.* Moscow: Nauka, 1979.

Sweeting, C. G. "How the Luftwaffe Kept 'Em Flying." *Aviation History* 22, 1 (September 2011): 36–41.

Szczepanski, Jan. *Polish Society.* New York: Random House, 1970.

Timin, M. "Otvetnyy udar: Deystviya Sovetskoy bombardirovochnoy aviatsii 22 iyunya 1941 goda." *Aviapark* 2 (2010).

Timokhovich, I. V. *Operativnoye iskusstvo Sovetskikh VVS v Velikoy Otechestvennoy voyne.* Moscow: Voyenizdat, 1976.

———. *Sovetskaya aviatsiya v bitve pod Kurskom.* Moscow: Voyenizdat, 1959.

Toland, John. *Adolf Hitler.* New York: Ballantine Books, 1976.

Tronko, P. T., ed. *Operation "Frantic": Collected Documents and Materials.* Kyiv: Ridny Kray, 1998.

Tsentralnyy Arkhiv Ministerstva Oborony Rossiyskoy Federatsii (TsAMO RF), fond 208, opis 2683, delo 47, list 44.

Vershinin, K. A. *Chetvertaya vozdushnaya.* Moscow: Voyenizdat, 1975.

VVS Rossii: Neizvestnyye dokumenty. Moscow: Izdatelskiy dom Vestnik Vozdushnogo Flota, 2005.

Werth, Alexander. *Russia at War, 1941–1945.* New York: Avon Books, 1964.

Zamulin, V. N. *Kurskiy izlom: Reshayuschaya bitva Otechestvennoy voyny.* Moscow: Yauza, Eksmo, 2007.

———. *Zasekrechennaya Kurskaya bitva. Sekretnyye dokumenty svidetelstvuyut.* Moscow: Yauza, Eksmo, 2007.

Ziemke, Earl F. *Stalingrad to Berlin: The German Defeat in the East.* Army Historical Series. Washington, DC: Office of the Chief of Military History, 1968.

Zlobin, Igor. "Spitfires over the Kuban." http://lend-lease.airforce.ru/english/articles/spit/index.htm (accessed September 18, 2010).

Zolotarev, V. A., ed. *Russkiy Arkhiv. Velikaya Otechestvennaya, tom 5(2), Stavka VGK. Dokumenty i materialy 1942 god.* Moscow: Terra, 1996.

————. *Russkiy Arkhiv: Velikaya Otechestvennaya, tom 12 (1-2), Nakanune voyny. Materialy soveschaniya vysshego rukovodyaschchego sostava RKKA 23–31 dekabrya 1940g.* Moscow: Terra, 1993.

————. *Russkiy Arkhiv: Velikaya Otechestvennaya, tom 15 (4-1), Bitva pod Moskvoy, Sbornik dokumentov.* Moscow: Terra, 1997.

————. *Russkiy Arkhiv: Velikaya Otechestvennaya, tom 16, 5(4), Stavka VGK. Dokumenty i materialy 1944–1945 god.* Moscow: Terra, 1999.

INDEX